SUCCESSFUL NEGOTIATION IN SCHOOLS

Y0-BDX-428

Successful Negotiation in Schools

MANAGEMENT, UNIONS, EMPLOYEES, and CITIZENS

Jerry J. Herman, Ph.D.

Educational Planning and Training Consultant

Janice L. Herman, Ph.D.

Professor and Department Head
Department of Educational Administration
College of Education
Texas A&M University-Commerce

TECHNOMIC
PUBLISHING CO., INC.
Lancaster · Basel

Successful Negotiation in Schools
a TECHNOMIC publication

Published in the Western Hemisphere by
Technomic Publishing Company, Inc.
851 New Holland Avenue, Box 3535
Lancaster, Pennsylvania 17604 U.S.A.

Distributed in the Rest of the World by
Technomic Publishing AG
Missionsstrasse 44
CH-4055 Basel, Switzerland

Printed in the United States of America
10 9 8 7 6 5 4 3 2 1

Main entry under title:
   Successful Negotiation in Schools: Management, Unions, Employees, and Citizens

A Technomic Publishing Company book
Bibliography: p. 365
Includes index p. 375

Library of Congress Catalog Card No. 97-62047
ISBN No. 1-56676-587-0

To our ongoing legacy—our newer grandchildren—in the hope that their educational experience will be the ideal described in these pages.
Connie, Matthew, Emma, Danielle, and Noah
and to the memory of Alec.

Introduction . . . . *xvii*

SECTION ONE: LIVING AND WORKING WITH INDIVIDUALS AND GROUPS

1. **WORKING TOGETHER WITH PEOPLE AND GROUPS**   3

Beliefs about People 3
Needs of People 6
Beliefs about Groups 6
Needs of Groups 9
Growth Patterns of Groups 9
Development of Groups into Winning Teams 11
Intergroup Formal and Informal Communications 11
Intergroup Relations 11
Summary 12
Exercises 13
References 14

2. **THE HISTORY OF AND REASONS FOR THE DEVELOPMENT OF UNIONS IN EDUCATION**   17

Union Preconditions in Education: The Fallow Ground 17
Reasons for the Existence of Unions in Education 18
Social Upheaval and the Unions: Suffrage, Depression,
    War, and Civil Rights 19
The National Education Association (NEA) 20
The American Federation of Teachers (AFT) 21
Union Influence and Power Since the 1980s 23
Summary 24
Exercises 24
References 24

3. THE HISTORY OF AND REASONS FOR EMPLOYEE EMPOWERMENT 25

Historical Theories and Research 25
Origins in Organizational Theory 28
Rationales for Empowerment 29
School-Based Management 31
Background of Teacher Empowerment and SBM 31
Vertical Work Teams 32
Focus Groups 33
Project Groups 33
Current SBM Practice 34
School-Based Management Interrogatory Checklist
  (A Reflective Aid to Be Used before Jumping Headlong
  into School-Based Management) 35
Quality of Work Life and Quality Circles 38
Total Quality Management 40
Similarities and Differences Among QWL,
  SBM, and TQM 41
Employee Recognition and the Creation and
  Maintenance of a Productive and Satisfying Work
  Environment for Employees 45
Collaboration as a Means of Developing Employee
  Ownership and Employee Leadership 46
Advantages of Employee Involvement, Empowerment,
  and Collaboration 46
Methods of Involving Union/Management Teams 48
Summary 49
Exercises 50
References 50

4. CONSIDERING THE STUDENTS, THE SCHOOL DISTRICT, AND THE COMMUNITY 53

Who Are the Stakeholders? 55
What Are the Clients' Needs and What Are the
  Responsibilities of the District's Management and
  Employees' Unions to These Clients? 58
How Do You Obtain Client Input? 60
How Do You Communicate with the School
  District's Clients? 62
Summary 63

Exercises 64
References 65

SECTION TWO: PREPARING FOR AND CONDUCTING COLLECTIVE BARGAINING

5. DETERMINING STRATEGIC AND TACTICAL PLANS RELATED TO COLLECTIVE BARGAINING 69

Definitions 69
Needs Assessments 70
Internal and External Scanning—Examples 71
Trend Analyses 73
Preferred Future Results 74
Strategic Planning: An Example 75
Union's Tactical Planning: An Example 76
Management's Strategic Planning: An Example 77
Management's Tactical Planning: An Example 77
Areas of Agreement and Disagreement between
  Union's and Management's Strategic Tactical Plans:
  An Example 78
The Approach to Strategic and Tactical Planning
  Differs When a Win-Win Environment Is in Place 79
Summary 79
Exercises 80
References 80

6. COLLECTING BACKGROUND INFORMATION IN PREPARATION FOR NEGOTIATIONS 83

What's Bargainable? 83
What Data Should Be Collected? 85
The Difference between Hard and Soft Data 92
The Importance of Conducting a Trend Analysis 92
Using Trend Data to Impact Upcoming Negotiations 93
Summary 93
Exercises 94
References 94

7. CHOOSING YOUR TEAM AND ANALYZING THEIR TEAM 97

Should There Be a Different View of Team Selection for
  Win-Win and Win-Lose Approaches to Negotiations? . . 97

Why a Negotiation Team?   98
What Should Be the Composition of the Team?   98
What Roles Should Each Team Member Play?   101
Factors That Impact the Timing of Team Selection   104
Negotiation Team's Behavioral Rules   106
Pre-Negotiations Training for Team Members   108
Support Groups and Individuals   110
Removing a Negotiation Team Member   110
Roles Played by Non-Team Members   111
Collecting Information about the Other Team's Members . .   112
Win-Win Procedures   113
Summary   113
Exercises   115
References   115

8. PREPARING TO GO TO THE BARGAINING TABLE   119

Taking a Different View of Win-Win and Win-Lose
    Approaches to Preparation   119
Determining How the Recognition Clause Should Read . . .   121
Preparing the Bargaining Notebook   123
Obtaining the Board of Education's Negotiation
    Guidelines   126
Deciding on Structures, Strategies, and Tactics   127
Preparing Proposals and Counterproposals   130
Preparing for Win-Win Negotiations   131
Summary   132
Exercises   133
References   133

**9. DOING IT: CONDUCT AT AND AWAY FROM
    THE TABLE   137**

Differences between Win-Win and Win-Lose Conduct
    at and Away from the Table   138
Establishing Ground Rules   139
Exchanging Contract Proposals   140
Presenting Proposals to the Other Party   142
Activities during at-the-Table Negotiating Sessions   144
Activities Away from the Bargaining Table   147
What Differences Would Exist if the Negotiating
    Environment Were a Win-Win One?   153

Summary 153
Exercises 155
References 156

**SECTION THREE: FINDING THE TROUBLE SPOTS AND LIVING TOGETHER
AFTER COLLECTIVE BARGAINING**

10. REACHING IMPASSE: TOO LATE FOR WIN-WIN   161

Preparing for Mediation 164
Fact-Finding 167
Interest or Contract Arbitration 169
Summary 172
Exercises 173
References 173

11. ARRIVING AT LOSE-LOSE   175

Preparing for a Strike 176
Preparing a Strike Plan 181
The Hard Place: Long Hours, the Big Stress Test,
    and Playing Chicken Until the End 182
Actions Following a Strike 183
Summary 185
Exercises 186
References · 187

**12. FINALIZING AND COMMUNICATING
THE SIGNED MASTER CONTRACT   189**

Reaching Tentative Agreement on a Contract 189
Presenting the Master Contract for Ratification 194
Printing and Publicizing the Contract 196
Summary 197
Exercises 199
References 199

**13. CONTRACT MANAGEMENT: LIVING WITH THE
CONTRACT THAT HAS BEEN NEGOTIATED   203**

Communicating and Interpreting the Ratified Contract
    during its Operational Stage 203
Training the Administrators in Contract Management 205
Establishing and Breaking Precedents 207

Disciplining Employees 209
A Typical Master Contract's Grievance Procedure 211
Progressive Discipline, Just Cause, and Due Process 213
Preparing for and Processing Grievances 217
Establishing a Continuing Win-Win Union/
    Management Working Environment 220
Summary 221
Exercises 222
References 223

SECTION FOUR: MISCELLANEOUS ITEMS AND SUMMARIZING

14. MISCELLANEOUS ITEMS   229

Agency Shops, Union Shops, and Closed Shops 229
Timing + Information = Power Management 230
Reality Versus Perception and Fact Versus Propaganda . . . 231
Union Support System 232
Contract Language Is Very Important 234
Importance of the First Negotiated Master
    Contractual Agreement 235
Information Leaks during Negotiations 236
When and Where Should Information Be Shared
    and to Which Groups 237
Reopeners and Zipper Clauses 238
Expedited Bargaining 238
Focused or Limited Bargaining 239
Forces That Influence Collective Bargaining 239
Recognition Clause 240
Certification and Decertification Elections 241
Unfair Labor Practice 242
Bad Faith Bargaining 242
Union/Management Conflict When School Districts
    Contract for Services with Outside Organizations 243
Summary 243
Exercises 245
References 245

15. SUMMARY OF COLLECTIVE NEGOTIATIONS   249

The Do's of Collective Bargaining 251
The Maybe's of Collective Bargaining 252

The Don'ts of Collective Bargaining 253
The Benefits of Collective Bargaining for Labor
   and Management 254
The Losses of Collective Bargaining for Labor
   and Management 256
The Benefits and Deficits of Adversarial Bargaining 256
The Benefits and Deficits of Win-Win Bargaining 257
School-Based Management and Its Impact
   on Collective Bargaining 257
Summary 258
Exercises 258
References 259

SECTION FIVE: APPLYING NEGOTIATION, MEDIATION, AND ARBITRATION
TECHNIQUES WITHIN THE BROADER SCHOOL DISTRICT ENVIRONMENT

16. DEALING WITH CONFLICTS INVOLVING INTERNAL INDIVIDUAL AND GROUP INTERESTS   263

Conflict Resolution as a Means of Positive Growth 263
Conflicts: Student Examples 264
Conflicts: Employee/Administration Example 266
Conflicts: Board of Education/Superintendent Example . . . 267
Conflicts: Board of Education Members—Internal
   Conflict Example 268
Extracurricular Activities Versus Academics 269
Communicating with the Community and the Media 270
Media Coverage as a Possible Determiner
   of Conflict Resolution Outcomes 271
Summary 272
Exercises 273
References 273

17. DEALING WITH CONFLICTS OF INTEREST BETWEEN EXTERNAL AND COMMUNITY PRESSURE GROUPS AND THE BOARD OF EDUCATION AND ADMINISTRATION   275

Definition of Conflict of Interest 275
Conflict of Interest Problem-Solving Techniques 275
Consensus-Building Techniques That Help Resolve
   Conflicts of Interest 277

Buying Houses to Build a New School:
  Avoiding Conflict 283
Conservative Groups Get Involved with
  Curricular Content 285
Closing a School Building 285
Changing Attendance Boundaries 288
Summary 290
Exercises 291
References 291

SECTION SIX: THE END PIECES

18. UNION/MANAGEMENT—THE END PIECE   295

The Past 295
The Present 296
The Projected Future 297
Moving from the Adversarial Historical Approach
  to the Preferred Collaborative Win-Win Approach 298
Getting to and Maintaining a Win-Win
  Labor/Management Environment 299
Summary 301
Exercises 302
References 302

**19. THE BROADER SCHOOL DISTRICT
ENVIRONMENT—THE END PIECE   303**

Getting to and Maintaining a Continuous Win-Win
  Environment with and between all Stakeholder
  Groups in the School District 303
Conflict Resolution Techniques with Various
  Stakeholder Groups 303
Conflict Resolution as a Means of Positive Growth 304
Means of Stopping Conflicts of Interest
  from Causing Harm 306
Unresolved Conflicts of Interest—Results 306
Evident Results If Conflict Resolutions Are Successful 307
Methods of Judging Whether or Not Conflicts
  of Interest Have Been Constructively Resolved 307
Summary 308
A Final Summary 308

Exercises 311
References 311

APPENDIX A: EXAMPLE PROVISIONS FROM LOCAL
SCHOOL DISTRICTS; MASTER CONTRACTS
RELATED TO INSUBORDINATION,
INCOMPETENCY, CONTRACT MANAGEMENT,
AND GRIEVANCE PROCEDURES   313

Policy for Insubordination, Incompetency, or Contract
   Mismanagement by Management Personnel 313
Grievance Procedure 313

APPENDIX B: EXAMPLES OF COST AND POWER
ANALYSES OF MASTER CONTRACT PROPOSALS   319

Example One 319
Example Two 320
Example Three 320

APPENDIX C: A FORMAT FOR ANALYZING
FRINGE BENEFITS AND THE COSTS OF MASTER
CONTRACT ARTICLES   323

APPENDIX D: MAIN POINTS OF KENTUCKY'S
REFORM ACT OF 1990 RELATED TO
SCHOOL-BASED DECISION MAKING   325

Kentucky Law: KRS Chapter 160, Sections 14 and 15 . . . 325

APPENDIX E: MAIN POINTS OF TEXAS' REFORM ACT
OF 1990 RELATED TO SCHOOL-BASED
DECISION MAKING   329

Senate Bill 1 (June, 1990) 329
House Bill 2885 (May, 1991) 330
Senate Bill 351 (April, 1991) 331

APPENDIX F: MANAGEMENT'S CONFIDENTIAL
CONTINGENCY PLAN FOR USE DURING
A STRIKE   333

APPENDIX G: UNION'S CONFIDENTIAL WORK
STOPPAGE, PRESTRIKE, AND STRIKE PLANS   339

Prestrike Tactics 339
Work Stoppages 340
Strike Plans 340

APPENDIX H: A CHECKLIST OF STEPS INVOLVED IN
SUCCESSFUL CONFLICT RESOLUTIONS   343

Glossary 345
Bibliography 365
Index 375
About the Authors 383

WHAT THIS BOOK IS ABOUT

PROBLEM solving between and among individuals and groups, especially during conflict of interest situations, is a dynamic, important, and very serious process. Preparing for it, accomplishing it, and living with its results will determine, in many aspects and to a large degree, the organizational structure that will exist in a school district and in the day-to-day procedures to be followed. Because of the impact on the school district's structure and procedures, the results of collective bargaining and conflict resolutions of other types will have a significant effect on the climate and culture of the school district. In addition, the processes utilized to conduct the resolutions of issues by union and management, by community and administration, and by individuals within and without the school district will determine the degree of success in the results achieved. These results will, consequently, strongly influence the attitudes of students, parents, taxpayers, employees, and the citizenry of the school district. It is extremely important that conflict of interest situations, regardless of the individuals or parties that are involved, be handled carefully and wisely by all involved in their resolutions.

Some of the material dealing with collective bargaining, although modified and stressing collaborative win/win bargaining techniques, is taken, with permission, from the 1993 Technomic Publishing Company book by Jerry Herman and Gene Megiveron entitled *Collective Bargaining in Education: Win/Win, Win/Lose, Lose/Lose.* With the advent of school-based or site-based management, which promotes the direct involvement of employees and citizens in management decisions related to the individual school buildings, both union and management representatives who are responsible for collective bargaining must be even more mature and sophisticated in their contract negotiations and contract management responsibilities. If the school district allows school-based management teams authority over the selection of employees, the structure of the school day, and some budgetary areas, the union and management representatives who are responsible for negotiating and managing the master school district contract must take these matters seriously when managing or renegotiating a master contract. Business-as-usual approaches will not suffice, because it is not a business-as-usual environment in which collective bargaining is taking place. Under these new and more complex situations, it will take sophisticated union and management leaders to resolve conflicts of interest that will arise between union and management and among union, management and community representatives.

This book is a how-to-do-it roadmap that presents practical details on the important aspects of collective bargaining at the local school district level. It sets the stage by discussing how administrators and employees live and work together in the school district environment. It then succinctly details all of the strategies, tasks, events, and influences that bear on the collective bargaining process from the initial certification election of a union through the preparation for, negotiation of, and administration of a union/management collective bargaining agreement.

In addition, it also presents sample case study actual incidents of nonunion and management conflicts of interests that involve various individual and groups (although the actual names of individuals and groups are fictionalized) that have been experienced by the authors or by professional colleagues of the authors. For the future operational health of any school district or any individual school building, a highly satisfactory rate of conflict resolution must be attained by those charged with the management responsibilities because this is a crucial element in the successful operation of a school environment.

It is about administrators, teachers, nonteaching employees, citizens, and students, and it is about union and management groups and community and school groups that participate in a dynamic, emotional, and intellectually stimulating and sometimes draining process applied to problem solving and conflict resolution situations. It is also about win-win, win-lose, and lose-lose situations that affect the individuals and groups that work and live within and outside of the school district, and it is about how the results achieved affect those who are served by the employees of the school district. That is, it is about successes, losses, hurts, and satisfactions felt by the individuals and groups of human beings who comprise the residents of a school district community, and it is about the individuals and groups who profit from the successful results of the processes and results achieved or who lose from the failed processes that are attempted to resolve conflicts of interest.

STRUCTURE OF THIS BOOK

While presenting a book written by experienced practitioners, this book includes numerous practical examples on a wide variety of situations that may be faced by the local school district employees or board of education members who are responsible for the conduct of collective bargaining or the resolution of conflicts of interests among a wide variety of individuals or groups who reside in or who interact with their school district. In addition, it includes exercises to assist the reader in participating in real lifelike situations.

The authors clearly favor a collaborative win-win approach to conflict resolution and to collective bargaining, whenever this approach is possible, but they also extensively explore the details involved in conflict of interest and major problem-solving situations that terminate in win-lose or lose-lose results for various individuals and groups involved in these conflict of interest situations. The book is broken into six sections, nineteen chapters, and ten appendices as follows.

Section One: Living and Working with Individuals and Groups includes Chapter 1, Working Together with People and Groups; Chapter 2, The History of and Reasons for the Development of Unions in Education; Chapter 3, The History and Reasons for Employee Empowerment; and Chapter 4, Considering the Students, the School District, and the Community.

Section Two: Preparing for and Conducting Collective Bargaining includes Chapter 5, Determining Strategic and Tactical Plans Related to Collective Bargaining; Chapter 6, Collecting Background Information in Preparation for Negotiations; Chapter 7, Choosing Your Team and Analyzing Their Team; Chapter 8, Preparing to Go to the Bargaining Table; and Chapter 9, Doing It: Conduct at and away from the Table.

Section Three: Finding the Trouble Spots and Living Together after Collective Bargaining includes Chapter 10, Reaching Impasse: Too Late for Win-Win; Chapter 11, Arriving at Lose-Lose; Chapter 12, Finalizing and Communicating the Signed Master Contract; and Chapter 13, Living with the Contract That Has Been Negotiated: Contract Management.

Section Four: Remembering Miscellaneous Items and Summarizing includes Chapter 14, Miscellaneous Items and Chapter 15, Summary of Collective Negotiations.

Section Five: Applying Negotiation, Mediation, and Arbitration Techniques within the Broader School District Environment includes Chapter 16, Dealing with Conflicts Involving Internal Individuals' and Groups' Interests and Chapter 17, Dealing with Conflicts of Interest between External and Community Pressure Groups and the Board of Education and Administration.

Section Six: The End Pieces includes Chapter 18, Union/Management: The End Piece and Chapter 19, The Broader School District Environment: The End Piece.

Appendices include: (1) examples from a local school district's collective bargaining agreement, (2) a cost and power analysis model, (3) a format for analyzing fringe benefits, (4) main points of Kentucky's Reform Act of 1990, (5) main points of Texas's Reform Act of 1990, (6) a management's confidential contingency plan for use during a strike, (7) a union's confidential work stoppage, prestrike, and strike plans, and (8) a checklist of steps involved in resolving conflict resolutions.

The book concludes with a Glossary and Bibliography.

FOR WHOM THIS BOOK IS WRITTEN

This book was written for three purposes. First, it is written as a self-contained, easily read, comprehensive manual for those administrators and board members and other school district employees who are inexperienced in the use of effective processes to resolve conflicts of interests between and among individuals and/or groups of any nature that interact with a school district and who are inexperienced in general labor/management relations and in the specifics of collective bargaining. Second, it is written as a university textbook for graduate education courses in dealing with the areas of conflict resolution and/or collective bargaining. Third, it is written for use as a reference book by anyone who is responsible for or who has an interest in resolving conflicts of interest between or among individuals and/or groups of any category that interact with a school district or who are involved with or who are interested in any phase of the collective bargaining process as it relates to the local school district level.

BY WHOM THIS BOOK IS WRITTEN

The authors have in excess of 60 years in education. They have been teachers, principals, central office administrators, superintendents of schools, university graduate professors in the areas of planning and administration, and state department of education officials. In addition, they have served as consultants to school districts, business organizations, universities, and foundations, and they also have extensively lectured and written on the matters discussed in this book.

Both authors have many years of experience and a wide variety of experiences with major problem solving and conflict resolution situations involving individuals and groups. These experiences span responsibilities as principals and central office administrators, as a schoollevel organizational representative, and as a superintendent of schools, and their experiences involve major problem solving and conflict resolutions situations, including board of education members, administrators, teachers, educational and trade unions, community groups, and a wide variety of pressure groups who have interacted with their schools and school districts.

In addition, their experience with collective bargaining began in 1965, in the state of Michigan, and it involved dealing with trade unions, municipal unions, teachers' unions, classified employees' unions, and administrators' unions in the states of Michigan and New York. Experiences included numerous contract negotiations as a spokesperson, as a negotiating team member, and as a CEO. One author also has much experience with the areas of mediations, arbitrations, fact findings, and strikes.

They share their wealth of on-line, practical experiences in a comprehensive, yet easily understood, manner. They write about major problem-solving methods, conflict resolution processes, and collective bargaining strategies and tactics through the eyes of a local school district's administrator, and they do this with real-life examples and with exercises that are designed to provide realistic practical experiences to be completed by the reader.

LIVING AND WORKING
WITH INDIVIDUALS AND GROUPS

Section One consists of four chapters. Chapter 1, Working Together with People and Groups, presents information about the beliefs one holds about individuals and groups, and discusses the needs of individuals and groups. It also discusses intergroup relations, communications among and between individuals and groups, and the development of groups into winning teams.

Chapter 2, The History of and Reasons for the Development of Unions in Education, briefly relates the history of the development of unions in education, and the reasons for their existence. The National Education Association and the American Federation of Teachers are described in greater detail and a perspective is provided on the contemporary climate of professional organizations and collective negotiations.

Chapter 3, The History of and Reasons for Employee Empowerment, outlines some historical theories and reasearch, covers the topics of employee empowerment, school-based management, and strategies for using groups to address issues. It describes employee recognition structures, methods of involving union/management teams, and models demonstrating the similarities and differences of some key concepts. It ends with a list of ways to create and maintain a productive and satisfying work environment.

Chapter 4, Considering the Students, the School District, and the Community, answers the following questions: Who are the stakeholders? What are the clients' needs? What is the responsibility of the district's management and the employees' union to the school district's clients? How is client input obtained? How do you communicate with the school district's clients?

Working Together with People and Groups

CHAPTER 1 develops a philosophical and pragmatic base about people and groups and about the development of an environment within which the educational and personal lives of students, employees, and management representatives will be affected. Chapter 1 discusses (1) beliefs about people, (2) needs of people, (3) beliefs about groups, (4) needs of groups, (5) growth patterns of groups, (6) development of groups into winning teams, (7) intergroup formal and informal communications, and (8) intergroup relations. This chapter also includes a summary, exercises, and references.

BELIEFS ABOUT PEOPLE

How one acts as a member of a group, collaborative team, task force, committee, or collective bargaining team, and how one administers or lives with the agreed-upon outcomes resulting from negotiated conclusions or consensus arrangements, to a large extent depends on what one believes about people—about individuals with opposing agendas or attitudes, about employees or board members and administrators, about members of the union or of management, about those persons who serve on the other party's collective bargaining team, and about those persons who are not immediately involved in conflict situations but who are seriously affected by the results of negotiated problem solving and collective bargaining. Also important is the way in which a negotiated master contractual agreement is administered. Therefore, it is very important to discern the beliefs, either by conversation or by analysis of actions, of all of the individual players in the school district.

If the parents and other stakeholders—teachers and administrators, board of education members, superintendent, and the collective bargaining team members—have positive beliefs about people and employees

3

they will exhibit behaviors during negotiation periods that will affirm the following beliefs:

- People are basically good, honest, and hardworking.
- Employees wish to perform well, serve students in a quality manner, and assist the school district in the achievement of its performance goals.
- Members of groups and teams have respect for the decision-making and conflict resolution processes, and keep acceptable closure/consensus as a goal.
- Union representatives want to be fair to their membership, fair to the students, fair to the community, fair to taxpayers, and fair to management.
- Union representatives prefer to approach negotiations of a master contractual agreement and day-to-day union business with management's representatives in a win-win, collaborative manner [1,2].

On the other hand, for example, if the union's collective bargaining team or, more importantly, the employees of the school district, feel that the board of education, or the school district administration, or the management's collective bargaining team harbors negative beliefs about people, employees, and the union, then collective bargaining will almost always be doomed to follow a hard line, win-lose relationship. At this point the threat of a lose-lose strike situation looms large as the collective bargaining relationship runs its course under adversarial interpersonal and intergroup relationships. If stakeholders, group or team members, and management harbor the following negative beliefs, or if, as in the example, the union's collective bargaining team feels that management harbors the following negative beliefs, labor and management are almost always doomed to a difficult, adversarial relationship:

- People are lazy, selfish, and have no concern for the quality of their work.
- Employees feel no loyalty to the school district's organization, nor to the students, nor to the community in which they work.
- Union representatives are not concerned about the quality of the students' environment, or the degree of achievement attained by the students.
- Union representatives are only concerned about power and money, regardless of the effect on students' programs or the community's, administration's, or board of education's attitudes towards the union [3,4].

If the individuals involved in the negotiation process hold the following beliefs, the collaborative and problem-solving environment will, in all likelihood, be a positive one [5]:

• Individuals and groups within the district respect and support each other as advocates for students.
• Board members appreciate the employees and trust them, realizing that employee unions represent an important and necessary countervailing force. They want to be fair to employees and provide them with good salaries, fringe benefits, and pleasing working conditions.
• Superintendents of schools believe employees are hardworking; that they wish to achieve; that they want to assist students and assist in improving all aspects of the school district; and that they want to be fair to students, to management, and to the community.
• Managers see themselves in the role of helpers of employees and students within a consulting and helping framework.
• Board collective bargaining team members desire to work in a collaborative, win-win environment that assists the union's bargaining team members in solving problems and in achieving reasonable union and employee collective bargaining goals [6,7].

On the other hand, if the administration, board members, employees, and union representatives hold the following negative beliefs towards each other, the environment within which conflict resolution and contractual negotiations takes place and within which the day-to-day personal and group interactions and union/management relations will function will probably be an adversarial, win-lose one. In all likelihood permanent, damaging enmity and a lose-lose strike situation will result [8].

• Conflicting individuals and groups within the district will make no attempt to find common ground and will polarize their respective positions and issues.
• Boards of education will adamantly refuse to share any power, and they will attempt to provide the lowest salaries and fringe benefit costs possible.
• Superintendents of schools and the board of education's chief negotiator will attempt to maintain control for the boards and they will attempt to keep new money expenditures to a minimum, whether the financial condition of the school district is average or of exceptional high wealth.

- Administrators play the roles of autocratic managers, not educational leaders, and they manage by "snoopervision" and intimidation.
- Board members, superintendents, administrators, and the board of education's collective bargaining team members believe that employees are lazy, selfish, not concerned about the students, not concerned about the school district, and not concerned about the community at large. They are only concerned about their own selfish interests and how much of everything their union representative can get from the board of education, management, and the taxpayers.

Not only will the beliefs that one holds about people influence the conflict negotiation, problem-solving, collective bargaining process, and labor relations in general, but the knowledge of and the consideration given to the needs of people will also influence these dynamics and processes within school districts. Crucial people needs must be addressed if one is to perform well within a collaborative and solution-seeking environment.

NEEDS OF PEOPLE

All persons have needs for security, social acceptance, and self-esteem. In addition, employees have needs for (1) adequate salary and fringe benefits, (2) job security, (3) interesting work, (4) opportunities for input into matters which affect them, (5) recognition by peers and management personnel, (6) opportunities for growth, and (7) self-satisfaction and self-actualization [9].

Whether one is dealing with a formal team or recognized group or dealing with employees on a day-to-day basis, these people needs are important variables that must be kept in mind. Individuals should recognize that even in the case of labor/management splits, identical or similar needs exist for both sides.

The way that individuals are treated depend on the beliefs one has about individuals. In addition, one must recognize the beliefs one holds about groups and about the needs of groups [10,11].

BELIEFS ABOUT GROUPS

If boards of education, stakeholders, employees, superintendents, and administrators hold the following beliefs about groups, they will act in a mature, collaborative, win-win manner during problem solving and conflict resolution, during the negotiations of a master contractual agreement, and during the day-to-day relations within the district:

- Group decision-making and collaborative conflict resolution processes are the best vehicle for reconciling diverse opinions and agendas.
- Unions' collective bargaining teams serve the legitimate purpose of representing all of its employees' interests.
- Unions' leadership groups are mature, logical, and fair.
- Unions' leadership groups will consider the financial ability of the district and the community; the leadership and legitimate leadership and management requirements of the board of education and the district's administrators; and, most importantly, the needs of the students [12].

On the other hand, if the boards of education, stakeholders, superintendents, administrators, and employees hold the following beliefs about problem solving and conflict resolution, they will act in an adversarial, win-lose mode that may eventually lead to permanent fissures in working relationships and, possibly, strikes by the school districts' employees:

- Group decision-making and collaborative conflict resolution processes are inefficient, create dissonance, and offer no opportunities for closure.
- Unions' collective bargaining teams are only concerned about getting more of everything regardless of any negative effect those moves may have on students, the taxpayers, community relations, or labor/management long-term relations [13].
- Unions' leadership groups are self-serving, power hungry groups whose only purpose is to increase their power and increase their own benefits. If the unions' membership receive gains through collective bargaining processes, those gains are incidental to the main goals of increasing leadership power, control, and benefits [14].

Stakeholders, employees, and other district individuals in general, react to management negotiation teams or representatives and to the board of education and the school district administration in a positive or negative manner based upon their beliefs about boards and administrators [15]. The following positive beliefs about these groups and individuals by stakeholders, employees, and union leaders will lead to a collaborative win-win approach to collective bargaining and to positive day-to-day labor/management and other relationships [16,17].

- Group decision-making and collaborative conflict resolution processes are superficial structures; rather, they are powerless, administratively designed, and offer no real opportunities for closure.
- School board members, administrators and management's collective bargaining team members believe that the union has a legitimate right to request working conditions that promote a positive, happy, and productive work environment for the employees it represents.
- They realize that it is necessary to provide good salaries, good fringe benefits, and a positive labor/management image in order to attract and retain excellent employees.
- They realize that a collaborative, positive, win-win approach in conjunction with union leaders is the best way to realize the goals of the school district and to enhance the probability of achieving the quality of education desired for all the district's students.
- School board members, administrators, and management's collective bargaining team members must represent the interests of students, taxpayers, and the community; but they will not do this by undermining or neglecting the legitimate interests of employees or the employees' union.

On the other hand, if the union leadership and the school district's employees harbor the following negative beliefs about boards of education, administrators, and management's collective bargaining team members, the result will be contracted and adversarial negotiations that may very well end in a lose-lose strike situation. In addition, these negative beliefs will probably lead to a day-to-day win-lose relationship between union leaders, employees, administrators, and board of education members [18].

- Board of education members are only concerned about keeping taxes low and pacifying community power figures in order to promote their own future political aspirations.
- Administrators view employees as lower level workers who must be closely monitored, given orders, and snoopervised.
- Management's negotiation team will lie, use dirty tricks, attempt to discredit union leaders, and do whatever they deem necessary to get a win for management and a loss for the union.

Not only are one's beliefs about individuals and groups, and the knowledge of the needs possessed by individuals and groups, predictors of one's potential future behavior, one's understanding of the growth patterns of groups will also determine the strategies and tactics one utilizes in dealing with labor/management situations.

NEEDS OF GROUPS

Whether one is dealing with a union group, a board/administrative group, or any other category of group, certain characteristics must exist if the specific group is to achieve its interests. In order to be successful, the group must identify and attend to the following needs: (1) to reach consensus on its mission and goals, (2) to develop effective and efficient strategies and tactics, (3) to clearly communicate with all members of the group, (4) to monitor the group's progress, and (5) to evaluate the degree of success it has achieved at various benchmark time periods, in accomplishing the specific goals it has established.

Each group must be cohesive, have a results-oriented agenda, and apply strategies and tactics that will receive the desired results. Once this has been accomplished, the group has greatly increased its probability of success when dealing with governmental organizations and other groups who do not share the mission or goals of the group.

GROWTH PATTERNS OF GROUPS

As individuals grow from birth through adolescence, adulthood, and old age, so do groups. It is crucial that those dealing with collaborative groups or teams carefully analyze the growth stage of the group with which they are dealing. Here are some of the major characteristics of the three stages in the growth pattern of groups:

During the *infancy stage* of group growth, a careful observer will see that (1) the group is not clear about the role of the individuals who comprise the group, (2) the group has no clear goals or objectives, (3) leadership within the group is undetermined, (4) strategies and tactics are not discernible, (5) communications are amoeba-like and lack clarity, and (6) problem-solving methodologies are nonexistent. Certainly during its infancy stage, the group (whether it be a labor or a management group) is ill-prepared to handle inter-group relations.

During the *adolescent stage* of group growth, a careful observer will recognize that the group (1) realizes the necessity of leadership, but the leadership role changes from time to time and from person to person, (2) has set goals but they are changed or modified frequently, (3) has knowledge of one another, and communications are beginning to be stabilized, (4) has developed strategies and tactics, but they are still moving targets, (5) only has short-term problem-solving abilities, and (6) is comprised of various members who are beginning to evolve in various roles.

During the *maturity stage* of group growth, even a casual observer will realize that (1) the roles of the various group members are clarified and stabilized, and they form the basis for the smooth operation of the group, (2) strategies and tactics are developed for both the short term and long term, (3) problem-solving techniques are highly sophisticated, and they successfully lead to the attainment of the desired results, (4) each person understands well the other members of the group, and each person understands the personality, strengths, and weaknesses of all other members of the group, (5) communications are clear and they are those of an open system, (6) leadership of the group is clearly identified, and the leadership is supported by all members of the group, (7) input is requested from all members and the members' input is accepted as valuable by all members of the group and (8) the group works as a cohesive unit which is well prepared to deal with inter-group relations in a professional and productive manner [19].

Once the adversarial or conflicting groups are in the maturity stage of growth, they can combine to create a mature, win-win, collaborative relationship. This relationship will serve both groups well as they collectively negotiate or problem solve a settlement or contractual agreement. This relationship will also serve both groups well in their day-to-day interpersonal and labor/management relations. However, the probability of successful win-win relations with adolescent groups is limited, and the potential for successful win-win, collaborative relations with immature groups is almost nonexistent [20,21].

When all groups reach the maturity stage, they are prepared, for all practical purposes, to become a single win-win, collaborative working group. Let's now briefly turn to the differences among a group, a team, and a winning team.

DEVELOPMENT OF GROUPS INTO WINNING TEAMS

A *group* is a collection of two or more people who are placed in a single environment for a period of time [22,23]. A group may be together for a short time period, and the group may not possess any goals. An example is a group of people at a shopping mall.

A *team* is comprised of a collection of two or more individuals who share a common purpose. An example is a sports team. The members of the team may have a common purpose and they may have agreed-upon goals, but the team may not achieve its goals and there might be dissension among the team members [24].

A *winning team* is comprised of two or more individuals who share a common purpose, have a set of agreed-upon goals and objectives, have a shared vision and mission, and who work together in a collaborative and positive manner to achieve its vision, mission, goals, and objectives. The individuals who comprise the team feel a sense of accomplishment and they also feel a sense of caring and respect from the other team members [25].

What follows are descriptions of the intergroup relations and communication patterns that identify an environment where individuals, stakeholders, union, and management form winning teams.

INTERGROUP FORMAL
AND INFORMAL COMMUNICATIONS

Intergroup relations within a win-win, collaborative, school district environment can best be described as one of mutual goal setting, mutual problem solving, and a high level of achievement related to the goals which were previously mutually established. In addition, a listing of those descriptors that identify, in detail, a winning team will further describe this more positive operation [26].

Formal and informal communications are open, honest, and frequent. Trust and understanding are fostered and the success of the group or team members is enhanced [27,28].

INTERGROUP RELATIONS

If any group sees those individuals or groups who do not share their interests as enemies, it will probably choose a confrontational warfare approach to achieve its interests. On the other hand, if the group sees those individuals or groups who do not share their interests as possessing legitimate but differing agendas, it can attempt to achieve its desired results by utilizing an educational and compromising approach with the other group. Providing information and logical argumentation, and attempting to locate and emphasize areas of agreement rather than disagreement, will go a long way in bringing the group credibility as a logical and collaborative entity. This is the only approach that any individual or group can logically take if they wish to become effective players in their environment over the long term.

SUMMARY

In order to be effective players within an environment of collaboration, conflict management, and collective bargaining, it is crucial that all participants work within their beliefs about people, stakeholders, groups, unions, members of the union's negotiation team, union leadership, and employees. It is just as crucial that employees and union leaders work within their beliefs about boards of education, superintendents, school district administrators, and management negotiation teams. In addition, it is important that both parties in any conflict or negotiation arrangement clearly understand the needs of individuals and of groups.

Indicators of the various stages of group growth were listed. The stages of group growth are *infancy, adolescence,* and *maturity.* Stress was placed on the fact that mature groups can combine into a single, win-win, collaborative, problem-solving, and program developing group. However, the probability of a win-win, collaborative environment existing is greatly diminished when the groups are in the adolescent stage of growth; and a win-win process is next to impossible when either of the groups are in the infancy stage of growth.

The differences among a group, a team, and a winning team were identified. A winning team is one which possesses: (1) an agreed upon vision, mission, goals, and objectives, (2) an open and clear system of communications, (3) strategic and tactical plans, (4) excellent problem-solving methodologies, and (5) a high level of achievement related to its vision, mission, goals, and objectives. The members of a winning team feel a sense of accomplishment, are individually productive, and feel a sense of caring, respect, and recognition from all other members of the team.

When a winning team, comprised of representatives of opposing groups or of management members and union members exists, informal and formal communications are positive, clear, and at a high level; and intergroup relations are those of respect, common concern, and caring. In addition, winning teams and winning team members:

- are comfortable in sharing leadership functions, and decisions are made within a collaborative atmosphere
- feel that a strong sense of interdependence is necessary if the vision, mission, goals and objectives are to be achieved at high levels
- solicit the best input from all members of the team
- participate consistently and comprehensively in communications on matters related to issues, goals, and problems
- are dedicated to creating a collaborative, win-win; rather than an adversarial, win-lose environment
- join forces to solve critical operating and long-term problems relating to the welfare of the district's students, the union's membership, and the district's management
- use informal as well as formal communications channels between ad hoc problem-solving and program development subgroups comprised of membership from conflicting sides, or from both union and management
- look at the level of positive functioning of the team, while each individual looks at her/his role(s) and performance(s) within the team as a means of assessing her/his level of performance as a team member
- feel a unity of purpose, a sense of ownership, and a requirement to be the best they can be as a unit and as members within the team

EXERCISES

1. Describe methods you can use to assist a group of individuals who are in the infancy stage of group development to quickly develop into a productive group.
2. Describe the methods you can use to assist a group of individuals who are in the adolescent stage of group development to quickly develop into a mature and successful group.
3. What techniques can you utilize to assess the level of achievement of a mature group and of the contribution(s) of each member.

4. Define the differences among a group, a team, and a winning team.

5. Describe the indicators that describe a winning team.

6. List your beliefs about people: stakeholders, union members, employees, boards of education, superintendents, administrators, members of a union's collective bargaining team, and members of a management's collective bargaining team.

7. What do you know about the needs of individuals and groups?

8. What type of informal and formal communications techniques would you use when dealing with union/management relations?

9. Describe some primary descriptors of the infancy, adolescent, and maturity stage of groups.

10. Think of specific instances in your experience when groups acted in an adversarial manner and when groups acted in a collaborative, win-win, manner. List the results achieved by each approach, and try to determine why each set of results occurred.

REFERENCES

1. McGregor, D. M. 1960. *The Human Side of Enterprise.* New York, NY: McGraw-Hill Book Co., pp. 33–34.

2. Herman, J. J. and J. L. Herman. 1991. *The Positive Development of Human Resources and School District Organizations.* Lancaster, PA: Technomic Publishing Co., Inc., pp. 183–184.

3. Herman, J. J. and J. L. Herman. 1991. *The Positive Development,* pp. 168–169.

4. Herman, J. J. and G. E. Megiveron. 1993. *Collective Bargaining in Education: Win/Win, Win/Lose, Lose/Lose.* Lancaster, PA: Technomic Publishing Company, pp. 3–11.

5. Kearney, R. C. 1984. *Labor Relations in the Public Sector.* New York, NY: Marcel Dekker, Inc., p. 237.

6. Helsby, R. D., J. Tener, and J. Lefkowitz, eds. 1985. *The Evolving Process—Collective Negotiations in Public Employment.* Fort Washington, PA: Labor Relations Press, p. 442.

7. Herman, J. J. and G. E. Megiveron. 1993. *Collective Bargaining in Education,* pp. 3–11.

8. Eberts, R. W, and J. A. Stone. 1984. *Unions and Public Schools.* Lexington, MA: D. C. Heath and Company, pp. 30–31.

9. Herman, J. J. and J. L. Herman. 1991. *The Positive Development,* pp. 138–139.

10. Barrett, Jerome T. 1985. *Labor-Management Cooperation in the Public Service: An Idea Whose Time Has Come.* Washington, DC: International Personnel Management Association, p. 30.

11. Morgan, G. 1989. *Creative Organizational Theory: A Resourcebook.* Newbury Park, CA: Sage Publications, pp. 41–48.

12. Helsby, R. D., J. Tener, and J. Lefkowitz, eds. 1985. *The Evolving Process,* p. 442.

13. Webster, W. G., Sr. 1985. *Effective Collective Bargaining in Public Education.* Ames, IA: Iowa State University Press, pp. 82–83.

14. Webster, W. G., Sr. 1985. *Effective Collective Bargaining,* pp. 10–13.

15. Webster, W. G., Sr. 1985. *Effective Collective Bargaining,* pp. 44–47.

16. Eberts, R. W, and J. A. Stone. 1984. *Unions and Public Schools,* pp. 30–31.

17. Coleman, C. J. 1990. *Managing Labor Relations in the Public Sector.* San Francisco, CA: Jossey-Bass Publishers, pp. 284–285.

18. Morgan, G. 1989. *Creative Organizational Theory,* pp. 121–123.

19. Herman, J. J. and J. L. Herman. 1991. *The Positive Development,* pp. 42–43.

20. Bacharach, S. B., J. B. Shedd, and S. C. Conley. 1989. "School Management and Teacher Unions: The Capacity for Cooperation in an Age of Reform," *Teachers College Record,* 91(1): 97–105.

21. "Are Trade Unions and Human Resource Management Incompatible?" 1995. *Manager Update,* 6 (3):25–27.

22. Johnson, D. W. and F. P. Johnson. 1982. *Joining Together—Group Therapy and Group Skills.* 2d ed. Englewood Cliffs, NJ: Prentice-Hall, p. 4.

23. Herman, J. J. and G. E. Megiveron. 1993. *Collective Bargaining in Education,* pp. 10–11.

24. Bucholz, S. and T. Roth. 1987. *Creating the High Performance Team.* New York, NY: John Wiley & Sons, pp. 30–31.

25. Bucholz, S. and T. Roth. 1987. *Creating the High Performance Team,* pp. 30–31.

26. Herman, J. J. and J. L. Herman. 1991. *The Positive Development,* pp. 182–183.

27. Guillén, M. F. 1994. "The Age of Eclecticism: Current Organizational Trends and the Evolution of Managerial Models," *Sloan Management Review,* 36(1): 75–86.

28. Castetter, W. B. 1996. *The Human Resource Function in Educational Administration.* 6th ed. Englewood Cliffs, NJ: Merrill, pp. 558–563.

The History of and Reasons for the Development of Unions in Education

CHAPTER 2 briefly relates the history of the development of unions in education, and the reasons for their existence. The National Education Association and the American Federation of Teachers are described in greater detail and a perspective is provided on the contemporary climate of professional organizations and collective negotiations. The chapter ends with a summary, exercises and selected references.

UNION PRECONDITIONS IN EDUCATION: THE FALLOW GROUND

It was the growth of cities and the centralizing of the public school systems which made unionization possible, changing the professional landscape from one of isolated, rural, community-dependent female teachers to one of a collective craft guild model. There was a sense of professionalism growing among the ranks that became an obstacle to unionization; the rank-and-file membership struggled with a conflict between career focus and craft pride and the imperatives of the bread-and-butter issues of compensation and benefits. A second obstacle was the political perception of teacher militancy as Communistic in overtone and instigation, with an attendant chilling effect on membership recruitment and retention. A third obstacle was the recurring financial crisis and cyclical fiscal restraints that have characterized the last decades of this century [1].

The sociology of teaching has also influenced the rise of unionism; the elevation of social status represented by joining this quasi–white collar profession represented a significant change in the personal and social class experience of, particularly, females and minorities. The historical profile of the teacher, especially during the last half of the nineteenth century, as one of feminine virtue and moral influence, coupled with low salaries/nonexistent benefits and limited scope of professional responsibilities, created a semi-professional underclass of low-paid females. Another factor in this profile was the rural and small-town setting of most schools, with the attendant dispersed functions and focus on community control. As urbanization increased in the last years of the century, the thrust of the growing national organizational activity— nascent unionism—was framed around gender issues. There was an old/new struggle between the dominance of the traditional male pedagogical professionalism and the emerging Progressive emphasis on female participation in the process. As centralization grew towards the end of the last century, "women schoolteachers stood at the boundaries between professionalism and unionism as they assessed the two movements that dominated educational discourse" [2].

REASONS FOR THE EXISTENCE
OF UNIONS IN EDUCATION

A close community environment and lack of professional/bureaucratic support and personal privacy isolated teachers and necessitated their conformity to local expectations. This degree of control was eroded by the common school movement of the mid nineteenth century, which sought to standardize practice and process, bringing a common body of knowledge to schools through centralization. At the same time, a feminization of the profession occurred through the exodus of the itinerant male instructors (frequently to school administrative levels) and the necessary (because of increased student numbers) increase in ranks of the lower-salaried and more "moral" women teachers. The "common school reformers sought longer terms of employment, higher pay, improved training, improved hiring procedures, and more communication through professional journals and associations. The issues of school centralization, professionalism, teacher militancy, and community resistance persisted throughout the Progressive Era. Teachers were now starting to band together to further the profession and their common interests" [3]. The primary issue was one of adequate compensation, since salary levels remained historically low, while administrators pushed for teachers to be better trained, more middle class in values, and nonpolitical. It is critical to keep in mind that the crucible of economic and political forces that shaped the emerging professional organizational movement predated women's suffrage; the absence of political pull for voteless women was key in the push for unionization. The only political clout possessed by urban teachers prior to formal organization was in their ties to the neighborhoods and communities they served (and from whose ranks they came; these high school and normal school–educated daughters of the blue collar classes). Ties to the wards and to the corrupt politicians running them, particularly in Chicago, created a need for school reformers who could disrupt this connection and make teachers conform to a new model of professionalism. (This need coincided with the rise in urban reform governments in both New York and Chicago.)

SOCIAL UPHEAVAL AND THE UNIONS: SUFFRAGE, DEPRESSION, WAR, AND CIVIL RIGHTS

Teachers were major players in the suffrage movement. The inherently feminine sense of self-sacrifice and the "higher calling" propaganda of fiscally pressed school boards was viewed as a tactic to suppress wages. In Chicago and other cities the women teachers were instrumental in organizing the women in other occupations, "milliners, packing house workers, box makers, musicians, chorus girls, laundry workers, domestic servants, department store workers, bookbinders, garment workers, and glove workers" [4]. This early cooperation created ties to the larger labor movement.

These early federations also addressed the right of married women to hold teaching positions, though a "family wage" mentality (the paternalistic attitude that a husband's wages were sufficient income) characterized early union male leadership. In fact, many of the early activities of the feminist movement in the unions were clearly aimed at attacking the male dominance of the profession. While they were frequently unsuccessful with the traditional leadership, they were supported by the rising young Progressive Era male superintendents, who opportunistically capitalized on the feminist energies to obtain their own agendas, while ultimately working to defeat the concept of teacher unionism.

The early years of the teachers' movement was amorphous. Teachers needed their local union affiliations to give them political power on the urban level, and they needed a national forum. There was mounting evidence that the NEA leadership would deliver neither and, pressured by business interests and beleaguered by teacher salary concerns, was becoming increasingly hostile to the teacher rebellion [5]. The birth of the American Federation of Teachers (AFT) was imminent.

THE NATIONAL EDUCATION ASSOCIATION (NEA)

Begun as a collective effort by ten state teacher organizations in 1857, the infant NEA (begun as the National Teachers' Association) merged with the National Association of School Superintendents in later years to become the National Education Association. The chartered purpose was to form a system of separate departments within the NEA (school administrators, college presidents, classroom teachers, etc.), which created a class structure; for years the real power and political influence was held by the elite male administrative membership side, while the larger female classroom teacher constituency held a tenuous position and was largely disenfranchised. Their participation in the emerging corporate industrial world and the new economic order was not envisioned. The decision-making process, the committee organizational structure, and the NEA leadership vision of the years before and after the turn of the century was characterized by gender inequality. Annual conventions were largely teacher institutes, with lectures and information provided by the male membership. A class struggle was developing between the larger female membership and the university/administrative elite, characterized by the leadership's (fearing a business support backlash) containment of the tax and salary issues. It was this growing discontent that provided the climate for the emergence of the AFT.

Membership in the NEA grew dramatically from the early 1900s to 1920, due to a campaign for membership focused on salary enhancement, garnering public support, and increasing the participation of teachers in school governance. (This organizing campaign closely followed the AFT's organization of its first meetings.) Simultaneously, the actual influence of teacher members was diluted by a change in the voting structure, which altered from a single-member, one-vote format to a politicized state delegate structure, which came to be dominated by the administrators until the upheavals and actionism of the 1970s.

Wartime patriotism became tied to NEA membership, and urban AFT member dismissals occurred due to harassment justified by "patriotic" causes. After World War I, with rising competition from the AFT, the NEA stressed large salary securement and promoted exclusive membership drives in districts. Due to the reorganization of schools, the changes in teacher population, and the power needs of new superintendents, the NEA changed not only its power structure but also managed to lure teachers away from the more radical union and to sell them on the professionalism and reputation of the larger organization [6].

During the Depression, membership numbers dropped, but the organization's sensitivity to teacher welfare issues was increasing. Postwar
development of focus on salary issues presaged the militancy of the
1960s and 1970s.

The organization entered the middle of the decade with an eighty-
five percent teacher membership. These members began to be concerned about NEA leadership, as positions of prominence were still
largely administrative, and growing adversarial in the changing meet-
and-confer environment, which was evolving into full-scale collective
bargaining.

The 1962 issuance of Executive Order 10988, through which
Kennedy gave federal employees the right to organize and bargain collectively, served as an impetus for the groundbreaking New York
teacher strike that spring [7]. The NEA initially supported sanctions
rather than walkouts, but as they and the AFT became competitors for
representation of local teacher affiliates, the AFT membership surged
and it won a number of elections. At the height of the 1970s, the NEA
was forced to survive through union-like negotiation tactics, even as
they clung to their image of professionalism and character.

THE AMERICAN FEDERATION OF TEACHERS (AFT)

Teachers in Chicago had organized in 1897 to protect teacher pensions, to gain a salary increase, and to democratize the administration
of the city schools. At the same time there was an influx of scientific
management of classrooms and schools by the new administrative con-
servatives, which caused much dissent among the teacher ranks. These
teachers resented the imposed view of progressive reformers, school
administrators, and business leaders that teaching was a selfless and
semi-religious calling, the true spirit and noble nature of which was in
direct conflict with the pursuit of "self-interests" symbolized by the
Chicago Teachers' Federation. The CTF, making an ideological break
with the male-dominated NEA, was primarily female in membership.
It successfully lobbied for the payment of corporate back taxes, but created a fatal precedent by affiliating with the Chicago Federation of
Labor. This action earned the enmity of the Chicago Board of Education and the Illinois Supreme Court; the latter upheld the Board's power
to require that all teachers not belong to an organization affiliated with
organized labor. The NEA officially censured the "revolutionists" of

the CTF and created a climate of accusation of protectionism and political activism, one which continued throughout the following decades of the AFT's ascendency. Shortly thereafter, the CFT reorganized and broke its ties with the Chicago Federation of Labor, substantially reducing its power and influence in the process.

Following the path of this prototype, a new organization formed by four local unions in Chicago in 1916 became the American Federation of Teachers. The election of male leadership, necessitated by the (pre-suffrage) members' need for access to power, created a primarily high school teacher membership base. Elementary teacher membership stayed at low levels for the first thirty years, reflecting a social class and academic preparation distinction between elementary and secondary teachers. This distinction was carried out in the salary differential between the two levels and the different political access and prestige they represented. The interchange of politics between the old CFT and the emerging AFT created a character difference that would set the early AFT apart from the NEA and the local community–connected, feminist elementary membership. Simultaneously, the NEA was strongly promoting a contrasting membership character focused on loyalty to the calling and based on professional solidarity and a "caste" implication. The postwar labor strikes and troubles of the early 1920s provided an opportunity for the demonization of the teacher unionization movement in the political arena and the popular press.

The Depression years transformed the AFT from a feminist gadfly union to the bread-and-butter organization of the 1960s. The early feminist local leadership gave way to a better educated professional group, which faced the economic collapse, fiscal crisis, and fight with the AFL in a context of continuing conflict [8].

The strains of the Depression affected both the NEA and the AFT; the loss of a viable public revenue base created strife. Both were further beset by social and economic pressures for a radical transformation of society and the beginning of federal intervention in youth training (which created the precedent for the national level programmatic and policy influences of the 1950s and 1960s).

In the interwar years the AFT lost membership; there was a perception of the union as a liberal and Communistic-leaning organization. The strains of conservative and liberal factions split the union's strength, it did not regain momentum until the political upheavals and strikes of the late 1960s and 1970s. In the interim, it was considered to be a radical alternative to the NEA.

UNION INFLUENCE AND POWER SINCE THE 1980s

These organizations have come to possess substantial human and financial resources; the political clout, both in effective lobbying (which has increased significantly since the 1960s), political contributions, and endorsements, and in the strength of the teacher voting bloc, has become significant. The financial resources of the NEA alone have exceeded those of the entire labor movement sector. The union influence is likewise strong at the state and local level.

The strong rivalry between the AFT and the NEA, traditionally aligned along social class and professional distinctions, kept the two organizations competing for membership numbers and political influence [9]. The NEA's altruistic profile and claims to selfless professionalism were altered by the need during the 1960s and 1970s to meet the challenge of the AFT, which had been more aggressive and successful in obtaining concessions and groundbreaking rights for its membership [10]. During the 1980s, the educational reform movement began with a series of state and national level reports of widespread mediocrity in the field and the disunity of the two organizations blocked what might have been a more cohesive and effective response to the tide of public criticism. Progressive forces within both organizations have pressed for a formal union and for the clout that would come with a three-million-member-strong coalition.

There is a push for professional unionism within the ranks, as the trend toward increased local control, collaboration, and teacher and other employee empowerment has increased within the field. The formation of community coalitions and substantial involvement in decision making at the individual school level have created a climate in which the reform goals of cohesion and collegiality are at odds with the traditional model of collective negotiations. The need for trust, open communication, and flexible operational and policy structures that characterize a restructured school environment run counter to the rulebound, centralized environment of a master contractual agreement. In the historical emphasis on membership benefits and economic issues, the unions have become "legally and psychologically distanced from the responsibility for meeting the general social goals of an educated citizenry. . . . A new relationship between school organizations must be developed," one that allows for "professionalism and the pursuit of teacher self-interest" [11].

SUMMARY

The social and economic conditions which created a climate for the seeds of unionism were described, as were descriptions of the historical sociology of the teaching profession. A brief description of the origins of the NEA and the AFT and their early connections to the larger labor movement of the century's earlier decades was included. A perspective of the recent challenges to the profession and the concurrent implications for the two organizations' merger and the changes required in an emerging collaborative educational system followed.

EXERCISES

1. Research the history of unionism in your school district. Why do you think the union(s) in your district evolved as it (they) did?
2. What obstacles and advantages do you see for a merger of the NEA and the AFT?
3. What do you see as the most critical need for a professional teacher organization in the current political climate?

REFERENCES

1. Murphy, M. 1990. *Blackboard Unions—The AFT & the NEA 1900–1980*. Ithaca, NY. Cornell University Press, p. 47.
2. Ibid.
3. Streshly, W. A. and T. A. DeMitchell. 1994. *Teacher Unions and TQE*, Newbury Park, CA: Corwin Press, Sage Publications, p. 5.
4. Murphy, M. 1990. *Blackboard Unions*, p. 79.
5. Ibid.
6. Berube, M. R. 1988. *The Influence of Unions*. New York: Greenwood Press: pp. 2–6.
7. Keane, W. G. 1996. *Win Win or Else: Collective Bargaining in an Age of Public Discontent*. Thousand Oaks, CA: Corwin Press, Sage Publications, pp. 4–6.
8. Spring, J. 1990. *The American School 1642–1990: Varieties of Historical Interpretation of the Foundations and Development of American Education*. 2nd ed. New York: Longman, p. 272–273.
9. Selden, D. 1985. *The Teacher Rebellion*. Washington, D.C.: Howard University Press, p. 82.
10. Streshly, W. A. and T. A. DeMitchell. 1994. *Teacher Unions and TQE*, 245.
11. Streshly, W. A. and T. A. DeMitchell. 1994. *Teacher Unions and TQE*, 66–68.

The History of and Reasons for Employee Empowerment

CHAPTER 3 discusses empowerment methodologies, and a variety of group and team configurations that can be used to implement a philosophy of employment empowerment. It also presents information related to historical theories and research, and discusses ways of creating and maintaining a productive and satisfying work environment. The chapter includes a discussion of methods of involving union/management teams in day-to-day problem solving and decision making. The chapter concludes with a summary, exercises, and references.

HISTORICAL THEORIES AND RESEARCH

The beginnings of empowerment as a concept lie in organizational theory and, more specifically, in private sector managerial innovation. Much of organizational theory has been developed over the last three decades; public sector–related research is even more recent. The idea of loosely coupled systems, and the resulting and inevitable cultural uniqueness of each individual school, supports the push for employee empowerment, decentralization, and the perception that the individual school can be a center for change [1]. More recent patterns found in productive businesses have included employee involvement, high levels of participation, a team approach, decentralization of decision making, and, most significantly, a downsizing of structure—scope, management, and governance [2].

The thrust of contemporary organizational theory and current corporate innovation has been one of participation, involvement, smallness, work teams, and decision making at the lowest level—these comprise various forms of self-determination which have decentralized the workplace. A common theme which runs through the body of contemporary corporate and managerial study is the key function of *decentralization,* in critical linkage with the increase of productivity. The striking absence of centralization and entrenched bureaucracies in lighthouse organizations is well documented [3,4].

In the Peters and Waterman 1982 study of the nation's "best-run companies," they identified *a shared sense of ownership* as a key ingredient of successful organizations. An increasing number of major corporations have adopted employee ownership, trading traditional line assembly for self-managing teams who assume responsibility for a larger scope of the production process or product [5].

Theories of how people work together effectively in organizations have been the focus for managerial research and practice for the past two decades. Downsizing as a pervasive application in scope, management, and governance/regulation has been a hallmark of the corporate field. Organizations are looking for ways to place responsibility closer to the activity; deciding which functions can be decentralized, and giving autonomy to units while also incorporating them into the overall operations [6].

In order to have a culture which involves employees in productive decision making and development, and which creates a sense of ownership, some essential components must be in place. If employees feel that (1) they are doing meaningful work, (2) they are recognized for their contributions, (3) they have opportunities for input into decisions affecting them, (4) they have security, (5) they are socially accepted, and (6) they have growth opportunities, they will want to improve their performance and the performance of the entire school district. Maslow has proposed that, for most workers, the first three levels of need are normally satisfied and are therefore no longer motivational in nature; however, satisfaction of esteem and self-actualization·are seldom completed, and will therefore serve as continual motivators [7]. The implication for educational organizations is that methods must be developed to better meet the higher-level needs of students, teachers, and administrators.

A more behavioral type of empowerment-connected motivational theory is based on philosophical assumptions about beliefs regarding human nature. McGregor's *Theory X,* primarily a negativistic view, includes assumptions held by supervisors and management about workers' inherent lack of motivation. It perceives them as instinctively disliking and avoiding work, and stresses the need to apply coercion, direction, threat, or consequence in order to have them work towards organizational goals or outcomes. There is an assumption that workers are essentially ambitionless; they require direction and lack responsibility. His *Theory Y,* by contrast, has a more positive view of human motivation as possessing a natural instinct and desire for both mental and physical effort. In supporting organizational goals, workers will employ self-direction and self-control if they feel commitment to the objectives, and that commitment is associated with the achievement of goals. Individuals instinctively seek responsibility, and will apply creativity, ingenuity, and imagination toward solving organizational concerns. These fundamental assumptions about the basic nature of human beings directly impacts relationships to work and to the human interactions within organizations.

The traditional and externally controlled managerial approaches of the early part of this century have been more *Theory X* in nature. The more self-controlled *Theory Y* belief is reflective of what is inherent in the individual worker, and that it is the nature of the tightly controlled organization that causes the need for external control; the experience of most workers has not tapped their motivational resources. Worker commitment and involvement with organizational objectives will result in the more fluid and consensus-driven type of managerial style suggested by *Theory Y* [8,9].

William Ouchi reviewed Japanese and American businesses and proposed that the notable successes in both environments were functions of a distinctive corporate culture, which was internally consistent and characterized by the shared values of intimacy, trust, cooperation, teamwork, and egalitarianism. The critical role of management was in the successful use of human resources rather than in any technological advantage. These *Theory Z* organizational cultures have distinctive hallmarks: employment security resulting in long-term personal investment in the organization; more opportunity for broadening experience and diverse career paths through slower promotion rates; participative and shared-consensus decision making, which requires cooperation, teamwork, common values, and mutual trust; and a pervasive concern for the whole employee [10,11].

These organizations possess the elements of a collective culture of shared core values and in the push for attainment of common goals. The overall design and orientation of these organizations is service-driven and, in that sense, facilitates the quality dynamics described previously. For employees to buy into the organization as true *owners*—the people who possess positional power [12] (the superintendent of schools and board of education; members at the school district level, and the building principal; or director at the site level)—must subscribe to positive beliefs about people and about the roles and motives of employees [13].

Barring these positive beliefs, the traditional top-down authoritarian model will prevail, to the detriment of the employees, administration, and, ultimately, the students.

An administrator who possesses positional power must truly believe that people are good, kind, trustworthy, and valuable [4]. She/he must also believe that employees possess these characteristics; but they also want to improve themselves, they want to assist other employees to improve, they want their school building and their district to be the best they can be, they want to assist in decision making which is intended to improve themselves and the school building's and school district's quality, and they want to do whatever they can to improve the education of their students [14].

An administrator who possesses positional power must truly believe that people are good, kind, trustworthy, and valuable. She/he must also believe that employees possess these characteristics; but also want to improve themselves; they want to assist other employees to improve, they want their school building and their district to be the best that they can be, they want to assist in decision making that is intended to improve themselves and the school building's and school district's quality, and they want to do whatever they can to improve the education of their students [15].

If the building principal truly feels positive about people and employees, she/he can use involvement and collaborative intervention strategies that will empower the employees. By promoting a collaborative empowerment culture, the principal will also experience a broadened leadership base within the building [16].

ORIGINS IN ORGANIZATIONAL THEORY

Decentralization and shared decision-making patterns among companies vary greatly, but the main issues of redesigning the American workplace are the challenges of rethinking the mission, doing more with less, and doing things better [17]. These challenges are common to both business and education, and may result in downsizing (reassigning central-level responsibility to the site-level manager) and blurring traditional lines of demarcation between labor and management, in order to assign that responsibility closer to the delivery point. Collaboration, as demonstrated in shared decision making, and the rewarding of performance, as shown in teamwork incentives for productivity and quality, are two powerful business concepts that underlie the concept of employee empowerment. The common theme that runs through contemporary corporate and managerial theory is the key function of *decentralization*. School-Based Management (SBM) as a governance strategy returns authority to the school, democratizing and effectively empowering the participants. SBM as a basic tool of restructuring is being reviewed by think tanks, and is viewed by both union leaders and government policy analysts as a prerequisite for enhanced teacher effectiveness. One of the strongest restructuring movements is teacher involvement, since change is best facilitated when those responsible for its implementation are involved in the process from the outset [18].

RATIONALES FOR EMPOWERMENT

Empowerment creates professionals out of educators, who are then accountable, possess a professional expertise, and progress intellectually [19]. School-Based Management as a restructuring tool can best facilitate these role changes by placing quality control at the lowest possible level. *Empowerment* has emerged as the banner word of the restructuring movement in response to the regulatory and compliance-ridden nature of the first wave of school reform; the issue has shifted from that viewpoint onto the treatment of educators in their own environments, especially in the provision of greater latitude over curricular and instructional decisions [20].

The concept of shared leadership within a school can be both current and controversial; touting teachers as leaders in contemporary times is occasionally a sensitive position. The removal of the present impediments to talent and the provision of conditions to enhance teachers' leadership tendencies is badly needed; the fate of such leadership in creating a community of leaders lies in the relationship between principals and their faculties [21]. Policymakers frequently withhold autonomy until they are assured of teacher accountability, and teachers resist accountability unless they have substantial control over service delivery. The bureaucratic management of schools stems from the view that teachers lack the talent or motivation to think for themselves. Within the context of a clear but limited set of student goals, teachers must be free to collaborate, to exercise collective professional judgment, thereby creating collegial communities that employ school-site budgeting and state deregulation. This empowerment of teachers does not mean the obsolescence of principal leadership; it is, rather, the enabling of teachers to participate in group decision making and to make key choices [22].

An AASA 1990 publication on empowerment in education indicates that schools are more effective places for learning because empowered individuals:

• Use their insights and experience to make better decisions,
• Have the flexibility and support to try new approaches and custom-fit what they do to meet the needs of schools and students,
• Learn and grow on the job,
• Work together to solve challenging problems. Empowerment creates "team" spirit among administrators, teachers, students, and citizens.
• Believe that improved instruction is everyone's responsibility [22].

Empowerment is practiced when authority and obligation are shared in a way that authorizes and legitimizes action, correspondingly increasing responsibility and accountability [23]. Teachers and principals must be put in charge of their practice, and schools must be allowed to create their own destiny. The empowerment process supports a shared covenant built by successful schools, where teachers and principals are free to do things that make sense to them as professionals, under the aegis of the shared values and requirements of the school covenant. SBM provides a place where students, parents, teachers, and other community leaders come together to support the learning process, to create a school community where teachers are regarded as professionals and exercise their own judgement in the facilitation of learning.

The common definitional element of teacher empowerment seems to be a culmination and fulfillment of professional status through the attainment of new levels of educational process efficiency and effectiveness [24]. Empowerment creates collegial communities, with the tradeoff of accountability for professional discretion and decision-making latitude. It is characterized by placing control at the lowest level of delivery and knowing what is needed for leadership at that level; by the removal of constraints on teacher expertise; and by the press for collective responsibility for educational decisions in a collegial and collaborative environment. The most distinctive application of this empowerment has been demonstrated in School-Based Management, also known as School-Based or Site-Based Decision Making.

SCHOOL-BASED MANAGEMENT

School-Based Management (SBM) is a structure and a process which delegates greater decision-making power over any or all of the areas of instruction, budget, policies, personnel, etc., related to governance to the local school building level; and it is a process that involves a variety of stakeholders, including employees, in the decisions which relate to the local individual school building's programs and operations [25].

SBM has borrowed from recent corporate practice. This tradition of local control of schools dates back to the last century, with separate boards of education for each school building, and has changed during this century to centralization, due to increasing district size and consolidation. Until the late 1960s, school-site decision making was done informally in the school's hallways, or through quick meetings between principal and staff. Authority in the schools became more centralized; the union conflicts of the decade impaired collegiality. During the 1960s and 1970s some early SBM forms began to appear in an attempt to respond to the changing profiles of desegregated and increasingly multicultural neighborhood and community schools [26]. Decentralization and some local-level budgeting innovations were present in scattered districts, adopted to give political power to local communities, to balance state authority, or to achieve an administrative efficiency gain. All of these initiatives preceded the substantial school-based management wave which occurred during the state and national level educational reforms of the 1980s.

BACKGROUND OF TEACHER EMPOWERMENT AND SBM

The bureaucratization of the teaching workplace is well documented and reflected in research. In 1987, Benson and Malone spoke of teachers' sensations of powerlessness, and of their sense of having a minor impact on influencing decisions [27]. Relatively little initial attention was paid to the role of teachers in school reform and restructuring during the first wave of reform in the early 1980s.

There is some historical teacher involvement in curricular decision making, but very little in more crucial areas such as evaluation, staff development, budget, and student policy development. She reported that a Michigan State University researcher feels that twenty years of top-down reform efforts have eroded the responsibility of students and teachers, insisting that instructional effectiveness is best accomplished by "creating schools in which teachers and students are expected as a condition of their work to take responsibility for their learning and to act on their knowledge."

There is a tradition of teacher isolationism and individual allegiance to union or district that may be the greatest weakness of the public school system. The history, culture, and physical structure of schools encourage this isolationism, however broken over the years it has been by such earlier successful innovations as team teaching, nongradedness, and differentiated staffing [28]. More recently, successful innovations have included subject area work teams, vertical curriculum teams, task forces, and faculty advisory groups—more broadly based governance structures. Development of a collegial professional climate is a philosophical shift, which is a prerequisite for shared decision making.

There is a cultural inhibition in the current labor–management climate that prevents many teachers from assuming empowerment and expanded responsibilities; a continuation of the "we–they" divisiveness prevails. Teachers and principals who would prefer to collaborate must confront and transform this ethic. Although some SBM models include parents and community members, all SBM models give a great deal of decision-making power to teachers. Teacher empowerment and employee empowerment is clearly a trend of the 1990s, but this trend has some precedental configurations; the first of these is that of vertical work teams.

VERTICAL WORK TEAMS

Historically, in school districts, vertical teams have been organized for relatively short time periods to accomplish a specific task. Traditionally, vertical teams of teachers, building administrators, and central office curriculum supervisors have been organized to develop a local school district's curriculum guides. Also, various categories of site-level employees, site-level administrators, and central-level administrators have been, voluntarily or mandatorily, formed into vertical teams for the purposes of training or staff development [29]. Another configuration is the vertical team, comprised of leadership, employee, and stakeholder representation from a pyramid of schools—a high school, its feeder middle and/or junior high schools, and their feeder elementary schools. The common attendance areas thus represented create a "neighborhood" or neighboring residential areas group; one which has some demographics and, presumably, some issues, concerns, and resources in common. Not only have vertical teams been historically utilized to involve employees, but focus groups have also been created as a means of involvement.

FOCUS GROUPS

Focus groups comprised of employees and management are usually assembled to deal with the problems facing the school district. Focus groups usually meet for very short periods of time. The task of a focus group is usually one of isolating a problem, analyzing the variables that impact the problem, and brainstorming possible solutions. This input is then utilized by management in arriving at an action plan to resolve the problem that has been discussed.

Another historical method of involving employees is that of assembling project groups.

PROJECT GROUPS

Project groups are comprised of a variety of employees who are relieved of their basic duties (part-time or full-time) for the length of time necessary to complete the project. In school districts, project groups or task forces may be comprised of teachers, classified employees, administrators, or a combination of the three. Also, in school districts, project groups may often meet after normal school hours or over the summer months [30].

This traditional form of employee empowerment utilizes the knowledge and skills of selected employees to develop program modifications, to solve problems, or to create innovative school building–level or school district–level services. Some examples of projects are (1) initiating a business/school partnership, (2) modifying the volunteer program to recruit a large number of retired community members, thereby lowering the adult/pupil ratio, and (3) modifying the existing school district's public relations program by creating a new marketing advisory committee comprised of representatives of each category of employee—this project group is charged with the responsibility of developing, implementing, and evaluating the success of the marketing efforts of each school building and of the school district as a whole.

CURRENT SBM PRACTICE

The legislatures of Kentucky and Texas have mandated School-Based Management through dramatic educational restructuring legislation. Also, many school boards and administrative leaders are mandating School-Based Management in their school districts; many teachers, teacher unions, principals, and superintendents are voluntarily entering the process [31]. Many of these districts are involving parents and community members, as well as teachers and other employees in the composition of their School-Based Management teams; but all SBM structures empower teachers in the process.

The most dramatic and far-reaching mandate so far was that passed by the Kentucky Legislature and entitled the *Kentucky Education Reform Act of 1990*. An elaboration of the provisions of the act related to School-Based Management will demonstrate Kentucky's commitment to using the SBM structure and process as a means of restructuring schools for the purpose of improving the education of children. The basic provisions of the *Kentucky Education Reform Act of 1990* are numerous. Those which impact local Kentucky school districts through what Kentucky has termed School-Based Decision Making (SBDM) are included in an appendix at the end of the book [32].

In response to societal concern for educational quality, Texas has experienced almost a decade of major change in the field. Beginning in 1979 with statewide student minimum mastery assessments, legislatively initiated changes included the passage of two significant bills; the *Educational Opportunity Act* (House Bill 72) and the adoption of a statewide curriculum for grades K–12 (House Bill 75). Not only was the content of the instructional program specifically defined, but virtually every operational aspect of the educational process was affected. This mass of detailed legislative mandates imposed constraints, which eventually served, at times, to rigidly inhibit innovative instructional strategies. There were some individual district initiatives during the 1980s aimed at meeting the needs of the increasingly diverse, majority/minority school population. There is now a second Texas wave of reform focused on *decreasing* the role of the state; the new outlook at the state level is to "clear the path for campus-based initiatives aimed at improving outcomes for all students." The details of this legislation are included in an appendix at the end of the book [33].

In consideration of the dramatic changes required in the implementation of School-Based Management, let's discuss the questions that anyone considering SBM should ask before entering into an SBM structure and process. The September, 1990 issue of the National Association of Secondary School Principals' *Bulletin* includes an article entitled "School-Based Management: A Checklist of Things to Consider." This checklist is repeated below as an aid for any school district's or school building's decision makers who are investigating the possibility of entering into the SBM structure and process.

SCHOOL-BASED MANAGEMENT INTERROGATORY CHECKLIST (A REFLECTIVE AID TO BE USED BEFORE JUMPING HEADLONG INTO SCHOOL-BASED MANAGEMENT)

(Answer "yes" or "no" to each question.)

(1) Do you really believe in shared decision making?

(2) Are you willing to take full responsibility (accountability) for your decisions?

(3) Have you decided which stakeholders should be given the power to make final decisions?

(4) Have you decided which stakeholders will be given a role in the decision-making process?

(5) Have the central decision makers reached agreement with the building decision makers on the policies, procedures, and methodologies to implement the process of school-based management?

(6) Have the local decision makers been given maximum decision making power and flexibility related to staffing, instruction, and operational budget decisions?

(7) Have you allowed sufficient time to reflect on all important decision areas before establishing a date to implement?

(8) Do you realize that this may cause an additional workload to be placed on the principal and the school building's employees?

(9) Have the local decision makers clearly defined, in operational terms, what they mean by school-based management; and have they developed the by-laws and policies which are necessary for implementation?

(10) Have you determined the outcome measures that will be assessed to decide whether or not your locally designed program

of school-based management is working well, or whether or not it requires modification?

(11) Are the roles of the central personnel and the building personnel crystal clear in each area of decision making?

(12) Is it clear, on the continuum of possible decision making possibilities, which decisions are totally school-based, which are totally district-based, and which are shared?

(13) Have you budgeted time and money to conduct training or staff development programs for those persons who are to become involved with school-based management for the first time?

(14) Have you decided upon methods to perform formative and summative evaluations?

(15) Will each school be able to develop its own school-based management procedures, or will there be a district structure applied to all school buildings within the school district?

(16) Do you have realistic expectations of what school-based management can do, and do you realize that it is not a "cure all" for everything that is happening in the schools?

(17) Do you realize that this is not a "quick fix", and that it will take considerable time and effort to implement and improve the process that you initially use?

(18) Do you realize that over a long time period, not only will the decision making process change; but that there will be a dramatic (hopefully, positive) change in the entire culture of the organization?

(19) Are you prepared to collect "hard" and "soft" data to make a yearly report of the degree of success of the school-based decision process in your school building?

(20) Do you really believe that the process of school-based management will improve the effectiveness and efficiency of your school and your school district, or are you involved simply because it is the thing to do?

(21) Do you believe that school-based management will improve communication, trust and collaboration between the school building and school district levels?

(22) Do you believe that school-based management will create a greater feeling of ownership and greater support from the employees and the community-at-large?

(23) Do you really like and respect people, and are you willing to depend on them to help you make important decisions?

(24) Do your employee union leaders and your board of education members buy into school-based management?

(25) Do you believe that dispersed leadership is the best type of leadership, and do you believe that school-based management nurtures and stimulates new leadership at all levels of the organization?

(26) Do you realize that school buildings and school districts are open systems, and that school-based management is a process that improves the schools' ability to become more open?

(27) Do you believe in "loosely coupled" organizations?

(28) Do you believe that school-based management can promote continuous school renewal?

(29) Do you believe in promoting entrepreneurial efforts?

(30) Again, do you really believe and trust people, and are you willing to share your decision making power?

(31) What types of training are you going to provide the school-based management team related to:
  (a) Communication skills?
  (b) Planning skills?
  (c) Decision making skills?
  (d) Problem solving skills?
  (e) Other skill areas?

(32) What specific procedures will you put in place to arrive at decisions related to:
  (a) Staffing?
  (b) Budget?
  (c) Instruction?
  (d) Building level governance?
  (e) Other? [34]

An important factor in any work environment is that of recognizing the positive contributions of individual employees and groups of employees, including union groups. Recognition of employees is only one factor in the creation and maintenance of a productive and satisfying work environment. We shall now discuss ideas related to employee recognition and the creation and maintenance of this type of work environment.

QUALITY OF WORK LIFE AND QUALITY CIRCLES

Another vehicle for empowering employees, initiated by some large American companies during the 1970s and 1980s, is entitled QWL (Quality of Work Life). QWL has a sub-category called Quality Circles. Some school districts in the 70s and 80s also developed QWL programs, and they found this structure and process, which was originally influenced by the success of Japanese industry, to be a very successful way of empowering employees.

A QWL process opens the communications system among employees and between employees and administration. It eliminates much of the top-down communication, and allows problems to be solved at the level at which the work is performed. It creates a team approach to planning, training, innovation, communication, problem solving, productivity, and quality control. It creates a collaborative approach between employee unions and the school district's management; rather than continuing an adversarial labor/management relationship. It also allows both labor leaders and administrators to feel successful, realizing that they assisted employees in improving their work environment; and creates an employee empowerment structure and process that allows for innovative programming, training, and problem solving, resulting in productive short-term operational and long-term strategic collaborative planning.

It allows for both district-wide and work site (Quality Circle) components, and is geared to improving the work climate at the individual employee, subgroup, and district levels. Being people oriented, process saturated, and success reinforced, it stresses the worth and dignity of the human element, and as a bonus, improves the organization's health [35].

Quality of Work Life can be defined as a *philosophy* that states that employees are capable of and desirous of improving their work environment and level of production; as a *goal* that attempts to make the work environment for employees the best possible work environment; and as a *structure and process* that involves employees in continuously improving the quality of their work life. *Quality Circles,* generally, are groups of six to eight employees who identify problems within their work place, develop potential solutions to each problem, present their proposed solution to management and, if management approves, implements its solution.

It is important to emphasize that this process is a voluntary one by employee unions or employee groups and management. QWL central groups, and their subset, Quality Circles, are also comprised of individual employees who volunteer their time to serve within this process [36]. Characteristics of Quality of Work Life include the following:

- It is voluntary.
- It is a long-term continuous process, *not a quick fix.*
- Union and nonunion employees, as well as management, must voluntarily work to evolve the specific form and substance to implement QWL within their own school district.
- Decisions are made by consensus and all participants have equal status.
- Activities of QWL groups should never infringe on any rights established by collective bargaining agreements.
- Participants should participate in ongoing leadership skills development and in training for interpersonal communications and problem-solving methodologies.
- The QWL groups should be provided with the necessary budgetary, temporal, and other resources that are required for them to be successful.
- A trained central liaison should be available to assist the elected leadership, to help with training needs, and to coordinate the building level Quality Circles.

Some of the detailed housekeeping that needs to be planned to enhance the probability of a successful implementation and maintenance of a QWL program include:

(1) Starting with a high-level activity to provide knowledge of and to enhance interest in the possibility of creating a QWL program for the school district

(2) Getting concurrent prior approval of the board of education, employee union leaders, and administrators to go ahead with the program

(3) Establishing budget accounts, naming the persons who are authorized to draw upon the budget, and determining the categories of activities for which expenditures can be made

(4) Hiring substitute employees when QWL or Quality Circle meetings are held on school district paid time

(5) Hiring consultants, especially during the initiation year, if the internal school district liaison or other school district employees are unable to provide members with the training required or desired

(6) Having the QWL central committee develop and adopt bylaws before starting the entire QWL program. These initial bylaws may need to be modified later, but they will provide clear-cut guidelines for the conduct of QWL business

(7) Conducting a needs assessment to determine the types of training required and desired by employees and management

The most important advantage of a QWL approach to employee involvement is that it improves employee/management relations by utilizing the full intelligence of every employee who volunteers to participate in improving the school district's work climate, which, in turn, improves the school climate for students and lets every employee know that she/he is valued, cared for, and respected.

TOTAL QUALITY MANAGEMENT

Total Quality Management has entered the restructuring considerations of school district decision makers through the successes experienced by business and industry in Japan, the United States, and Europe. It is being heavily promoted by the American Association of School Administrators, and many other school-related national and state associations are promoting this restructuring program. Awards, like the Deming Award, given by Japan, and the Baldridge award, presented by the United States to businesses and industries that meet an extensive list of quality standards, are also heightening interest among school people.The Total Quality Management movement, sometimes merely called Quality, can prove a guiding quest in a holistic approach to educational quality management. TQM utilizes simple ideas, but it demands a long-term commitment to change and to the development of a more productive and positive organizational culture [37].

The core ideas incorporated within TQM include the following clear conceptual beliefs:

- Quality results are expected in *every product.*
- *Value is to be added* at every step in the process of developing a service or a product.
- Stakeholders who are to develop the products and deliver the services are to be empowered with decision-making authority.
- Data collection and feedback are continuous.
- Planning is continuous based upon data collection and feedback.

- Customer satisfaction with the product and service is the ultimate challenge.

Total Quality Management is a customer-focused, strategy-driven approach that makes new and profound demands on every organization, creating the personal obligation of everyone, not merely a specific department. The products and services must meet or exceed customer expectations. It demands a proactive culture within the organization that addresses quality on both the sourcing and delivery ends of the supply chain. With specific reference to collaboration and to union–management interactions, adversarial relationships are replaced by partnerships with employees, suppliers, and customers, and employees *at all levels* are empowered to make decisions that allow them to provide superior quality and service [38]. When TQM concepts are applied to education, there are some collaboration-related points for applications of TQM:

- Educational customers include all internal (students and employees) as well as all external (parents, residents, and other agencies that interact with the schools) stakeholders.
- TQM should focus on processes that are designed to continuously produce quality products at each step and to all customers. It has a value-added dimension, in that every step of the process will lead to an improved output; and quality is added to each step.
- Extensive two-way communications between all stakeholders is required to define the quality specifications to be used by the schools or schools districts.
- TQM involves a systems approach, and TQM school districts' or school buildings' decision makers should constantly improve the quality of their systems or processes.
- Employees are empowered through communication, training, and encouraging leadership. Many times problem-solving teams are utilized to remove glitches in the systems or processes.
- TQM is about change, and change involves causing changes in behaviors.

SIMILARITIES AND DIFFERENCES AMONG QWL, SBM, AND TQM

When reviewing the key concepts of QWL, SBM, and TQM, we discover that a complementary approach to these concepts permits the development of a holistic approach to positive systemic and transformational change in schools. Using the essential concepts as the basic structural means of developing a holistic approach that includes all currently favored restructuring and school improvement approaches, it is possible and profitable to unite the concepts of QWL, SBM, and TQM. It is very clear that *strong evidence* exists to prove the commonality, in most programs, of the concepts of:

• empowerment
• needs assessment
• strategic goals

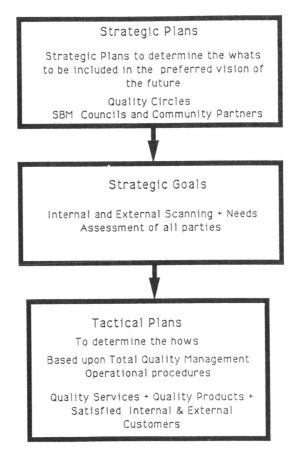

FIGURE 3.1. Tying total quality management, school-based management, quality of work life, strategic planning and tactical planning together.

- objectives
- action programs
- data collection and feedback
- recycling phase
- planning
- strong leadership
- collaborative decision making
- conducive support climate [39]

At the school district— or school building—level, understand that it makes a great deal of sense to locate the common elements in each plan for school collaboration and improvement; rather than using them as independent programs. Figures 3.1–3.4 illustrate these commonalities.

TOTAL QUALITY MANAGEMENT

1. Vision of continual improving quality
2. Quality goals
3. Value added concept of quality at each juncture
4. Quality results in products and services
5. Empowers stakeholders
6. Planning is continuous
7. Data collection and feedback
8. Customer satisfaction

QUALITY OF WORK LIFE

1. Vision of continuing quality improvement in work environment
2. Quality goals developed
3. Outcome/results driven
4. Empowered stakeholders
5. Data collection and feedback - MIS (management information system)
6. High achievement expectations
7. Supportive work climate

SCHOOL-BASED MANAGEMENT

1. Authority and accountability shifted to school site level (empowerment shift)
2. Collaborative decision making is the process used
3. Stakeholders are involved in school site decision making
4. A conducive support climate exists

FIGURE 3.2. Key planning concepts.

PLANNING STEPS

STRATEGIC PLAN

A. Vision
B. Beliefs and values
C. External and Internal Scanning
D. Critical Success Factors
E. Needs assessment
F. Mission
G. SWOT Analysis
H. Strategic goals
I. Specific objectives for goals
J. Evaluate and recycle

TACTICAL PLAN

K. Decision rules to determine priorities

L. Action plans:
   (a) Brainstorm
   (b) Force field Analysis
   (c) Cost/benefit Analysis
   (d) Select best alternative
   (e) Allocate resources and operate plans

M. Evaluate and recycle

KEY CONCEPTS

Total QUALITY MANAGEMENT

1. Vision
2. Goals
3. Empowerment
4. Continuous planning
5. Data collection and feedback
6. Value added at each juncture
7. Quality results (services and products)
8. Customer satisfaction

Quality of Work Life

1. Vision of preferred future
2. Quality goals developed
3. Outcome/results driven
4. Supportive work climate
5. Empowered stakeholders
6. Data collection and feedback
7. High achievement expectations

SCHOOL-BASED MANAGEMENT

1. Empowerment to the school site
2. Stakeholders' involvement in decisions
3. Collaborative decision making
4. Conducive support climate

FIGURE 3.3. Interface between key concepts and planning steps.

DIRECTIONS: Place a large X when the characteristic is an absolute, and place a small x when the characteristic is applicable but not absolute.

KEY CHARACTERISTICS	SBM	TQM	QWL	STRAT &TACT PLANNING
STRATEGIC & TACTICAL PLANNING				
1. Vision	x	x	x	X
2. Empowered stakeholders	X	X	X	X
3. Needs assessment	X	X	X	X
4. Goals	X	X	X	X
5. Objectives	X	X	X	X
6. Action programs	X	X	X	X
7. Data collection and feedback	X	X	X	X
8. Recycling	X	X	X	X

FIGURE 3.4. Holistic matrix for systemic transformational change.

44

EMPLOYEE RECOGNITION AND THE CREATION AND MAINTENANCE OF A PRODUCTIVE AND SATISFYING WORK ENVIRONMENT FOR EMPLOYEES

For a work environment to be both productive and satisfying, it must maintain a positive balance between the *positive feeling tone* among employees and a *positive level of quality outputs and outcomes*. An environment with a positive feeling tone, but with a low level of outputs and outcomes, is one which eventually will lead employees to a feeling of defeat, and it will also lead to a reduction in the feeling tone about their own contributions and about the quality of the school district in which they work. On the other hand, an environment that produces acceptable outputs and outcomes, but which leaves employees with an attitude that no one recognizes their contributions or is concerned about their well being, will eventually become an organization with low morale and low productivity [40].

To create and maintain a positive work environment, employees must feel that they:

- are trusted by their peers and by the administration
- have interesting work to do
- feel they are wanted, cared for, and respected
- feel they have an opportunity for self growth
- have security in their positions
- are provided the opportunity to give input into matters concerning them and into matters of importance to their school and school district
- feel that they are challenged and are making an important contribution
- understand that they are crucial elements in a high quality school district that produces high achieving students, productive employees, and a community that supports and respects the educational efforts of the school district

Finally, it is important that management plan celebrations for employees' successes and plan for recognition of good contributions by individual employees, groups of employees, and the employees' unions. Although the administrators and boards of education of school districts can develop recognition programs such as employee of the week or month, designation as a master employee, or merit or performance pay, the more significant and accepted forms of employee recognition are those wherein the administration creates programs where students, parents, business and industry groups, and professional groups find specific ways to recognize employees. The most important source of employee recognition, however, is one in which management creates a program where employees select and publicize individual employees and groups of employees who perform in an extraordinary manner [41].

Now that we have discussed ways of empowering employees, let's discuss a formal means of empowering members of the employee unions and management representatives to avoid potential union/management problems or to solve existing problems within their school districts.

COLLABORATION AS A MEANS OF DEVELOPING EMPLOYEE OWNERSHIP AND EMPLOYEE LEADERSHIP

If the building principal or other leader promotes a culture of involvement and empowerment and the employees are not accustomed to the freedom and to the opportunity to involve themselves in decisions that affect them and the school building's operation, the leader must *sell* this new culture until the employees buy in and develop an *ownership* mindset. By utilizing collaborative intervention strategies, not only are better and fully owned decisions made, but, over time, a dispersed ownership will develop. In other words, each employee, within a culture that promotes collaborative involvement, will eventually be provided with and will assume a leadership role within the school building or school district [42].

ADVANTAGES OF EMPLOYEE INVOLVEMENT, EMPOWERMENT, AND COLLABORATION

Employee involvement can exist without empowering the employees with final decision-making responsibility, and involvement and empowerment can exist without utilizing a collaborative structure of employee decision making. However, it is clear that all of these elements must co-exist if the maximum advantages are to be reaped by the employees and the school building's operation. The major advantages are listed below.

- Employee accountability is evident when they are given authority.
- Employees enjoy working in an environment that provides them with opportunities for input, improvement, and leadership.

- Employees enjoy the opportunity to improve themselves, to help improve their colleagues, and to improve the school building's operation.
- Employees take pride in high quality outputs and outcomes, which come about because of their efforts.
- Employees use contributions by their colleagues and their principal.
- Employees are motivated when they feel they are a valued part of a collaborative employee team.
- Leadership builds more leadership, and diversified leadership is more productive than positional leadership by a single person—the principal.
- Positive experiences in leadership promote additional leadership desires and opportunities.
- Employees prefer to be partial owners of an institution that believes in utilizing all of its human resources to form a productive work family that achieves high quality results.

Now that the advantages are clear, what are some of the characteristics of productive employee collaborative teams? If one wishes to measure whether or not a productive collaborative employee team exists, she/he should be able to observe the following characteristics as one visits the school building and talks to the employees:

- Employees listen to and are open to the ideas of others.
- Employees take pride in the employee team's achievement.
- They are free with their praise of one another.
- There is a feeling of ownership, work family, and empowerment.
- They are alert to ways in which they can assist and support each other.
- Employees act as a unified group by using a diagnostic and positive approach to problem solving and program development.
- Employees look for opportunities to share with one another.
- Each employee operates as a full and valued member of the employee team.
- Each employee feels successful and feels that she/he is an integral part of a successful work family.
- The team exhibits distributed skillful and positive leadership.
- The team has clearly defined goals and objectives.
- The team members have many creative and innovative ideas that prove to be successful.
- They have a well-developed structure for realistic planning and conflict resolution.

- They exhibit positive, effective, and persuasive communication techniques.
- They exhibit success, which leads to the desire for greater success [43].

To this point we discussed (1) the beliefs about people and employees that are required to have a winning employee team, (2) how collaborative structures develop ownership and leadership among employees, (3) the advantages of employee involvement, empowerment, and collaboration, and (4) the advantages to the school building's operation when employees are involved and empowered in collaborative efforts.

Now that we have discussed ways of empowering employees, let's end by discussing a formal means of empowering members of the employee unions and management representatives to avoid potential union/management problems or to solve existing problems within their school districts.

METHODS OF INVOLVING UNION/MANAGEMENT TEAMS

Although QWL diminished, to some degree, the power of union leaders and school district administrators in school districts that have officially recognized unions, one of the bylaws that control QWL structures and processes always states that QWL activities cannot conflict with or replace any activities reserved to the union under a collective bargaining master contractual agreement. On the other hand, School-Based Management structures and processes, especially if they involve parents, taxpayers, and some of the community's power people, have the potential to seriously impact the environment within which collective bargaining takes place. This potential, if activated, may cause conflict within the school district, lessen the power of union leaders and school district administrators, and may impact both board of education policies and collective bargaining master contractual agreements. These master contracts may be impacted during the process of negotiations, and they may be impacted during the operation of a previously negotiated master contract. To realize the potential impact on collective bargaining and union/management relations, one only has to review the current state of affairs related to SBM legislation.

Union/management teams are various-sized groups comprised of official representatives of the employees' union and the official administrative representatives of the school district. The union/management teams meet for a variety of time periods depending on the issue upon which the team is focusing. This approach allows for continuous and formal communications between union and management, and promotes trust and respect between the union's and management's official representatives as they work collaboratively, rather than adversarialy, to improve conditions for employees and to improve the operations of the local school district [44].

Some major tasks that can be undertaken by union/management teams are:

- to solve employee grievances without getting into adversarial positions or going to grievance arbitration
- to discuss items that might well be problem areas in upcoming contract negotiations prior to formally sitting across the table from one another
- to discuss and resolve union/management problems that currently exist in the school district
- to plan specific approaches to improving the school district
- to jointly collect accurate information related to specific grievance situations and upcoming potential collective bargaining issues; and to collect comparative information from comparable school districts about salary, fringe benefits, and other matters related to teachers and classified employees

Through a myriad of cooperative endeavors, both the union and management officials will avoid negative feelings towards one another. They will provide a model of conduct for the employees and administrators within the district to emulate and will display a mature, professional approach to union/management operations that will be recognized and appreciated by the school district's patrons.

SUMMARY

After providing a background in human and organizational development theory and research, this chapter discussed a variety of means of empowering employees. An extensive presentation was provided on School-Based Management, its origins, rationales, state mandates, current practice, and implementation considerations. A brief discussion about various group participation and decision-making structures— vertical teams, focus groups, and project groups—followed. Lengthy descriptions were provided about Quality of Work Life and its subset technique, Quality Circles.

The importance of recognizing the contributions of employees was emphasized, and the factors important in creating a productive and satisfying employee work environment were presented. Although management's involvement in employee recognition programs was mentioned, stress was placed upon the belief that the strongest role of management is one in which management assists other groups, especially employees themselves, in developing programs that recognize the positive contributions of individual employees and groups of employees, and in the creation of a supportive work environment.

The chapter ended by stressing the advantages of creating union/management teams that collaboratively explore problem solutions and program improvements. The resultant improvement in day-to-day union/management relations when union/management teams are operative was emphasized.

EXERCISES

1. What form of employee empowerment exists in your organization, and what forms do you feel can be added to improve the employees' work environment?
2. What detailed steps would you place in your plan if you wished to install a QWL (Quality of Work Life) and Quality Circles operation in your school district?
3. What categories of stakeholders would you involve in an SBM (School-Based Management) team in your school district, and why would you include each category?
4. How would you go about initiating an SBM program in your school district?
5. What measures could you use to measure the impact of a QWL or SBM program in your school district?
6. What are the advantages of creating collaborative stakeholder teams or union/management teams in your school district?

REFERENCES

1. Bailey, W. J. 1991. *School-Site Management Applied.* Lancaster, PA: Technomic Publishing Co. Inc., pp. 24–26, 37.

2. Ibid.

3. Peters, T. J. and R. H. Waterman. 1982. *In Search of Excellence: Lessons from America's Best-Run Companies.* New York: Warner Books, pp. 112, 121–213, 312.

4. Bennis, W. and B. Nanus. 1985. *Leaders: The Strategies for Taking Charge.* New York: Harper & Row, pp. 16–18.

5. Toch, T. 1991. Public Schools of Choice. *American School Board Journal,* 178(7): 18–21.

6. Lewis, A. 1988. *Restructuring America's Schools.* Alexandria, VA: American Association of School Administrators, pp. 20–25, 143–150, 152–169, 184.

7. Hampton, D. R., C. E. Summer, and R. A. Webber. 1987. *Organizational Behavior and the Practice of Management.* Glenview, IL: Scott, Foresman and Company, pp. 179–180.

8. Hampton, D. R., C. E. Summer, and R. A. Webber. 1987. *Organizational Behavior,* pp. 43–44.

9. Rush, H. M. F. 1987. "The Behavioral Sciences," in *Training and Development Handbook,* edited by R. L. Craig, 3rd edition. New York: McGraw-Hill, pp. 135–167.

10. Hoy, W. K. and C. G. Miskel. 1987. *Educational Administration,* 3rd ed. New York, NY: Random House, pp. 250–251.

11. Herman, J. 1989. "Strategic Planner: One of the Changing Leadership Roles of the Principal," *The Clearing House,* 63(2): 56–58.

12. Hampton, D. R., C. E. Summer, and R. A. Webber. 1987. *Organizational Behavior,* p. 197.

13. Lewis, A. 1988. *Restructuring America's Schools.* Alexandria, VA: American Association of School Administrators, pp. 233, 236–237.

14. Ibid.

15. *Challenges for School Leaders.* 1988. Alexandria, VA: American Association of School Administrators, pp. 11–12.

16. Killion, J. P., J. P. Huddleston, and M. A. Claspell. 1989. "People Developer: A New Role for Principals," *Journal of Staff Development,* 10(1): 2–7.

17. Lewis, A. 1988. *Restructuring America's Schools,* pp. 233, 236–237.

18. Ibid.

19. Bailey, W. J. 1991. *School-Site Management,* pp. 24–26, 37.

20. Glickman, C. 1990. "Pushing School Reform to a New Edge: The Seven Ironies of School Empowerment," *Phi Delta Kappan,* 72(1): 68–75.

21. Barth, R. 1990. *Improving Schools from Within.* San Francisco, CA: Jossey Bass, Publishers, p. 145.

22. AASA. 1990. *A New Look at Empowerment.* (AASA Stock Number 021-00278). Washington, D.C.: American Association of School Administrators.

23. Sergiovanni, T. J., and J. H. Moore. 1989. *Schooling for Tomorrow.* Boston: Allyn & Bacon, pp. 108–109.

24. *America 2000: Voices from the Field.* 1991. Washington, D.C.: William T. Grant Foundation Commission on Work, Family, and Citizenship, and the Institute for Educational Leadership.

25. Herman, J. J. and J. L. Herman 1993. *School-Based Management: Current Thinking and Practice,* Springfield, IL: Charles C. Thomas, Publisher, p. 13.

26. Taylor, B. O. and D. U. Levine. 1991. "Effective Schools Projects and School-Based Management," *Phi Delta Kappan,* 72(5): 394–397.

27. Benson, N. and P. Malone. 1987. "Teachers' Beliefs About Shared Decision Making and Work Alienation," *Education,* Spring: 244–251.

28. Herman, J. J. and J. L. Herman. 1993. *School-Based Management,* p. 48–50.

29. Herman, J. J. and J. L. Herman. 1991. *The Positive Development of Human Resources and School District Organizations.* Lancaster, PA: Technomic Publishing Co., Inc., p. 159–160.

30. Herman, J. J. and J. L. Herman. 1991. *The Positive Development,* pp. 30, 33.

31. Lewis, A. 1988. *Restructuring America's Schools,* pp. 173–175.

32. Miller, M. H., K. Noland, and J. Schaaf. 1990. *A Guide to the Kentucky Education Reform Act.* Frankfort, KY: Legislative Research Commission.

33. Herman, J. J. and J. L. Herman. 1993, *School-Based Management,* pp. 187–188.

34. Herman, J. J. 1990. "School Based Management: A Checklist of Things to Consider," *NASSP Bulletin,* 74(527): 67–71.

35. Herman, J. J. and J. L. Herman. 1991. *The Positive Development,* pp. 208–209.

36. Herman, J. J. and J. L. Herman. 1991. *The Positive Development,* pp. 153–162.

37. Herman, J. L. and J. J. Herman. 1995. "Total Quality Management (TQM) for Education," *Educational Technology,* 35(3): 14–18.

38. Herman, J. J. 1993. "TQM for Me: A Decision-making Interrogatory," *School Business Affairs,* 59(4): 28–30.

39. Herman, J. J. and J. L. Herman. 1991. *Educational Quality Management: Schools Through Systemic Change.* Lancaster, PA: Technomic Publishing Co., Inc., pp. 150–157.

40. Herman, J. J. and G. E. Megiveron. 1993. *Collective Bargaining in Education: Win/Win, Win/Lose, Lose/Lose.* Lancaster, PA: Technomic Publishing Co., Inc., pp. 24–25.

41. Ibid.

42. Herman, J. J. and J. L. Herman. 1991. *The Positive Development,* pp. 150–151.

43. Herman, J. J. and J. L. Herman. 1991. *The Positive Development,* pp. 152–153.

44. Herman, J. J. and J. L. Herman. 1991. *The Positive Development,* pp. 168–171.

Considering the Students, the School District, and the Community

CHAPTER 4 addresses the following questions: (1) Who are the stake-holders? (2) What are the client's needs and what are the responsibilities of the district's management and employees' union to the clients? (3) How do you obtain client input? (4) How do you communicate with the school district's clients during normal day-to-day school district operations and during negotiations of a master contractual agreement? The chapter ends with a summary, exercises, and references.

To provide a brief historical note, the loss of confidence in management, in administration, in leadership, in supervision of personnel, and in American education came about soon after the loss of confidence in big business management and the management of the labor unions during the early 1960s. Costs began to spiral, and legislatures began to feel the pinch of financial demands from the schools. Higher salary needs to meet marketplace expenses and basic survival needs became reasoned and reasonable expectations. Management in education (superintendent and central cadre) was tied to the public coffer of property, income, and sales taxes and had little recourse but to expect those at the state level to more adequately fund the education process. With the increasing cost of goods and services needed to operate the very broad education spectrum (food service, office materials, books, transportation, insurance, construction, renovation of facilities, and oftentimes the largest payroll in town), there was not enough money left for salary increases. State efforts had to be increased, but it was not enough. Therefore, the states passed legislation to permit public sector employees to reap the same benefits as those employed in industry. Conditions of work and salary could then be bargained. The results, in terms of success and failure, were varied [1].

The impact of conflict on a school system, particularly between district employees and the community or special interest groups, can be a permanently damaging and divisive experience. Once a state legislature approves a collective bargaining law for public school employees [2],

53

the result of each local contract negotiation can vary in accordance with the skill, attitude, and ability of both the union and board players. What are the possible results of each conflict resolution or each contract negotiation in terms of the stakeholders? Who loses when the conflict or bargaining ends in a lose-lose arrangement?

- *Win-win* is the result when there is a collaborative approach to problem solving by conflicting sides. The outcome effect results in students experiencing a better school environment, the employees having an improved work environment, and the community attitude remaining at the status quo stage or improving in support of the school district [3,4].
- *Win-lose* is the result of an adversarial approach to conflict or to contract negotiations, wherein each party wins some and loses some. In this case, the outcome usually results in students losing opportunities because of ever-tightening contractual mandates, employees losing some control over their individual day-to-day professional destinies, administrators and the board of education losing some control over the operation of the district for which they hold ultimate responsibility, and the community, perhaps, developing a decreasing attitude of support when strategies and tactics used during the negotiation process imply that either the conflicting sides or the board/administrative representatives are dishonest, greedy, do not care about students, and use negative strategic or tactical publicity.
- *Lose-lose* is usually the result of an adversarial approach to conflict resolution or negotiations that has gotten out of control. The negotiations have entered a serious impasse, which may even end in a strike. In this case the outcome effect on all stakeholders is a negative one, and the negativism may linger for years. Students lose a great deal as employees may refuse to perform those duties related to students that are normally expected. In addition, the environment in which students are to learn is one that is extremely negative. Employees' focus will be on real or perceived grievances, union tactics, and their own job security. The board of education and its administrative staff will be under great stress as employees lose morale and professional cooperation, use work-to-rule tactics, picket meetings, or utilize other similar strategies. Finally, the community, especially parents who have children attending the district's schools, will become upset with the employees and the board of education for not achieving a reasonable outcome or

contractual settlement without involving everyone in a complicated negative situation. The effects on attitudes, due to this serious impasse condition, can well hinder progress of the school district's programs and negatively affect the human relationships of the various stakeholders for years to come.

Now that we have explored the potential results of win-win, win-lose and lose-lose conflict resolution, let's discuss in more detail who these stakeholders are and what their interests are in the school district.

WHO ARE THE STAKEHOLDERS?

Stakeholders may consist of individuals and of groups. The community residents are stakeholders, but, in a larger sense, the entire population of the nation is comprised of important stakeholders. Often during national and state-level political races those running for office talk about the importance of education and the importance of improving our current system of education. Indeed, some presidential candidates and gubernatorial candidates market themselves as the "education candidate."

Obviously, community residents and civic, business, industrial, and other community organizations are immediate stakeholders because they pay taxes to support schools. Parents and other community members are stakeholders who reside in the local school district. They may be satisfied with the quality of their schools, or they may be upset with the way the district is operating and with the skills and knowledge that the students possess upon graduation. They may vote additional taxes to enrich an already sound educational system, or they may withdraw financial support if they do not feel they are getting their money's worth. Businesses, industrial, civic, and other organizations are stakeholders because they must have excellent schools in order to attract the quality of employees they desire; and, to a large extent, the quality of their employees will determine the quality and profitability of their products [5].

Students, of course, are the most important of all stakeholder groups. They are the future, and when they are amassed across the entire United States, they truly become our "nation in waiting." They will provide the energy and knowledge to propel the nation into a preeminent position among the nations of the world, and they will be the determining factor in our maintaining that leadership for succeeding generations. At the local community level, they will assume leadership, and, in large measure, will determine the quality of life that will exist in the communities in which they choose to reside [6].

Teachers, classified employees, and administrators, when grouped together, are another important stakeholder group. The working conditions under which they work are crucial to their meeting basic economic, social, and professional needs. If the negotiated resolution of differences and the negotiated contract improves upon these needs, the employees can spend more time and energy on improving educational delivery systems. If the negotiated resolution or contract negotiation process negatively affects these needs, the employees will spend more time and energy on satisfying these needs. Also, if these settlements are perceived as negative, morale, efficiency, and effectiveness will suffer [7].

The final group of important stakeholders is the board and its individual members. If the conflict resolution and the contractual negotiations are conducted in an atmosphere of trust and cooperation and if a fair contractual settlement is reached as the end product of that collaborative environment, the board and its members will retain and perhaps increase the respect they have in the eyes of the general public and in the eyes of their employees. If, however, the process of resolution becomes adversarial and bitter, and the outcome or the negotiated contract is either unfair to the employees or the community, the board and its members will be the recipients of complaints, distrust, and disrespect. The conditions could deteriorate to the point that board members would resign or a totally new board would be elected as soon as elections are held [8].

Looking at the best result we find that the resolutions achieved and the contract negotiated is a fair one to all parties and it is designed to assist students and to satisfy both employee and community needs. Finally, let us assume that the contract was negotiated through the collaborative efforts of the union and the board representatives. If these are true statements, what then are some elements of a positive scenario that would immediately result from this contractual settlement. From our wide-lens view of the school district, we can observe the following:

- The school year starts on time.
- Teachers and other employees are anxious to assist students to learn.
- New and returning students are eager to begin their classes and participate in co-curricular activities.
- Preschool and kindergarten students are dressed in their finest clothes and wondering what this new adventure is all about.

- Parents are anxious for their children to once again begin their formal learning; and those parents who are working outside of the home are relieved to be free of child care costs and the concern about where their children are and what they are doing.
- The community at large begins a more normal pattern that will last approximately nine months of the year.
- Parents and nonparents begin to support the school district's students by becoming volunteers or members of booster groups for various types of student activities.
- Businesses, industrial firms, civic groups, and nonprofit groups assist the school district by offering student visits, by offering lecturers to classes, by participating in "adopt-a-school" programs, or by involvement in a wide variety of other supportive activities [9,10]

Now let's turn to elements of the negative scenario that occurs when the parties to negotiation have reached an impasse, and negotiations have become adversarial and negative in tone. From our wide-lens view we can perceive the following elements:

- Conflicting members or individuals allow the disagreement to extend to other areas of activity or interaction.
- Teachers refuse to sponsor sports teams and other co-curricular activities because the union has decided this is a tactic that can be utilized to apply pressure on the board of education.
- School sites are picketed before and after normal school hours, as are all meetings of the board of education.
- The opposing sides put a spin on communications and produce media releases that paint the other party as the villain. Extremely negative press results from the dramatization of the nature and distance between the opposing points of view.
- Employees "work to rule." That is, they refuse to give homework, refuse to attend meetings, or eliminate any voluntary activity. They only do what is absolutely legally required.
- Students are upset because employees have poor morale, refuse to give students extra help when it is requested, and spend a lot of time and energy on non–student-related matters.
- Parents and nonparents are disgusted with the situation, and are complaining about the leadership of the district.
- Civic, business, industrial, and other community groups are concerned about their community's reputation and what effects a tarnished reputation will have on the community's future.
- Media sources have a field day [11].

If a negative scenario exists, all parties must pull together after some resolution has been achieved, or after a master contractual agreement is finally signed, in order to get the district back on a positive note. Although all parties have a stake in recreating a positive environment, the individuals who will have the most direct impact on the situation are those who work directly in each individual school building. Important players may include the union steward for the building and the school principal. Working together they can improve the morale of the staff and the school building's climate. The principal's actions will also, to a large degree, determine whether or not the parents and residents of that school attendance area will again buy into a supportive stance.

Now that we have elaborated upon the stakeholders' identities, let's turn more directly to the clients' needs. Clients are the customers, or recipients, of what the schools in that district deliver.

WHAT ARE THE CLIENTS' NEEDS AND WHAT ARE THE RESPONSIBILITIES OF THE DISTRICT'S MANAGEMENT AND EMPLOYEES' UNIONS TO THESE CLIENTS?

At the local school district level, the clients are the students and the taxpaying residents of the local school district. The needs or rights of the clients should be adequately met by the providers, who consist of the employees of the school district and the board of education. For example, the students need to be assured that the school to which they are assigned is ready for their occupancy. The school must be neat, clean, in good repair, bright, and cheerful. They ought to expect other needs to be satisfied as well: the need (or right) to be educated by the best staff using the latest and best equipment and supplies; a supportive setting or learning environment in which to learn and recreate; and resources that are spent in the best manner they can in order to derive the most from them. They need to have the proper time (both clock and calendar) allotted for the educative process. Diagnostic, instructional, assessment, or evaluative tools need to be at their disposal to assure each is obtaining the highest level of assistance from the education. In short, students need and should be provided a minimum of the following:

- a safe and healthy learning environment in which to learn
- teachers and other school employees who care about them and respect them

- teachers and other school employees who have high aspirations for each student's academic achievement and social behavior, and who demand the best efforts from each student
- teachers and other school employees who possess a high degree of skill and knowledge related to subject areas taught and also related to the psychological, physiological, and social growth patterns of children and youth
- an expectation that when they graduate from high school, they will be able to obtain a good job and perform that job well; or that they will be well prepared to enter and succeed at an institution of higher education

If the above represent the needs of student clients, what, then, are the needs of the clients of the district—the residents of the community? These clients need to be considered by any concerned individuals or interest groups in the district, including the union leadership and the administrative staff. It is usually the management group that bargains for the Board of Education, and thus represents the community and students by virtue of management's position during the year and throughout bargaining. The clients, from both sides of the table, have a responsibility to both sides to be considerate of clock and calendar, curriculum and course, time and teachers, finances, fair play for the employees, and, certainly, a contract completed on time.

The needs of the school district's clients include the following:

- They need to receive a product equal to or in excess of their investment. In other words, the community should expect that those responsible for the education of the community's students should turn out productive citizens who contribute in a positive manner to the community. They should be academically well educated, economically productive, and socially conscious of their societal responsibilities.
- They should expect the employees of the school district and the members of the board of education to see the school district as an integral and important part of the larger community, and be cooperative with other elements in the community.
- The financial and other resources provided the school district by the residents of the community are to be spent wisely, efficiently, effectively and productively [12,13].

Both the students' needs and the needs of the community's residents are the responsibility of all of the district's employees. In the case of collective negotiations, the two parties must work together to reach a contractual master agreement that allows the needs of these clients to be met to the highest degree possible. To do otherwise is to neglect their collective responsibility and to renege on an important professional obligation.

Now that we have identified stakeholders and discussed their needs, let's turn our attention to ways of obtaining client input.

HOW DO YOU OBTAIN CLIENT INPUT?

Prior to negotiating a conflict situation and seeking settlement, and prior to sitting down at the table to negotiate a master contractual agreement between the board of education and the union, it is wise to determine the expectations that the clients have for the school district. For the board of education, the clients are the community residents and input should include the quality of school district they desire, and the components they expect to be delivered by their school district [14]. Although many times forgotten in the heat of negotiations, the most important clients are the students of the school district. Both union and management share the responsibility of assuring that the student clients' needs are adequately represented during the negotiations dialogue.

Although obtaining reliable and useful input is a difficult task for both sides in a conflict situation, in this case the union and management negotiation teams, it appears to be an even more difficult task for management than for the union. Time and information are the two elements of formal contractual negotiating power, and both of these elements generally favor the union. Flexibility with the time factor is not an option for management because of the historical calendar, and funds are not an issue, since the law dictates much of the total expenditure allocation. Information, while available through legal and public access channels, is often difficult for nonschool persons to obtain, due to the somewhat specialized and dispersed nature of educational and district data.

Much of the information used by administration—the number of days of attendance, for example—in most, if not all of the states, is hard to protect due to the public nature of the operation of the district. The district's open budget, enrollment, and programmatic data are examples of this. The management team brings few surprises to the table beyond its undisclosed outer concession limits. On the other hand, what the union brings to the table is not known in advance to management; the surprise element is essentially one-sided.

Once adequate input information is gathered, both sides should establish specific objectives to be achieved during the upcoming negotiations. Once the objectives are clearly in mind, they should both go about the tasks of developing tactics and support materials designed to achieve those objectives.

The union negotiators usually have three sources of information related to their objectives for an upcoming contract negotiation. Through a national network, the union negotiators can obtain information on national trends, comparative national data, and any priorities that the national union wishes their local affiliates to address. Through the union's state organization, the negotiators can obtain information on state-level contract trends, suggested language for proposals, comparative state contractual data, and any priorities that the state's union leadership wishes the local units to address. [Indeed, in many local school districts, a state representative ("Uniserve Director") is an integral part of the local negotiation team's membership.] Finally, the local union leadership usually conducts a needs assessment by polling or discussing priorities with all its local members. Traditionally, this is achieved by a questionnaire or by a series of meetings with focus groups. Following the needs assessment, the leadership decides on the priorities, goals, and objectives for the upcoming negotiations. The local union negotiators will also collect comparative information from other local districts in their geographical region.

The board's negotiating team receives its directions from the board of education. However, the negotiating team can collect data on the history of negotiations in the district, an analysis of grievances filed during the current and previous master contractual agreements, and comparative information from other local school districts in their geographical area or in their state.

The board of education and its administrative staff may also wish to collect broader-based information from the public at large, in the case of nonbargaining disagreements [15]. Some of the possibilities for this broader-based input are as follows:

(1) The board of education may distribute questionnaires containing items that can be ranked or prioritized by its clients—students and community residents. These results must be prioritized if they are to be used as negotiation input. The negotiation team needs to be clear on the direction to take at the bargaining table.

(2) Another technique is that of placing questions in newspapers to which the board asks citizens to respond by mail back to the

school district's administrative offices. A caution has to be stressed at this point: children should not be used to deliver negotiation-related materials home, or to "courier" information back to the administration or board members.

(3) Another means of obtaining input is to survey the business and civic clubs by attending their meetings and asking to be placed on their agendas to obtain suggestions and feedback related to the school district, to existing controversies, or areas of concern, or about the upcoming contract negotiations [16].

Once the board of education has collected information from the various sources available to them, it must establish its goals, objectives, and priorities for the upcoming contract negotiations. Once this is done, the board provides this information to its negotiating team, and the negotiating team develops language proposals, strategies, and tactics to achieve the goals and objectives outlined by the board of education. Once they have received input from their clients, the board must develop a plan to communicate with those clients [17].

HOW DO YOU COMMUNICATE WITH THE SCHOOL DISTRICT'S CLIENTS?

In the case of collective negotiations, the union again has a much simpler task in that it can call meetings at any time and directly communicate with its total membership. In addition, because it usually has a state union representative sitting in as part of its negotiation team, the union has access to all union contractual activities in the entire state. In addition, in many large population areas unions establish phone banks during negotiations. The local unions report on their progress by phone during each negotiation session, and anyone can call into the area union negotiation's communication media center to receive up-to-date comparative information on every other local district's position.

On the other hand the board of education and its negotiation team have a much more diverse and complex variety of clients with whom they have to communicate. This complexity can be understood by outlining the four phases of the collective bargaining process during which the board of education and administration may communicate. The four phases are: (1) before negotiations begin, (2) during the process of negotiations, (3) when conflict flares into the public eye and an impasse is declared, and (4) after the master contract is agreed to and ratified by both the union and the board of education [18].

Before contract negotiation begins it is wise for the board of education to inform the community of the needs identified in the upcoming budget year. The focus should be on program needs, maintenance needs, and capital outlay needs. Obliquely, the message should be given that there is uncertainty over the costs of fringe benefits and employee salaries as it is a year when a new contract has to be negotiated with the union(s) [19].

During the process of negotiations it is generally wise not to provide any information to the media or the public while contract negotiations are moving forward. However, if an impasse is reached, it is wise to have a news release that outlines the areas of disagreement between the board of education and the union. It is also important at this time to stress the progress that has been made to date.

During the impasse stage, which usually consists of mediation, fact finding, and contract arbitration, it is crucial that a status report is given to the public at each stage of the impasse process. These reports should be limited to a factual account of the items in contention between the board of education and the union.

After the master contract is ratified by the union and the board the public has a right to know any significant agreements which were agreed to in the contract. They especially should be given information about the financial cost of the contractual settlement for each year of the contract if the contract is for multiple years [20].

SUMMARY

This chapter discussed the involvement of stakeholders, clients, and the greater community. The outcomes of negotiated conflict and the legislated bargaining process will impact these participants differently, depending on the nature of the union and management relationship, and the quality and amount of collaboration that exists between the two. The corresponding results of win-win, win-lose, and lose-lose on the public are the product of positive attitudes, decreasing support, or extreme negativism.

The definition of stakeholders was enlarged to include all parent and nonparent community residents, students, civic, business, industrial, and other community organizations, as well as district employees and board members. These last stakeholders will respond particularly well to a win-win situation by exhibiting improved morale, efficiency, and effectiveness.

Scenarios were proposed that outlined the contrast between positive and negative collective negotiations. The needs of the clients—climate, academic achievement, teacher expertise, and readiness for job entry—were described. The needs of the community—"product" quality, district integration with the community, and wise financial expenditure—were likewise described.

Client input via expectations was outlined for both the clientele of union membership and the clientele of the community. Broader-based community and historical information can be gathered to support the normal data and information gathered by both negotiating teams. Such input can be sought, for example, from the previous master contractual agreements, through questionnaires or media coverage, or through civic organizations. The board can then provide this information to the negotiating team.

The diversity and complexity of the board's clientele prevents constant, effective communications with those clients during the negotiations process, compared with the more sophisticated network available to the less restricted union. Four phases of collective bargaining—before negotiations, during negotiations, impasse declaration, and ratification of the master contract—were described; and the opportunities for communication with the board's clients were enumerated for each phase of bargaining.

EXERCISES

1. Identify the groups that management can go to for input at the initiation of the bargaining schedule. Record the group name, and investigate the access channels to reach them.

2. Identify the significant "groups" in your community that need as much insider information as is plausible during a conflict or negotiations process.

3. Develop a memo to management team members to secure information to be used on any type of personnel contract (teachers, secretaries, etc.) that can be used to develop specific proposals in bargaining.

4. What would be the most feasible ways to obtain issue-response or pre-negotiations input from your community?

5. What communications structures (communication fan-outs) could you put into place to disseminate accurate information to all members of the management team?
6. What communications structures could you initiate to keep the public updated during negotiations?
7. How would you go about presenting important pre-negotiation information to the board of education, and how would you advise the board members to establish negotiation guidelines?

REFERENCES

1. Keane, W. G. 1996. *Win Win or Else: Collective Bargaining in an Age of Public Discontent.* Thousand Oaks, CA: Corwin Press, Sage Publications, pp. 7–9.
2. Freeman, R. B. and C. Ichniowski. 1988. *When Public Sector Workers Unionize.* Chicago, IL: The University of Chicago Press, p. 41.
3. Barrett, Jerome T. 1985. *Labor-Management Cooperation in the Public Service: An Idea Whose Time Has Come.* Washington, D.C.: International Personnel Management Association, p. 30.
4. Barrett, Jerome T. 1985. *Labor-Management Cooperation,* p. 29.
5. Webster, W. G., Sr. 1985. *Effective Collective Bargaining in Public Education.* Ames, IA: Iowa State University Press, pp. 166–167.
6. Herman, J. J. and G. E. Megiveron. 1993. *Collective Bargaining in Education: Win/Win, Win/Lose, Lose/Lose.* Lancaster, PA: Technomic Publishing Company, pp. 7–8.
7. Coleman, C. J. 1990. *Managing Labor Relations in the Public Sector.* San Francisco, CA: Jossey-Bass Publishers, pp. 20, 104.
8. Helsby, R. D., J. Tener, and J. Lefkowitz, eds. 1985. *The Evolving Process—Collective Negotiations in Public Employment.* Fort Washington, PA: Labor Relations Press, pp. 460–461.
9. Webster, W. G., Sr. 1985. *Effective Collective Bargaining,* pp. 52–53.
10. Webster, W. G., Sr. 1985. *Effective Collective Bargaining,* pp. 44–45, 48.
11. Smith, S. C., D. Ball, and D. Liontos. 1990. *Working Together—The Collaborative Style of Bargaining.* Eugene, OR: ERIC Clearinghouse on Educational Management, University of Oregon, pp. 47–48.
12. U.S. Department of Education—Office of Educational Research and Improvement, Programs for the Improvement of Practice. 1993. *A Guide to Developing Educational Partnerships.* Special report prepared by Naida C. Tushnet, Southwest Regional Laboratory. GPO, October, pp. 3–13.
13. Panasonic Foundation. 1994. "Using Internal and External Coalitions," *Strategies for School System Leaders on District-Level Change,* 1(2): 1–12. Seacaucus, NJ: Issue series of the Panasonic Foundation in collaboration with the American Association of School Administrators.

14. Herman, J. J. and G. E. Megiveron. 1993. *Collective Bargaining in Education,* pp. 207–209.

15. Guthrie, J. W. and R. J. Reed. 1986. *Educational Administration and Policy— Effective Leadership for American Education.* Second Edition. Boston, MA: Allyn & Bacon, pp. 43–44.

16. Keith, S. and R. H. Girling. 1991. *Education, Management, and Participation— New Directions in Educational Administration.* Boston, MA: Allyn & Bacon, pp. 268–269.

17. Herman, J. J. 1991. "The Two Faces of Collective Bargaining," *School Business Affairs,* 57(2): 10–13.

18. Webster, W. G., Sr. 1985. *Effective Collective Bargaining,* p. 73.

19. Webster, W. G., Sr. 1985. *Effective Collective Bargaining,* pp. 121–122.

20. Webster, W. G., Sr. 1985. *Effective Collective Bargaining,* p. 76.

PREPARING FOR AND CONDUCTING COLLECTIVE BARGAINING

Section Two consists of five chapters. Chapter 5, Determining Strategic and Tactical Plans Related to Collective Bargaining, discusses union and management strategic and tactical planning processes, and locating areas of agreement between the union and management plans. Examples are included.

Chapter 6, Collecting Background Information in Preparation for Negotiations, presents a discussion of the various types of background information that should be collected prior to entering into the act of negotiating a new or replacement master contractual agreement between an employees' union and the school district. The information to be collected includes information about the collective bargaining laws and procedures that govern negotiations in that particular state, financial information, comparative information about other school districts, historical information related to prior negotiations and grievances, and information about needed or desired changes suggested from the existing contract.

Chapter 7, Choosing Your Team and Analyzing Their Team, deals with the topics related to choosing, organizing, training, and operating the negotiating team. It also includes a discussion of the advantages of analyzing the other party's team and its members. It ends with a comparison of the difference in behavioral rules that would govern the negotiations when dealing with a win-win, rather than an adversarial negotiating environment.

Chapter 8, Preparing to Go to the Bargaining Table, discusses the areas of drafting at-the-table proposals, anticipating and analyzing the other party's proposals, establishing the strategies and tactics that will be used during negotiations, determining the negotiation guidelines, and establishing a pre-negotiations tone. The chapter ends with differences that would exist in the preparation for win-win negotiations instead of adversarial negotiations.

Chapter 9, Doing It: Conduct at and away from the Table, discusses ground rules, methods of exchanging proposals, controlling personality conflicts, selecting the spokesperson, establishing a communications hotline, and timing the negotiations moves. This chapter also discusses projecting multi-year costs, being flexible and creative, setting a tone, posturing and positioning, presenting proposals, analyzing proposals and using quid pro quos, and participating in side bar bargaining. The chapter ends with a discussion of establishing priorities, drafting counterproposals, keeping a notebook, and reaching closure.

Determining Strategic and Tactical Plans Related to Collective Bargaining

CHAPTER 5 will present definitions of terms used in strategic and tactical planning, the importance of conducting a needs assessment, present information about internal and external scanning, and trend analyses. It also will present examples of union and management strategic and tactical planning. The chapter ends with a summary, exercises, and selected references.

DEFINITIONS

Frequently terms are unclear or misused because of the lack of agreement on their definitions and usages. To avoid misunderstanding of the terms used in this chapter, the following definitions will be applied. In addition, we will discuss the importance of determining a preferred future, and examples of strategic and tactical plans from both the union's and management's viewpoints will be presented. Areas of agreement and disagreement between the union and management will be identified.

(1) *Strategic planning* is a process designed to develop a vision of what should be or what could be at some point, usually five or more years in the future. It is comprised of all the elements that the visionary desires to be present, and it can be simply defined as a series of desired *whats*.

(2) *Tactical planning* is the process of deciding upon the means that will be utilized to achieve the desired strategic vision of the future. It is comprised of all activities that provide the *hows* to achieve the whats of the strategic plan.

(3) *Needs assessment* is a process used to determine the discrepancies that exist between what should or could be and what is. That is, the present state is compared to the desired future state, and the

gaps identified between the two states provides a list of needs to be addressed.

(4) *Scanning* is the process of collecting and analyzing information.

(5) *External scanning* is the process of collecting and analyzing information that is external to the group or organization that is collecting the scanning information.

(6) *Internal scanning* is the process of collecting and analyzing information that is internal to the group or organization that is collecting the scanning information.

(7) *Trend analysis* is a process that reviews the internal and external information that has been scanned to locate trends that will be studied to determine the effect they might have on upcoming contract negotiations.

(8) *Preferred future* is the process utilized to spell out all details that the group wishes the organization and the organization's collective bargaining environment to look like at some point in the future.

(9) *Strategic goals* are those items that are derived from the overall strategic plan, and are general directional outcomes to be achieved in the future.

(10) *Strategic objectives* are those items that are derived from the strategic goals and are specific directional results to be achieved.

(11) *Action plans* are the listing of specific activities to be completed over a specific time period and by specific named persons in order to achieve the specific strategic objectives, which combined will lead to achievement of the strategic goal to which those objectives apply.

(12) *Monitoring* is the process of studying the progress of action plans, the status of goals and objectives, and continuous scanning of the internal and external environments for the purpose of reacting to changes in the environment or for the purpose of making modifications in the action plans as they become necessary [1–3].

NEEDS ASSESSMENTS

A need is a gap or discrepancy between what is (current state) and what should or could be (preferred future state). A needs assessment is the task of collecting data that identifies what the group desires and then comparing these data to what is currently in place [4]. Thus, it is the assemblage of a listing of gaps between the specific desires of a group and the actual existing degree to which those specific desires are currently being met.

The union may conduct an interactive needs assessment to use in planning upcoming contract negotiations by asking its members to indicate the items they want removed from the current contract, the items they wish modified, and the items they wish to be added. The board of education's negotiating team would conduct a similar needs assessment, but, obviously, using different sources [5].

A needs assessment could be conducted by any one of the district's stakeholder groups—employees, parents, students—to determine the collective response to the described gaps between the specific desires of a particular group and the actual existing degree to which those specific desires are currently being met [6].

INTERNAL AND EXTERNAL SCANNING—EXAMPLES

As defined previously, external scanning is the process of collecting and analyzing information that is external to the collecting group or organization, while internal scanning is the process of collecting and analyzing information that is internal to the group or organization [7]. Examples of information sources and areas of investigation that could be targeted by various groups within the district or by the district as a whole include the following demographic, political, social, and economic factors:

External Data
(1) Future business and industry plans
(2) Community attitude towards schools
(3) Federal, state, and local governmental legislation that has an impact on the schools
(4) District-applicable court decisions
(5) Population shifts related to age, race, and socioeconomic level that will have an impact on schools
(6) Trends in such matters as private school enrollments and parental choice [8]

Internal Data

(1) An increase in single parent homes, and homes where both parents work

(2) A decline in parent and community attendance at school-sponsored activities

(3) A reduction of state financial support

(4) An increase in the percentage of student dropouts [9]

In preparation for upcoming master contract negotiations, both union and management should conduct internal and external scans. Examples of the data scanned for by both union and management in preparation for upcoming master contract negotiations will clarify this activity [10].

The union's negotiating team will probably collect the following examples of data and attempt to determine trends that will impact the upcoming master contract negotiations:

External Data

(1) Comparative employee salaries from neighboring school districts

(2) Comparative fringe benefits (types and costs paid) from neighboring school districts

(3) Suggested contract clauses from the state and/or national union with whom the union is affiliated

(4) Attitudes of the residents of the community (soft data, see Chapter 6)

Internal Data

(1) The historical records of past contract negotiations

(2) The specifics of any employee grievances filed during the operation of the current master contract agreement

(3) The needs assessment data collected from any interactive needs assessment that was recently conducted with the union's members [11]

The board of education's negotiating team will probably collect the following data and from it attempt to determine trends that will impact the upcoming contract negotiations:

External Data

(1) The attitudinal data from the survey of community residents (soft data)

(2) Comparative data on the salaries paid like employees in neighboring school districts

(3) Comparative data on like employee fringe benefits (type and amount) paid by the school district) in neighboring school districts

(4) Copies of neighboring school districts' master contract agreements for like employees

Internal Data

(1) The current tax effort (in terms of voted millage) voted by the taxpayers of the district to be used for comparison with those of neighboring school districts

(2) The current income from national, state, and local sources, and the percentage of the total for each to be used for comparative purposes to those categories of statistics in neighboring school districts

(3) The history of proposals, counterproposals, and contract clauses approved during all previous negotiations of master contracts

(4) The total cost per employee of salary and fringe amounts expended, and the percentage of the total budget expended for this purpose

(5) The history of grievances (types and resolutions reached) that were filed during the administration of the current master contractual agreement [12]

TREND ANALYSES

The conduct of intensive trend analyses is an important activity that groups within the district participate in to locate those trend items that might impact the overall vision and goals of the district. Those trends that appear to potentially have a negative impact should be directly addressed with an intent to remove, or, at the very least, neutralize them.

Those trends that appear to potentially have a positive impact should be utilized to the fullest when presenting a group's negotiating positions and rationales. As an example, a few of both the negative and positive trends from a union's and a management's point of view will emphasize the importance of each group conducting a trend analysis prior to sitting down at the table to negotiate a new master contract [13].

(1) It is clear that taxpayers are reluctant to vote additional taxes upon themselves for any purpose, including schools.

(2) It is clear that federal aid is consistently being reduced.

(3) It is clear, from attitudinal surveys of the community, that community residents are not pleased with the results achieved by the school district.

(4) It is clear that neighboring districts are more successful in hiring the type of new employees that the school district desires to hire.

(5) It is clear that businesses in the district are planning to expand, and this will provide a larger tax base.

(6) It is clear that the state is increasing its tax base, and this will mean additional state aid for the school districts in the state.

(7) There is a trend toward businesses and industries becoming more supportive of school districts with their willingness to adopt a school, provide speakers for classes, and allow high school junior and senior students to work in their businesses and industries during the summer.

(8) There is a trend toward districts involving their residents in community education programs.

(9) There is a trend toward school districts involving senior citizens in their schools as speakers for classes and as tutors for students.

PREFERRED FUTURE RESULTS

Once an initial collective bargaining master contract agreement has been signed, it is very seldom that the union is decertified by election. It is also uncommon for any significant change to occur in the membership or participation of key decision-making groups. Therefore, both parties to collective bargaining should look upon the process as one very similar to a marriage for life. There will be occasional disagreements, occasional emotional outbreaks, and many compromises reached.

Because this is a very long-term relationship it is important that both labor and management determine the preferred future results that they desire to achieve. This preferred future may very well, among parties of good will, lead to a cooperative, collaborative, and win-win continuing relationship [14]. However, if the overall district or collective bargaining environment is an adversarial one, each group should still make certain that it spells out the preferred results it intends to achieve.

The beliefs and visions held by stakeholders that relate to students, parents, community, instructional and co-curricular programs, governance, and many other matters, should be incorporated into the operating vision. Reaching this stage may take a considerable period of time, since any group will probably vary in the types and amounts of beliefs and values held by its individual members. Eventually, a consensus will be reached on those core beliefs and values which must be incorporated into the preferred future vision for the school or school district [15].

STRATEGIC PLANNING: AN EXAMPLE

Strategic goals are the final task of a strategic planning committee before it turns its information over to a tactical planning group. A few strategic goals (samples of outcomes from stakeholder groups) are listed below. It must be emphasized, however, that strategic goals are the whats to be achieved, and the details are left to the tactical planners [16].

- Lower the student drop-out rate.
- Increase collaboration and/or partnership with the other organizations within the community.
- Increase the school climate scores.
- Provide for the at-risk students.
- Increase the investment earnings of the district.
- Prove that all students are learning.
- Increase the enrollments in math, science, and foreign languages [17].

It is incumbent upon any union to clearly spell out those elements it wishes to include for its members in the future. The combination of these elements comprise the preferred future vision for the union. This vision must then be broken down into strategic goals and strategic objectives; and action programs must be devised, initiated, and carried out with the intention of achieving those specific results that are desired. A few examples from the union's viewpoint will illustrate this matter.

Goal example one: The teachers of this district shall be paid the highest salaries in the area.

Objective: By 1998, the district's teachers shall be paid a salary that is in the top ten percent of the salaries paid to teachers in all school districts in the region.

Goal example two: The employees of this school district shall add additional fringe benefits to their fringe package.

Objective: By 1999, the employees of the school district will add optical, hearing, and disability insurance to the paid fringe benefit package.

Goal example three: The employees will be granted the opportunity to have greater input into decisions made by the school board.

Objective: By 2000, the school board will agree that all proposed policies will be distributed to the employees for comments prior to adoption. The union will be given an opportunity to present its views on the proposed policy at a publicly called official board of education meeting prior to the policy being acted upon by the board of education.

UNION'S TACTICAL PLANNING: AN EXAMPLE

A useful format for devising any tactical plan is listed below, and one limited example from the union's view will demonstrate its usefulness. Of course, a tactical plan should be devised for each strategic objective.

Specific Objective: By 1997, to have the board of education agree to and put into operation a site-based management plan that is agreeable to the union.

Task	Chronology	Person Responsible	Time	How Measured
Study	2	Advisory committee	2 months	Data collected
Visit	1	Key officials	3 weeks	Best ex. selected
Develop plan promote	4	Leadership	6 months	Teachers accept
Sell	3	All members	7th month	All members accept
Present to board	5	Leadership	8th month	Board adopts
Assist to implement	6	All members	1st and 2nd years	All members accept

Unless the action plan lists all the tasks (the example greatly abbreviated this), and unless the plan pins responsibility to specific persons and establishes time limits and ways to measure results, there will be no method of measuring progress and level of achievement. Therefore, monitoring by the leadership is crucial to achievement. By monitoring, the leadership can determine if the assigned individuals have completed their tasks, if the time frame has been successfully followed, if there are reasons to adjust the action plan, and the degree to which the desired results have been achieved [18]. This, in turn, will accomplish the specific strategic objective, which, then, helps accomplish the goal, which, finally, accomplishes a segment of the preferred future vision. They all tie together and if these procedures are not followed, the union will never know if it was successful or not because its results were not predetermined. The union will find itself in a predicament similar to the driver who wanted to go to San Francisco, but ended up in Chicago because she/he wasn't clear about the destination nor had a roadmap (plan) to get to that destination.

MANAGEMENT'S STRATEGIC PLANNING: AN EXAMPLE

It is also incumbent upon any board of education to clearly spell out the elements that it wishes to achieve in the future. The combination of those agreed upon elements comprise the preferred future vision for the board of education and administration [19]. This vision must then be broken down into strategic goals and strategic objectives; and action programs must be devised, initiated, and carried out with the purpose of achieving those specific desired results. A pair of examples from management's viewpoint will illustrate this matter.

Goal example one: To initiate joint labor/management advisory committees.

Objective: By 1998, to get agreement with the union that joint labor/management advisory committees will be organized to study problems that affect the school district and to recommend solutions to the identified problems.

Goal example two: To initiate School-Based Management committees into the school district's decision-making processes.

Objective: By 1999, to put in place School-Based Management committees at all sites, whose membership will include teachers, classified employees, principals, parents, and community members.

MANAGEMENT'S TACTICAL PLANNING: AN EXAMPLE

To repeat, a useful format for devising any tactical plan is listed below, and one limited example from a management's viewpoint will demonstrate its usefulness. Remember that a tactical plan should be devised for each strategic objective.

Specific Objective: By 1999, to implement School-Based Management committees into the school district.

The format below will, once again, be utilized to (1) determine every task that has to be completed to achieve the objective, (2) place the tasks in chronological order so that the plan stays in a reasonable sequence of accomplishments, (3) to identify a specific individual or group that is responsible for each of the listed tasks, (4) to establish time limits by which each task is to be completed, and (5) to determine how the degree of achievement (completion) is to be measured. Finally, someone or some persons must attend to the very serious function of monitoring the progress as the action plan is being completed [20].

Task	Chronology	Person Responsible	Time	How Measured
?	20	?	?	?
?	8	?	?	?
?	3	?	?	?
?	etc.	?	?	?

AREAS OF AGREEMENT AND DISAGREEMENT BETWEEN UNION'S AND MANAGEMENT'S STRATEGIC TACTICAL PLANS: AN EXAMPLE

Even when the union/management environment is adversarial in nature, it behooves both parties to clearly identify areas of agreement and disagreement. As areas of agreement are identified, both parties ought to be mature enough to help one another accomplish the desired goals where agreement is present. A good example would be that of School-Based Management. For example, by agreeing to implement SBM, the union will achieve its strategic goal of having more input into decisions, and the board of education and management will achieve its goal of having a broad-based group of employees, the principal, parents, and community members assist in making decisions that impact the local school building [21]. Obviously, if agreement exists on the goal of implementing SBM and if agreement is reached on the specific objective to be achieved by a specific date for said implementation, both parties should be able to collaboratively develop an action plan that would result in the successful implementation of SBM into the school district's decision-making structures.

THE APPROACH TO STRATEGIC AND TACTICAL PLANNING DIFFERS WHEN A WIN-WIN ENVIRONMENT IS IN PLACE

When the union's leadership and the management's leadership approach collective bargaining from a cooperative, collaborative, and win-win mindset, they still need to (1) develop a preferred future vision, (2) develop strategic and tactical plans, (3) establish strategic goals and objectives, (4) conduct internal and external scanning exercises, (5) develop action plans, and (6) monitor the in-process results of action planning, as well as make changes when scanning trends indicate the need to do this. However, in a win-win situation, both the union's leadership and the management's leadership approach these tasks as a unified body [22].

They develop a vision that is desirable for the students, employees, and the school district as a whole. They try to develop salaries, fringe benefits, and power-sharing agreements that consider the tax efforts made by residents. They determine the value of expenditures for all items that are included in the budget, not just employee salaries and fringe benefits. They assess the availability of funds and the appropriate balance of decision-making power with a clear eye towards the legitimate roles of management and labor [23]. With clear strategic goals and objectives agreed to by consensus, they can jointly scan the external and internal environment for trends that might positively or negatively affect the school district, and can jointly develop action plans to achieve their strategic objectives and strategic goals. Finally, they can monitor the action programs and the trends, and work together to make sensible and required modifications in strategic or tactical plans as the opportunity or requirement to do this arises.

SUMMARY

This chapter presented definitions of key terms related to strategic and tactical planning and discussed conducting a needs assessment of the district's stakeholder groups. It provided examples of internal and external scanning from the viewpoints of the union and the board. It described negative and positive trend examples, and defined beliefs and visions as related to preferred future results. An example of strategic planning was followed by an example of union tactical planning of a site-based management plan. Similar examples were provided for management, preceding a description of the areas of agreement and disagreement, again framed around SBM. A descriptive outcome of a win-win cooperative approach to planning was provided.

EXERCISES

1. Place yourself in the role of a union leader, and decide upon the strategic plans that you would put in place for collective bargaining purposes.
2. Place yourself in the role of the board of education, and decide upon the strategic plans that you would put in place for collective bargaining purposes.
3. Decide how you would go about doing a union's needs analysis before beginning contract negotiations.
4. Decide how you would go about doing the board of education's needs analysis before beginning contract negotiations.
5. Place yourself in the role of a union leader, and decide what external and internal scanning information you would collect.
6. Next, decide how you would utilize the trends you have identified during your scanning exercises to support your negotiating positions.
7. Place yourself in the role of the chief negotiator for the board of education, and decide what external and internal scanning information you would collect.
8. Next, decide how you would utilize the trends you have identified during your scanning exercises to support your negotiating positions.
9. Place yourself in the role of a union leader, and decide what tactics you would utilize during the negotiation of a master contract.
10. Place yourself in the role of the chief negotiator for the board of education, and decide what tactics you would utilize during the negotiation of a master contract.

REFERENCES

1. Kaufman, R., J. J. Herman, and K. Watters. 1996. *Educational Planning: Strategic, Tactical, Operational.* Lancaster, PA: Technomic Publishing Co., Inc., pp. 259–269.
2. Herman, J. J. 1993. "Conducting a SWOT Analysis: Strategic Planning for School Success," *NASSP Bulletin,* 77(557): 85–91.

3. Herman, J. J. 1994. "Determining the Critical Success Factors," *NASSP Bulletin,* 78(559): 108–110.

4. Herman, J. J. 1989a. "School District Strategic Planning (Part I)," *School Business Affairs,* 55(2): 10–14.

5. Herman, J. J. and G. E. Megiveron. 1993. *Collective Bargaining in Education: Win/Win, Win/Lose, Lose/Lose.* Lancaster, PA: Technomic Publishing Co., Inc., pp. 31–41.

6. Kaufman, R. and J. J. Herman. 1991. *Strategic Planning in Education: Revitalizing, Restructuring, Rethinking.* Lancaster, PA: Technomic Publishing Co., Inc., pp. 27–29.

7. Herman, J. J. 1989b. "External and Internal Scanning: Identifying Variables That Affect Your School," *NASSP Bulletin,* 73(520): 48–52.

8. Herman, J. J. and J. L. Herman. 1994a. *Making Change Happen: Practical Planning for School Leaders,* Thousand Oaks, CA: Corwin Press, Sage Publications, pp. 30–31.

9. Herman, J. J. 1988. "Map the Trip to Your District's Future," *The School Administrator,* 45(9): 16, 18, 23.

10. Herman, J. J. and J. L. Herman. 1994b. *Educational Quality Management: Catalyst for Integrated Change.* Lancaster, PA: Technomic Publishing Co., Inc., pp. 50, 122–124.

11. Ibid.

12. Genck, F. H. and A. J. Klingenberg. 1991. *Effective Schools Through Effective Management.* rev. ed., Springfield, IL: Illinois Association of School Boards, pp. 67–71.

13. Kaufman, R. and J. J. Herman. 1991. *Strategic Planning in Education,* p. 104.

14. Herman, J. J. 1989c. "Site-Based Management: Creating a Vision and Mission Statement," *NASSP Bulletin,* 73(519): 79–83.

15. Herman, J. J. 1989d. "A Vision for the Future: Site-Based Strategic Planning," *NASSP Bulletin,* 73(518): 23–27.

16. Kaufman, R., J. J. Herman, and K. Watters. 1996. *Educational Planning,* p. 175.

17. Herman, J. J. 1989e. "Strategic Planning—One of the Changing Leadership Roles of the Principal," *The Clearing House,* 63(2): 56–58.

18. Herman, J. J. 1990. "Action Plans to Make Your Vision a Reality," *NASSP Bulletin,* 74(523): 14–17.

19. Kaufman, R. and J. J. Herman. 1989. "Planning that Fits Every District: Three Choices Help Define Your Plan's Scope," *The School Administrator,* 46(8): 17–19.

20. Herman, J. J. 1992. "Strategic Planning: Reasons for Failed Attempts," *Educational Planning,* 8(3): 36–40.

21. Herman, J. J. and R. Kaufman. 1991. "Making the Mega Plan," *American School Board Journal,* 178(5): 24–25, 41.

22. Herman, J. J. 1989g. "A Decision-Making Model: Site-Based Communications Governance Committees," *NASSP Bulletin,* 73(521): 61–66.

23. Herman, J. J. 1989h. "School Business Officials' Roles in the Strategic Planning Process (Part II)," *School Business Affairs,* 55(3): 20, 22–24.

Collecting Background Information in Preparation for Negotiations

CHAPTER 6 will answer the following questions: (1) What's bargainable? (2) What data should be collected? (3) What is the difference between hard and soft data? (4) What is the importance of conducting trend analyses? and (5) Why use trend data to impact upcoming negotiations? This chapter will also address such topics as: What is the role of "past practice"? What are the at-the-table issues that have not reached closure during prior contract negotiations? What are comparable school districts providing and doing? What can you afford? How do you get suggestions and opinions from those persons in the trenches (principals, supervisors, and other administrators) about what problems they are encountering and about existing contract provisions they feel require changes? When and under what conditions do you wish to settle the contract? and what are the differences, if any, in the preparation for and the information collected prior to bargaining when planning a win-win instead of an adversarial strategy? The chapter also includes a summary, exercises, and references.

WHAT'S BARGAINABLE?

The first step in collecting information prior to negotiations is to obtain an updated copy of state law and the rules and regulations (if they exist) adopted by the state agency appointed to oversee collective bargaining in the state. In many states this agency is called the PERB, which stands for the Public Employee Relations Board [1]. With information in hand, in particular, the manner of determining bargaining units, the scope of bargaining, impasse procedures, and grievance resolution provisions, it should become clear to the board of education's collective bargaining team which items are bargainable and which conditions have been predetermined by statute or by a public governing body. The search of governing laws and rules and regulations for the state in which the local school district is located should also provide clear information about which items are (1) *mandated* subjects of bargaining, (2) *permissive* subjects of bargaining, and (3) *prohibited* subjects of bargaining [2]. Most states distinguish among those items which are mandated, permissive, and prohibited [3]. A few examples will clarify the differences among these areas.

Mandated subjects of collective bargaining usually include matters of salary and fringe benefits. Other items will vary from state to state.

Prohibited subjects normally include the right to strike. In some cases such items as hiring, supervision, job assignment, recruitment, discharge of employees, and evaluation of employees are prohibited.

Permitted subjects include practically anything that can be agreed to by both parties, and are not contradictory to any existing law. These items vary greatly from state to state to a greater extent than those items that are mandated or prohibited. In the absence of specific inclusion within the state law governing collective bargaining, the state public employee relations board's rulings or case law defines the area and range of permitted subjects. Some items in this category could include class size, agency shop (see below), and/or selection of instructional materials. Proposals and counters are significant here; being proposed and left on the table does not make them bargainable.

Briefly, let's define, at this juncture, the differences among the following terms: (1) agency shop, (2) union shop, (3) closed shop and (4) meet and confer; three of these categories exist within the states; one category is prohibited. The specific category under which the local district falls is an important determiner of the strategies and tactics utilized during the negotiation of a new or replacement master contract.

Union shop refers to a situation wherein teachers or other school district employees are required to join whichever majority union organization has been recognized by the board and by the National Labor Relations Board or comparable state governing agency as the exclusive employee representative. The employee must remain a member for the term of the collective bargaining agreement(s).

Agency shop refers to a situation wherein all employees are required to pay a service fee to the union, but they are not required to become members of the union [4]. The fee is intended to cover all the costs of the union when the union is representing the employee in collective bargaining matters.

Closed shop refers to a situation wherein any person wishing to become employed by the school district must become a member of the union prior to being hired. Closed shops are prohibited [5].

"Meet and confer" refers to those few situations wherein a state permits collective bargaining or the meet and confer approach depending on the preferences of the majority of the teachers or other employees within each school district [6].

In most states, either the union shop or closed shop provisions dictate the approach used. Again, it is important that the board of education's negotiating team clearly understands which legal positions control the negotiating process in their local school district.

Now that we have stressed the importance of the specific laws and conditions governing the local collective bargaining process, let's turn to the topic of the data that should be collected prior to beginning negotiations.

WHAT DATA SHOULD BE COLLECTED?

In addition to the legal framework collective bargaining must adhere to, many other areas of information should be collected including (1) existing personnel policies and practices, (2) existing board policies and the accompanying rules and regulations, (3) financial conditions of both income and expenditures—past and present, (4) past practice in the district, (5) history of grievances and grievance arbitrations, (6) prior at-the-table issues which were not resolved during previous master contract negotiations, (7) history of prior contractual negotiations, (8) comparable school districts' contractual provisions and current negotiating status, and (9) other miscellaneous sources of useful data [7,8]. Let's begin by investigating existing personnel policies and practices.

Existing personnel policies and practices are important documents to review prior to negotiations for two basic reasons. First, if management has workable policies, the board of education's negotiating team wants to make certain that nothing is agreed to at-the-table that will interfere with the operation of the school district under the direction of those policies. Second, they can guide the board of education's negotiation team by developing proposed contractual articles that will provide added management decision-making authority in important areas not covered by policy [9].

Some of the major areas of concern within the framework of collective bargaining are those areas dealing with the recruitment, placement, and evaluation of employees. These activities should be regarded as management rights, and should be held as sole management decision making areas [10,11].

Existing board of education policies and the accompanying rules and regulations are also very important documents to be reviewed by management's negotiating team. These policies provide the philosophical and broad directional operating orders under which the administration administers the district. The major concern, here, is that the management's negotiating team not unknowingly agree to anything at-the-table that would interfere with the district's operation under the existing policies (and the rules and regulations which supplement and complement those policies) [12,13].

Present and past income and expenditures/financial conditions should be studied to determine the sources of national, state, and local income, the trendlines of the various sources, and the predictability of the various sources in the future. Funding source verification is significant. Many unit members will receive funds from different sources (i.e., local, state, and/or federal funds are usually designated as directly applicable only to specific programs, grants, and foundation gifts). Each "program's" funding must be categorized by the team so that they are aware of whence the money comes, dates of receipt, and whether the funds are reimbursed monies or budget monies. It is important to determine the percent and dollar expenditures of the various accounts within the district. An analysis of the amounts and percentages expended for administration, instruction, fixed charges, and the other budget accounts will display the various current expenditure priorities, and it will also display the trends in the various categories of expenditures over a five year or longer time period. This information provides an important database, which will assist management's negotiating team in determining what money is available to settle the upcoming master contract [14].

Of course, the key sub-areas of data involve an analysis of the current and historical salaries, salary schedules, and fringe benefits related to employees. This, coupled with information about the cost-of-living index, the placement of existing employees, the length of the work day, the length of the work year, and estimates of where newly hired employees would be placed, provides the most useful database with which to enter negotiations with any employee union [15]. The gathering of this information can be distributed across the members of the managerial team [16].

Next, let's visit the area of past practice. This is an area which may well determine what happens with at-the-table strategies and tactics, and it becomes crucial information if an impasse is reached that terminates with mandated contract arbitration of unresolved issues between the union and management.

Past practice has important implications for future union/management issues. Virtually all activities related to union/management issues can be viewed from the perspective of past practice. Past practice shows how consistently administrators, on a day-to-day basis, operate within policies, rules and regulations, and existing master contractual agreement. Any discrepancies between what exists in writing and what occurs during the operation of the school district can lead to problems. Also, if all administrators do not operate within these parameters, troublesome precedents can be established. Erosion of the contract or policies by administrators who choose to ignore, stretch, or misinterpret policy can be devastating to table bargaining. The union can negotiate a point they want in the contract by providing extensive documentation about the past practice of even one administrator, if there has been a method of operation contrary to policy. These situations become even more demanding if grievance arbitrations have produced rulings for or against specific operational procedures.

The flip side of past practice damage is one in which management (or the union) breaks a troublesome past practice without the union filing a grievance [17]. Past practice can also be neutralized if various and contradictory rulings on identical or similar items have been rendered by arbitrators during a variety of grievance arbitrations.

In any case, analysis of past practice can lead to existing contractual language being challenged (or perhaps even changed). If the language is not changed, it can lead to an impasse which could ultimately become an issue in contract arbitration.

The history of grievances and grievance arbitrations should be studied for the purpose of locating potential trouble spots as one prepares to enter the negotiation phase of collective bargaining. Grievance arbitration is the study of mandated or suggested rulings by an arbitrator when there is disagreement about specific management actions that may or may not violate the actual wording or intent of the master contractual agreement. The mandated or suggested rulings depend on the state's laws and regulations, or they depend on what is agreed to within the master contract agreement [18].

This differs from contract arbitration, which involves an outside arbitrator coming into the school district as a step in an impasse procedure. In this case, the union and management cannot reach agreement on one or more proposed master contract articles, and an arbitrator is hired to come in to resolve the outstanding contractual issues in order that a total master contract agreement can be reached and ratified. It should be stressed, however, that contractual arbitration can be mandated or permissive, depending on state laws and regulations governing collective bargaining and/or the specific local agreement resolving contractual impasses by both the union and management [16].

Although the seriousness of contract arbitration has already been stressed, the importance of studying the types and numbers of grievances on file has not been sufficiently emphasized. In addition, it is even more important to study the history of arbitrators' rulings related to grievances that have been processed through arbitration [17].

Grievances are caused when management exercises its right to operate the district. When the union feels that management has operated in a manner that is not in accordance with the letter or the intent of a master contract agreement, the union can file a grievance [18]. A grievance, depending on the governing conditions in each local school district, can be filed by an individual union member, or the union may file a class grievance on behalf of a group of union members. The basic rule is that management can demand an employee to comply, and the employee must comply or be considered insubordinate and subject to discipline [19]. The only two exceptions are situations that are considered illegal or immoral.

When a grievance is filed, it alleges that management has violated a specific contract article. It is then dealt with as an alleged grievance until it is proven or resolved.

A study of currently existing grievances and a history of union grievances filed against the management of the school district is important. It identifies trouble spots and areas of disagreement that will likely be attended to through contract article proposals at the negotiation table, if they are not resolved prior to the beginning of master contract negotiations [20].

A history of at-the-table issues not resolved during previous master contract negotiations is another important area of data gathering [21]. Those items placed on the table but not agreed to by both parties, and the strategies and tactics used during the negotiations on those items, provide a potential list of what could be placed on the table during the upcoming negotiations [22]. It may be advisable to reserve this area for the chief negotiator, providing that she/he was the person responsible for the contract being reopened. If this is the first contract, the job of collecting these data should be distributed among the team members, who should contact neighboring districts for comparable information.

Obviously, both parties will attempt to strengthen the next contract. Knowledge of the progression of unresolved issues in prior negotiations provide a roadmap, in many cases, to the future [23,24]. Inadequate research into the issues and the background of these issues will put the bargaining team at a serious disadvantage. Without this research, the management negotiating team will perhaps do the following: (1) put items on the table which are duplications of previous effort, (2) introduce or react to items that are never going to be resolved, except through mandatory contract arbitration, (3) reveal a lack of basic knowledge of what has been important in the eyes of the union's negotiating team, and (4) introduce items or react to items which have previously been proven unnecessary or relatively unimportant.

In some cases, the union's or the management's negotiating team introduces new ideas during negotiations that they know will not be accepted by the other party, but are introduced to get them on record as items to be dealt with during future contract negotiations. This is a technique that is very useful to either party in outlining future at-the-table negotiation agendas [25].

Assuming that there has been discussion of policies, past practices, finance, grievances, and prior negotiation history, the following information from school districts will serve as an important measure of comparability in at-the-table discussion of provisions.

Comparable school district contractual provisions provide basic data to bring to the table; these data provide the ammunition to back up the rationales for the offers being made during at-the-table negotiation sessions. These data also become crucial during mediation, arbitration, and fact-finding impasse procedures, as third parties serving in these impasse roles will give much weight to the provisions provided by comparable school districts.

Not only should data be collected about the existing master contract conditions in each of the comparable districts, but data should also be gathered about what is being placed on the negotiation table by union or management if current contractual negotiations are taking place [26–28].

The major categories of data should include the following:

- school district income from federal, state, local, and other sources: Both the actual dollar amounts and the percent of budget income from each source should be collected [29].

- school district effort information: Effort can be determined by the amount and percent of the budget raised through local property taxes or other local tax sources [30].
- the amount and percentage of the total budget expended for salaries and fringe benefits for the employees of the various unions and for non union employees' various job categories [31].
- the specific types of fringe benefits offered members of the various employees' unions, and the cost per union employee of each fringe benefit: In this category, some districts provide fringe benefits covering spouses and families, rather than just the specific employee; it is crucial that this level of detailed information be collected [32].
- the present pupil enrollment of the district, with a breakdown by grade level: This detail is important as it is traditionally more expensive to offer secondary programs than to offer elementary programs. Also, related to this matter, there should be an analysis of pupil-teacher ratios for the various grade levels and the various instructional programs offered by the districts [33].
- the numbers and types of present specialized program offerings: Offerings such as special education categories often have very small class sizes, and teacher aides are also required [34]. Other conditions, such as a student weighting (for example, a weighting of four times the actual number of students being considered for a class in severely mentally retarded handicapped students) are oftentimes negotiated into a master contract agreement [35]. In addition, vocational classes, gifted and talented classes, and other specialized program offerings provide important data that should be collected prior to beginning negotiations of a new or replacement master contract agreement [36].
- the numbers and types of co-curricular (athletic and other nonclassroom offerings) and the costs related to the same [37]: The additional salaries and contractual conditions related to the coaches and sponsors of co-curricular offerings are many times a point of deliberation and/or disagreement during the negotiations process.
- five-year trends in assessed property valuations within the district [38]: These data will provide the negotiators with information related to the future potential increase or decrease of the property tax income.
- review of the current bonded indebtedness of the district: The amount of taxes levied to pay off bonds issued by the school district certainly will impact the total taxes available to settle a future

master contract. If there is a large amount of tax levied to pay off the principal and interest related to bond issues, the probability of increasing the tax rate to support the operational programs of the school district would be very limited at best [39]. Bonded indebtedness cannot be used for salaries this fact needs to be emphasized.

- the salary schedules and the array of teacher data on the salary schedules: These data are important, because if your district is one in which nearly all of the teacher or other employee union groups are at the top of the salary schedule, and you are comparing the data with districts who have most of their teaching staff or other employee union groups at the beginning steps of the salary schedule, your district will already possess a higher mean (average) salary and will have a larger percentage of the total budget expended for salaries [40].

  In addition, if your school district has a step salary schedule, as do most school districts, it will make a difference in the new money that can be allocated to improve the schedule; it will also guide management's negotiating team in devising its proposals to meet the obvious array of teachers or other union employees along the existing salary schedule. For example, if the district has a lot of beginning employees, the money required to move them up steps on the existing salary scale will be a significant amount; and there will be far less money available to improve the salary schedule, per se. If, on the other hand, most of the employees are at the top of the schedule, the salary schedule can be modified because very little of the available funds will have to go to support movement of the employees up the stepped increments. In the case of teachers, the same analysis would be true if the district provides a differential for various degree levels or certifications held by employees.
- collection of the employee work day and work year: Obviously, if one district requires a greater number of work hours in the day or a greater number of work days in the year, these data should be factored into the comparisons being made. This also relates to the salary breakdown-per-day-worked comparison among comparable school districts [41].

Now that the standard data collection categories have been discussed, let's turn to other sources of useful information. These may be information sources related to national, state, or regional trends.

Other miscellaneous sources of data might prove helpful, including: (1) data on the number of students, cost of tuition, salaries paid, and fringe benefits provided by private competitive schools in the specific district's area, (2) extent of general support or lack of support for labor unions in the specific community in which the school district is housed, and (3) specific targeted proposal items (such as a "no-layoff" clause) suggested by national, state, or regional groups with which the specific local union is affiliated.

Finally, it should be stressed that not only is it important to collect data about contracts that currently exist in comparable school districts, it is imperative that you establish an information network to gather daily information about the at-the-table give-and-take agreements reached by other school districts who are negotiating master contractual agreements concurrently with those of your own local school district. Negotiations are comprised of a series of give-and-take agreements that are reached over time. Many of the items being negotiated move slowly, while others may move or change overnight. To be lacking updated information on what is taking place in other negotiation venues is to imitate the heavyweight boxer who attempts to win the championship with one hand tied behind his back.

THE DIFFERENCE BETWEEN HARD AND SOFT DATA

Although they differ in type, both hard and soft data can be very useful during negotiations. Either or both can be used to verify substance for the party's at-the-table use. Hard data is factual data, such as salary schedule patterns, pupil-teacher ratios, or percentage of budget expended for employee benefits. Soft data, on the other hand, is opinion-related or attitudinal in nature. Examples could include school climate data and employee or community opinions, or other opinion or attitudinal-related sources of information that could prove helpful in reinforcing the points a party wishes to impress upon the other party during negotiations.

THE IMPORTANCE OF CONDUCTING A TREND ANALYSIS

Another matter, that of conducting a trend analysis, should be emphasized. Trends such as citizen attitudes towards any of the following: tax increases, student test results, union/management contract provisions from comparable school districts, employee turnover, numbers of employee candidate applications, days of sick leave, and other like matters, will indicate what negotiation strategies and tactics to use to take advantage of the positives and eliminate the negatives in advance of negotiations.

USING TREND DATA TO IMPACT UPCOMING NEGOTIATIONS

Once trends are analyzed, it is crucial that articles are devised, positions are taken up, and strategies and tactics are organized to improve the probability of achieving successful results at-the-table. Whether it be the union's negotiating team or the management's negotiating team, advanced analyses of trends and advanced detailed planning must take place to enhance the possibility of successfully concluding a negotiated contract [42]. A party cannot plan too much; and if a party doesn't plan, it will probably be a big loser in the process of collective bargaining and the negotiation of a master contract.

SUMMARY

Determining the current state laws related to bargaining and the scope of possible negotiations is a critical first step in collecting background information. Mandated, prohibited, and permitted subjects were described in terms of collective bargaining. Key terms were identified— union shop, agency shop, closed shop, and meet and confer. These dictate the approach used in negotiations.

Prior to bargaining, data should be gathered regarding existing personnel policies and practices, existing policies and accompanying rules and regulations, and present and past income and expenditures. Past practice has important implications for future negotiations in the setting of precedent by management, which may later become an area of negotiation or grievance.

The history of grievance arbitration as a potential (types and numbers of grievances filed) trouble source in negotiations was discussed. Contract arbitration as a step in previous procedures must be considered in data gathering. The history of previously unresolved issues could reveal upcoming overtures in future negotiations.

Comparable school district contractual provisions provide basic data on such major categories as district income, tax effort, budgetary salary expenditure, benefits, enrollment, programs, co-curricular offerings, property valuation trends, current bonded indebtedness, actual salary arrays, and employee work day and work year.

All of this information, gathered collectively and cooperatively by the administration and negotiating team members, must be compiled and organized to provide base data for at-the-table considerations. Provisions must also be made for a continuous update of these data, during negotiations, via an information network.

EXERCISES

1. Investigate the applicable bargaining law in your state, and determine its requirements and specifications. Also, investigate the controlling state's administrative body (PERB or other) and its requirements and specifications.

2. Collect a sample of existing personnel policies and practices in the district, and project which policies might be challenged or renegotiated in upcoming negotiations.

3. List a minimum of ten (10) sources of hard data and ten (10) sources of soft data that you could utilize during negotiations.

4. Survey your district for any identifiable trends or random policy noncompliance occurrences in past practice.

5. Develop a brief history of grievance and arbitration in your district, and investigate any previous negotiation issues which were unresolved.

6. Using the list of comparable school district data categories, develop a master contract profile fact sheet for three neighboring districts.

REFERENCES

1. Eberts, R. W. and J. A. Stone. 1984. *Unions and Public Schools.* Lexington, MA: D. C. Heath and Company, p. 27.
2. Ross, V. J. and R. MacNaughton. 1982. "Memorize These Bargaining Rules Before You Tackle Negotiations," *American School Board Journal,* 169(3): 39.
3. Eberts, R. W, and J. A. Stone. 1984. *Unions and Public Schools,* p. 20.
4. Helsby, R. D., J. Tener, and J. Lefkowitz, eds. 1985. *The Evolving Process—Collective Negotiations in Public Employment.* Fort Washington, PA: Labor Relations Press, pp. xii–xxxi.

5. Ibid.

6. Helsby, R. D., J. Tener, and J. Lefkowitz, eds. 1985. *The Evolving Process,* p. 5.

7. Schwerdtfeger, R. D. 1986. "Labor Relations Thrive When You Control Collective Bargaining," *American School Board Journal,* 173(10): 41.

8. Keane, W. G. 1996. *Win Win or Else: Collective Bargaining in an Age of Public Discontent.* Thousand Oaks, CA: Corwin Press, Sage Publications, pp. 31, 33.

9. Seifert, R. 1990. "Prognosis for Local Bargaining in Health and Education," *Personnel Management,* 22 (June): 54–57.

10. Herman, J. J. and G. E. Megiveron. 1993. *Collective Bargaining in Education: Win/Win, Win/Lose, Lose/Lose.* Lancaster, PA: Technomic Publishing Co. Inc., pp. 65–75.

11. Janes, L. 1984. "Collective Bargaining," *NASSP Instructional Leadership Booklet.* Reston, VA: National Association of Secondary School Principals, pp. 22–23.

12. Schwerdtfeger, R. D. 1986. "Labor Relations Thrive," p. 40–42.

13. Ross, V. J. and R. MacNaughton. 1982. "Memorize These Bargaining Rules before You Tackle Negotiations," *American School Board Journal,* 169(3): 39–41.

14. Granof, M. 1973. *How to Cost Your Labor Contract.* Washington, D.C.: The Bureau of National Affairs, Inc., p. 32.

15. Streshly, W. A. and T. A. DeMitchell. 1994. *Teacher Unions and TQE,* Thousand Oaks, CA: Corwin Press, Sage Publications, pp. 31, 33.

16. Elkouri, F. and E. A. Elkouri. 1973. *How Arbitration Works.* 3rd ed. Washington, D.C.: Bureau of National Affairs, Inc., pp. 389–392.

17. Ibid.

18. Lavan, H. 1990. "Arbitration in the Public Sector: A Current Perspective," *Journal of Collective Negotiations,* 19(2): 154.

19. Fox, M. J., Jr. and D. Cooner. 1990. "Arbitration: Preparing for Success," *Journal of Collective Negotiations,* 19(4): 254.

20. Neal, R. G. 1988. "At Arbitration Hearings, Justice Favors the Well Prepared," *Executive Educator,* 10(11): 17–18.

21. Trotta, M. S. 1976. *Handling Grievances—A Guide for Management and Labor.* Washington, D.C.: The Bureau of National Affairs, Inc., p. 2.

22. Paterson, L. T. and R. T. Murphy. 1983. *The Public Administrator's Grievance Arbitration Handbook.* New York, NY: Longman, Inc., pp. 14–16.

23. Herman, J. J. 1991. "The Two Faces of Collective Bargaining," *School Business Affairs,* 57(2): 11.

24. Ibid.

25. Webster, W. G., Sr. 1985. *Effective Collective Bargaining in Public Education.* Ames, IA: Iowa State University Press, p. 83.

26. Webster, W. G., Sr. 1985. *Effective Collective Bargaining,* pp. 133–135.

27. Eberts, R. W, and J. A. Stone. 1984. *Unions and Public Schools,* pp. 32–34.

28. Ibid.

29. Bascia, N. 1994. *Unions in Teachers' Professional Lives: Social, Intellectual, and Practical Concerns,* New York: Teachers College Press, pp. 1–8.

30. Urban, W. J. 1985. "Merit Pay and Organized Teachers in the U.S.A.," In *Politics of Teacher Unionism: An International Perspective,* edited by M. Lawn. New York: Croom Helm, pp. 193–210.

31. Castetter, W. B. 1996. *The Human Resource Function in Educational Administration.* 6th ed. Englewood Cliffs, NJ: Merrill, pp. 581–582.

32. Webb, L., et al. 1987. *Personnel Administration in Education—New Issues and New Needs in Human Resource Management.* Columbus, OH: Merrill Publishing Company, pp. 170–171.

33. Webster, W. G., Sr. 1985. *Effective Collective Bargaining,* p. 119.

34. Webb, L., et al. 1987. *Personnel Administration,* pp. 195–196.

35. Huber, J. and J. Hennies. 1987. "Fix on These Five Guiding Lights and Emerge from the Bargaining Fog," *American School Board Journal,* 174(3): 31–32.

36. Webster, W. G., Sr. 1985. *Effective Collective Bargaining,* pp. 123–124.

37. Granof, M. 1973. *How to Cost Your Labor Contract,* pp. 83–95.

38. Ibid.

39. Herman, J. J. 1991. "The Two Faces," p. 11.

40. Bascia, N. 1994. *Unions in Teachers' Professional Lives,* pp. 1–8.

41. Urban, W. J. 1985. "Merit Pay and Organized Teachers," pp. 193–210.

42. Kaufman, R. and J. Herman. 1991. *Strategic Planning in Education,* Lancaster, PA: Technomic Publishing Co., Inc., pp. 21–29.

Choosing Your Team and Analyzing Their Team

CHAPTER 7 discusses the following: (1) Should there be a different view for team selection for win-win and win-lose approaches? (2) Why a negotiating team? (3) What should be the composition of the collective bargaining team? (4) What roles should each team member play? (5) What behavioral rules should govern the team members? (6) What types of pre-negotiations training should be provided for team members? (7) What categories of individuals or groups should be made available to support the negotiation team? (8) When should a team member be replaced? (9) What roles can or should be played by non–team members such as the superintendent, board members, lawyers, business official, staff, and line administrators? (10) What information should you acquire about the other party's team members, and how will this information be of benefit during the negotiations process? and (11) How would the team membership and your procedures differ if you were involved in win-win negotiations rather than adversarial negotiations? The chapter ends with a summary, exercises, and references.

SHOULD THERE BE A DIFFERENT VIEW OF TEAM SELECTION FOR WIN-WIN AND WIN-LOSE APPROACHES TO NEGOTIATIONS?

Before any other matter is decided by the union's or the management's negotiating team, a judgement has to be made as to whether the negotiating will be of a win-win or win-lose nature. This is a crucial threshold decision that must be made.

If it is determined by either or both parties that the negotiations will be adversarial (due to a lack of trust in the other party, or due to a previous history of adversarial negotiations), the team selected will include wording experts, financial experts, communication experts, observational experts, data gathering experts, and others, who, from time to time, will be judged beneficial to the negotiating team. On the other hand, if both parties predict that the negotiations will be one of cooperative and collaborative decision making, the team members will differ significantly from those selected as members of an adversarial team. The collaborative approach will stress the selection of team members who are friendly, knowledgeable, and cooperative, who will work in partnership with the other party's team members, who will make judgements based upon sound data, and who will arrive at a master contract that is fair and equitable to both parties. In other words, the end result will be a win-win arrived at by sincere, honest, intelligent, and cooperative members of both the negotiating teams. A contrast of this is shown in Figure 7.1

WHY A NEGOTIATION TEAM?

The law in many states is very clear as to the right of the employees in public school districts to bargain for wages, hours, and conditions of employment. When such a law is passed, a legal representative union is selected, and management is notified that there is a willingness to have a negotiated contract put into place. This necessitates the forming of a management team.

Like a sports team, the degree of success of a negotiating team will depend upon the skill, attitude, and degree of knowledge possessed by the team members. Also, like a sports team, a negotiation team will only be effective and efficient if the individual team members ably fulfill their individual roles, and the team, as a whole, becomes a positive and high achieving body. Therefore, selecting a team and determining how it will operate within the negotiating environment is a very important and crucial step in preparing to negotiate a master contractual agreement. The steps are numerous, but they should begin with the task of selecting the team members.

WHAT SHOULD BE THE COMPOSITION OF THE TEAM?

The composition of the negotiating team will depend somewhat on the type of union group with which the management team is to negotiate. For instance, the membership and role of a school district's management negotiation team may well differ when the team is dealing with a teachers' union (AFT or NEA) than when the negotiation team is dealing with the Teamsters, ASCME, AFL, UAW, or some other group representing food service employees, custodial or maintenance employees, transportation employees, or some other non-teacher group. The team members chosen would also have somewhat different characteristics and roles if the negotiations were to be conducted in a win-win rather than an adversarial union/management negotiation environment.

One of the more significant tasks the board of education, the superintendent, and the chief negotiator has is selecting the proper team for bargaining with teachers or other unions in the school district. It is a significant choice; the team members need to complement each other and enable the chief negotiator to do an efficient job. The chief negotiator can be effective using skills he/she already possesses, but to be efficient takes a strong support cadre of personnel as dedicated to improving the instructional program as they are to their positions in the district. To be on the team ought to rank as high as any other honor bestowed upon an administrator.

The number of members on the team will vary with the requirements of each set of negotiations. The general guide is to have as few members as possible to do the job well, and to include as many members as are required to do the job well. A good target number is six members. If you have too small a team, all the skills needed will probably not be covered; if the team is too large, communications and actions become overly complicated and burdensome.

Those individuals who are responsible for selecting the board of education's negotiation team should initially select the membership based upon general selection criteria that have been predetermined. The more important criteria should include:

- persons having a knowledge of the specific state laws that control the collective bargaining process in that state
- those who have a knowledge of the history of labor relations in the school district and a knowledge of the current labor/management relations
- persons who have a knowledge of the school board's policies
- persons who have an understanding of the income sources and the expenditure patterns of the school district's budget
- those who know and understand the reasons for the various curricular and co-curricular offerings of the school district
- persons who can control their emotions at the table; good poker players who do not give away their hand

- those who have a lot of patience, as this process often includes many long and tedious meetings.
- persons who care about the quality of the education offered students who know the degree of effort of the taxpaying public, and who honestly care about the welfare of the district's employees
- those who possess well-honed listening skills
- persons who can present proposals in a clear, complete, and convincing manner
- those individuals who will subordinate their personal interests to those of the negotiation team when a divergence of views comes about
- persons who are honest, considerate, and ethical

If the negotiation is to take place in a win-win environment, the criteria of being a collaborative decision maker should be added as a most important criteria. In win-win, where joint problem solving is the key, a collaborative attitude is a prerequisite [1,2].

Now that we have outlined general criteria to be used in the selection of negotiation team members, let's discuss the appropriate number of team members and the roles that those members should play. In addition, let's add a few comments on who should probably *not* serve on the negotiation team, and also add a few comments on the membership and roles of the members if there are negotiations taking place with multiple unions during the same time frame.

The size of the negotiation team depends on the specific character of the current negotiation, and can vary if the district is involved in multiple contractual negotiations. However, it is probably not wise to have more than six team members sitting at the negotiations table, although other representatives may briefly be brought to the table for a very specific sharing of knowledge. Alternates should also be appointed in case one of the regular team members is incapacitated or cannot make some of the meetings [3].

Significant purposes and tasks for team members could include the following:

(1) Read critically all proposals of the union
(2) Read critically all counters to the management proposals
(3) Study the members of the opposing team in order that she/he can be understood in confrontational settings
(4) Prepare proposals representing the sub-group being represented at the table

(5) Prepare suggested counters to the opposing team's proposals, with emphasis on the area being represented

(6) Do research on assigned topics for documentation to counters or proposals espoused by the CBA

(7) Record comments made by "their" opposing team member in discussions at the table

(8) Keep alternates well informed of the work being done in the bargaining process

(9) Suggest a caucus at a propitious time to share findings or observations that will assist the CBA [4]

WHAT ROLES SHOULD EACH TEAM MEMBER PLAY?

Each, perhaps all, team members must be a good and accurate observer of the process. The chief negotiator cannot watch all the other team members as they react to the discussion. It is good to assign each team member to observe a specific member of the union team. It is also wise to switch observed members so that there is no tipping of the hand of the administration as to the process the members are pursuing. In any event, the observation of the other team must be done and individual reports to the chief negotiator are important as she/he frames the counters with the team. Therefore, the observation of the opposite team, the ability to "read" the expressions and subtle nuances of the members' behavior (both verbal and nonverbal) is significant.

Each member ought to be in contact with the group of administrators they represent. They must be able to rapidly contact each member of the group—a list of home and work phone numbers should be obtained and available for polling purposes—especially as the process begins to be finalized and the intensive item bargaining begins. Each member ought to be able to speak for his/her group and speak with authority. Perhaps at each administrative council meeting some time could be set aside for this purpose.

In general, the team members and the roles they should cover are as follows:

(1) The *spokesperson* is the most important team member. This is especially true if the negotiations are of an adversarial nature and if there is to be a single spokesperson for the board of education's negotiation team. The role of this person is one of complete control over communication at the table. This person must possess the

ability to think on her/his feet, be able to manage conflict and disagreement within the team and between the union and management teams, possess leadership skills that will cause consensus among the team members, and share responsibility for the training and overall preparation for upcoming negotiations with the various team members [5,6].

(2) The *wordsmith* is another important member of the team. The wordsmith carefully prepares the wording of each proposal offered by the management's negotiation team, and is responsible for the detailed analysis of every word of every proposal brought to the table by the union's negotiation team. A simple example of the importance of words can be seen when one realizes that the common words *shall* and *will* are mandatory, while the words *could* or *should* are permissive.

(3) The *cost/benefit analyst* is crucial to the team because that individual carries the basic responsibility of determining the financial cost of every potential proposal being developed by management's negotiation team. This person will also be responsible for determining the financial cost of every at-the-table proposal being made by the union's negotiation team. She/he not only determines the immediate cost, but also projects the financial cost of each proposal into future years [7,8]. Finally, this person can work with the other management team members to decide whether or not the benefit received through agreement with the proposal exceeds the financial costs involved. A prime example could be the proposal by the union to lower the pupil-teacher ratio, based on the rationale that each teacher could be more effective by giving each student more individual attention. While it would be difficult to argue with the desirability of small classroom size, it could be extremely costly. In fact, if the average class size was twenty-five students and the proposal was to reduce it to twenty students, new teachers would have to be hired. In fact, this expenditure could well be more than that available to the district for all negotiation purposes [9].

(4) The *recorder* has the responsibility for accurately and comprehensively keeping a written record of every significant discussion or agreement point made at-the-table by the union, management, or both parties [10].

(5) The *observer* is responsible for observing the behavior of the other team's members. Many people telegraph their feelings by

verbal cues or by tone of voice. The observer may note that a head nodder is giving away the fact that she/he is agreeing with management's position, or that someone on the union's team may display a very emotional tone of voice when she/he is angry about a statement made or a position taken by management's team. These cues can be helpful to the management team's spokesperson, because they allow the spokesperson to discern unstated agreements or hidden agendas, or to disrupt the union's spokesperson by triggering anger from one of the union's team members [11].

(6) The *instruction expert* is the one who knows the what and why of the instructional programs being offered in the district, and can alert the management team to the impact, positive or negative, of any proposal that the team is considering bringing to the table as well as the impact on instructional programs of any proposal brought to the table by the union's team. Obviously, this expert position would be filled by different members of management if one were dealing with food services, transportation, secretarial and clerical personnel, aides, custodial and maintenance personnel, or any variety of union groups with whom management would negotiate [12].

In all probability, it is not wise to have the superintendent or a board member serve on the district's negotiation team. These are people to whom the team reports and from whom management's negotiation team will get its guidelines. In any case, if the negotiations are adversarial in nature, there is the potential liability of losing a good superintendent or a good board member through adverse pressure or through political manipulations [13]. It may or may not be wise to have an attorney serve as the team's spokesperson, depending on the expertise possessed by the full-time administrative staff and the personality of the attorney. In any case, even though it is generally not a good idea to have a board member or a superintendent of schools serve on the district's negotiation team, they should be placed on the team if they are the only ones who possess the necessary negotiation skills [14].

The team membership may vary when multiple negotiations with a variety of unions are taking place within the school district during the same time period. In this case, the board of education's negotiation teams should all have a skilled spokesperson, wordsmith, recorder, and observer, but the expert may vary with each team. In addition, the cost/benefit analyst may be used as an advisor to all the teams, rather than being seated as a member of just one.

Alternates can be good resource persons to whom the chief bargainer turns for non-emotional observation. By not being at the table, the alternates can offer a fresh perspective for the development of proposals or counters. Alternates can be placed in a group assigned the task of writing proposals and, therefore, they will be able to speak with little emotion tied to their comments.

FACTORS THAT IMPACT THE TIMING OF TEAM SELECTION

There are several and differing influences on the date of appointment of the management team.

(1) The purpose of the bargaining needs to be set first. If the contract is to be changed dramatically, the team needs to be in place for at least two months and meet at least eight to ten times before bargaining begins at the table.

(2) If the management team has to prepare proposals, they need to get organized and hold discussions based upon a survey of needs. If the team is only to develop counters to the union's proposals, it can be formed literally just before the first session.

(3) Frequently the two chief negotiators will meet to discuss the upcoming process and set a date to initiate joint at-the-table bargaining. If this is done, the tone will be set, and the magnitude and purpose established. In any event, the team ought to be appointed at least two weeks before the first session.

(4) Contracts often stipulate the date to begin bargaining a new contract. In this case, the judgement of the chief negotiator will prevail, realizing the full impact of the task ahead.

(5) Contracts often stipulate the narrowing down of the numbers of items each side can bargain. This is particularly true, in a larger sense, with annual single contracts. If the wording is correct in the current contract, the alterations necessitated to be "reopened" can be done during the year, so the need to get an early start is lessened.

(6) If the contract indicates that only reopeners, and not new proposals, will be entertained, the need for an early formulation of a team is less likely than at a later date. The number of reopeners will affect the need for early assignment.

WIN/LOSE	WIN/WIN
SPOKESPERSON	ALL MEMBERS SPEAK
WORDSMITH	COLLABORATIVE WORDING
COST/BENEFIT ANALYSIS	MUTUAL BUDGET AND COST ANALYSES
RECORDER	JOINT MINUTES
OBSERVER	NO OBSERVER
INSTRUCTIONAL EXPERT	ON CALL IF REQUIRED
FINANCIAL EXPERT	ON CALL IF REQUIRED
PERSONNEL EXPERT	ON CALL IF REQUIRED
ADVERSARIAL MINDSET	COLLABORATIVE MINDSET
SECRETIVE INFORMATION	MUTUAL INFORMATION COLLECTION
ONE WINNER	ALL WINNERS

FIGURE 7.1. A comparison of negotiating team selection characteristics for win-win and win-lose approaches.

(7) Boards annually provide for a meeting schedule. Once known, the superintendent usually has a list of essential items for each agenda as much as a year ahead of schedule. On one of these lists, the authorization for team selection should be placed.

(8) There will be other work being done by the administrative cadre. As this is usually calendarized, the chief negotiator may well want to wait until the total termination of this process before making any appointments in the areas upon which scrutiny is being focalized.

(9) Another factor may be the "age" or experience of the team members. Some districts appoint a totally new team every time so that all administrators get trained, on the job, to handle confrontation and collaboration in negotiations.

(10) The total effort involved in the amount of work to be done by the chief negotiator is highly significant. During the time the contract is in effect, the chief negotiator will be making marginal notes in the contract already bargained. Things that go well and things that require adjustment are noted throughout the year to prepare for the next round of negotiations. The chief negotiator will undoubtedly develop some new proposals based upon any application of

the grievance procedure. These proposals may be in the form of new statements to be added to an article in the contract or prepared as a counter to one which is already spelled out. Summarily, the chief negotiator ought to be ready to assume leadership when the bargaining is slated to start.

(11) Expectations of the superintendent and the board of education need to be considered in terms of when to appoint the team. If the superintendent and board desire large-scale changes in the contract, the chief negotiator needs to ensure success by having the team appointed early.

(12) Lastly, the chief negotiator may wish to appoint the "new" team as soon as the contract is ratified, which takes away some of the mystery and allows for constant contact as she/he develops new strategies, proposals, or counters. This may be particularly helpful to a group who has not served before. However, the team being appointed "too" early may have some concerns as they come under pressure from the union. There is no harm done in applying several different techniques to see which is best for the district. Be aware, however, that the union also changes leadership, and such change may well call for a different counterstrategy by the board and its team [15].

Now that we have discussed the composition of the collective bargaining team, the roles various team members should play, and the timing of appointing the team, let's turn to the topic of the behavioral rules that should govern the board of education's negotiation team—at the table and away from the table.

NEGOTIATION TEAM'S BEHAVIORAL RULES

The choice of rules by which any negotiation team operates depends on the directions given by the official body (board of education, in the case of management's negotiation team) the overall guidelines provided to the negotiation team, and to the specific style and role to be played by the negotiation team's chief negotiator and spokesperson [16]. There are three at-the-table rules, the choice of which will depend on the intensity of the negotiation's session, the degree of adversarial attitudes, and the experience level of the negotiation team's members. The three choices are (1) no one speaks at the table but the chief negotiator, (2) all persons are free to speak at any time, and (3) other members beside the chief negotiator can speak at-the-table, but only if they send the chief negotiator a note asking permission to make a certain comment. If the chief negotiator sees the comment as helping management's discussion, permission will be granted [17].

With reference to this communication, it is also helpful to consider the shape of the table for bargaining. The chief negotiator needs to be able to make eye contact with his/her team members at any and all times. A straight alignment of chairs will not facilitate this; with practice and judicious chair arrangement, the bargaining team should be able to operate comfortably when the sessions begin.

During caucuses within a negotiation session, each member is encouraged to give her/his full views and suggestions on all topics being considered. However, between negotiation sessions, only the board's chief negotiator and the union's chief negotiator should communicate. To allow otherwise is to add confusion and complication to an already complicated process.

The chief negotiator ought to encourage the team members to be as nonreactive to issues and items as they can be. The very idea that the nonverbal reading gives away some tone of the discussion is one which needs to be covered in depth. The other behavior which may be desirable is to have the team be prompt in attendance and supportive when issues develop.

If there is truly a win-win attitude during negotiations, all persons on both teams should be free to express opinions freely and completely. This open format will serve win-win negotiations well, as it encourages collaborative problem solving, with a goal of reaching a fair and equitable master contractual agreement [18,19].

With regard to the presence of visitors or observers, the authors have bargained both ways. The difficulty is that the union will maintain the same right to have observers in the room. Whereas one author feels that there is no room for observers in the process, the other feels that it is to the advantage of the bargainers to have a fresh viewpoint after an observation. Both authors, however, agree that for the initial or single contract bargaining, there is little or no room for observers. Observers do become less than disinterested in the process, and, like other situations in education, an observer in the room changes the chemistry between the chief negotiators and team members. This is particularly true when a visitor is credentialed (such as a superintendent or a board member), and when that person may be involved in a later process. The exposure via observation could affect their means of thinking about the entire contract later. Alternates could attend sessions, which might also affect their potential involvement.

Now that we have discussed the negotiation team's composition, team member roles, and behavioral rules, we must address the important matter of pre-negotiations training for negotiation team members [20].

PRE-NEGOTIATIONS TRAINING FOR TEAM MEMBERS

If there are negotiation team members who are new to the process, it is crucial that they be given pre-negotiations training. Also, if any significant amount of time has elapsed since the last contract negotiations, it is wise to review the negotiation procedure with experienced members of the team.

The types of training that prove most helpful for negotiation team members include (1) communications, (2) language analysis, (3) review of applicable laws, (4) review of the history of previous negotiations and the history of employee grievances, (5) methods of acquiring helpful comparative data from other school districts, (6) financial status and implications for negotiations, (7) at-the-table behavior, and (8) strategies and tactics to use at-the-table and outside the negotiation sessions. Let's briefly explore each of the training areas.

Communications training should include the skills of (1) active listening (listening for emotional tone, not just the spoken word), (2) nonverbal cueing (facial and other mannerisms which telegraph what the person is thinking), (3) paraphrasing (the repeating by the listener of what was said to make certain the meaning is clear), and (4) wait time (not immediately responding, but allowing time to think and react before commenting) [21].

Language analysis training is important, as all members of the negotiation team need to be very alert to the actual meaning and potential for multiple meanings of each word in every article proposed by their team or by the other team. Again, the use of the words "will" and "shall" (mandatory words) instead of "could" and "should" (permissive words) provides a dramatic example of the importance of training in this area [22].

Methods of acquiring comparative information is a training area that is important for negotiation team members. For the most part, unions—especially teacher unions—have access to a bank of comparative information on every school district in their region, their state, and the nation. It is incumbent upon management's negotiation team to acquire the detail of economic provisions and non–economic provisions of every master contract from comparative districts within their geographical area, or from those districts to whom they will have to be ultimately compared. Salary structures, fringe benefits, and contractual language are all important. Also, it behooves the management negotiation team to establish a network with those districts who will be involved in negotiations during the same time frame, in order to immediately discern the current status of negotiations on each important contractual area being proposed in those districts.

Financial status and its implications for negotiations is another key area of training. Each negotiation team member should fully understand the income and expenditure status of the budget, its historical allocations, and the amount of money available for all purposes—including negotiations [23].

At-the-table behavior training is crucial. If members of a team do not behave in accordance with the pre-decided standards, the at-the-table and away-from-the-table bargaining can become a comic disaster, with very serious consequences for employees, management, the school district, the community and, most importantly, the students [24].

Useful strategies and tactics to be employed during the negotiations should be discussed and clearly identified. Simulation training for the negotiation team members will assist them in perceiving how various strategies and tactics may or may not be effective during the upcoming negotiations [25]. It may be a good idea to have the previous year's management team come to the table and role play the opposition. Keep in mind that more caucuses will need to be called during the first actual sessions as the chief negotiator spots things that should be discussed and clarified while fresh in team members' minds [26].

As an additional consideration, different team choices may need to be made to meet the demands of win-win versus adversarial bargaining. If the situation is deemed to be a no-win situation for management, it is advisable to arrange for those who are not intimidated by conflict to be appointed to the team. There are frequently those in administrative positions who are not highly regarded by the union. They should not be included on the bargaining team if the atmosphere is adversarial.

Let's turn now to a discussion of the individuals and groups who should be made available to support management's negotiation team.

SUPPORT GROUPS AND INDIVIDUALS

Although the administrative negotiation team members will be the primary messengers, they may require support help from the board of education, the superintendent, the business manager, the director of instruction, the director of food services, the athletic director, the director of library and media service, and other specialized members of the administrative staff. They also require the advice of principals, assistant principals, and department heads [27]. The type of support required is of three varying categories. First, they require advice on what should be placed on the table to improve the ability to effectively operate the district ; second, they require advice on what should be taken out of the existing master contractual agreement, and third, they require advice on the potential impact on instruction and the management of the district related to any at-the-table proposal made by the union's negotiation team. All administrators need to be considered as significant support cadre members for the chief negotiator and team.

Now, let's turn to a discussion of situations that may justify removing a member of management's negotiation team from active participation in the negotiations process.

REMOVING A NEGOTIATION TEAM MEMBER

Removing a member from a negotiation team is a very serious decision, and is one that should not be taken lightly. Removal discredits that person as a viable and valuable member not only for the current negotiations, but also, in all probability, for consideration as a member of any future negotiation team. This extreme action should only be taken under the following circumstances:

- During long and stressful adversarial negotiations a member of the team becomes too physically or psychologically exhausted to continue. In such case, it is best for the individual and the team to remove the member [28].
- The team member has a serious personality conflict with a key member of the union's negotiation team, and that personality conflict is hindering progress towards reaching a ratified master contractual agreement.
- The team member telegraphs, by non-verbal behavior or voice tones, her/his attitude at-the-table, which becomes a detriment to the poker-like attitude that is required of the team.

- The team member becomes so emotional and/or aggressive that she/he cannot abide by the pre-determined behavioral rules established.

Let's next turn to the roles that can or should be played by non-team members such as (1) the superintendent of schools, (2) board of education members, (3) the school attorney, (4) the school district's business manager, and (5) other staff and line administrators.

ROLES PLAYED BY NON-TEAM MEMBERS

Significant controlling or helping roles can be played by the board of education, individual board members, and various non-team administrators during the process of negotiating a new master contractual agreement with an employee union. Some of the more important roles by management position follow.

The board of education as a whole, initially provides the overall guidelines that direct the strategic goals of the negotiating team [29]. These guidelines always include financial guidelines, but they sometimes include non-financial guidelines as well. In addition, the board of education must react to requests from their negotiation team to modify the original board of education's guidelines. Finally, the board will have to vote in an officially called board of education meeting to ratify the contract that has previously been ratified by the union.

If the district enters the impasse stages of mediation, fact finding, and arbitration, the board of education must again provide guidelines within which the negotiation team must operate [30]. Also, since these impasse procedures are many times strung out over a long time period, the board may have to modify its guideline instructions to fit the stage in which the impasse procedures are entered.

Individual board members may also have crucial roles to play [31]. During adversarial bargaining, the president of the board of education, or some other board member should be designated as the sole spokesperson for the board when communicating with the media or general public [32]. This person should also be apprised of the negotiation situation on a day-to-day basis, through the superintendent.

The superintendent should be available for consultation with the management team's chief negotiator at any time, and she/he should assist the chief negotiator in communications with the board of education members [33,34].

The school attorney should be available to the negotiation team to read over any language proposed by either negotiation team before the article is TA'd (tentatively agreed to) at-the-table. The attorney can determine if any of the language puts the district in a position of illegality [35].

The business manager, when sitting as a member of the negotiation team, is a most valuable support resource. The business manager can inform the negotiation team of the amount of money available to settle the contract negotiations, and she/he can price out the cost of all at-the-table proposals by both management and labor [36].

Other non-team administrators can provide valuable insights to the negotiation team regarding the potential impacts of any proposal made by either the management's team or the union's team on instruction and management in their particular area of specialty and work assignment [37].

Let's turn now to the topic of the information that should be collected about the union's team members.

COLLECTING INFORMATION ABOUT THE OTHER TEAM'S MEMBERS

Collecting information about the other team's members is important. It is also important to discover if the control person on the team, who may not necessarily be the local union's spokesperson, is a regional, state, or even a national official (in cases where it is pre-determined that the union has established the district as a target district—one in which the union wishes to set some precedent).

It is desirable to place members on the team who have not, prior to selection, been too vociferous about the intended outcome of the contract. The management team must also assign one of its members to observe the other team's members and "read" them throughout the negotiations, by noting any changes of expression or displays of sympathy or opposition to any cause or issue presented by either team.

It is important to discover if the team is primarily comprised of employees with long years of service to the district, or if it is composed of younger employees. In the case of the teacher's union, it is important to discover if most of the team members are coaches, music teachers, guidance counselors, or some other identifiable potential control group. It is also important to discover the specific interests and personalities of the union's team members. Finally, it is important to discover whether or not certain members have previously filed grievances against the district, and it is equally important to discover the specific types and number of grievances involved [38].

All of this information will assist management's negotiation team to deal more effectively with the individuals on the union's team. Management's team will have a good idea about the specific job categories represented at the table, and they will know about the personalities and interests of the union's team members [39].

Let's end this discussion by stating the difference in the procedures utilized if management were to deal with a union who has bought into a total win-win approach to contractual bargaining.

WIN-WIN PROCEDURES

Much of what has been previously said can be modified if management's negotiating team knows that the union's negotiating team will pursue the current negotiations from a total win-win collaborative approach. In this case, the primary characteristic to be possessed by management's team members is an attitude of cooperation and collaboration in mutual problem solving. Also, all team members will be free to speak to any topic being discussed at any time.

In addition, much of the data gathering about comparable districts' contractual provisions can be a shared task, as well as the pricing out of each contractual article [40,41]. The district's budget should be an open book, and both parties should agree to the total dollars available to settle the contract being negotiated [42].

It is also feasible that the negotiation teams will agree to break into subcommittees comprised of membership from both teams. These subcommittees will have the task of arriving at the wording of specific articles and the study of the article's impact [43]. Once these tasks are performed, the subcommittee will bring the proposed article back to the total group for at-the-table TA (tentative agreement) and for sign-off by both teams.

Since a great deal of information relating to negotiation teams has been covered, let's turn to a summary of what has previously been covered.

SUMMARY

The composition of the bargaining team, as one possessing skills, attitude, and degree of knowledge, strongly affects the success of negotiations. Choices of team membership are affected by the positive or adversarial nature of the negotiations. Team members should be versed in the law and procedures of bargaining, as well as possess a collaborative, patient, and calm attitude. Effective interpersonal interaction skills are critical. The optimum size of the team is impacted by the need to cover such team roles as spokesperson, wordsmith, cost/benefit analyst, recorder, observer, and instructional expert. The experience demands a skilled chief negotiator backed up with a viable, symbiotic, supportive cadre of team members.

Behavioral rules must be established within the team, with the focus and control resting on the chief negotiator. A range of at-the-table intercommunication is possible, with caucus interchange being much more open. If a win-win attitude prevails, an open format of interaction should be adopted.

Pre-negotiation training is desirable if there has been a gap in team experience or if neophyte members are assigned to the team. The types of training described as most helpful were communications, language analysis, methods of acquiring comparative information (through research and investigation of comparative districts), financial status and implications, at-the-table behavior, and strategies and tactics. The types of responsibilities—significant purposes and tasks (such as the compiling of background information)—appropriate for team members was discussed.

The roles team members play, in addition to the specifically assigned ones such as cost/benefit analyst, require an assigned observational match with a union team member, and the necessity to stay linked with the team and administration for the constant channeling of communication. Consideration should be given to the need for total membership discretion on discussion issues while negotiations are underway, and on the pros and cons regarding observer presence during sessions.

The time frame for team formation was considered in light of a number of factors, including the breadth of desired contractual change, in-place contract requirements, board and administrator calendar and workload demands, and the experience needs of team members. Ample lead time for preparation is important.

Support groups were described as "deep" background resources for the negotiation team, supplying the supportive and specific factual information related to contractual items under consideration. The impact of financial, temporal, and personnel resource on potential agreements must be assessed by these content-area experts. The role of such credentialed but nonparticipating individuals as board members, superintendents, and school attorney was outlined. Removing a team member was also discussed.

The chapter concluded with a rationale for the collection of information about the other team's members. The professional profile of the teaching professionals on the union's team and information about their interests and previous personnel interactions is valuable information. A perspective about the data gathering procedure and coalition subcommittee formation during win-win negotiations was presented.

EXERCISES

1. Select an imaginary bargaining team and justify your choices by discussing the strengths needed and how these members can complement the entire team.

2. Name a chief negotiator and respond to the criticism of other administrators as to why this person should be selected.

3. Hold a mini bargaining session, with roles carefully defined, and see if an audience can identify particular roles.

4. Conduct a mock caucus, following a mini bargaining session, to involve team members in the debriefing process.

5. Design a pre-negotiations training session for new team members, focusing on one of the types of training described in the chapter.

6. Determine whether adversarial or win-win bargaining (or meet-and-confer sessions) has been the norm in your district, and select two imaginary teams to deal with both situations.

7. Develop some articles to propose at-the-table. Do this as if you represented management, and also as if you represented the union.

REFERENCES

1. Coleman, C. J. 1990. *Managing Labor Relations in the Public Sector.* San Francisco, CA: Jossey-Bass Publishers, pp. 124–125.

2. Keane, W. G. 1996. *Win Win or Else: Collective Bargaining in an Age of Public Discontent.* Thousand Oaks, CA: Corwin Press, Sage Publications, pp. 13–22.

3. Webster, W. G., Sr. 1985. *Effective Collective Bargaining in Public Education.* Ames, IA: Iowa State University Press, p. 144.

4. Webster, W. G., Sr. 1985. *Effective Collective Bargaining,* pp. 139–140.

5. Neal, R. 1980. *Bargaining Tactics—A Reference Manual for Public Sector Labor Negotiations.* Richard G. Neal Associates, p. 28.

6. Streshly, W. A. and T. A. DeMitchell. 1994. *Teacher Unions and TQE,* Thousand Oaks, CA: Corwin Press, Sage Publications, pp. 86–89.

7. Neal, R. 1980. Bargaining Tactics, pp. 26–27.

8. Castetter, W. B. 1996. *The Human Resource Function in Educational Administration.* 6th ed. Englewood Cliffs, NJ: Merrill, pp. 570–571.

9. Granof, M. 1973. *How to Cost Your Labor Contract.* Washington, D.C.: The Bureau of National Affairs, Inc., pp. 20–22.

10. Herman, J. J. 1991. "The Two Faces of Collective Bargaining," *School Business Affairs,* 57(2): 10–13.

11. Herman, J. J. 1991. "The Two Faces," pp. 10–13.

12. Tait, R. C. 1995. "Contract Negotiations Without Ill Will," *School Administrator,* 52(9): 30–31.

13. Neal, R. 1980. Bargaining Tactics, p. 34.

14. Webster, W. G., Sr. 1985. *Effective Collective Bargaining,* pp. 24–26.

15. Cloyd, S. 1990. "Involving School Board Members in Negotiations," *School Business Affairs.* 56(12): 24–27.

16. Schwerdtfeger, R. D. 1986. "Labor Relations Thrive When You Control Collective Bargaining," *American School Board Journal.* 173(10): 41–42.

17. Coleman, C. J. 1990. *Managing Labor Relations,* pp. 125–126.

18. Helsby, R. D., J. Tener, and J. Lefkowitz, eds. 1985. *The Evolving Process—Collective Negotiations in Public Employment.* Fort Washington, PA: Labor Relations Press, pp. 220–222.

19. Heisel, W. D. 1973. *New Questions and Answers on Public Employee Negotiation.* Washington, D.C.: International Personnel Management Association, p. 72.

20. Namit, C. 1986. "The Union Has a Communications Strategy—And Your Board Should, Too," *American School Board Journal.* 173(10): 30–31.

21. Herman, J. J. 1991. "The Two Faces," pp. 10–13.

22. Herman, J. J. and G. E. Megiveron. 1993. *Collective Bargaining in Education: Win/Win, Win/Lose, Lose/Lose.* Lancaster, PA: Technomic Publishing Co. Inc., pp. 45–61.

23. Huber, J. and J. Hennies. 1987. "Fix on These Five Guiding Lights and Emerge from the Bargaining Fog," *American School Board Journal.* 174(3): 31.

24. Coleman, C. J. 1990. *Managing Labor Relations,* pp. 127–128.

25. Ibid.

26. Ibid.

27. Neal, R. 1980. *Bargaining Tactics,* p. 20.

28. Namit, C. 1986. "The Union," pp. 30–31.

29. Ibid.

30. Granof, M. 1973. "How to Cost," pp. 20–22.

31. Herman, J. J. 1991. "The Two Faces," pp. 10–13.

32. Schwerdtfeger, R. D. 1986. "Labor Relations Thrive," p. 41.

33. Cloyd, S. 1990. "Involving School Board Members," pp. 24–25.

34. Kennedy, J. D. 1984. "When Collective Bargaining First Came to Education: A Superintendent's Viewpoint," *Government Union Review,* 5(1): 26.

35. Herman, J. J. 1991. "The Two Faces," p. 11.

36. Schwerdtfeger, R. D. 1986. "Labor Relations Thrive," p. 41.

37. Ibid.

38. Webster, W. G., Sr. 1985. *Effective Collective Bargaining,* pp. 55–56.

39. Ibid.

40. Neal, R. 1980. *Bargaining Tactics,* pp. 182–183.

41. Attea, W. J. 1993. "From Conventional to Strategic Bargaining: One Superintendent's Experience," *School Administrator,* 50(10): 16–19.

42. Keane, W. G. 1996. *Win Win or Else,* pp. 13–22.

43. Plauny, L. 1992. "Compared to What? Developing a Teacher Compensation Comparison Standard," *School Business Affairs,* 58(8): 16–20.

Preparing to Go
to the Bargaining Table

CHAPTER 8 discusses the following topics, framed around a different view for win-win and win-lose approaches. It includes information on determining how the recognition clause should read, how to draft your proposals and counterproposals, and how to determine your fall-back positions and your last best offer. The preparation of quid pro quos, how to anticipate the other team's proposals, and the reaction their team may have to your proposals are discussed. The study of existing and prior agreements for directional thrusts, determining what you wish to keep and what you wish to change or eliminate, and holding firm on management's rights are covered. Also included are how to establish your pre-negotiation tone with employees and community members, how to determine throw away issues, and how to determine the absolutes or strike issues. Information is provided on getting your parameters from the board of education, how to develop bargaining structures, how to prepare your bargaining notebook, bargaining strategy, and tactics, and how to prepare differently for win-win negotiations than for adversarial ones. These topics refer to both preparing for the initial bargaining session and for all subsequent negotiating sessions throughout the sometimes lengthy and tedious process of arriving at a ratified master contractual agreement between union and management. The chapter ends with a summary, exercises, and references.

TAKING A DIFFERENT VIEW OF WIN-WIN AND WIN-LOSE APPROACHES TO PREPARATION

A totally different approach to preparation for upcoming negotiations takes place when the parties to negotiations take a win-win view of the process rather than a win-lose, adversarial one. In the adversarial, win-lose approach, preparation is secretive; each party collects data, rationale, and argumentation to win their viewpoint in opposition to any viewpoint held by the other party to the negotiations that may be contrary to that held by itself. Data collection may well include information about the contract articles successfully included, and whether or not they fit the school district in which both parties live. These articles, then, become the asking, negotiating, and pressuring points for the dual purpose of frustrating the opposition's team and obtaining as much as possible within each contract negotiated. In addition, each party will plan strategies, such as newspaper releases, accusing the other party's negotiating team of, for example, bad faith bargaining, unfair labor practices, not caring about the students, or other even more derogatory claims [1].

The other, and much more preferred, win-win approach will see both parties to the negotiation sitting down and determining what data are needed to allow a civilized and analytical look at solving any existing contractual problems or satisfying any of the differing needs or interests of either or both parties. This data collection, data analysis, problem sharing, and consideration of interests will take place in an environment that leads to cooperative and collaborative actions by both parties. It will not be unusual to have joint subgroups of members from both the union's and management's teams structured to (1) gather and analyze data that both parties have agreed needs to be collected and investigated, (2) resolve the differing interests of both parties, and (3) resolve the problems that are faced by both parties [2].

The results of this win-win approach are evident: (1) all members of both parties display a trusting, caring, and respectful attitude to members of each other's negotiating team, (2) negativism and dirty tricks are totally absent, (3) students and community are spared the negativism that exists when adversarial bargaining is the choice of the parties to the negotiations, (4) a fair and equitable master contract is consummated, (5) both parties give credit to all members, and (6) a climate has been created that bodes well for the union/management relations in the extended future.

Although it is not directly related to preparation for at-the-table sessions, the determination of the wording of the clause that recognizes the union as the formal representative of the employees is an important initial document, and is most important when written into the initial contract. Let's begin this chapter by addressing this prerequisite topic.

DETERMINING HOW THE RECOGNITION CLAUSE SHOULD READ

Initial recognition of a specific union as the sole representative of an employee group for collective bargaining purposes usually takes place (in those states which possess collective bargaining statutes) under one of two methods. In the first method, the board of education, with the understanding that most, if not all, of the members of the employee group would prefer or vote for a specific union to represent them, may grant exclusive recognition to that union. The second method is one wherein the PERB (Public Employment Relations Board) or whatever body is established to implement the state's collective bargaining law, conducts an election upon petition by a group of employees or the employer [3]. Usually, if more than fifty percent of the employees who vote do so for a specific union, that specific union serves as the official representative of that group for all matters related to the negotiations and operational procedures involving the master contract between the union and management. The only way to change the specific union which represents the employees is to have a decertification election [4].

In districts that have employees who are members of various unions, it is very important that the recognition clause is crystal clear. If it is ambiguous, many difficulties and much confusion could arise.

A typical recognition clause would read as follows:

In accordance with the provisions of the 1991 Public Employees' Fair Employment Act of the State of _____, the Board of Education of _____ School District recognizes the _____ union, affiliated with the regional, state and national _____ as the exclusive representative for all professionally certified personnel, exclusive of those in management positions, for the purposes of collective bargaining as outlined in the Public Employees Fair Employment Act of 1991.

The wording of this clause clearly recognizes a single specified union to be the sole representative of all professionally certified personnel for the purposes outlined in that state's collective bargaining law [5]. By this language, the union is restricted to representing the certified employees to the provisions of the Act of 1991, and the union has no authority to operate outside of the provisions of the Act of 1991.

In addition, the language clearly excludes the union from representing management personnel who also possess professional certification [6]. Obviously, this language also prohibits the union from representing management employees who may not be required to possess certification. It is very important to exclude management personnel from inclusion with other employee groups whom they may manage.

Next let's turn to establishing your pre-negotiation tone with the employees within the specific union and with the community at large. Obviously, the long-term tone between union and management, as perceived by the employees who are members of the union, and by the community at large, will depend on the long-term, day-to-day union/management relationship. If the relationship is adversarial, a lack of trust will exist between union and management, and the community will probably think that their children suffer as a result. On the other hand, if harmonious day-to-day relations exist between union and management, the members of both groups will possess a high level of trust in the members of the other party, and the community will probably feel that, at the very least, the children are not subject to the after-effects of poor morale and lack of cooperation among those hired to teach and manage their schools [7,8].

The time just prior to entering into a specific contractual negotiations process is the optimal time to attempt to establish a tone that will carry on throughout the contract negotiations process [9]. Below is an example of a correspondence read by the board of education president and adopted by the board of education at a formal board meeting. Following this meeting, the correspondence was distributed to all teachers, to the teacher union officials, and to the media.

This attempt to establish a tone for negotiations was a method used by one of the school districts where the author served as superintendent of schools. It clearly specifies the intent of the board of education in a school district that traditionally had poor labor/management relations.

Board of Education Approach to Teacher Contract Negotiations

Theme of Cooperation

It is the desire of the Board of Education to approach teacher contract negotiation in a spirit of cooperation. We believe that our goals for improving the instructional programs in _____(name of school district) are shared by most teachers. The only way to attain the improvements we desire is to work cooperatively at a professional level.

Our Challenge

There are many myths about what is good for education, and there are constraints which can impede learning. It is clear, however, that all of us in education must unite in common pursuit to overcome the obstacles to successful teaching and learning. This is our challenge.

Some of the undeniable elements of a strong educational system are:

1. effective staff development and training,
2. well-defined objectives for every course of instruction,
3. a system for evaluating the extent to which instructional programs meet their objectives,
4. cooperative learning environment,
5. professional employees who assume assignments where they can be of the greatest help to students,
6. students engaged in instructional tasks a high percentage of their time,
7. students challenged consistent with their abilities, and
8. flexibility of goals and practices to accommodate change and student differences.

We need to work together to build these elements into the _____ (name of school district) education system.

Working Principles

The board of education believes in the following working principles and will approach teacher contract negotiations with these as a guidance:

1. Teachers deserve fair pay and a professional working climate.
2. Teachers' assignments and student loads should be reasonable.
3. Teachers' assignments should be made to best use their strengths.
4. The district should provide and teachers should partake of development and training programs to strengthen and develop teaching skills.
5. Student learning should be measured and monitored as a means for improvement.
6. Teachers should be involved in the evaluation of instructional programs and school climate.
7. Use of technology should be employed to increase the effectiveness of learning and teaching time.
8. The ratio of benefit to cost of what we do should be maximized.

Once the pre-negotiation tone has been established, a collective bargaining notebook should be prepared. This notebook should contain any documents and information that will be helpful as one prepares to enter the formal negotiating sessions.

PREPARING THE BARGAINING NOTEBOOK

The bargaining notebook is a very important reference document that will serve the negotiating team well throughout the entire negotiations process. It should consolidate all of the information that the local bargaining team feels it will require as reference information during the process of negotiations [10]. The major items to be included in all notebooks are:

- a copy of the state's collective bargaining law, and a copy of the collective bargaining implementation rules and regulations promulgated by the state's PERB or the body that has been created by the state to manage the state's collective bargaining law
- copies of the current master contract agreement between the union and the school district, and copies of prior master contract agreements between the union and the school district
- copies of the board of education's policies, and copies of the rules and regulations promulgated to implement those policies
- copies of all grievances and grievance arbitration rulings for the past five years, and copies of any grievances that are currently pending or that are in the process of grievance arbitration
- copies of the minutes from prior negotiations, and copies of correspondence between the union and the management negotiation team or the board of education related to the current upcoming negotiations [11]
- copies of the adopted budgets for the past five years detailing income, sources of income, expenditures, and categories of expenditures, including a projection of income and expenditures for the next three years
- copies of financial audits over the past five years, which, when compared to the adopted budgets, will indicate any discrepancies, and the degree of these discrepancies, between the adopted budget, the actual income received, and the actual expenditures made
- information about the union's team members that could prove helpful, the key persons being the union's negotiating team spokesperson and any state or national union representatives who may be part of the team, or who may be influential in terms of the union team's strategies, tactics, or the signing-off of contractual articles [12]
- a listing of the current salary schedule and number of employees on each vertical (years of service) step or horizontal (degree level for teachers) step of that schedule, which will provide cost information on built-in costs of automatic step schedule changes
- data collected on the historic increases in salary and fringes provided by the district, which should be compared with the consumer price index for the geographic region's trends over the

same time frame and which should also be compared to a rational index of the taxpaying public's ability to pay versus its historical effort made to financially support the school district: Such information might well be obtained from a database or management information system [13]

- historical data on any prior mediation, fact-finding or contract arbitrations that have taken place; and the results of such impasse sessions or rulings [14]
- a listing of each fringe benefit and the cost to the district of each of these fringe benefits: It is also important to find out from the suppliers or estimate the anticipated cost increase associated with large outlay benefits like health insurance coverages. In this area it is also important to break down the information, where appropriate, into cost data for the individual employee, the individual employee and the spouse, and/or for the individual employee and family [15]. A simple scheme will serve this purpose well, as this outline of a comparative table demonstrates:

Benefit Title	Coverage	Current Cost	Estimated Future $

As the negotiations proceed, the following will be added to the notebook:

- guidelines given management's negotiating team by the board of education
- analysis of the current master contractual agreement, of management's operational problems, and of management's desired changes to the existing contract, which is usually done by having all of the school district's administrators, in a series of meetings, review the existing master contract and offer suggestions for changes that are in the interest of the district's ability to manage well the day-to-day instructional and support programs [16]
- minutes of every negotiation session and any pertinent correspondence between the union and management, or the board of education
- a copy of all proposals and counterproposals offered by either party to the negotiations: Each item passed across the table, from both the union and management, needs to be dated, timed, and recorded for later impasse reference
- an analysis of the master contractual agreements of all comparable school districts, and an update on the status of the specifics of negotiations in those comparable districts undergoing negotiations

during the same time frame: It is helpful to record changes proposed or heard from other districts on a separate entry page; each article can be "logged" as to the impact the negotiations might have on each item
- information about any directions or suggestions provided by the regional unit, the state's unit, or the national unit with which the local union is aligned
- other information, as determined by the local management's negotiation team, which should be collected and which will prove useful during the process of negotiating a new or renewed master contractual agreement with the union [17,18]

Once the notebook is prepared, it should be used when meeting with the board of education to obtain those guidelines governing the parameters of the upcoming negotiations as far as the management's negotiating team is concerned. Once these guidelines are issued, they cannot be exceeded by management's negotiating team unless they go back to the board of education and officially receive approval to modify or exceed the original guidelines.

OBTAINING THE BOARD OF EDUCATION'S NEGOTIATION GUIDELINES

If the board of education and the management team anticipate a serious, adversarial negotiating environment, it is wise for the board to provide guidelines for the *last best offer* of the board under the most adverse circumstances [19]. This worst-case scenario would then give management's negotiating team the greatest amount of flexibility at-the-table. On the other hand, the board of education, having provided guidelines for its last best offer, can then direct management's negotiating team to attempt to get a master contract settlement on more reasonable terms.

Obtaining worst-case scenario guidelines accomplishes three major purposes. First, it provides management's negotiating team the greatest flexibility in its day-to-day negotiations with the union's negotiating team. Second, it eliminates a lot of unnecessary and very complex tripartite bargaining between and among the members of management's negotiating team, between management's negotiating team and the union's negotiating team, and between management's negotiating team and the board of education. Third, it avoids the suffering and untold long-term damage done by a serious employees' strike when the board of education eventually exceeds the guidelines which were given to its management negotiating team [20]. Why punish the employees, the students, and the community, if the board of education will eventually change its mind under pressure from the local union, union members, and officials from the regional, state, and national levels?

Once the board of education guidelines are provided, the administrators of the district have analyzed the current master contractual agreement and provided management's negotiating team with their suggestions, and the bargaining notebook has been prepared, management's negotiating team can study the existing and prior agreements for directional thrust and prepare the desired structures, strategies, and tactics to be utilized in the upcoming negotiations with the union [21,22].

DECIDING ON STRUCTURES, STRATEGIES, AND TACTICS

The structural decisions that should be decided prior to entering the actual contract negotiations include decisions such as (1) Should the team have subcommittee structures [23]? (2) Should the team allow for side bar (away from the table) discussions [24]? or (3) Should the team have a larger referent group to which they will report progress and receive suggestions [25]? These decisions can be modified while negotiations progress, but it is wiser to have these structural decisions made prior to sitting down at the table. Obviously, these decisions may become even more important if negotiations enter the impasse stages of mediation, fact finding, and/or contract arbitration.

Strategies are the *whats* and tactics are the *hows*. Strategies deal with broad directional statements, such as, "We can give no more than five percent new money for employee salaries and fringes; and this new money will be on the base of the current expenditures for these purposes." Obviously, if there are increases in fringe costs from some of the suppliers of benefits, there will be less than the five percent of new money available for improvement in employee salaries or fringe benefits structures. On the other hand, there may be a desire to protect or increase control of non-economic areas, such as the power of administrators to make employee assignments from contractual obligation or union interference [26].

The strategies must be broken down into specific measurable objectives in order to be of maximum benefit [27]. Once the specific objectives for each strategic goal have been identified, management's negotiating team can develop specific action programs or tactics to attempt to accomplish the specific objectives and the strategies established. Having well-timed, preconceived, at-the-table concessions is an example of a tactic [28]. It is crucial to realize, however, that bargaining strategies, objectives, and tactics are interdependent. Strategies may guide the bargaining team to the development of specific negotiation objectives, and tactics, if successfully employed, should lead to the attainment of strategic outcomes or results.

Some likely bargaining objectives may well include those related to money and those related to decision-making authority [29]. In either case, the objectives must be clearly stated and measurable in order to determine, at some future date, whether or not the specific objective(s) or result(s) desired have been attained. In addition, it is wise to allow flexibility in the objectives to be achieved, or the negotiation's give-and-take will become too rigid [30].

It is wise to state the objectives in three priority categories such as (1) maximum achievement, (2) realistic achievement, and (3) minimum achievement [31]. The simple example of increased salary provisions from both a union's and a management's point of view could well appear as stated below:

ITEM: EMPLOYEES' SALARY INCREASES

	Minimum	Realistic	Maximum
Union	4%	5%	8%
Management	2%	4%	5%

In this example, one can see that the possibility of a settlement exists at somewhere between 4% and 5%. If the negotiation was held in a win-win environment, this structure would not be necessary, as both parties would share information as to what new money was available [32], and would go about the resolution of the final dollar amount by collaborative problem solving.

Some tactics which will be faced or utilized during master contract negotiations may very well include the following:

• asking for the moon: This tactic is based on the assumption that starting big, even though the initial request or offer may be unreasonable even to the party which proposes it, will serve well when compromises have to be reached in the future [33].

- use of public sentiment: This tactic is utilized in the hope of getting the general populace to agree with the party's positions; and with the hope that the general population will put pressure on the other party to give into, or at least come closer to, the position presented [34].
- planning for impasse: This tactic assumes that third parties (mediators, fact-finders, and/or contract arbitrators) will provide a settlement closer to the demands of the union than that which could be achieved by dealing directly at-the-table with management's negotiation team [35].
- use of media releases and letters to the editor: Newspaper and television coverage of a party's biased report of the status of negotiations can become an effective tactic to arouse the public in support of the union's or management's position. Also, letters by friends of the union or the board of education, although obviously not identified as such, can get the message out. These tactics are frequently used during impasses [36].
- hot issues, which are sometimes headlined and dramatized to provide a biased perception that all issues are of this nature [37].
- promoting popular, high-cost items as non-cost items that are good for students: Such items as reducing class size or pupil-teacher ratios comes under this tactical category.
- reducing the other parties' expectations: To accomplish this tactic, the negotiating team has to provide a strong rationale coupled with convincing data to move the other negotiating team away from its original demand(s) [38].
- items for the future: Since most collective bargaining arrangements are like a good marriage—they go on forever—a useful tactic is to introduce new desired items into current negotiations, though not expecting to achieve those demands. This, however, does establish a future agenda which can be pushed during subsequent contractual negotiations of replacement master contractual agreements between union and management [39,40].
- presenting proposals equivalent to the best conditions present in master contract agreements of other school districts: This is a tactic frequently used by unions, especially as the first at-the-table proposal [41].
- other tactics as devised by either party to the current negotiations.

Now that we have emphasized the importance of strategies, objectives, and tactics, let's turn to the topic of proposals and counterproposals.

PREPARING PROPOSALS AND COUNTERPROPOSALS

There are two rules to follow when preparing proposals and counter-proposals. First, any and all proposals should be accompanied by a comprehensive and logical rationale, and second, each and every proposal should be supported by comprehensive and convincing data.

It is very wise to prepare alternatives (fall-back proposals), for each of your original at-the-table proposals; this advance preparation will permit you to respond in a reasoned manner without being under the sometimes intense pressure that accompanies the actual negotiation sessions [42]. These alternative proposals may or may not always be used, but it is wise to have them available before starting the initial negotiations, and they are best developed inbetween sequential at-the-table negotiation sessions [43].

The actual proposals prepared will be determined by management's negotiating team, from information collected previously, including the board of education's guidelines, the administrative staff's analysis and suggestions, and the materials in the bargaining notebook [44,45].

Management's negotiating team's proposals should include all the following considerations:

- Propose those items you wish to retain, and those items you wish to eliminate from the current master contract agreement [46].
- Propose strengthening the management's rights clause in the current master contract agreement.
- Make at-the-table proposals that will strengthen management's and the board of education's decision-making prerogatives in important instructional and management areas.
- Determine your fall-back positions in advance of the initial negotiating session, and make any required modifications inbetween at-the-table negotiating sessions.
- Anticipate the union's proposals and the potential reactions that the union's negotiating team may have to your proposals. Playing the "what if" game can be very valuable when the management team must react quickly under pressure [47].
- Prepare quid pro quo proposals. This basically has the negotiating team analyzing what they can obtain of equal or greater value than what they would give as a compromise to the other team. This analysis should take place between each and every at-the-table negotiating session.

- Prepare throw-away proposals. These are proposals which are seriously presented, but which are not considered absolutely necessary to secure before reaching a contractual settlement. These proposals will assist in the give-and-take that accompanies every negotiations.
- Determine absolutes and potential strike items. These should be determined by the board of education, with the guidance of management's negotiating team. They might deal with such items as the right of administrators to evaluate the degree of employee performance, the right of management to make employee assignments, or the amount of new dollars that will ultimately be allocated to settle the contract with the employees' union.
- On the other hand, the union will probably have its own list of absolutes or strike items. These may include such matters as improving the salary schedule to keep up with comparable districts, an agreement to receive a certain degree of pay for extra duties performed, or the specific conditions under which an employee can be transferred by management [48–50].

Keeping in mind all the details previously discussed, let's turn to the differences that would exist if management's and union's negotiating teams were preparing for win-win rather than adversarial, negotiations.

PREPARING FOR WIN-WIN NEGOTIATIONS

Probably the first major difference would be that both parties would agree to cooperate in the collection and analysis of the data required to intelligently approach the negotiations of a new master contract agreement [51]. What has previously been called the *bargaining notebook* would now become a *joint databased notebook.*

The second major difference would become one of deciding upon strategies, objectives, and tactics. In the case of win-win negotiations, the strategy would be one of collaborative decision making; the objectives would become specific measurable desired results agreed to by both the union's and management's negotiating team members. The tactics used could be joint media releases, joint progress updates, and subcommittee study committees comprised of membership from both union and management [52].

The final major difference would become one of an atmosphere in which every individual from union or management would speak freely, make recommendations, and advise the total unit of both union members and management personnel. In actuality, the labels of union and management would disappear in favor of one problem-solving team of professionals.

SUMMARY

In preparing to go to the bargaining table, consideration must be given to the specific content of the union recognition clause in order to determine the level of exclusive representation, recognition of multiple unions, and the type of certification election required. A distinction was made regarding the representation of certified management personnel.

The long-term relationship between union and management affects the pre-negotiations tone, and efforts should be directed to establish a positive tone. An example of such effort was provided.

The development of a notebook containing documents and information was described as a key strategy. This book will serve as a reference throughout the negotiations process. Major items to include are the state collective bargaining law and other pertinent regulations, the current master contract agreement, board policies, historical grievance mediation and arbitration rulings, prior years' minutes, prior adopted budgets and financial audits, profiles of the union's team members, and current and historical salary/benefits schedule information. The notebook is augmented during the process with board guidelines, analysis of desired changes and proposals/counterproposals, current minutes, and comparable district information. Additionally, the board should provide the negotiating team with the *last best offer* in order to maximize flexibility, achieve agreement, if possible, and conserve time.

Structures, strategies, and tactics for negotiating should be made in advance, such as the option for subcommittees and side bar agreements. Broad directional statements underlie strategies, and are broken down into specific objectives, such as those related to money or decision-making authority. These objectives can be categorized and prioritized as maximum, realistic, and minimum. Examples of tactics to support these objectives were given and include inflated initial requests, use of public sentiment, planning for impasse, media release use, emphasis of controversial or hot issues, reduction of expectations, "planting" of future issues, and comparable district data contrasts.

Rationales and supportive data must support all of the proposals and counterproposals, and alternative proposals must be available. Consideration must be given to the retention and/or elimination of current agreements, the strengthening of managerial rights, preparation for anticipated union proposals, the development of quid pro quo and throwaway proposals, and the determination of the absolutes, or bottom line.

In a win-win atmosphere, all of the strategies, objectives, and tactics would become collaborative, communication would become joint, and the objectives would be developed by both teams in a professional, problem-solving format.

EXERCISES

1. Identify the union recognition clause, if any, in your district and clarify its meaning.

2. Assuming that negotiations were to begin tomorrow, how would you describe the union-management tone in your district? How would it affect negotiations?

3. Collect samples of data for a bargaining notebook, such as copies of the state law, the current master contract and other helpful information.

4. After investigation, how would you characterize the district's history of grievance, arbitrations, and prior negotiations?

5. Obtain a salary/benefits schedule with arrayed employee numbers, and compare it to that of comparable neighboring districts. What are the implications for future negotiations?

6. List some desired managerial changes or additions to the master contract; then list some possible union-proposed changes.

7. Which of the strategies and tactics described would be most successful in your district's negotiations?

REFERENCES

1. Keane, W. G. 1996. *Win Win or Else: Collective Bargaining in an Age of Public Discontent.* Thousand Oaks, CA: Corwin Press, Sage Publications, pp. 4–7.

2. Keane, W. G. 1996. *Win Win or Else,* pp. 40–42.

3. Kearney, R. C. 1984. *Labor Relations in the Public Sector.* New York, NY: Marcel Dekker, Inc., pp. 66–67.

4. Kearney, R. C. 1984. *Labor Relations,* p. 323.

5. Coleman, C. J. 1990. *Managing Labor Relations in the Public Sector.* San Francisco, CA: Jossey-Bass Publishers, pp. 64–65.

6. Helsby, R. D., J. Tener, and J. Lefkowitz, eds. 1985. *The Evolving Process— Collective Negotiations in Public Employment.* Fort Washington, PA: Labor Relations Press, pp. 140–141.

7. Bacharach, S. B., J. B. Shedd, and S. C. Conley. 1989. "School Management and Teacher Unions: The Capacity for Cooperation in an Age of Reform," *Teachers College Record,* 91(1): 97–105.

8. Cimini, M. H., S. L. Behrmann, and E. M. Johnson. 1994. "Labor-Management Bargaining in 1993," *Monthly Labor Review,* 117(1): 20–33.

9. Huber, J. and J. Hennies. 1987. "Fix on These Five Guiding Lights and Emerge from the Bargaining Fog," *School Board Journal.* 174(3): 31.

10. Coleman, C. J. 1990. *Managing Labor Relations,* p. 127.

11. Webster, W. G., Sr. 1985. *Effective Collective Bargaining in Public Education.* Ames, IA: Iowa State University Press, pp. 133–135.

12. Tait, R. C. 1995. "Contract Negotiations Without Ill Will," *School Administrator,* 52(9): 30–31.

13. Plauny, L. 1992. "Compared to What? Developing a Teacher Compensation Comparison Standard," *School Business Affairs,* 58(8): 16–20.

14. Schwerdtfeger, R. D. 1986. "Labor Relations Thrive When You Control Collective Bargaining," *American School Board Journal.* 173(10): 41–44.

15. Davis, W. M., et al. 1990. "Collective Bargaining in 1990: Health Care Cost a Common Issue," *Monthly Labor Review,* 113(1): 3–10, 27–29.

16. Cimini, M. H. 1995. "Negotiated Changes in State and Local Government Contracts," *Monthly Labor Review,* 117(8): 3–10.

17. Kearney, R. C. 1984. *Labor Relations,* pp. 106–107.

18. Sleemi, S. 1995. "Collective Bargaining Outlook for 1995," *Monthly Labor Review,* 118(1): 3–21.

19. Herman, J. J. and G. E. Megiveron. 1993. *Collective Bargaining in Education: Win/Win, Win/Lose, Lose/Lose.* Lancaster, PA: Technomic Publishing Co., Inc., pp. 84–86.

20. Ibid.

21. Herman, J. J. 1991. "The Two Faces of Collective Bargaining," *School Business Affairs,* 57(2): 11–12.

22. Castetter, W. B. 1996. *The Human Resource Function in Educational Administration.* 6th ed. Englewood Cliffs, NJ: Merrill, pp. 566–569.

23. Herman, J. J. 1991. "The Two Faces," pp. 11–12.

24. Helsby, R. D., J. Tener, and J. Lefkowitz, eds. 1985. *The Evolving Process,* p. 222.

25. Heisel, W. D. 1973. *New Questions and Answers on Public Employee Negotiation.* Washington, D.C.: International Personnel Management Association, p. 86.

26. Herman, J. J. and G. E. Megiveron. 1993. *Collective Bargaining in Education,* pp. 100–103.

27. Bacharach, S. B. and E. J. Lawler. 1984. *Bargaining—Power, Tactics, and Outcomes*. San Francisco, Ca: Jossey-Bass Publishers, pp. 42–43.

28. Neal, R. 1980. *Bargaining Tactics—A Reference Manual Used for Public Sector Labor Negotiations*. Richard G. Neal Associates, p. 147.

29. Nickoles, K. W. 1990. "Future Shock: What's Coming to the Bargaining Table," *School Business Affairs*, 56(12): 36–38.

30. Richardson, R. C. 1985. *Collective Bargaining by Objectives: A Positive Approach*. Englewood Cliffs, NJ: Prentice-Hall, Inc., p. 168.

31. Herman, J. J. 1991. "The Two Faces," p. 11.

32. Huber, J. and J. Hennies. 1987. "Fix on These Five Guiding Lights," p. 31.

33. Neal, R. 1980. *Bargaining Tactics*, pp. 177–178.

34. Namit, C. 1986. "The Union Has a Communications Strategy—And Your Board Should, Too," *American School Board Journal*. 173(10): 30–31.

35. Ross, V. J. and R. MacNaughton. 1982. "Memorize These Bargaining Rules before You Tackle Negotiations," *American School Board Journal*, 169(3): 39–41.

36. Namit, C. 1986. "The Union Has a Communications Strategy," pp. 30–31.

37. Ibid.

38. Neal, R. 1980. *Bargaining Tactics*, pp. 181–182.

39. Herman, J. J. 1991. "The Two Faces," p. 12.

40. Herman, J. J. and G. E. Megiveron. 1993. *Collective Bargaining in Education*, pp. 88–90.

41. Schwerdtfeger, R. D. 1986. "Labor Relations Thrive," p. 42.

42. Neal, R. 1980. *Bargaining Tactics*, pp. 140–141.

43. Herman, J. J. and G. E. Megiveron. 1993. *Collective Bargaining in Education*, pp. 101–106.

44. Streshly, W. A. and T. A. DeMitchell. 1994. *Teacher Unions and TQE*, Thousand Oaks, CA: Corwin Press, Sage Publications, pp. 77–79.

45. Panasonic Foundation and the American Association of School Administrators. 1994. "Building Labor and Management Coalitions," *Strategies for School System Leadership on District-Level Change*, 1(1): 1–5.

46. Webster, W. G., Sr. 1985. *Effective Collective Bargaining*, p. 85.

47. Aaron, B., J. M. Najita, and J. L. Stern. 1988. *Public Sector Bargaining*. Washington, D.C.: Industrial Relations Research Associates, p. 132.

48. Coleman, C. J. 1990. *Managing Labor Relations*, pp. 127–132.

49. Webster, W. G., Sr. 1985. *Effective Collective Bargaining*, pp. 87–92.

50. Neal, R. 1980. *Bargaining Tactics*, pp. 165–168.

51. Coleman, C. J. 1990. *Managing Labor Relations*, p. 245.

52. Hendrickson, G. 1990. "Where Do You Go after You Get to Yes?" *The Executive Educator*, 12(11): 16–17.

Doing It: Conduct at and Away from the Table

CHAPTER 9 discusses all the important details that must be attended to during the period within which contract negotiations is taking place. These details include differences between win-win and win-lose conduct at and away from the table, establishing ground rules, exchanging proposals, keeping up with the other party's moves, and controlling personality conflicts. It addresses selecting your at-the-table and away from the table spokesperson(s), establishing a communications hotline, timing your moves, projecting multi-year proposal costs, being flexible and creative, and setting the at-the-table tone. Also included are carrying out each member's role(s), posturing and positioning, presenting your proposals and demands, analyzing and using quid pro quos, packaging your proposal, participating in side bars, and analyzing proposals for power and costs. Consideration is given to placing yourself in the other party's shoes, prioritizing your proposals and their proposals, drafting counterproposals, observing verbal and non-verbal behavior, and identifying the real issues, the giveaways, the musts and the bargaining chips. More detail is provided regarding cutting deals, working with the other team's members, developing strategies and tactics for each negotiation session, and keeping score by analyzing results immediately after each negotiation session. Such strategies as dividing and conquering, reaching closure on articles and getting TA's (Tentative Agreements), arriving at total contract at-the-table TA, and emphasizing the differences in at-the-table behavior if the negotiations take place in a win-win environment. The chapter concludes with a summary, exercises, and references.

This discussion begins with the establishment of ground rules. Usually, the first discussion that takes place when the union team and management team first sit down at the bargaining table is one which establishes the rules for the negotiations.

DIFFERENCES BETWEEN WIN-WIN AND WIN-LOSE CONDUCT AT AND AWAY FROM THE TABLE

Behavior at and away from the table of parties negotiating from a cooperative and collaborative approach is a joy to behold. Members of both the union's and management's teams work as co-workers to accomplish a just and equitable master agreement between the two parties. Subgroups that meet away from the negotiating table will be developed for the following purposes: (1) to gather and analyze data of interest to either or both parties, (2) to develop the language of the contract, (3) to resolve any problems of conflicting interests between the two parties, and (4) to jointly sell the negotiated master agreement to the employees and to the board of education for the school district, although in many cases this fourth joint effort may be eliminated.

At the table, every member of the negotiating teams may discuss matters, bring data and rationale, raise questions, and openly communicate with everyone there. On the other hand, in win-lose, adversarial bargaining, each party would have a sole spokesperson, the only person to speak unless the spokesperson gives permission to another member of the negotiating team. If ideas are to be shared with the spokesperson, they are communicated by written notes or during an away-from-the-table caucus.

Both teams in a win-lose adversarial negotiating environment are very secretive. They collect data in secret, they develop proposed contractual language in isolation, they develop strategies and tactics in meetings before and after at-the-table sessions or in caucuses, and they hardly ever share their ultimate settlement goals until the final contract language is agreed upon by both parties.

Win-win can be described as an environment of trust, respect, honesty, cooperation, joint problem solving, and total collaboration. On the other hand, win-lose can be described as secretive, mistrusting, and self-serving, and exists in an environment designed to defeat the other party to the negotiations [1].

With these differences clearly identified, let's turn to the establishment of ground rules to be used during the conduct of negotiations. It is crucial, especially in the case of adversarial negotiations, to clearly specify these in writing and to have both parties to the negotiations sign-off on these ground rules.

ESTABLISHING GROUND RULES

At the initial at-the-table meeting of the two negotiation teams, the union team will propose a set of ground rules for bargaining, and the management team will propose its own set of ground rules [2]. Bargaining begins in earnest as both teams propose and counterpropose ground rules under which the bargaining will proceed. Sometimes agreement on ground rules may take multiple meetings. Regardless of the number of meetings needed, agreement on ground rules must ultimately be reached before discussion of contractual articles begins. These sessions are critical in that they set a tone and determine detail as to rules favoring management and/or labor; hence, the meetings are highly significant in their shaping of and in their ultimate impact on the actual bargaining sessions.

Ground rules will vary from school district to school district, and they may even vary within the same district during various replacement contract negotiations. However, most ground rules will include rules similar to the following:

- The place of meeting shall alternate for each session, one meeting being at the administrative offices and the next being at the union's offices [3].
- The time of meeting shall be after normal working hours unless management agrees to pay for the time expended by the union's team members, or the union agrees to pay the district an amount of money equivalent to its team members' pay during the time these members are involved in negotiation sessions [4].
- There will be a time limit of four hours on meetings unless both parties agree to continue beyond that time [5].
- The union and management will exchange total contract proposals during a specific meeting, and negotiations will be limited to the items submitted in these initial proposals. No additional items are permitted to be added during these contract negotiations [6].
- Both parties shall be allowed to bring resource persons to specific meetings when they notify the other party in advance. Only one resource person at a time can be brought to a specific negotiating session, and the resource person must add information to or clarify some substantial aspect of the current negotiation [7].
- Observers to the negotiations will not be permitted [8].

- There shall be no media releases during the negotiations process unless impasse is reached [9]. During the time of impasse, each party will notify the other party of their intent to issue a media release in advance of releasing it. These rules are agreed to in the great majority of situations, since history has suggested that releases to the media, observers to the negotiations, and other intrusions on the process appear to lengthen and make more complex the task of reaching contractual agreement [10].
- Both parties shall keep their own minutes of the sessions, unless there is agreement that an official set of minutes shall be accepted. If official minutes are agreed upon, both parties generally date and sign the official meeting minutes at the beginning of the next negotiating meeting [11].
- Both parties agree to sign-off each article as that article is agreed to, or they agree not to sign-off any article until the total contract document is TA'd (Tentative Agreement). It may be more desirable to discourage individual sign-off of each article; a package sign-off could be a very significant managerial gain [12].
- Other ground rules as agreed upon by both parties to the negotiations in each school district.

Now that the ground rules have been established, the negotiating teams can get down to exchanging contract proposals. Contracts are broken down into various subsections, called articles, and proposals may include (1) the introduction of a new article, (2) a modification of an existing article, or (3) the elimination of an existing article [13].

EXCHANGING CONTRACT PROPOSALS

Procedures for exchanging proposals vary. Sometimes both parties exchange total initial proposals at the same session. Occasionally the union will submit its total set of proposals first, management will be required to submit its total set of proposals within two weeks, and sometimes the non-economic and the economic proposals will be submitted at different times [14]. In the case of non-economic and economic proposals, the economic proposals are usually held until the non-economic proposals are settled, or an impasse has been reached on them [15]. This impasse may be resolved without the help of a third party, since many times there will be trade-offs between economic and non-economic proposals as the negotiations proceed [16].

At this juncture, it should be stressed that as proposals and counter-proposals are presented and discussed, there is no requirement in the collective bargaining laws that either party has to agree. The only requirement is that both parties negotiate *in good faith*. Good faith implies listening to the other party's proposals and giving them serious consideration. It also implies that both parties continue to meet and negotiate with one another, and that their proposals are honest ones based on data and rationale [17].

Initial proposals usually include three types of items: (1) proposals that are absolutely necessary to achieve in order to ratify a contractual agreement, (2) proposals which are meant to be giveaways or bargaining chips, and (3) proposals which are intended to introduce a new item in order to establish an agenda item for future contract negotiation, but on which the party does not actually expect to attain agreement during the current negotiations. One example of each type will help to define the differences among the three proposals.

- A *required proposal* by the union may be to achieve complete board of education paid health coverage for the entire family; whereas the board of education currently only pays for the individual employee [18].
- A *bargaining chip proposal* by management's negotiation team is to have teachers attend a week of staff development workshops each year before the start of the actual student school year, and to do this for substitute teacher wages instead of the normal teacher wage [19].
- A *new item proposal* by the union may include adding dental, optical, and auditory care to the health package of fringe benefits. This will be introduced because of the trend in comparable districts towards improved health benefits for employees [20,21].

Now that we have discussed the three major types of proposals, let's examine the scope of proposals that comprise a complete labor/management contractual document. Obviously, the specifics will vary with the category of employee, the type of union, and the specific items included in each school district's master contract agreement. In general, however, most master contract agreements will include the following definitive articles:

- Article One—Recognition
- Article Two—Employee and Union Rights

- Article Three—Employment Conditions
- Article Four—Employee Evaluation
- Article Five—Employee Termination
- Article Six—Employee Compensation
- Article Seven—Employee Fringe Benefits
- Article Eight—Employee Leaves
- Article Nine—Grievance Procedure
- Article Ten—Negotiation Schedule and Procedures
- Article Eleven—Duration of the Agreement
- Article Twelve—Management Rights [22]

Now that the types of proposals have been discussed, let's look at presenting proposals and the activities and considerations that take place during at-the-table negotiating sessions. Both the method and tone of your presentation and the activities of your team during the session are important to the success of each at-the-table session.

PRESENTING PROPOSALS TO THE OTHER PARTY

It is crucial that you have a knowledgeable and effective chief negotiator, as this is the person who will make all the initial contract proposals and all counterproposals [23]. The chief negotiator should (1) know the laws affecting negotiations in the state, (2) know the details of the activities and work performed by the employees and administrators of the school district, and (3) have at hand all the pre-negotiation information collected and arrayed in the bargaining notebook.

Each proposal presented should have a rationale and supporting facts and argumentation. Let's look at the following examples of proposals from both union and management:

Example—Union's Proposal

Article Sixteen—Salary to be modified as follows:

(1) The initial step of the teacher's salary schedule be increased from $16,000 to $22,000.
(2) Each step on the salary schedule be increased by $200.
(3) An eleventh step be added to the current ten-step salary schedule.
(4) The differential between a BA degree and an MA degree be increased from its current $500 to $1,000.

(5) The differential between an MA degree and a Ph.D. or Ed.D. degree be increased from $500 to $1,500.

Rationale

There are two excellent reasons for this proposal. First, the district has had difficulty in getting candidates to fill teacher vacancies during this time of a national teacher shortage. Secondly, the board of education has consistently indicated that they want excellent employees and that they desire to treat all employees fairly.

Factual Data

In comparing our teachers' salary and salary schedule with the twenty districts both parties have agreed will be those used for comparative purposes, we find that (1) The beginning salaries in all but six districts are at the level or higher than we are requesting in our proposal. (2) Our step increments are anywhere from $50 to $400 dollars lower than twelve of the districts. (3) The average increments in the salary schedule in our comparable districts is twelve steps. (4) The differential between the BA or BS degree and the MA or MS degree average in the comparable districts is $900, with three districts exceeding $1,500. (5) Although only two districts have a salary differential between the MA or MS degree and the Ph.D. or Ed.D. degree, one district allows a differential of $2,500, and the other allows a $4,000 differential. In addition, we feel the board of education should agree with an action which will encourage more teachers to go on for advanced education which ultimately will accrue to the benefit of the students and the district.

Example—Management Proposal

Article Seven: Fringe benefits be modified as follows: Although the board of education pays the complete cost of Green Bills Corporations' hospital and medical insurance, management's negotiating team proposes that (1) all hospital and medical insurance be bid and the business be given to the lowest bidder, (2) only HMO (Health Maintenance Organization) organizations be asked to bid, and (3) the employee pays for the first $100 of benefits received.

Rationale

The reason for this three-part proposal is to provide substantial health coverage for the school district's employees, and to do so at the lowest cost. By achieving the lowest cost, additional money can be allocated to other important employee and school district needs, while maintaining the current level of protection.

Factual Data

In comparing the cost of our health insurances over the years and in comparing our health insurance coverages with other districts, we find:

(1) Our premiums have increased an average of twenty percent (20%) per year over the past ten years. This has happened while the additional income received by the district over the same ten year period has only averaged four and one-half percent (4 1/2%).

(2) Districts who have bid their health insurance packages have experienced a reduced premium cost of five percent (5%) per year.

(3) Districts who have gone strictly to HMOs for their health insurance indicate that they have experienced a yearly savings of fifteen percent (15%).

(4) Although we agree that very few employees take advantage of the full coverage paid by the board of education, by causing employees to pay for the first one hundred dollars ($100) of coverage, those employees who will misuse the policy coverage will be discouraged from further misuse. This also would have the possibility of lowering the district's premium costs as our policies' premiums are set on an experienced use basis [24].

Once initial proposals have been presented, attention is turned to the activities that take place during at-the-table negotiating sessions. Let's turn now to a discussion of these activities.

ACTIVITIES DURING AT-THE-TABLE NEGOTIATING SESSIONS

Earlier, in Chapter 4, we discussed the roles of the various team members. It is important that the spokesperson controls the dialogue, that the recorder keeps an accurate account of the happenings, that the wordsmith does her/his homework and alerts the spokesperson of concerns about the other team's wording of proposals, that the observer cues the spokesperson whether any of the other team's members are telegraphing their attitudes, and that the finance expert alerts the spokesperson to any hidden financial implications in the other party's proposals.

While the team members are performing their roles, it is also important that they work together as a smoothly operating whole, wherein all of the players do their roles well, thereby strengthening the entire team and allowing it to be the best it can be [25]. For only if the members help each other and work in tandem can the team successfully implement its at-the-table strategies and tactics.

Other important at-the-table items to consider include (1) being flexible and creative, (2) establishing the tone of each session, (3) timing proposal movements, (4) posturing and positioning, (5) dividing and conquering, and (6) controlling personality conflicts.

To a large extent, these moves will not only depend on the activities that take place during a specific at-the-table session, they will also depend on the power relationship of each party to the negotiations [26]. For example, if taxpayers have consistently refused to vote an increase in the local property tax, and state aid to the district has been decreasing over the past five years, it will be extremely difficult for the union's negotiating team to achieve large, if any, expenditures related to employees' wages or fringe benefits [27]. On the other hand, if the school district has accumulated an unnecessarily large end-of-year fund balance, it will be very difficult for management's team to have enough power to keep fairly substantial increases in salary and fringe benefits from taking place.

At this point, let's return to the six items listed above:

(1) Flexibility at the table is a great asset to a negotiating team. Flexibility will allow agreement on a contested proposal by modifying the initial proposal or counterproposing a logical modification in the other party's proposal [28]. For instance, in our health insurance example, the proposal may be modified in the following ways: (1) Instead of the employee paying for the first one hundred dollars ($100) of benefits, the sum could be reduced to twenty-five dollars ($25), and this would establish a future agenda for increased employee contributions. (2) The proposal to allow only HMOs (Health Maintenance Organizations) to bid could be dropped from the original proposal.

Being creative is another means of becoming more effective at the table. For instance, if the union would agree to having each employee contribute twenty-five dollars toward her/his health insurance costs, the school district would add fifty dollars ($50) to another category of employee fringe benefits [29].

(2) Establishing the tone of each session is another important skill that will enhance the team's chance for success. If the team and its chief negotiator perceive that the other team will not make any movement at the session, the team should establish a tone of courteous listening and intelligent questioning of the other team's comments and proposals, and make an effort to hide a no-give demeanor.

(3) If the team senses the timing is right for movement, it should establish a tone of flexibility and sincere interest in making progress through give and take with the other team's and its own proposals. One reason for the timing being right might be after receiving information indicating where other districts in the process of contract negotiations have settled on the item in dispute.

(4) Posturing and positioning are important tactics to be utilized at the table. Posturing implies presenting an artificial position or attitude in order to pretend that you feel strongly or take seriously an item about which you do not feel strongly or about which you are truly not serious. Like a feinting move by a boxer, posturing is intended to throw the opponent off balance in her/his deliberations [30].

Positioning implies the ability to arrange an order to things; the relative position within the whole, when controlled, presents a tactical advantage for the negotiating team when compared to the positioning of the other team. Like the track star who draws the inside lane position for the race, controlling the position of your team and the other party's team will give you a big advantage during each negotiation session. This tactic of positioning can be used as a technique for pairing proposals, for faking proposals, or juxtapositioning proposals.

(5) Dividing and conquering is a useful technique to use when the union's team members represent different interests. For example, in dealing with a teachers' union, one might realize from pre-negotiation information collected on the union's team members that many of them are at the top of the salary schedule, and forty percent of the members are coaches. Management's negotiating

team may make initial proposals that would not increase the top of the salary schedule, but which would increase the additional salaries paid to coaches by fifty percent (50%). This approach would probably cause serious disagreement among members of the union's negotiating team, and management could use this dissension to come up with an entirely creative proposal in the future. The importance of having in-depth knowledge about members of the opposition's team cannot be emphasized sufficiently.

(6) Controlling personality conflicts is a skill that must be exercised by the chief negotiator. Controlling involves triggering anger in one of the other party's team members whenever one wants to because of a dislike by that person of the chief spokesperson or another member of the negotiating team. It also involves observing the team members to make certain they are not losing their cool. Finally, it involves the chief negotiator's maintaining a calm and collected appearance in the midst of a serious personality conflict with the other party's chief negotiator.

Now that we have discussed at-the-table activities, let's turn to the activities that take place away from the bargaining table. These areas include (1) packaging proposals, (2) analyzing proposals by putting yourself in the other party's shoes, (3) prioritizing proposals and counterproposals, (4) drafting counterproposals for quid pro quo, (5) cutting deals through side bar discussions, (6) developing strategies and tactics for each negotiation session, (7) costing proposals for power and financial impact and for immediate and long-term impact, and (8) analyzing the results of each collective bargaining session [31].

ACTIVITIES AWAY FROM THE BARGAINING TABLE

Packaging Proposals

The collective bargaining process often involves the negotiation of a large number of issues. One way to expedite negotiations is to package proposals and counterproposals [32]. Packaging involves combining those items which have some relationship into one group, and insisting that all interrelated items are bargained for as a unit.

If management were to receive proposals involving (1) increased sick leave, (2) child care leave, (3) sabbatical leave, (4) paid holidays, (5) life insurance, (6) hospital insurance, (7) medical insurance, (8) accidental death and disability insurance, (9) dental insurance, (10) optical insurance, (11) maternity leave, and (12) salary increases, these items could then be packaged for bargaining purposes [33].

Management could insist on dealing with all cost and *possible* non-cost items as separate packages [34]. In the above case only two items, those of maternity and child care leaves are non-cost items. If, on the other hand, management wanted to package them according to categorical areas and insist that each category be negotiated as a unit, all leaves would become a package, all insurances would become a package, and salary increases would stand alone [35].

The advantage of packaging is that it puts pressure on the other party to look at a group as a whole, and it allows for reasoned give-and-take. This technique should increase rationality over separate item bargaining, and it should expedite the negotiations process.

Analyzing Proposals by Putting Yourself in the Other Party's Shoes

One of the best ways to analyze your proposals and counterproposals and the other party's proposals and counterproposals is by putting yourself in the other party's shoes. That is, management takes the union's viewpoint and addresses the "what ifs" (What, if I were the union, would I do in reaction to management's proposal or counterproposals?). This technique allows management to anticipate the items which may be approved by the union, and it will also allow management to anticipate areas of disagreement [35]. Of course, the union's negotiating team members will benefit by utilizing the same procedure.

Prioritizing Proposals and Counterproposals

Every proposal or counterproposal made by management is not of equal worth, and every proposal made by the union is not of equal value. It is wise to prioritize the proposals and counterproposals that management presents on some scale such as (1) required, (2) desired, or (3) wishful thinking [36,37]. It is wise to do the same analysis of the union's proposals and counterproposals. Within each rating category, it is also wise to prioritize all items within each category; this procedure will allow you to maximize your strategies, objectives, and tactics on those items which are the most important negotiation proposals.

Drafting Counterproposals for Quid Pro Quo

Drafting counterproposals should be done by each negotiating team, with the wordsmith and the financial resource person taking the lead. The key to drafting counterproposals is making certain that the counterproposal achieves a quid pro quo (that is, the negotiating team will receive equal or greater value than what is given to the other party) [38]. Counterproposals can be limited to a single item, or the negotiating team can propose giving something in one proposal area in exchange for something of equal or greater value from another proposal area.

An example of a single-item counterproposal might be one where management offers a better comprehensive health insurance coverage if the employees will pay the first one hundred dollars ($100) of the premium for coverage. An example of a multiple-item counterproposal might be agreeing with the union's request for fully board-paid improved comprehensive health insurance in exchange for employees reporting for three days of staff development at substitute pay and the union's agreeing to drop its request for adding a salary step to the existing salary schedule.

Cutting Deals through Side Bar Discussions

Side bars refer to actions taken away from the official negotiation meetings [39]. An example would be the chief negotiators for both management and union meeting at a restaurant with no others present to see if they can talk about ways to resolve an item that is stalemated at the official sessions. If a successful compromise is worked out at this meeting, it will then be presented by one of the chief negotiators at an official negotiating meeting, and both chief negotiators will attempt to get their negotiating teams to agree to the proposal.

Developing Strategies and Tactics for Each Negotiating Session

Not only should overall strategies, objectives, and tactics be determined prior to the initial negotiation session, but they should also be arrived at prior to each collective bargaining session [40]. Negotiations, many times, present an amoeba-like moving target; and that is the primary reason for taking time between negotiation sessions to plan the strategies, objectives, and tactics for the next upcoming negotiation session.

Strategies are the "whats" that the team wishes to achieve, the objectives are the specific measurable results to be achieved, and the tactics are the "hows" of achieving the strategies and objectives [41]. An example of a management strategy might be the lessening of the escalating cost of health insurance that the board of education pays for employees. A specific objective might be to limit the cost increase to five percent (5%) over the next three years. The at-the-table tactic might be to offer to provide the union with a much-desired win in another proposal area to achieve the slowdown of cost escalation in the area of health insurance.

Costing Proposals for Power and Financial Impact and for Immediate and Long-Term Impact

The teacher's union has proposed increases of five hundred dollars ($500) to each step on the existing one thousand dollar ($1,000) salary step increment on the schedule, moving the starting salary from its current twenty thousand dollars ($20,000) to twenty-two thousand dollars ($22,000), and adding another step to the existing ten-step salary schedule at the master's degree level. The union also wishes to increase the current one thousand dollar ($1,000) differential between the bachelor's and master's level to four thousand dollars ($4,000).

Let's examine the current step salary schedule and the placement on that schedule of the current employees. Also, the union's proposals will be placed in parentheses opposite the current salary schedule steps. The example in Table 9.1 is limited to a five and added sixth step (instead of the added eleventh step) for the sake of brevity. The cost increase for future year increase if the union's proposal were accepted can be computed as shown in Table 9.2.

Total new money costs for the first future year would equal $1,383,000. In addition, for the subsequent year, the costs would increase dramatically by moving all employees on steps one through four at the bachelor's level and steps one through six on the master's level. As these employees are placed forward one step on the salary schedule, each employee would receive a $1,500 step increment increase in salary, which is built into the schedule. This amounts to one hundred and forty teachers each receiving $1,500, or a total built-in increase of $210,000. This does not consider any increase in the basic salary schedule, any addition to the step increments, or any additional steps being added to the schedule for the second year of the master con-

Table 9.1.   Wonderful School District's Current Teachers' Salary Schedule.

Step	No. of Tchrs	Bachelor's	No. of Tchrs	Master's
1	12	$20,000 ($22,000)	4	$21,000 ($26,000)
2	10	21,000 (23,500)	8	22,000 (27,500)
3	12	22,000 (25,000)	20	23,000 (29,000)
4	2	23,000 (26,500)	32	24,000 (30,500)
5	4	24,000 (28,000)	40	25,000 (32,000)
New	0		18	0 (33,500)

tract's duration. Each year into the future, the built-in cost increases from year one will keep carrying forwarded [42,43].

Let's turn now to a non-economic example of a proposal that will have a long-term impact on the management of the school district. In this example, the transportation union's negotiating team has proposed that all bus routes be bid on the basis of seniority. In analyzing this proposal, management's negotiating team did some *"what if"* thinking. The management team said *What if* a bus driver that had seniority bid to drive a bus with handicaped students, and the driver was too old to assist in their placement on, in, and off of the bus? The management team said *What if* a bus driver with a lot of seniority, who did not like nor could handle little children, bid for the kindergarten bus run; and

Table 9.2.   Cost Increase for Future Year.

	Current Year	Future Year	Difference
Bachelor's			
Step 1	$ 240,000	$ 264,000	+$ 24,000
2	210,000	235,000	25,000
3	264,000	300,000	36,000
4	46,000	53,000	7,000
5	96,000	112,000	16,000
Master's			
Step 1	$ 84,000	$ 104,000	$ 20,000
2	176,000	220,000	44,000
3	460,000	580,000	120,000
4	768,000	976,000	208,000
5	1,000,000	1,280,000	280,000
New	00	603,000	603,000

that driver replaced a person who loved small children, and was very gentle and kind to them? These *what ifs* pointed out the long-range damage that could be done to the children and to the reputation of the district within the community at large.

Analyzing the Results of Each Collective Bargaining Session

It is important to analyze the degree to which the negotiating team had achieved its specific objectives in relation to its strategies, and the degree of success the negotiating team had with the tactics it utilized during each session. This analysis should be conducted as soon after the negotiating sessions end as is practical; the sooner the analysis is conducted, the better will be the team members' memories of what took place during the session [44]. Also, it is important to keep a running account of the status of negotiations after each session. This procedure will quickly identify for the team where the negotiations have been, the current status of negotiations, and the potential opportunities for future negotiating sessions.

A running diary of the status of proposals during negotiations will prove, along with the bargaining book that was previously prepared, to be a very valuable asset to the negotiating team. A simple format outlining status proposals will demonstrate this aid.

Negotiations' Status Notebook

Article	Proposed by	Agreed	Compromisable	Objectionable
Recognition	Union			X
Management Rights	Mgt.		X	
Employee Evaluation	Mgt.	X		

Once the negotiating team has analyzed the status of each proposal, it should set about establishing means of reaching closure on the articles for which agreement has not yet been reached. As agreement is reached on each proposal and each contractual article, both parties should TA (Tentatively Agree) and sign-off and date that agreement. This being accomplished, all the TAs can then be reviewed before the entire contractual agreement is TA'd, and both parties would then bring the TA'd contractual agreement to their referent groups for official ratification [45].

Having dealt with the tentative agreement of contract articles, it is important to briefly indicate the differences that would take place in the conduct of at-the-table and away-from-the-table negotiations if the negotiating climate were win-win rather than adversarial.

WHAT DIFFERENCES WOULD EXIST IF THE NEGOTIATING ENVIRONMENT WERE A WIN-WIN ONE?

The basic differences that would be clearly evident if there were win-win negotiations rather than adversarial negotiations include the following:

- Pre-negotiation preparations would be a joint venture by both the union and management negotiating teams [46].
- The negotiating discussions would not be controlled by the chief negotiation spokespersons; rather all parties would add their comments and suggestions during each and every negotiating session.
- Joint official minutes would probably be utilized.
- There would be no need for side bar bargaining as all members of both groups would be privy to all information and to all discussion.
- Subcommittees, comprised of members of both the union team and management team, would be used to investigate any area of study; they would also be used to draft proposals that could be presented at-the-table to both the union and management teams.
- A collaborative problem-solving process would be used, and this would be the greatest and most significant difference from the process used during adversarial negotiations [47,48].

SUMMARY

The establishment of ground rules is a negotiations process in itself, as both teams will make proposals prior to the actual discussion of contractual articles. Ground rules usually include locations and schedules for meetings, the specific packaging of proposals, media update agreements, minutes keeping, and any Tentative Agreement arrangements.

Procedures for exchanging proposals range from initial total proposal submission by one or both teams, to the splitting of economic and non-economic proposals. The specific division of proposals may set the stage for later impasse trade-offs. Good-faith bargaining, implying integrity of intent and accuracy of data, is required at this stage. Initial proposals usually include three types of items: required proposals, bargaining chips, and new items. In general, most master contract agreements will include such standard articles as recognition, employee and union rights, employment conditions, employee evaluation, employee termination, employee compensation, employee fringe benefits, employee leaves, grievance procedures, negotiation schedule and procedures, duration of the agreement, and management rights.

The presentation of proposals requires a chief negotiator who is knowledgeable in negotiations law and in the employment details of the district. Examples of such proposals, both union and management, were provided, accompanied by rationales and supported by factual data. The importance of team members' roles, as critical functions in a smoothly running process, are combined with successful at-the-table strategies. (Power relationships intervene as well, particularly as they reflect the relative resource strength of the district). Suggested strategies include flexibility to maximize proposal modification, creativity in proposal modification, and control of personality conflicts. Establishing the tone of each session, sensing optimum timing for proposal give and take, and dividing and conquering (to cause union inter-team stress), were described. Positioning and posturing, to feign attitudes aimed at throwing the opposition off balance and to arrange proposals for maximum advantage by controlling the position of both teams, are additional strategies.

Proposal packaging involves combining similar issues into groups, through categorical or cost/non-cost clustering, for example, thus creating negotiation units and allowing for reasoned give-and-take within the package.

Analysis of proposals can be done by assuming the union viewpoint and addressing the *"what ifs,"* in order to anticipate counterstrategies. Proposals likewise need to be prioritized, and counterproposals drafted in order to achieve quid pro quo (equal value). Side bar agreements are actions taken informally, away from the table, usually for the purpose of addressing stalemated package items.

These and other strategies must be orchestrated and a game plan determined prior to each negotiation session, bearing in mind that the strategies are what the team wishes to achieve. Objectives are the measurable results, and tactics are the processes used to attain them. A cost example was provided to show the financial impact of a salary proposal, and a non-cost example of a procedural item was described.

Analysis of each session must be conducted soon after its conclusion, and a running diary or ledger-like account kept to maintain a negotiations status record. Strategies for achieving closure on each of the proposal items can then be planned, and Tentative Agreement reached and mutual sign-off accomplished.

The occurrence of all this in a win-win climate would likely result in joint venture pre-negotiation preparations, open and free interchange discussions, joint minutes and subcommittee investigative efforts, and the presence of a collaborative, problem-solving atmosphere.

EXERCISES

1. Describe what you feel would be optimum ground rules for a negotiations session in your district.

2. With regard to past contractual agreements in your district, what would be the likeliest mandatory proposal items, and which might be bargaining chips or new items?

3. Select a management package proposal and create a rationale for it, supporting it with factual data.

4. Select a union package and create a rationale for it, supporting your package with factual data.

5. Which of the at-the-table tactics described do you feel would be the most effective in your district's negotiations? Which would be the least effective?

6. What would be the best packaging for a proposal in your district? Describe how you would pair, group, and prioritize items for maximum effect.

7. Investigate one previous negotiation's salary proposal, and determine the impact of it on the district's existing salary schedule.

8. Investigate one no cost or power proposal, and determine its impact on the school district's operation.

9. Explain how you would approach an adversarial bargaining environment.

10. Explain how you would approach a win-win, collaborative bargaining environment.

REFERENCES

1. Herman, Jerry J. 1991. "The Two Faces of Collective Bargaining," *School Business Affairs,* (57)2: 10–13.

2. Kearney, R. C. 1984. *Labor Relations in the Public Sector.* New York, NY: Marcel Dekker, Inc., p. 106.

3. Ibid.

4. Webster, W. G., Sr. 1985. *Effective Collective Bargaining in Public Education.* Ames, IA: Iowa State University Press, p. 149.

5. Herman, J. J. 1991. "The Two Faces," p. 12.

6. Helsby, R. D., J. Tener, and J. Lefkowitz, eds. 1985. *The Evolving Process—Collective Negotiations in Public Employment.* Fort Washington, PA: Labor Relations Press, p. 225.

7. Feiock, R. C. and J. P. West. 1990. "Public Presence at Collective Bargaining: Effects on Process and Decisions in Florida," *Journal of Collective Negotiations,* 19(1): 69.

8. Ibid.

9. Ordovensky, P. and G. Marx. 1993. *Working with the News Media.* Alexandria, VA: American Association of School Administrators, pp. 11–12.

10. Namit, C. 1986. "The Union Has a Communications Strategy—And Your Board Should, Too," *American School Board Journal,* 173(10): 30–31.

11. Neal, R. 1980. *Bargaining Tactics—A Reference Manual for Public Sector Labor Negotiations.* Richard G. Neal Associates, p. 138.

12. Herman, J. J. 1991. "The Two Faces," p. 9.

13. Streshly, W. A. and T. A. DeMitchell. 1994. *Teacher Unions and TQE,* Thousand Oaks, CA: Corwin Press, Sage Publications, p. 64.

14. Webster, W. G., Sr. 1985. *Effective Collective Bargaining,* pp. 151–152.

15. Ibid.

16. Ibid.

17. Coleman, C. J. 1990. *Managing Labor Relations in the Public Sector.* San Francisco, CA: Jossey-Bass Publishers, p. 119.

18. Kearney, R. C. 1984. *Labor Relations,* p. 14.

19. Coleman, C. J. 1990. *Managing Labor Relations,* p. 16.

20. Ibid.

21. Herman, J. J. and G. E. Megiveron. 1993. *Collective Bargaining in Education: Win/Win, Win/Lose, Lose/Lose.* Lancaster, PA: Technomic Publishing Company, p. 98.

22. Gorton, R. A., G. T. Schneider, and J. C. Fisher. 1988. *Encyclopedia of School Administration & Supervision.* Phoenix, AZ: Oryx Press, pp. 62–63.

23. Richardson, R. C. 1985. *Collective Bargaining by Objectives: A Positive Approach.* Englewood Cliffs, NJ: Prentice-Hall, Inc., p. 167.

24. Ventner, B. M. and L. A. McFerran. 1992. "Don't Use Our Health Insurance: Paying Employees to Forgo Dual Coverage," *School Business Affairs,* (58)2: 10–13.

25. Herman, J. J. 1991. "The Two Faces," p. 11.

26. Bacharach, S. B. and E. J. Lawler. 1984. *Bargaining—Power, Tactics, and Outcomes.* San Francisco, CA: Jossey-Bass Publishers, pp. 206–208.

27. Webster, W. G., Sr. 1985. *Effective Collective Bargaining,* pp. 162–163.

28. Ross, V. J. and R. MacNaughton. 1982. "Memorize These Bargaining Rules Before You Tackle Negotiations," *American School Board Journal,* 169(3): 39–41.

29. Herman, J. J. and G. E. Megiveron. 1993. *Collective Bargaining in Education,* p. 103.

30. Webb, L. Dean, J. T. Greer, P. A. Montello, M. S. Norton. 1987. *Personnel Administration in Education—New Issues and New Needs in Human Resource Management.* Columbus, OH: Merrill Publishing Company.

31. Helsby, R. D., J. Tener, and J. Lefkowitz, eds. 1985. *The Evolving Process,* pp. 227–228.

32. Webster, W. G., Sr. 1985. *Effective Collective Bargaining,* p. 85.

33. Sleemi, S. 1995. "Collective Bargaining Outlook for 1995," *Monthly Labor Review,* 118(1): 3–21.

34. Webster, W. G., Sr. 1985. *Effective Collective Bargaining,* p. 85.

35. Fisher, R. and W. Ury. 1981. *Getting to Yes—Negotiating Agreement Without Giving In.* Boston, MA: Houghton Mifflin, pp. 114–128.

36. Kearney, R. C. 1984. *Labor Relations,* pp. 106–107.

37. Coleman, C. J. 1990. *Managing Labor Relations,* pp. 122, 169.

38. Neal, R. 1980. *Bargaining Tactics,* p. 167.

39. Kerchner, C. T. 1988. "A New Generation of Teacher Unionism," *Education Digest,* L111 (9): 52–54.

40. Kearney, R. C. 1984. *Labor Relations,* pp. 106–107.

41. Kaufman, R., J. J. Herman, and K. Watters. 1996. *Educational Planning: Strategic, Tactical, Operational.* Lancaster, PA: Technomic Publishing Co. Inc., pp. 60–69.

42. Granof, M. 1973. *How to Cost Your Labor Contract.* Washington, D.C.: The Bureau of National Affairs, Inc., pp. 2–3.

43. Herman, J. J. 1992. "School-based Management: Staffing and Budget Expenditures," *School Business Affairs,* 58(12): 24–25.

44. Herman, J. J. 1991. "The Two Faces," p. 12.

45. Helsby, R. D., J. Tener, and J. Lefkowitz, eds. 1985. *The Evolving Process,* pp. 227–228.

46. Venter, B. M. and J. Ramsey. 1990. "Improving Relations: Labor Management Committees in School Districts," *School Business Affairs,* 56(12): 20–23.

47. Nyland, L. 1987. "Win-Win Bargaining Pays Off," *Education Digest,* L111(1): 28–29.

48. Keane, W. G. 1996. *Win Win or Else: Collective Bargaining in an Age of Public Discontent.* Thousand Oaks, CA: Corwin Press, Sage Publications, pp. 1–3.

FINDING THE TROUBLE SPOTS AND LIVING TOGETHER AFTER COLLECTIVE BARGAINING

Section Three consists of four chapters. Chapter 10, Reaching Impasse: Too Late for Win-Win, covers information related to mediation, arbitration, and fact-finding.

Chapter 11, Arriving at Lose-Lose, discusses preparing for a strike, conduct during a strike, and follow-up after a strike. It also refers to the stresses that take place during a strike, and presents a case for consistent and accurate communications before, during, and after a strike.

Chapter 12, Finalizing and Communicating the Signed Master Contract, discusses reaching a tentative agreement, presenting the contract for ratification, giving the other party credit, and printing and publicizing the master contract agreement that has been negotiated and ratified by both parties.

Chapter 13, Contract Management: Living with the Contract That Has Been Negotiated, discusses the topics of communicating and interpreting the contract, training administrators for contract management, setting and breaking precedents, and disciplining for contract violations. This chapter also discusses preparing for and conducting grievances and preparation for and conduct during grievance arbitration.

Reaching Impasse:
Too Late for Win-Win

CHAPTER 10 covers the detailed planning that is required when an impasse is reached and management and union groups are processed through the impasse resolution methods of mediation, fact-finding, and arbitration. It also provides an example of one state's impasse procedures. The chapter concludes with a summary, exercises, and references.

An impasse may be deemed to exist if union and management fail to reach a total contract agreement, usually after lengthy negotiations. States vary on impasse procedures; some allow either party to declare an impasse and request a mediator from the state's PERB (Public Employment Relations Board) or other state agency designated to oversee the collective bargaining of public agencies in the state. Other states provide a different structure [1,2].

For example, New York State's Taylor Law defines an impasse as what occurs when both parties fail to achieve an agreement at least one hundred and twenty days prior to the end of the fiscal year of the public employer. In this case, public employers may enter into written agreement with the recognized employees' union about specific measures to end impasses. Such written procedures can include submitting the unresolved issues to impartial arbitration. If there is not such a written agreement between both parties, PERB will appoint a mediator, upon request of either party or by PERB's own motion, who will attempt to arrive at a voluntary resolution of items in dispute. If mediation does not end the dispute at least eighty days prior to the end of the public employer's fiscal year, or by such other date determined by PERB to be appropriate, PERB shall appoint a fact-finding board of not more than three members. Finally, if the fact-finding board's recommendations are made public and the impasse is still not resolved, PERB has the power to take whatever steps it deems necessary to resolve the dispute [3].

Another example comes from the State of Iowa's impasse procedures. To quote from *An Introduction to Iowa's Public Employment*

Relations Act, which was prepared on the basis of an address by the PERB Chairperson:

> PERB (Public Employment Relations Board) has general responsibility for the administration of mediation, fact-finding, interest arbitration, and grievance arbitration. Mediation is provided without cost to the parties and is performed by full-time staff, part-time "ad hoc" mediators, and commissioners of the Federal Mediation and Conciliation Service (FMCS).
>
> The expenses incurred in impasse services other than mediation are shared by the parties. PERB selects the individuals that serve on the fact-finding and arbitration panels. Lists of these individuals are provided the parties from which a selection is made through a striking procedure. Although the following sections deal only with "statutory" impasse procedures, parties may substitute their own mutually-agreed-upon "independent" procedures.
>
> Either party in a dispute may request the services of a mediator. The request must be dated and signed, filed with the Board, and served upon other parties to the negotiations. Although only ten days are allocated for the mediation process, the Board has determined that the day of the first meeting is the "date of appointment" which commences that time period.
>
> Fact-finding is a compulsory component of the impasse procedures unless the parties mutually agree to eliminate it. In the event mediation efforts are unsuccessful, the statute requires the Board to appoint a fact-finder. Recently the Board has adopted a policy of allowing the parties to select fact-finders from a list provided by the agency. It is on this basis that the appointment is made by the Board. The fact-finder conducts a hearing and issues findings and recommendations for the parties' consideration. After the fact-finder issues the report the parties either accept or reject it. If the dispute remains unresolved ten days after hearing, PERB makes the report public.
>
> The advocates of fact-finding argue that it encourages settlement, or at least reduces the issues between the fact-finding and arbitration stage. In Iowa, fact-finding is particularly significant because it becomes a third option for the arbitrator to consider.
>
> Increasingly, states are enacting public laws which require interest arbitration (sometimes called contract arbitration). In Iowa, there is final offer arbitration on an issue by issue basis. If the fact-finder's recommendations are not accepted, either party may request arbitration.
>
> Following a request for arbitration, the parties are required to exchange their final offers on each issue at which they are at impasse. The parties may opt to have one arbitrator or a tripartite arbitration panel hear the dispute. If the parties cannot agree upon a neutral arbitrator, PERB supplies a list of names from which to make the selection.

The arbitrator is required by statute to consider certain criteria in making his or her award. Included within these criteria are a comparison of wages, hours, and conditions of employment of the involved public employees with other public employees doing comparable work; past contracts between the parties; the employer's power to levy taxes and the ability of the employer to finance economic adjustments.

The award must be issued within fifteen days of the hearing, unless the parties have otherwise agreed. The arbitrator is prohibited by statute from mediating the dispute. An arbitrator's award is subject to judicial review as agency action under Chapter 17A, *The Code* (1981).

The main function of PERB in grievance arbitration cases is to provide panels of arbitrators upon request. PERB offers staff grievance arbitration services based on an hourly fee rate, shared by the parties and paid to the State [4].

Other states have different impasse structures. Before the discussion moves to another topic, some specific clarifications should be made:

(1) Interest arbitration (sometimes called contract arbitration) refers to an impasse procedure *during* the negotiations process. Grievance arbitration, on the other hand, refers to a third party investigating an alleged violation by management of the terms of an *existing* master contract agreement as claimed by the union [5].

(2) In some states arbitration precedes fact-finding.

(3) In some states, arbitrators attempt to mediate the resolution, but in all situations, arbitrators or fact-finders are not utilized until mediation has been exhausted.

(4) Arbitration and/or fact-finding can be done by a single person serving as an outside party or by a panel serving as an outside body.

(5) The cost for arbitration and/or fact-finding is usually shared equally by both union and management, although it is possible for other agreed-upon payment structures to be used.

(6) Both fact-finding and arbitration can be compulsory or voluntary, depending on the individual state's laws and rules and regulations, and depending on the agreement between both parties when the state's laws do not restrict the parties to a specific method.

(7) Interest (contract) arbitration, if compulsory or voluntary, can be item-for-item or total last best offer [6]. If arbitration is item-by-item, the arbitrator is free to select the position of either party on

each contractual item that remains in dispute, and may rule in favor of one party on some items and in favor of the other party on other items.

(8) If, however, arbitration is of the last best offer type, the arbitrator must rule in favor of a single party's total last best offer. There can be no decisions on the merits of either party on the individual contractual items in dispute [7].

Now that an overlay of impasse situations has been provided, let's turn to the topic of preparing for impasse. This section will discuss the preparations recommended for each of the impasse situations of mediation, fact-finding, and arbitration.

PREPARING FOR MEDIATION

When you enter this initial impasse stage, it is important that you have kept a complete record of every matter that has been discussed or presented by either party during the negotiations that have taken place to this point [8]. Also, this is where all the pre-negotiations information collected for your bargaining book, the information on the actual status of each article discussed at the table, and the updates of information from comparable districts who are currently involved in negotiations becomes crucial.

Usually a mediator is assigned by the state's PERB or by some other state's body that has the responsibility for overseeing public collective bargaining in the state, upon the written request of the local school district's employer or the local school district's union [9]. At this point, it is wise to check on the track record of the mediator to determine the degree of success the person has in resolving disputes.

If, after a few sessions with the assigned mediator, one is not pleased with the mediator's performance, it is wise to request a change of mediators. PERB, however, may or may not grant the request for a change.

The mediator, whose role it is to simply try to resolve the dispute, is not concerned with the values involved in the dispute, nor is the mediator attempting to get a necessarily fair settlement. The mediator's sole role is to obtain a settlement which will be agreed to by both parties in the dispute [10].

The scenario of a hypothetical mediation might very well follow the sequence illustrated here:

(1) The mediator contacts the bargaining teams and sets up appointments for her/him to meet with both the union's negotiating team and management's negotiating team.

(2) At the initial mediation meeting, the mediator will meet separately with both the union and management negotiating teams. At this meeting, the mediator will review the mediation procedure. Also, at this meeting, the mediator will ask each party to stipulate the specific items in dispute and to clarify the party's current offer on each item. Finally, the mediator will ask for the underlying rationale for the party's position on each item, and she/he will listen to any data that the party feels strengthens the case for the party's current position.

(3) After meeting separately with each party to the dispute, the mediator will conduct a joint meeting of both parties to review the state's collective bargaining law and the applicable rules and regulations as these apply to the impasse procedure entitled mediation. The mediator will also outline the items in dispute and her/his understanding of each party's position on each item. At this session the mediator, hopefully, can get the agreement of both parties that the items reviewed are those in dispute; and that the positions of both parties on each disputed item are clear.

(4) At this point, the mediator will generally conduct a series of meetings with the individual parties to the dispute, and will occasionally bring both parties together for meetings. During the meetings with each party, the mediator will explore areas of flexibility, and suggest a variety of compromise solutions. These are exploratory discussions, and are not binding on either party.

(5) If the mediator feels, after a series of meetings with the union and management negotiating teams, that she/he is in a position to make a proposed settlement, she/he may call both teams together and present her/his proposal. If the proposal is accepted, it should be signed-off by both parties, and the impasse is resolved. Oftentimes, the mediator may feel it prudent to present additional compromise recommendations, if the original recommendations are rejected by either party or by both parties.

(6) If mediation is unsuccessful after a reasonable period of time, the mediator, or PERB, may declare an end to mediation, or either party (or both parties) may terminate the mediation process [11].

With this sequenced mediation scenario in mind, let's return to the type of preparation the negotiating team should undertake prior to meeting with the mediator. First, the team should clearly identify the items in dispute and prepare its rationale and factual arguments for its position on each one. Second, it should clearly identify for the mediator on which items the team will be flexible and the degree of this flexibility, and the areas for which there will be absolutely no flexibility. Third, the methods of presenting this information to the mediator should be predetermined. Finally, the negotiating team should decide how much they will tell the mediator about their ultimate position, especially on financial items [12]. This caution refers to the fact that if the entire available amount of money to reach a final settlement is revealed to the mediator and the mediation is not successful, there will be no flexibility left for further stages of the impasse process.

Let's review the preparation for mediation of two items in dispute: a financial example and a non-financial example.

A non-financial example is one in which the union proposes that management will have to obtain the agreement of the individual employee before that employee can be transferred to another site or another position. In this situation, management would present the following rationale and data:

- Management must retain the right to assign employees, otherwise the entire school district could end in chaos. Specific scenarios would be presented to illustrate this point.
- There is not evidence from comparable school districts that any board of education has ratified a master contract agreement incorporating such restrictive language.
- The position of management's negotiating team on this item is one of absolute rejection.

A *financial example* is one in which the union proposes a ten percent increase in the amount of money allocated to the salary schedule of teachers. Management's response to the mediator includes the following:

- The board of education wants to pay teachers a fair wage, but it cannot afford to increase the salary of teachers by ten percent.
- The cost of living index for the district's region is only four and one-half percent, and a ten percent increase in teachers' salaries is uncalled for at this time.

- Management's negotiating team has offered a five percent salary increase, and this offer is one-half of a percent in excess of the cost of living.
- Management's five percent offer will retain the teachers' salary ranking at fourth place, when compared to the area's twenty other districts.
- The public last year voted a two mill increase in property tax for school purposes, and the effort made by the citizens of this community, when compared with the taxable base available to it, indicates that the district ranks fifth of the twenty-one districts in its financial effort to support its schools.

Assuming that the information shared above by management's negotiating team and the information shared by the union's negotiating team, coupled with the efforts of the mediator, did not end the impasse, the process will move to the fact-finding stage. It should be remembered that this is not the sequence or procedure followed by all districts, or one that is mandated in all states that have collective bargaining legislation.

FACT-FINDING

Fact-finding is the step in the impasse resolution process that usually follows an unsuccessful mediation attempt. It is sometimes conducted by a single fact-finder or by a fact-finding panel; occasionally, the panel is selected by each party selecting one member of the fact-finding panel and agreeing on a method of selecting the third member [13,14].

Although it is sometimes used as a tactic, it is poor practice for either party to artificially push negotiations into fact-finding with the hope that the fact-finder will give them a better deal than the one that could be achieved through at-the-table negotiations, or through the impasse procedure of mediation [15].

In states where fact-finding is advisory, the results of the fact-finding are published if the parties cannot agree. Also, in some states, the fact-finders make recommendations for settlement, and these recommendations may also be published. The publication of the recommendations is intended to put public pressure on either or both parties to settle the disputed areas [16]. In states where fact-finding is binding, this publication step is not required.

During fact-finding, each party presents written documentation and oral arguments which best present its case. Witnesses can be called, and the fact-finder may legally subpoena witnesses. Also, fact-finders will interrogate the testimony of witnesses, and oftentimes a court recorder will be hired to take and transcribe a verbatim transcript of the fact-finding. Generally, fact-finders will also allow written rebuttals of the opposite party's presentations following the fact-finder's hearing; at times, the fact-finder will allow the parties to file post fact-finding hearing briefs [17].

In general, fact-finders will use a set of criteria upon which to collect facts and on which to make recommendations. A reasonable set of criteria would include (1) the impact on the education program, (2) equity for both parties, (3) practicality of the issues and of their resolutions, (4) future implications of the settlements, (5) ability of the school district to pay, (6) comparative standards with other school districts, and (7) compromises which assist each party [18].

Don't expect the fact-finder to speak to the merits of your position. Her/his recommendations will almost certainly be profoundly influenced by the facts you present and by the effectiveness and relevance of the presentations made on the issues in dispute [19]. Also, remember that if you do not fully understand the fact-finder's report, phone her/him to get clarification prior to deciding on a course of action.

The kind of information you should be prepared to give the fact-finder will include the following:

- a copy of your operating budget and last year's audit
- a list of items that are in contention, and the cost of each of the economic items in contention with both the union's demands and management's offers
- gross budgetary increases represented by the union's demands and management's offers
- impact of the tax rate of each of the demands and offers
- impact of anticipated changes in revenues from local, state, and federal sources
- demographic data about the school district and its students
- such data as per pupil expenditures, student enrollment, and the socioeconomic level of the community at large is always helpful to the fact-finder
- a statement of the first proposals made by the union and the first counterproposals made by management
- any change of position on the contested items, which were made during the mediation process, especially listing those items for which there was tentative agreement

- a clear statement of each party's *last best offer* on each item in contention [20]

Usually, a fact-finder's written report will include sections such as (1) background information, (2) the criteria used in decision making or in acceptance of the facts submitted by the parties, (3) a listing of all items in contention, with both the union and management positions clearly stated, (4) a summary of all pertinent facts related to each item in contention, and (5) a final section including decisions, findings, and recommendations (this section usually contains the rationale utilized by the fact-finder in making her/his recommendations) [21].

Assuming that the state in which the school district is located permits both parties to the negotiations to either accept or reject the fact-finder's report and recommendations, and assuming that one or both parties reject the fact-finder's report, the next step would lead to the impasse process of arbitration. Let's now turn to a discussion of this step in the impasse procedure.

INTEREST OR CONTRACT ARBITRATION

Whether arbitrators or arbitration panels are controlled by PERB or whether the parties to the negotiations apply to the American Arbitration Association for a list of arbitrators, both parties usually can select some names and reject others until agreement is reached [22]. In cases where agreement is not reached, some states permit PERB to select the arbitrator. In all cases, the parties to the negotiations would be wise to locate sources of information about each proposed arbitrator and about the rulings that she/he has issued to date, especially rulings on cases involving the specific items that are in contention during the current negotiations [23]. Besides the PERB morgue, a person could search the Bureau of National Affairs' *Labor Arbitration Reports* or the information about arbitrators listed in the *Martindale-Hubbell Law Directory,* or in the *Summary of Labor Arbitration Awards,* or any other similar sources of information about arbitrators [24].

Even though arbitration is requested on items in contention, the question of arbitrability of some of the items can be questioned by either party [25]. If the question of arbitrability is raised and a review by the arbitrator of existing contractual language, the state's collective bargaining laws, and its supplemental rules and regulations causes the arbitrator to rule that a certain item is not arbitrable, the party who questioned the arbitrability of the item scores a big tactical win. Most times, however, the arbitrator will not be questioned on the arbitrability issue and when she/he is, the ruling generally is one that states the item is arbitrable. It is becoming more prevalent in contracts that a ruling of arbitrability is made by a court prior to submission to arbitration. Judges only rule on the arbitrability and not on the case itself [26].

In many ways, the preparation for arbitration and the conduct of the arbitration hearing are very similar to those of fact-finding. Again, the arbitration can be voluntary or mandatory, and the hearing can be conducted by a single arbitrator or by a panel. In arbitration states, it is permitted that the same person serve as a mediator and an arbitrator within the same case [27]. In the opinion of the authors, this method truly puts the arbitrator in the position of becoming a super mediator, and it weakens the mediation step in the impasse procedures.

Even though there are many similarities in the preparation for and the conduct of arbitration and fact-finding, let's terminate this discussion on impasse procedures by outlining the steps the party to negotiations should take in preparation for contract arbitration. Also, let's discuss the likely procedures that will be used in conducting the arbitration.

It is important to note that most of the arbitration cases management loses are lost due to poor planning and preparation. The steps that should be used in planning for arbitration are (1) pre-deciding on the written data to be presented—these should be mostly identical to those prepared for fact-finding, including the initial information that was included in the fact-finding report, if that report favors your party's views; and (2) preparing the oral presentation and deciding on the person(s) who will give the oral presentation [28]. Also, if post-arbitration hearing briefs are permitted by the arbitrator, the briefs should be carefully planned and expertly prepared.

Now that the parties have prepared for the arbitration, let's briefly outline a scenario of the probable structure of the arbitration hearing:

- The first step will probably involve the introduction of all parties, a short review of the purpose of arbitration, and a review of the items in dispute.
- A decision will be made as to whether or not the hearing shall be opened or closed. If both parties agree to an open meeting, the arbitrator may or may not agree, and if either party objects to an

open hearing, the arbitrator will definitely conduct a closed hearing. Most experts in the field recommend closed hearings.

- If both parties agree to accept the testimony of outside parties, the arbitrator will probably rule in favor of this; but if either party disagrees on this item, outside party testimony will probably not be allowed.
- The arbitrator may decide to tape the hearing, or there may be an agreement among the parties that a court recorder be hired to take a verbatim transcript of the hearing. In cases where a transcript is allowed, there should be a prior agreement as to which parties besides the arbitrator are to receive transcripts, and who will pay the expenses of the court recorder and for the preparation and distribution of the transcripts of the hearing.
- Some arbitrators insist that all persons testifying do so under oath.
- Opening statements are presented by both parties. In general, either the union or the party who initially requested the arbitration is the first party to present.
- The parties present their written exhibits and their oral arguments. Sometimes both parties will agree to joint stipulations of the issues being contested, and they will agree to filing joint exhibits related to the items stipulated.
- Either party is sometimes permitted to cross-examine the other party's witnesses, but in all cases, the arbitrator will interrogate the witnesses for clarification and additional detail.
- In some states, the arbitrator is given power to subpoena witnesses or records if information which may be pertinent to the case is not forthcoming.
- Closing arguments are presented by both parties.
- The arbitrator ends the hearing, and may allow both parties to file post-hearing briefs.
- Within a reasonable period after the hearing, or within a few weeks if a verbatim transcript is required, the arbitrator will make the mandates for settlement known (in situations where arbitration is mandatory) or the arbitrator will make the recommendations for settlement of the outstanding issues in contention known (in situations where arbitration is voluntary arbitration).
- If arbitration is mandatory, the issues are resolved and a master contract agreement is issued. This terminates the negotiations and the impasse procedures [29].

SUMMARY

Impasse may be deemed to exist if the union and management fail to reach a total contract agreement. State impasse procedures vary in the structures that determine which party, or agency, may declare impasse. Examples from New York and Iowa illustrated the language and statutory provisions of impasse. Also addressed were such issues as expenses, mediation participant selection, compulsory fact-finding, contract arbitration, and criteria for awards.

Interest arbitration refers to an impasse procedure during negotiations. Grievance arbitration refers to allegations of violations of existing contracts. In some states, fact-finding precedes arbitration; in others, the opposite occurs. These procedures may be done by a panel or by an individual, vary in expense assignment, and be compulsory or voluntary. Arbitration can also consider settlement item-by-item, or by total last best offer.

Preparing for mediation requires referral to the bargaining book, to updated information on at-the-table items, and to information about comparable districts. Disputed items should be clarified and further preparation done on proposals, rationales, supporting facts, and possible areas of flexibility. The track record of the mediator should be investigated. The procedure itself usually involves separate mediator meetings with the two teams to get a perspective on their proposals, followed by a joint meeting with both parties to review the law and to outline disputed items. A series of individual team meetings follow to allow exploration of flexibility, and a proposed settlement is made. Examples of financial and non-financial proposals were provided. It should be remembered that the mediator's sole role is to obtain a mutual (not necessarily fair or equitable) settlement.

Fact-finding is the impasse resolution that usually follows an unsuccessful mediation attempt. This can be done by an individual, or by a panel of fact-finders. Each party presents written documentation and oral arguments for its case, and the fact-finders may expand upon that information by subpoena of witnesses or interrogation of witnesses. In general, a set of criteria is used for collecting facts and making recommendations. Teams usually provide the fact-finders with budget information, proposal item costs, revenue and demographic data, and a summary of the preceding negotiations process. Sometimes fact-finding is used as a tactic by one party to obtain a better settlement than could be achieved through negotiations. In some states, the results of fact-finding are publicized, particularly if fact-finding is not binding.

Parties to the negotiations usually have the option to select or decline arbitrators. The arbitrability of some items in contention may be questioned. The preparation for interest (contract) arbitration is much the same as that for fact-finding. Care must be given to the preparation of the information and to the presentation of the brief. The procedure (usually closed to the public) will usually involve a review of the items in dispute, the submission of any outside party testimony and subsequent cross-examination, the presentation of each party's proposals, maintenance of a transcript of the proceedings, the presentation of closing arguments, and the filing of post-hearing briefs. The arbitrator will, within a reasonable period, provide mandates for settlement (or recommendations for settlement, if arbitration is voluntary).

EXERCISES

1. Investigate the impasse procedures in your state. What is the order of those procedures, and is arbitration compulsory or voluntary?

2. Investigate the record of any fact-finding or mediation process that involved a district in your state.

3. With reference to the last proposal package prepared by either party in your district, which individual items do you think might have been used as flexibility areas during mediation procedures?

4. With reference to the last proposal package prepared by either party in your district, which individual items in dispute might have been factually supported by the testimony of expert witnesses? How would those witnesses have been found?

5. Locate the sources in your state of important information about the rulings of individual arbitrators and fact-finders.

6. What information would you present at the impasse stages of mediation, fact-finding, and arbitration?

REFERENCES

1. Helsby, R. D., J. Tener, and J. Lefkowitz, eds. 1985. *The Evolving Process—Collective Negotiations in Public Employment.* Fort Washington, PA: Labor Relations Press, p. 16.

2. Castetter, W. B. 1996. *The Human Resource Function in Educational Administration.* 6th ed. Englewood Cliffs, NJ: Merrill, pp. 582–585.

3. New York State Public Employment Relations Board. 1983–1984. *The Taylor Law.* Albany, NY: New York Public Employment Relations Board, pp. 13–15.

4. Beamer, J. B. 1985. "An Introduction to the Public Employees Relations Act," Address by the Chairman of the Public Employment Relations Board of Iowa. *Public Employment Relations Act,* pp. 13–18.

5. Elkouri, F. and E. A. Elkouri. 1973. *How Arbitration Works.* Third Edition. Washington, D.C.: Bureau of National Affairs, Inc., pp. 44–48.

6. Herman, J. J. and G. E. Megiveron. 1993. *Collective Bargaining in Education: Win/Win, Win/Lose, Lose/Lose.* Lancaster, PA: Technomic Publishing Co. Inc., pp. 119–120.

7. Elkouri, F. and E. A. Elkouri. 1973. *How Arbitration Works,* pp. 2–8.

8. Webster, W. G., Sr. 1985. *Effective Collective Bargaining in Public Education.* Ames, IA: Iowa State University Press, pp. 250–253.

9. Kearney, R. C. 1984. *Labor Relations in the Public Sector.* New York, NY: Marcel Dekker, Inc., pp. 250–253.

10. Kearney, R. C. 1984. *Labor Relations,* p. 253.

11. Coleman, C. J. 1990. *Managing Labor Relations in the Public Sector.* San Francisco, CA: Jossey-Bass Publishers, pp. 217–219.

12. Brock, J. 1982. *Bargaining Beyond Impasse—Joint Resolution of Public Sector Labor Disputes.* Boston, MA: Auburn House Publishing Company, pp. 53–54, 71–76.

13. Zack, Arnold. 1980. *Understanding Fact Finding and Arbitration in the Public Sector.* Washington, D.C.: U.S. Department of Labor, Labor Management Services Administration, p. 2.

14. Streshly, W. A. and T. A. DeMitchell. 1994. *Teacher Unions and TQE,* Newbury Park, CA: Corwin Press, Sage Publications, pp. 101–102.

15. Neal, R. 1980. *Bargaining Tactics—A Reference Manual for Public Sector Labor Negotiations.* Richard G. Neal Associates, pp. 229–230, 232.

16. Kearney, R. C. 1984. *Labor Relations,* pp. 255–256.

17. Helsby, R. D., J. Tener, and J. Lefkowitz, eds. 1985. *The Evolving Process,* pp. 242–243.

18. Webster, W. G., Sr. 1985. *Effective Collective Bargaining,* p. 162.

19. Neal, R. 1980. *Bargaining Tactics,* pp. 232–233.

20. Webster, W. G., Sr. 1985. *Effective Collective Bargaining,* p. 162.

21. Coleman, C. J. 1990. *Managing Labor Relations,* p. 220.

22. Webster, W. G., Sr. 1985. *Effective Collective Bargaining,* pp. 165–166.

23. Elsea, S. W., D. A. Dilts, and Haber, L. J. 1991. "Factfinders and Arbitrators in Iowa: Are They The Same Neutrals?" *Journal of Collective Negotiations,* 19(1): 61–67.

24. Helsby, R. D., J. Tener, and J. Lefkowitz, eds. 1985. *The Evolving Process,* pp. 252–253.

25. Zack, Arnold. 1980. *Understanding Fact Finding,* pp. 58–59.

26. Herman, J. J. and G. E. Megiveron. 1993. *Collective Bargaining in Education,* pp. 125–126.

27. Zack, Arnold. 1980. *Understanding Fact Finding,* p. 3.

28. Zack, Arnold. 1980. *Understanding Fact Finding,* pp. 39–40.

29. Kearney, R. C. 1984. *Labor Relations,* pp. 258–260.

Arriving at Lose-Lose

CHAPTER 11 discusses the following topics: (1) preparing for a strike, (2) conduct during the strike, (3) follow-up after the strike, (4) developing of and carrying out the strike plan, (5) selecting a spokesperson(s) to communicate with the community, the board of education, the administration, the employees, and the media, (6) establishing a "hot line", (7) long hours and the big stress test, and (8) playing "chicken" until the end. The chapter ends with a summary, exercises, and references.

For demonstration purposes, the incident of a teachers' union strike will be used throughout the chapter, as teachers comprise the largest and probably the most powerful union group within the local school district. However, most of the illustrations in this chapter will be presented from a board of eduction's or management's point of view.

Let's begin by discussing strike preparation. It is important to realize that the worst case scenario in collective bargaining is that of a strike. If a strike exists in a school district, no one wins. At best, a strike is a temporary lose-lose situation, but most often it is a long-term lose-lose situation for everyone involved.

Prior to a teachers' union strike the students are subjected to an unhappy environment, and they see their teacher role models picketing and behaving in a manner that is not conducive to appropriate modeling behavior. In a state such as Michigan, which prohibits teachers from striking, if many teacher strikes still take place without any punishment to the individuals and the union leadership, it gives some students the impression that if teachers can break the law, they have a similar option to disobey district or classroom rules [1,2].

Once the parties arrive at the strike stage, propaganda proliferates. Many times the community does not know who is telling the truth, and they lose faith in both parties [3–5]. This community image damage often continues long after the strike is settled.

Finally, the employees are frustrated because they are concerned about their livelihood, concerned about repercussions, and are sometimes not certain where the current situation is headed. Many times, they become emotional; and some employees are forced, because of pressure from other union members, to participate in a strike, picket the school board and administrative office, and do other tasks that are totally opposed to their traditional value system [6,7].

Once all other efforts to reach agreement during at-the-table negotiations—mediation, fact-finding, and arbitration—have failed and the parties are presumably headed for a strike, it is crucial that a detailed and comprehensive strike plan is prepared. Without a strike plan, one party is at the total mercy of the tactics of the other party; and sometimes those tactics can become rather severe. Prior to initiating the strike plan and prior to experiencing a strike, management can do much to prepare.

PREPARING FOR A STRIKE

There is only one certain key to surviving a strike, and that key is preparation, preparation, and more preparation. *Management cannot over-prepare for an upcoming strike.* The best means of preparation includes playing *"What-if" scenarios,* with the board of education, the administrators, and management's negotiating team taking part. In addition, management should establish strategies, objectives, tactics, and countertactics. What-if scenarios can be developed by exploring the experiences of districts that have undergone strikes. Also, if the district has previously experienced a strike and the union leadership is still in place, many of the union's tactics will be repeated. Some of the What-if scenarios for which management should prepare include the following:

- *Sick outs* happen when all the teachers use sick leave or personal leave on the same day in the hopes that the normal school day will be interrupted. Sometimes there will be a staggered use of this tactic wherein the teachers in one building will all call in sick or take personal leave one day, and another building's teacher staff will do this on another day, and so forth [8].

  Management's response to this scenario could be to (1) increase the number of substitute teachers that the district normally retains on its payroll, (2) hire some of the substitute teachers to a short-term, full-time rotating teaching position, or (3) have all administrators who are certified as teachers report to the local schools to do large group instruction or to take the students on field trips with instructional goals. In each case, an action plan should be prepared in advance of the job action; in the case of the field trip alternative, a lesson plan should be prepared with instructional outcomes stated [9].

- *Work-to-rule actions* happen when teachers are instructed by the union leaders to refuse to perform any duties that are not specifically mandated by the contract [10]. In many cases, this means that teachers will not provide homework, will not meet with students who require help after normal school hours, and will not meet with parents to discuss their child's progress at any time other than normal school hours.

  About the only response management can have to these job actions is (1) appeal to the professional instincts of the teachers, (2) suggest to parents who complain that this will be a short and temporary situation, and (3) state that you are sorry for the inconvenience and lack of normal services caused by this work-to-rule action.

- *Nonfulfillment of coaching and after normal school hours sponsoring activities* is another possible job action that management might very well face. The students who are involved in these activities will be very vocal; their parents will become very angry; and the general public, in a school district that has football, band, basketball, or some other activity that brings pride and recognition to the community, will become very upset with all parties to the negotiations [11].

  Occasionally, coaches, band directors, or the sponsors of some other high visibility, co-curricular activity will not march by the union's directives, and will be severely ostracized by the union leadership. They may also suffer daily harassment by the other teachers in the school district. Management can do three things to help combat this job action scenario: (1) protect the coaches and sponsors from harm by cancelling all co-curricular activities until after a master contractual agreement is reached. If such action is to be taken, the media and community should be informed. The community should also be informed if the reason for the action was that some coaches and other co-curricular sponsors would continue their after school duties, but others would not continue. Also, rather than only having some students receive the advantage of after school activities, the board of education should decide to cancel all after school activities until a master contract agreement with the teachers' union has been ratified. (2) People who wish to coach or be a co-curricular sponsor but who work for other school districts, or other persons who wish to and are able to coach or sponsor an activity can be hired as replacements. If the board of education authorizes this approach, every new coach or co-curricular sponsor should be told, in advance, of the pressure they will probably receive from members of the school district's teachers' union. (3) In anticipation of a possible job action, the board of education could authorize the administration to prepare and offer written contracts to each coach or co-curricular sponsor providing the same salary and job assignments as those written into the expiring master contractual agreement. A clause should be inserted stating that any additional benefits which may accrue to that specific coaching or co-curricular sponsorship will be passed on to the coach or sponsor once the successor master contractual agreement is ratified. This approach will put the situation under contract law, and it will provide those coaches and sponsors who wish to continue with an excuse—they cannot violate a signed personal contract.

- In the case of *boycotts of business establishments* or other situations where the school district's board members have an interest [12], about the only thing that can be done is to collect data as to the harm done, then hire a lawyer to sue the union leaders, individually, for damages. In all probability this technique will not be ultimately successful, but it may cause some concern among the union leadership.

- The *picketing* of board of education meetings, picketing schools before and after normal school hours, or picketing the administration building and individual school buildings [13] demands that management had better be prepared to communicate with the media, as the media is definitely going to cover any potential conflict situation [14]. The union's spokesperson will certainly have contacted the media and given the union's side of the story, and management should be prepared with a truthful and clear response. Management, in this situation, should do two things: (1) provide a clear statement of the board of education's current position in relation to union/management contract negotiations [15], and (2) alert the police department to be on call in case the picketing becomes unpleasant and gets out of hand. It should be clear to the police, however, that their presence on campus should only take place after a call from a specific administrator, as the presence of police can incite a riot [16].

These and other job actions will only prove to be successful if the union receives almost unanimous teacher member compliance. In a school district which has multiple unions, the support of other labor unions is also important. A school district wherein most of the adults belong to unions is an aid to the teachers' union [17]. The timing of the job actions is important, as is the element of surprise.

Now that we have reviewed the most serious job actions that could be taken by a teachers' union and the possible planned responses of management, we are still left with a variety of other tactics, which are not job actions, for which management will have to enact What-if scenarios. Some of the most likely tactics and some possible plans that could be enacted by management are:

- Union notifies the administration that they will be taking a strike vote, or has others spread the word that there might be a strike. If state laws prohibit a strike, the administration, with prior approval of the board of education, could issue a news release and organize a mailing to each household in the school district (and a copy of both to the union's leadership) stating something similar to the following:

"Rumor has it that a teachers' strike is imminent in our district. Since the state's collective bargaining statute prohibits strikes by public employees, it is our hope and belief that the school district's teachers will not participate in an illegal strike action. However, in order to protect the students and the school district, the board of education has made the decision to start the school year two weeks later than normal next year unless a master contract agreement with the teachers' union has been ratified prior to the beginning of the normal school year. We assure you that students will be provided a full contingent of days of instruction, because the two week late start of school will be made up by taking an equivalent amount of days from the normal mid-year and spring vacation schedules."

It is important to note that the authors disagree on this particular tactic.

- Writing letters to the editor is another tactic that management is likely to face. In this case, friends of the teachers' union, although not identified as teachers from other districts or relatives of teachers, will write letters indicating that the board of education and the administration are unfair to the teachers. These letters will also indicate that the teachers are merely asking for wage and fringe benefits comparable to employees of other organizations, and that many of their union's proposals, such as a reduction in class size, are being proposed to improve the quality of education given the students of the district [18]. Management's most likely response is to have friends of the board of education, who are not identified as such, send letters to the editor supporting the board of education's views. These letters should indicate the fairness of the board of education's proposals, and the concern that the board of education has for fairness to the taxpayers and for the welfare of students and the school district's employees.

- Packing board of education meetings occurs when union members from other school districts act as if they are parents of students in the district or portray concerned citizens of the district. This is an especially effective technique when the state's sunshine laws call for open meetings and the bylaws of the board permit public comment during each officially called board of education meeting. The board of education's meeting agenda may not have a spot for negotiations-related discussion (most states with sunshine laws permit executive sessions for this purpose), but the audience can certainly ask critical questions or make derogatory statements when called upon by the board chairperson. Also, if the teachers and union members from other school districts report to the site early enough to fill the room so that no room remains for the general public or for supporters of the board of education's position, meeting control shifts to the advantage of the union and its supporters [19]. In all likelihood, the media will be tipped off in advance by the union; and both newspaper and TV media representatives will be present to record the proceedings of the board of education meeting. Management can probably only do two things in this situation: (1) ask each audience participant to respond as to whether or not they are a resident of the district and whether or not they are a teacher. In most cases, the person will not respond, but the media will at least get some message which can then be pursued after the meetings, and (2) pack the meeting with friends of the board of education's position.
- Have supporters hold informal neighborhood meetings sponsored by teachers or by teacher union supporters. The most likely tactic

that management can devise in this situation is to attempt to get a person who supports the board of education's position to attend the neighborhood meeting. This person should not be readily identified as a supporter of the board of education's position, and the person should report the content and tenor of the meeting to management. This information will assist management in developing countertactics to be used in the future [20].

Now that we have discussed some of the job actions and some of the tactics that may be used by a teachers' union prior to actually going on strike, and some of the potential countertactics that might be used by the board of education and its administrators, let's turn to the topic of a strike plan. The focus shall continue on a teachers' union and on management's planning [21].

PREPARING A STRIKE PLAN

Once a strike is evident, it is important that a comprehensive strike plan be developed and that this plan not be shared with many people until a strike actually occurs [22]. It would be wise to inform the board of education members and all administrators that a plan has been developed, and that a meeting will be called to share the details of that plan as soon as a strike takes place. It is suggested that the board members and the administrators be told that it is wise to keep the plan confidential to the last minute to avoid accidental leaks to the teachers' union of information about the details of the plan. It is suggested that only three persons have knowledge of the strike plan's details; and that those three persons be the board of education president, the superintendent of schools, and the chief negotiator of management's negotiating team.

A copy of an actual strike plan used by the board of education and management personnel in a Michigan school district during an illegal strike is replicated below. This plan was shared at a meeting with board of education members and with all administrative personnel when it was certain that a strike would take place. The identity of the district is purposely concealed. In this case, not only did the State of Michigan, in its collective bargaining law, prohibit strikes by public employees, but every prior master contractual agreement that was ratified, signed-off, and dated by both the union's officials and the board of education included a "no strike" clause as an article.

During any strike situation, administrators and board of education members are under a great deal of stress. Now that we have our strike plans in place, let's discuss the conduct of board of education members and administrators during the strike.

THE HARD PLACE: LONG HOURS, THE BIG STRESS TEST, AND PLAYING CHICKEN UNTIL THE END

During a long and very adversarial strike, participants will feel that they are between a rock and a hard place. Long hours will be the order of the day, as protecting the interest of the district on a twenty-four hour basis, while many times conducting all day and night meetings with the other party, will sap the energy of even the strongest participants. In addition, the stress level of the participants will be greatly increased because of disparaging remarks made by various members of the community and sensationalized reports presented in the media [23].

Finally, both parties will probably participate in a game of chicken (not revealing the final moves) until the last minute before settling the contract. The union will usually want an agreement that any charges against its members or its leaders will be dropped [24], and all salary improvements will be given retroactively [25]. Although the union will undoubtedly attempt to pressure the board and superintendent into a non-reprisal agreement, it is wise to have this decision made ahead of time. After all, illegal acts should not go unpunished; such action would show that the Board is selective as to which laws it supports. As role models they will be uncomfortable, but that comes with the job. With a courageous superintendent making the recommendations the pressure is somewhat off the board, they only have to support or deny support for upholding the law. The superintendent may wish to have the school board attorney frame the recommendations for the board. Charges against the union leaders may have to be made, and its leaders will be involved. The charges (if already made) may be dropped, but to expect no reprisal is inappropriate, when the law has clearly been violated. As for salary, none must be given retroactively. Any improvements conceded to will be made effective the day the strike ends and normalcy returns.

During this stressful period, it is important that management not portray the participating teachers or the union as villains; because once the strike is settled, the members of the community will still have to be supportive of teachers, administrators, and the board of education if the district is to survive a strike with the least amount of long-term damage [26].

It should be stated that the school district can request injunctive relief, or cease and desist orders from the courts. However, these orders are very seldom issued.

Finally, the strike has ended, the collective bargaining agreement has been presented by the union's leaders to its membership, and it has been ratified. Following this, the district's chief negotiator has presented the TA'd agreement to the board of education with the recommendation that it be ratified. After both parties have ratified it, the master contract agreement is signed and dated by the officials designated to represent both parties, and the immediate crisis comes to an end.

At both of the meetings to ratify, it is wise for the union leadership and the school district's chief negotiator to give credit to each other's professionalism and hard work. This will help end the adversarial relationship between the two parties; and it will bring some credibility to the settlement in the eyes of the general public.

Once the ratification activities and the summary speeches have been made, the district's management has to focus its maximum effort on repairing the damage done within the community and repairing the damage done within the employee group and between the employees and administrators and the board of education. The final discussion in this chapter focuses on the actions to be taken following the ending of a strike and the ratification of a master contractual agreement.

ACTIONS FOLLOWING A STRIKE

Once a strike is terminated, the efforts of both sides must focus on repairing the damage done by the strike. Some suggestions for repairing the damage done during a strike include:

- Immediately after the master contract agreement is printed, the chief negotiator and the superintendent of schools should have an all-day meeting with the administrators of the school district for the purpose of explaining every page and detail of the contract. If the intent of any language is unclear, that intent should be clarified at this meeting. A long question and answer period should be planned and added to the meeting's agenda. Sometimes the parties desire nebulous language that allows for flexibility in future dealings between the parties. In such a case, the language should not be clarified to any great extent. Occasionally there is unfavorable language that has appeared in past contracts and which is carried over into the current contractual agreement. In this case, the rule is to leave it alone if it hasn't caused problems [27].

- If there is unclear language that is of concern to management, a written memorandum should be sent to the union's chief negotiator clarifying management's intent of the language in the specific contract article(s) involved [28]. If the union does not disagree with management's interpretation, management's interpretation shall hold, until it is grieved and adjudicated differently.

- A meeting should be held between the superintendent of schools and the president of the union to see if there are actions that can quickly be taken to start building an environment of trust and respect between the union and management; and between teachers and administrators. Such tactics as having weekly meetings between the superintendent, the chief negotiator, selected administrative representatives, and the union leadership can help keep a continuous dialogue going. Also, both the union's leadership and management's leadership can create a series of curricular or other types of study committees comprised of teachers and administrators.

- Management and the union can devise means of publicly recognizing the excellent contributions of individual teachers and other employees.

- Management's leadership and the union's leadership can join together with members of visible community groups to assist in community projects. These types of efforts will display to the community members the camaraderie between the school district's administrators, the board of education's members, and the union leaders, and will display the willingness of all school district related parties to participate in activities that will improve the community at large.

- Finally, union and management leadership should encourage all their members to be involved in devising innovative means of recognizing the value of one anothers' members, and in devising creative ways of redeveloping community support for the school district's schools, for the school district's employees, and for the board of education [29–31].

SUMMARY

The worst-case scenario in collective bargaining is that of a strike, which creates an unfortunate and unhappy environment for all members of a school district, including the community. Emotionalism and hostility can mark the experience, and the damage may take years to heal. However, when facing the inevitable, administrators must operate with the intent of damage containment. Preparation is critical; "What-if" job action scenarios that must be considered are sick outs, work-to-rule actions, nonfulfillment of after-hour activities, and picketing. Management responses to these tactics include substitute teacher and co-curricular sponsor hiring, assignment of administrators to teaching duties, the provision of public relations to assuage the adverse parental/community reaction, and the release of accurate and persuasive information to the media.

Other union tactics include the spread of a strike rumor, media editorials claiming administrative contract inadequacies or mistreatment of employees, packing board meetings with union-sympathetic citizen input commentary, and holding informal neighborhood meetings to sway public opinion. Management responses to these tactics include publicizing late-summer contingency plans to delay the opening of school, responsive and proactive media editorials, calling for identification of public speakers (who are frequently union activists or nonresident "plants") at board meetings, packing those meetings with supporters of the board's position, and infiltrating, for observational and reporting purposes, the neighborhood meetings.

If a strike is imminent, a comprehensive strike plan should be developed, with details being available to only a few administrators to minimize leakage of tactical details. A copy of an actual strike plan used in a Michigan district outlined recommended critical tactics and strategies. Both an administrative and public "hotline" must be established for rumor and information clearinghouse purposes. Building administrators must file a daily report on teacher or picket presence. Questions or visits from the media are to be supervised and reported, and all contacts with union members recorded and reported.

Clear lines of communication to the attorneys, board president, and other governmental agencies must be drawn, with official spokespersons identified. Any services for which the district has contracted or is providing to non-public schools must be rearranged, if necessary. Contingency plans to provide for emergency student supervision if employees do not report for work or leave early, and financial/employment arrangements made for any necessary layoffs of non-striking employees and for payroll adjustment of fringe benefits. Security must be provided if all buildings close down completely, and incidents, such as unruly picketing, fully documented. If the strike appears likely to continue for a period of time, then long-term arrangements must be made for downsizing costs and for alternate provision of instruction.

Whatever the outcome of a strike, it is a stressful and damaging process, and its conclusion must lay the groundwork for repairs to begin. Adequate question and answer meetings must be held for all administrators; collaborative meetings between the superintendent and union president should focus on planning mutual trust-building activities, individual teacher and administrator contributions should be recognized, and visible effort made for both sides to join with community groups in mutual projects.

EXERCISES

1. As a building administrator, what contingency procedures could you employ in dealing with sick outs, work-to-rule actions, or nonfulfillment of sponsorship activities?

2. Create an emergency administrative plan for notifying key media personnel and community members about a pending strike. What proactive information could be supplied for the editorial pages?

3. Visualize your board of education meeting's format and procedures, and devise a contingency plan to control citizen input and attendance problems.

4. Create a communications chart, indicating lines of connection and authorized official statement sources for your district's administrators.

5. With reference to a particular school in your district, create a step-by-step emergency plan to supervise students in case of a mid-morning teacher walkout.

6. What would be the most productive ways for teachers/employees and administrators in your district to come together in the "repair" process after a strike?

7. Review the strike plan presented in this chapter, and decide whether or not you agree with each item presented.

8. What would you add, delete, or modify to improve the strike plan presented in this chapter?

REFERENCES

1. Doherty, R. E. and W. E. Oberer. 1967. *Teachers, School Boards, and Collective Bargaining: A Changing of the Guard.* Ithaca, NY: New York State School of Industrial and Labor Relations, Cornell University, p. 120.

2. Streshly, W. A. and T. A. DeMitchell. 1994. *Teacher Unions and TQE,* Thousand Oaks, CA: Corwin Press, Sage Publications, pp. 11–13.

3. Donley, M. O., Jr. 1976. *Power to the Teacher.* Bloomington, IN: Indiana University Press, p. 109.

4. Webster, W. G., Sr. 1985. *Effective Collective Bargaining in Public Education.* Ames, IA: Iowa State University Press, p. 168.

5. Braun, R. J. 1972. *Teachers and Power—The Story of the American Federation of Teachers.* New York, NY: Simon and Schuster, pp. 107, 112.

6. Kerchner, C. T. 1988. "A New Generation of Teacher Unionism," *Education Digest,* L111 (9): 52–54.

7. Bascia, N. 1994. *Unions in Teachers' Professional Lives: Social, Intellectual, and Practical Concerns,* New York: Teachers College Press: pp. 1–8.

8. Murphy, M. 1990. *Blackboard Unions—The AFT & the NEA 1900–1980.* Ithaca, NY. Cornell University Press, p. 226.

9. Castetter, W. B. 1996. *The Human Resource Function in Educational Administration.* 6th ed. Englewood Cliffs, NJ: Merrill, pp. 583–585.

10. Doherty, R. E. and W. E. Oberer. 1967. *Teachers,* p. 100.

11. Ibid.

12. Webster, W. G., Sr. 1985. *Effective Collective Bargaining,* p. 167.

13. Braun, R. J. 1972. *Teachers and Power,* pp. 112–113.

14. Ibid.

15. Doherty, R. E. and W. E. Oberer. 1967. *Teachers,* p. 297.

16. Herman, J. J. and G. E. Megiveron. 1993. *Collective Bargaining in Education: Win/Win, Win/Lose, Lose/Lose.* Lancaster, PA: Technomic Publishing Co. Inc., pp. 132–135.

17. Webster, W. G., Sr. 1985. *Effective Collective Bargaining,* p. 52.

18. Webster, W. G., Sr. 1985. *Effective Collective Bargaining,* pp. 167–168.

19. Braun, R. J. 1972. *Teachers and Power,* pp. 112–113.

20. Donley, M. O., Jr. 1976. *Power to the Teacher,* p. 109.

21. Herman, J. J. and G. E. Megiveron. 1993. *Collective Bargaining in Education,* pp. 135–137.

22. Castetter, W. B. 1986. *The Personnel Function in Education.* New York, NY: Macmillan Publishing Company, pp. 170–171.

23. Smith, S. C., D. Ball, and D. Liontos. 1990. *Working Together—The Collaborative Style of Bargaining.* Eugene, OR: ERIC Clearinghouse on Educational Management, University of Oregon, p. 18.

24. Webster, W. G., Sr. 1985. *Effective Collective Bargaining,* p. 168.

25. Helsby, R. D., J. Tener, and J. Lefkowitz, eds. 1985. *The Evolving Process—Collective Negotiations in Public Employment.* Fort Washington, PA: Labor Relations Press, p. 416.

26. Webster, W. G., Sr. 1985. *Effective Collective Bargaining,* p. 168.

27. Webster, W. G., Sr. 1985. *Effective Collective Bargaining,* pp. 134–135.

28. Elkouri, F. and E. A. Elkouri. 1973. *How Arbitration Works.* Third Edition. Washington, D.C.: Bureau of National Affairs, Inc., pp. 296, 303.

29. Smith, S. C., D. Ball, and D. Liontos. 1990. *Working Together,* pp. 58–59.

30. Miron, L. F. and R. K. Wimpelberg. 1992. "The Role of School Boards in the Governance of Education." In *School Boards: Changing Local Control,* edited by P. F. First and H. J. Walberg. Berkeley, CA: McCutchan Publishing, p. 170.

31. Herman, J. J. and G. E. Megiveron. 1993. *Collective Bargaining in Education,* pp. 139–141.

Finalizing and Communicating the Signed Master Contract

CHAPTER 12 discusses the topics of reaching a Tentative Agreement (TA), presenting the contract for ratification, and printing and publicizing the contract document. The chapter ends with a summary, exercises, and references.

The negotiations between the union and management may be of short duration, or may be very lengthy and drawn out. The negotiations may result in settlement of the contract without assistance from third parties, or become a situation in which both parties experience a long and bitter impasse, causing them to go through the impasse procedures of mediation, fact-finding, and arbitration. Also, the negotiations may be of a serious adversarial nature, or may have taken place within a collaborative win-win negotiating environment [1].

Regardless of the length and character of the negotiations, the union's negotiating team and management's negotiating team, sooner or later, end the at-the-table negotiating by TA'ing (Tentatively Agreeing) to a comprehensive master contract document [2]. At this point, while there is a sigh of relief that the negotiation has been concluded, there is anticipation of the relative difficulty of presenting and recommending the TA'd master contract to the total union membership for a vote and to the board of education for ratification at a formally called board of education meeting [3].

REACHING TENTATIVE AGREEMENT ON A CONTRACT

Let's pause for a moment and examine two word scenarios of how the TA'ing of the master contract probably came about. The first scenario will outline the steps leading to a TA within a win-win negotiating environment, and the second will outline the steps leading to a TA within a severely adversarial union/management environment [4].

The path to reaching a TA within a win-win environment, regardless of the time expended, requires a serious, hard working, and trusting effort by the union's negotiating team and management's negotiating team [5]. In fact, if one could view the meetings through a window, it would be difficult, if not impossible, to determine which persons at the meeting represented the union and which represented management.

As subgroups—comprised of members of both union and management—present their findings and recommendations to the total body, and as joint minutes are kept, which provide the official reference document of prior discussions, the two parties end up agreeing on each contractual article's content and wording [6].

At the point of agreement on each article, both parties may officially vote a tentative agreement on the specific article upon which agreement has been reached, or there may merely be a general agreement that the article is acceptable in form and content. In some instances, the chief negotiator for both the union and management will officially sign and date each article as tentative agreement is reached on that specific article. On the other hand, the parties may wait until the entire contractual document is in its finalized and agreed-to form before TA'ing the entire master contract agreement. At this point, the chief negotiators for both parties will definitely sign and date two copies of the TA'd agreement, with one copy kept by the union's negotiating team and the other copy retained by management's negotiating team [7,8].

The path to achieving a tentative agreement within a severe adversarial environment will probably be a very long, stressful, negative, and sometimes painful experience. It will usually begin by high ball and low ball proposals being presented (an example would be the union asking for a twenty percent increase in salary each year of a proposed three-year contract, and management responding by proposing a one-year contract and a one percent salary increase for that contract year). Also, even though this may be the renewal of a master contractual agreement [9], preceded by fifteen years of prior master contractual agreements between the two parties, every single one of the twenty (or possibly as many as fifty) contract articles will have to be renegotiated, because each article in the master contract has proposed changes—thus reopening negotiations on the entire master contract agreement.

Since both parties remain very adversarial and antagonistic to one another, and since there is a lack of trust present in both parties, many long, vociferous, and vituperative negotiating sessions result in very little progress. After months of meetings and a great deal of positioning and posturing in the community and in the media, an impasse is declared. A mediator is assigned by the state's PERB (Public Employment Relations Board) [10].

The mediator meets separately with both parties and discovers that a personality conflict exists between the chief negotiators for the union and management, and practically no agreements have been reached on any contract article [11]. At this point in one particular case, the mediator considered informing both parties that she/he would not return to assist in resolving the impasse until the parties had narrowed the points of contention to no more than three areas [12]. However, the mediator decided to attempt to assist, even though the entire contract remained in contention.

The mediator, after meeting with both parties, called a joint meeting. During this meeting the mediator informed them of the collective bargaining laws and of the purpose and process of mediation. The mediator also warned both parties that she/he would only continue to meet with them if continuing progress towards settlement was being made [13]. Following this joint meeting, the mediator again met separately with both parties.

When the mediator met with the union's negotiating team, she/he discovered that even though the team had initially requested a three-year contract with a twenty percent increase in salary demanded for each year of the contract, they did this with the idea of splitting the difference with the management team. This tactic would, the team hoped, produce a ten percent to a twelve percent raise, and the union could prove that it gave up more of its initial request than management if the ten percent raise were the settlement point [14]. Also, the union identified the proposal by management to increase the rigidity of the employee evaluation procedure as an area where it would absolutely not compromise [15].

When the mediator met with management's negotiating team, she/he discovered that the team didn't really expect to settle the contract for a one percent increase in salary, but was reacting to the ridiculously high twenty percent per year for each of the three years proposed by the union's team. Also, the mediator discovered that management's negotiating team would also prefer a three-year contract, but the team countered with a one-year contract proposal because the union's team proposed a three-year contract. Management's team felt this approach would give them some flexibility for future trade-offs [16]. Finally, the mediator discovered that management's negotiating team was under a strict board of education guideline that the employee evaluation system and its accompanying contract language had to be strengthened.

The mediator met many times with both parties in joint sessions, and she/he finally was able to receive some flexibility from both parties in two areas: (1) both union and management agreed that the length of the contract would be a flexible area for future discussion, and (2) the union reduced its salary increase demand to fifteen percent per year for each year of the contract length under agreement, and management increased its salary increase offer to three percent per year for each year of the contract length under agreement. All other matters remained in contention, and the mediator pulled out of the district, while indicating to both parties and to PERB that she/he had assisted as much as possible [17].

At this point a fact-finder was called into the district to collect the facts and write a fact-finder's report [18]. Since neither party had to accept the fact-finder's report and recommendations for settlement, this fact-finding was voluntary.

Upon entry into the school district, the fact-finder established a hearing. At this hearing, each party presented its evidence and rationale for its position on each unresolved issue. The fact-finder accepted the written documents and recorded the oral presentations, then allowed post-hearing briefs to be filed within two weeks of the hearing. The fact-finder also indicated that the written fact-finding report would be issued within one month of receipt of the written post-hearing briefs [19]. Although the fact-finder dealt with all issues in contention, let us address three areas as examples of recommendations made by the fact-finder in the written report. The fact-finder recommended that a (1) a six percent raise be given for each year of the contract, which would keep the district's employees' salary ranking sixth out of the twenty-one comparable districts; (2) the master contract would be two years in length; and (3) the language related to employee evaluation was to remain the same as that in the prior master contractual agreement, which had just expired.

Since neither union or management accepted the fact-finder's recommendations, the fact-finder published his findings and recommendations in the newspaper that covered the school district. This technique was used at this stage of impasse in order to let the general public know the exact condition of the current negotiations and the recommendations made by the fact-finder to resolve the items that remained unresolved [20]. This technique was utilized to allow the general public to bring pressure on both parties to settle the contract.

Since neither party accepted the fact-finder's recommendations, and the community was vociferously condemning the board members, the administration, and the teachers for not settling their expired master contractual agreement, both parties agreed to contact AAA (American Arbitration Association) for the assistance of an arbitration panel. Both parties agreed that the panel would be selected from the names submitted by the AAA, with the union selecting one member, management selecting the other member, and the third arbitrator being selected by agreement between the union and management [21]. However, it was agreed that if no agreement could be reached on the third arbitrator, the other two arbitrators selected would select the third arbitrator.

The AAA submitted a list of potential arbitrators, and both teams, who were experienced in negotiations, did research on the prior arbitration rulings of each of the arbitrators who were submitted. After both parties had stricken numerous names from the original list, the arbitration panel was selected and the arbitration hearing was conducted [22].

Because of the history of bad relations between union and management in this district, the arbitration panel and the parties agreed that a court recorder would be hired and each party would pay for one-half of the cost of the recorder and five sets of transcripts (one for each member of the arbitration panel, one for the union, and one for management) [23]. Each person who testified at the hearing did so under oath. At the hearing each party reviewed its perception of the history of the negotiations up to this point, presented written evidence that supported its position on each item in contention, and orally presented the rationale and data defending its position. Cross-examinations were permitted, and the arbitration panel permitted post-hearing briefs [24].

Within four weeks of receipt of the post-hearing briefs and the verbatim transcript of the arbitration hearing, the arbitration panel provided its rulings on each master contract item that remained unresolved. At this point, both parties' negotiating teams, tiring of the long and unpleasant negotiations, agreed to bring the arbitration panel's recommendations to their referent groups with recommendations for approval. The union met with its membership, its negotiating team made its case for acceptance, and management's negotiating team recommended to the board of education that it accept the arbitration panel's recommendation [25]. In each case, the teacher membership and the board of education agreed to the recommendations of the arbitration panel, but they held final ratification approval until they had the entire newly written contract in their hands for an adequate time period prior to a vote for contract ratification.

PRESENTING THE MASTER CONTRACT
FOR RATIFICATION

The union's chief negotiator, the union's president, and the union's negotiating team would do well to plan its strategy and tactics for presentation of the master contractual agreement in advance [26]. This advance planning is important regardless of whether tentative agreement is attained at the negotiating table or at any other stage of the impasse procedures [27]. To use the teachers, again, as an example, it is important that the union's leadership come out strongly in favor of ratification, for if they do not, the contract agreement may be voted down [28].

Depending on the attitude of the union leadership, they will either strongly sell a contract agreement they feel is the best compromise agreement they could negotiate during the current negotiations, or they may present the TA'd agreement without recommendation if they feel the need to leave the decision totally in the hands of the general membership [29]. Finally, because of increasing pressure, due to public condemnation of both parties, or because of having already passed through all of the impasse procedures, the union leadership may agree to bring the recommendations to the total membership, but behind closed doors recommend that the membership reject the proposed contract and request a strike vote authorization [30].

The strategy and tactics utilized by the union's leadership will vary depending on the outcome they desire when the contract is presented to the total membership. In general, if the leadership wishes ratification, it will not permit dissidents to speak prior to making the sales pitch, and the leadership will limit the time for questions. Also, the leadership will not submit the written TA's to the membership, as it is easy to quibble over words in a lengthy document; rather they will provide an overview of the gains they have received for the membership and ask for a ratification vote [31,32].

Since the union usually ratifies the TA'd agreement before the board of education does (this procedure is wise because the union leadership may not be willing to sell the agreement and the membership may refuse to ratify it), the management's chief negotiator, the superintendent of schools, and management's negotiating team will await the result of the teacher union's general membership vote before approaching the board of education. Obviously, if the teacher union's general membership refuses to ratify the TA'd contract, it is back to the bargaining table, or back to an impasse procedure; and there is no reason to make a presentation to the board of education [33].

Assuming, however, that the teacher union's general membership has ratified the contract, the board of education should then be presented with the TA'd agreement, and management's chief negotiator, the superintendent of schools, and management's negotiating team members should strongly support ratification. In the case of the three example items presented earlier, the board would probably be told of the hard fought, at-the-table battles and how this is the best agreement they could get during this round of negotiations [34].

On the three specific example items, the board of education members might very well be told the following: (1) The salary increase is well within the district's ability to pay, it keeps the district in its relative salary position in relation to the other comparable districts, and it maintains a salary level that is sufficiently attractive for recruitment of new employees. (2) The two-year contract is better than a one-year contract because it keeps the district out of contract negotiations and away from potential harm for a two-year period rather than a single year. It also allows expenditure predictability for budget planning purposes for two years into the future [35]. (3) The lack of movement to agree caused the resultant retention of the expiring master contract's language related to the employee evaluation article. This was the best that could be achieved during the current negotiations, and established an emphatic negotiating position and an agenda of items for future negotiations. This last item would have to be a very hard sell, since this was a serious demand under the guidelines provided the negotiating team by the board of education [36,37].

Immediately after, the board of education would agree to ratify the contract in executive session (which is legal for the purposes of discussing negotiations-related items in most states that possess both collective bargaining and sunshine law statutes) [38]. The board would come into public session during a legally constituted board of education meeting. At this time, the chief negotiator and the superintendent of schools publicly request ratification by the board of education for this fair compromise, which would become the master contractual agreement governing union/management actions for the next two-year period [39]. At this public meeting, much praise would be given to the members of both negotiating teams for their hard work at arriving at a fair and equitable master contract. Obviously, the media would attend this meeting; and the union's leadership, management's leadership, and the board members should echo the congratulations to both teams for all their efforts and express their pleasure over reaching a fair and equitable settlement. At this point, the contract is moved to the printing stage [40].

PRINTING AND PUBLICIZING THE CONTRACT

Once both parties have ratified the contract, the actual contractual document will be printed and distributed. It is common for the board of education to take responsibility for seeing that the document is typed, carefully proofread, and printed. It is also common for the union and the board of education to equally share the cost of producing the printed contract document.

At this stage a caution is offered. Print the contract in an awkward size, which will prohibit female union members from carrying it around in their purse, and male union members from keeping a copy handy in their pants pocket. If the climate continues to be an adversarial one between the union and management, the less ready access that each employee has to the printed master contractual agreement, the less probability of an increased magnitude of contract grievances being filed. Once the contract has been printed, it is important that management's chief negotiator and the superintendent of schools meet with all of the school district's administrators to go over each page and each word of the ratified master contractual agreement [41]. At this meeting, the specific wording should be discussed as well as the intent of the contract wording, and all questions that the administrators may have will be answered. This is an important meeting, because the management of the negotiated master contractual agreement is as important, if not more important, than the act of negotiating the master contractual agreement.

On the other hand, a similar procedure should be followed by the union's chief negotiator and the president of the local union. This meeting should be conducted for the union's stewards—the dialogue should explain the intent of all the contract's wording and a good deal of time should be spent on answering procedural questions related to the responsibility of the union's stewards under the ratified master contractual agreement [42].

In addition, union leaders, administrative officials, and board of education members should contact the media and/or respond to media queries in a manner that will place the agreement, the employees, the administrators, and the board of education in the best possible light. For once the negotiations are completed, it is important that all parties work hard to repair any damage done between union and management. It is also important that community support is retained at the highest possible level [43].

The best way to achieve both of these results is to make certain that the students of the district are well served instructionally and cared for as valued young people. It should be clear to all parties that schools were not created to provide jobs for teachers and other union and non-unionized employees, or for board of education members or administrators. The only reason that any school district exists is to educate youngsters, and the quality of that education and the obvious caring concern for students is the best approach to creating a positive school district environment. This is also the best way to obtain and increase community support for the school district, the individual schools, and the people who are employees of the school district.

SUMMARY

The negotiations process, whether lengthy, adversarial, mediated, or win-win and collaborative, usually ends with Tentative Agreement to a comprehensive master contract document. This recommended contract is then submitted to total union membership and to the board of education for a ratification vote.

Two scenarios can characterize this Tentative Agreement process. Reaching a TA within a win-win environment is accomplished through a shared effort in an environment of trust. Information is collaboratively collected and analyzed, and joint minutes kept. This collegial process results in an agreement that may be generally approved, or approved article by article, prior to TA'ing the entire master contract agreement.

Achieving Tentative Agreement within a severe adversarial environment will most likely be a long and stressful process. Extreme proposal items (high ball and low ball) may be introduced by both sides, and every single one of the existing contract articles may be reopened for negotiation. The bargaining sessions may be marked by discord, personal dissent, and unfavorable media coverage. Impasse may be declared, and a mediator assigned by the PERB may have to direct the parties to narrow the points of contention. Joint and separate meetings with the parties are conducted, during which time the mediator may be able to discover the real threshold of proposal items, and determine the range of flexibility for eventual settlement.

Despite this intervention, contract matters may still remain in contention, and a fact-finder may be called upon to investigate the evidence and rationales for each unresolved issue. Recommendations are then made by the fact-finder with regard to each area of contention, and, upon the decline of the recommendation package by both parties (the example being one of non-binding arbitration), the package is publicized by the fact-finder to bring public pressure to bear on both sides.

Both parties may then agree to request the assistance of an arbitrator or an arbitration panel. After the selection of arbitrators (after investigation of their arbitration records by both parties), a hearing is held. Each side reviews its perceptions of the process and presents written and oral evidence to support proposal rationales and data. Cross-examination of witnesses and the submission of post-hearing briefs may be permitted. The arbitration panel provides rulings on each master contract item that remains unresolved, and union ratification and board approval can follow.

The presentation of the master contractual agreement requires strategy on the part of the union leadership, depending on the leaders' assessment of the document. They may strongly recommend ratification (limiting the amount and detail of member input and inquiry), or withhold recommendation without actually condemning the document, thereby leaving the issue up to the membership. In response to public pressure to settle, they may bring a public recommendation for ratification to the total membership, but may privately recommend rejection and a strike vote authorization.

Usually, it is advisable that the recommendation and union ratification process precedes that of the board, in case of non-ratification and a return to impasse procedure. Following union ratification, the board is then presented with management's recommendation to approve the agreement, accompanied by details as to the contract items' cost and non-cost impacts. Appropriate media information and management/ union visible support should follow the ratification of the contract.

The costs for printing and distribution of the contract are usually shared by union and management, and meetings should be held wherein management's chief negotiator, the superintendent, and all administrators discuss the contractual wording intent and implementation and procedural detail of the agreement. A similar procedure should be followed by the union's leadership and stewards.

EXERCISES

1. Visualize a win-win negotiation scenario in your district, and describe the group members, subcommittees, information search collaborations, and joint media release procedures that could occur during negotiations, impasse procedures, and ratification procedures.

2. Investigate the public record on any mediated adversarial negotiations session in your district or a neighboring district. Trace the process through the stages of impasse, mediation, fact-finding, and arbitration.

3. Obtain a copy of a master contract from a school district, and review the individual articles. What strategies could have been utilized to "sell" the items to the board and to the community?

4. Investigate the arbitration process in your state. What is the linkage with the American Arbitration Association?

5. What public channels of information could the union and management use to co-publicize a new contract and what strategies would convince the public that the parties intend to work together collaboratively under the new agreement?

REFERENCES

1. Cimini, M. H., S. L. Behrmann, and E. M. Johnson. 1994. "Labor-Management Bargaining in 1993," *Monthly Labor Review,* 117(1): 20–33.

2. Helsby, R. D., J. Tener, and J. Lefkowitz, eds. 1985. *The Evolving Process— Collective Negotiations in Public Employment.* Fort Washington, PA: Labor Relations Press, p. 413.

3. Herman, J. J. 1991. "The Two Faces of Collective Bargaining," *School Business Affairs,* 57(2): 12.

4. Nyland, L. 1987. "Win-Win Bargaining Pays Off," *Education Digest.* L111(1): 28–29.

5. Huber, J. and J. Hennies. 1987. "Fix on These Five Guiding Lights and Emerge from the Bargaining Fog," *School Board Journal,* 174(3): 31.

6. Tait, R. C. 1995. "Contract Negotiations Without Ill Will," *School Administrator,* 52(9): 30–31.

7. Herman, J. J. 1991. "The Two Faces," p. 12.

8. Koppich, J. E. 1993. "Getting Started." In *A Union of Professionals: Labor Relations and Educational Reform,* edited by Kerchner, C. T. and J. E. Koppich. New York: Teachers College Press, pp. 194–195.

9. Neal, R. 1980. *Bargaining Tactics—A Reference Manual for Public Sector Labor Negotiations.* Richard G. Neal Associates, pp. 158–159.

10. Brock, J. 1982. *Bargaining Beyond Impasse—Joint Resolution of Public Sector Labor Disputes.* Boston, MA: Auburn House Publishing Company, pp. 13–16.

11. Neal, R. 1980. *Bargaining Tactics,* p. 66.

12. Brock, J. 1982. *Bargaining Beyond Impasse,* pp. 155–156.

13. Helsby, R. D., J. Tener, and J. Lefkowitz, eds. 1985. *The Evolving Process,* pp. 236–238.

14. Neal, R. 1980. *Bargaining Tactics,* pp. 158–159.

15. Rynecki, S. B. and J. H. Lindquist. 1988. "Teacher Evaluation and Collective Bargaining—A Management Perspective," *Journal of Law & Education,* 17(3): 489–490.

16. Aaron, B., J. M. Najita, and J. L. Stern. 1988. *Public Sector Bargaining.* Washington, D.C.: Industrial Relations Research Associates, p. 148.

17. Webster, W. G., Sr. 1985. *Effective Collective Bargaining in Public Education.* Ames, IA: Iowa State University Press, p. 161.

18. Zack, Arnold. 1980. *Understanding Fact Finding and Arbitration in the Public Sector.* Washington, D.C.: U.S. Department of Labor, Labor Management Services Administration, pp. 8–13.

19. Zack, Arnold. 1980. *Understanding Fact Finding,* pp. 50–51, 89–91.

20. Zack, Arnold. 1980. *Understanding Fact Finding,* pp. 90–91.

21. Elkouri, F. and E. A. Elkouri. 1973. *How Arbitration Works.* Third Edition. Washington, D.C.: Bureau of National Affairs, Inc., pp. 88–89.

22. Neal, R. 1980. *Bargaining Tactics,* pp. 117–118.

23. Neal, R. 1980. *Bargaining Tactics,* pp. 217–218.

24. Neal, R. G. 1988. "At Arbitration Hearings, Justice Favors the Well Prepared," *Executive Educator,* 10(11): 17.

25. Coleman, C. J. 1990. *Managing Labor Relations in the Public Sector.* San Francisco, CA: Jossey-Bass Publishers, pp. 222–223.

26. Herman, J. J. 1991. "The Two Faces," p. 12.

27. Helsby, R. D., J. Tener, and J. Lefkowitz, eds. 1985. *The Evolving Process,* p. 237.

28. Webster, W. G., Sr. 1985. *Effective Collective Bargaining,* p. 25.

29. Maier, M. M. 1987. *City Unions.* New Brunswick, NJ: Rutgers University Press, p. 157.

30. Ibid.

31. Helsby, R. D., J. Tener, and J. Lefkowitz, eds. 1985. *The Evolving Process,* pp. 59–60.

32. Eberts, R. W., and J. A. Stone. 1984. *Unions and Public Schools.* Lexington, MA: D.C. Heath and Company, p. 175.

33. Castetter, W. B. 1996. *The Human Resource Function in Educational Administration.* 6th ed. Englewood Cliffs, NJ: Merrill, pp. 586–588.

34. Herman, J. J. 1991. "The Two Faces," p. 12.

35. Muhl, C. 1995. "Collective Bargaining in State and Local Government, 1994." *Monthly Labor Review,* 118(6): 13–17.

36. Castetter, W. B. 1996. *The Human Resource Function,* pp. 586–588.

37. Cimini, M. H. 1994. "Negotiated Changes in State and Local Government Contracts, 1993." *Monthly Labor Review,* 117(8): 3–10.

38. Feiock, R. C. and J. P. West. 1990. "Public Presence at Collective Bargaining: Effects on Process and Decisions in Florida," *Journal of Collective Negotiations,* 19(1): 69–70.

39. Helsby, R. D., J. Tener, and J. Lefkowitz, eds. 1985. *The Evolving Process,* p. 228.

40. Herman, J. J. and G. E. Megiveron. 1993. *Collective Bargaining in Education: Win/Win, Win/Lose, Lose/Lose.* Lancaster, PA: Technomic Publishing Co. Inc., pp. 151–152.

41. Smith, S. C., D. Ball, and D. Liontos. 1990. *Working Together—The Collaborative Style of Bargaining.* Eugene, OR: ERIC Clearinghouse on Educational Management, University of Oregon, p. 59.

42. Brock, J. 1982. *Bargaining Beyond Impasse,* pp. 80–81.

43. Herman, J. J. 1991. "The Two Faces," pp. 12–13.

Contract Management: Living with the Contract That Has Been Negotiated

CHAPTER 13 will include discussions on communicating and interpreting the contract during its operational stage; training the administrators in contract management; setting and breaking precedents; disciplining for contract violations; insubordination, incompetence, and disciplining progressively; and the contractual items of providing due process, establishing just cause, preparing for grievance arbitration of the active contract (voluntary or mandatory), and following grievance procedural steps. Paying for the grievance arbitrator and related expenses, the handling of employee grievances, and union class grievances are covered and an example of a contractual grievance clause is included. Information is also provided on how to judge by the lowest common denominator, and how to observe time limits. Also included: a checklist for a grievance arbitration hearing, information on how to follow contractual procedures for grievance resolutions, and how to establish a continuing win-win union/management working environment. The chapter concludes with a summary, exercises, and references.

COMMUNICATING AND INTERPRETING THE RATIFIED CONTRACT DURING ITS OPERATIONAL STAGE

Once the contract has been finalized and all articles have been TA'd (Tentatively Agreed), management needs to call the entire management team together and go over the contract to bring about a basic understanding of the document. In some districts, this is done in a joint meeting with the Board and administration. In other districts, the Board needs to review first. Then, with approval, the superintendent and the chief negotiator present the contents to the administrators. The communication between the chief negotiator and the management team at this point should be an overview to the document and its implications.

It is not, at this unratified stage, a full-scale review of every article and item in the contract.

It often happens that union and management leaders expend great energies on the negotiation of a new or replacement master contract document, and once the new contract has been ratified, they breathe a sigh of relief and go into a long rest period and relax from the rigors of negotiations. This is a *big mistake*. A well-managed contract will prevent grievances from developing and facilitate labor/management relations, and will eventually provide a positive labor/management attitude when the parties head into successor contractual negotiations.

Good contract management is a very important element in the overall collective bargaining agenda, and the first step is that of communicating and interpreting the contract [1,2]. Once the newly negotiated master contract agreement has been printed and distributed to employees, administrators, media, and significant community groups, a central authority, such as the chief negotiator or the director of personnel, should meet with all administrators and any media groups or community groups who request further discussion or interpretation of the contract [3]. Of course the employees' union should do the same with its membership.

Interpreting the contract is something different from communicating the contract to the administration. This is done after both sides have ratified the contract. Once ratified, the document must be explained to the managers to leave less room for individual interpretation of the contents.

During a series of meetings with all the school district's administrators, the central authority should review the contract page by page and word by word [4,5]. There should be lengthy question and answer periods, if necessary, where questions are answered and interpretations are provided by the central authority. If there are numerous questions about the interpretation of a specific article, it is wise for the central authority, immediately following the meeting, to forward a written memo to all administrators clarifying the article in question. In addition, it should be made clear to every administrator that should a grievance occur, or should there be a further question about interpretation, the administrator must, before answering, contact the central authority for interpretation. This is the only method of consistently ensuring uniform interpretations of the negotiated contract's articles and wording. Some things that need to be highlighted include the glossary of terms, an explanation of the background for each item's inclusion, timelines used, applicability of individual interpretation, avoidance of misapplication, and the necessity of following the exact wording. In order to avoid erosion of the contract, any doubt about the meaning of an item or attention of a term calls for the chief negotiator's immediate attention and clarification.

Now that the importance of communicating and interpreting the negotiated master contractual agreement has been discussed, let's focus a little more closely on some of the specific items that should be stressed with the school district's administrators, who will be responsible for implementing and interpreting the ratified master contract on a day-to-day basis [6].

TRAINING THE ADMINISTRATORS IN CONTRACT MANAGEMENT

Training the district's administrators in contract management is not a one-shot event. If the negotiated master contractual document is perceived as an instructional tool, it should be treated as such when the chief negotiator or the director of personnel meets with the district's administrators [7,8]. Everything in the contract document can and usually does impact all aspects of the district's operations. It impacts the budget, decision making, student instruction, personnel policies and procedures, the allocation of time and of personnel, and, frequently, student relations and public relations [9,10].

How well the administrators—especially the building principals in the case of teachers who are members of a union—administer the contract at the site level pretty much determines the school climate at it relates to teachers and students. If the contract is administered well, an effective working relationship between the teachers and the principal will be maintained. This effective working relationship will ensure accountability for both teacher and principal actions under the master contract. If, however, the administration of the contract is weak, day-to-day relationships will become strained, a proliferation of grievances will probably result, many of the contract's articles will be violated, and numerous unintended precedents will be established that will affect the next round of contract negotiations.

During these training sessions, the areas that should be thoroughly explored, discussed, and interpreted are those which practically every administrator will have a duty to interpret during the term of life of the negotiated master contract. These high stress areas will definitely include most of the following articles for most employee unions, and they will include all of them for a teachers' union [11]:

- union rights
- managements rights
- academic freedom
- employee assignments
- employee transfer
- employee evaluation
- unit membership
- grievance process

In addition, school site administrators must be careful not to cause complications in administering the contract. Things to avoid include:

- attempting to negotiate at the school site level
- resolving grievances without first checking with the district's chief negotiator or the director of personnel
- interpreting a master contract clause that is being questioned by an employee or the union without first checking with the district's chief negotiator or the director of personnel
- giving the impression that they are anti-union or opposed to the terms of the negotiated master contract
- allowing themselves to be intimidated by a strong willed employee or union official from taking action that is called for within the negotiated master contract
- circumventing the school district's policies or the intent of the articles in the negotiated master contract for the purpose of enhancing her/his personal popularity [12]

In addition to the regularly scheduled contractual training sessions, management's chief negotiator or the director of personnel should initiate a newsletter for the school district's administrators providing information about any activity, any change in board of education policy, and any contract interpretation about which union and management disagree and which may impact the day-to-day interpretation of the contract [13]. Only by taking contract management as a serious and important function [14], and only by perceiving contract management as an ongoing activity during the entire term of the negotiated master contract, will the contract be competently and consistently administered. And only by consistently managing the contract will problems be avoided and positive union/management relations be improved and retained.

Once the training regimen has been established, management should be constantly on the alert for precedent setting activities. A permanent place on the administrative agenda should be reserved for review of any recent actions (grievance or otherwise) that develop, and a rapid information dispersal system made accessible to the chief negotiator. Precedents can certainly influence arbitration decisions if grievances arise, and they can add complexity to the next round of contract negotiations. Also, the chief negotiator must constantly stay in touch with the union officers to make sure that the interpretations are agreed upon by the union leadership [15].

ESTABLISHING AND BREAKING PRECEDENTS

Past practice is a term used when a certain action has consistently taken place over a significant length of time [16]. Past practice can, especially during grievance arbitration, obliterate the wording and intent of the negotiated master contract provision under question if past practice is in opposition to the contract language. Therefore, the establishment of precedental past practices is an area that should be constantly kept under management's microscope as the day-to-day management of the negotiated master contract is continued [17].

Erosion of the existing master contract will take place whenever an administrator deviates from the standards embodied in the contract. If the administrator relinquishes authority under the contract in order to be seen as a friend, or exceeds her/his authority, erosion of contract begins and contractual problems soon follow.

To establish a precedent, an administrator has only to make an interpretive decision not necessarily covered by the contract, or which exceeds or is in opposition to the contract document. For example, if the contract allows an employee to take one day per year for personal business, and an administrator unofficially permits even one employee to take more than one day without deducting a day's pay or disciplining the employee for a contract violation, a precedent has been started [18].

Usually, a precedent is committed without forethought or malice; it is normally caused by an administrator who doesn't carefully attend to the negotiated master contract, or by an administrator who is deemed lenient in the interpretation of the contract [19]. In either case, the damage is done, and the bargained limitation or requirement is of no value, not only in the immediate unit, but throughout the district. It would be better to adhere rigidly to the contract; and through the grievance process, bring about an allowable exception. This can be done with the firm statement that the allowance is without precedent and is for specific and stipulated reasons. Precedent-setting actions by any of the school district's administrators should be a serious concern to upper level management. For precedence, one of the mainstays of our legal system, basically indicates that one must continue the precedential action or decision as actions or decisions are taken in similar future situations. In other words, all administrators are almost always bound by the actions of one of its own—no matter how ill-conceived or inconsiderate that action was.

Once a precedent has been established, management is usually bound to act in accordance with that precedent [20]. If the precedent is seen as one that is having a harmful effect on the operation of the school district, management may wish to set a course to break the precedent. Of course, the union may take the same tactical approaches to breaking a precedent that they feel is harmful to their members or to the union's operation.

Precedents can be broken in three ways. First, during new master contract negotiations, language can be written into the contract (assuming this language remains in the contract when finally ratified) that has the effect of eliminating the undesirable precedent. Second, management may proceed to make a variety of different contract interpretations of the same item, or may take a variety of actions applied to an identical situation. This diversity will, for all intents and purposes, break the precedent because there is no consistency in the actions or interpretations taken over a reasonable span of time [21,22]. Third, management may notify the union, in advance of taking action, that it intends to change a standing past practice. This third method is not recommended by the authors.

Next, let's move to a discussion of disciplining an employee for contract violations, insubordination, or incompetency. Usually, any disciplinary action by management immediately brings the union into a confrontational position with management [23]. It should be stressed, however, that the union leadership are compelled to represent their members. In fact, even if they feel management has acted correctly and responsibly, they will represent the employee if the employee requests the union leadership's support [24]. There have been cases where the union leadership has not come to the defense of the employee, and the employee has successfully sued the union leadership for lack of representation [25].

DISCIPLINING EMPLOYEES

If a union employee violates the contract, there must be specific and clear language within the negotiated master contract that completely and irrefutably spells out the means and steps involved in conducting the disciplinary process. Incompetency of performance, especially in the case of a teacher, is often very difficult to prove; but insubordination or a violation of the specific terms of the negotiated master contract is not.

The key to successfully disciplining an employee is documentation. Documentation must take place at every step of the disciplinary process, and the documentation must be in writing, with a copy placed in the employee's personnel file and a copy given to the employee.

Incompetency refers to the inability of an employee to perform up to the expected standard. For all practical purposes that standard is set at the lowest common denominator. In other words, the employee in question must perform at a level lower than any other employee who is not being disciplined [26]. In many cases, termination will eventually be decided by the state's tenure commission. At this hearing, management will present its specifications for termination, prove that the employee has been informed of the specific areas to be improved, given assistance in the improvement effort, and given a reasonable time period in which to demonstrate improvement [27]. The union, generally, will defend the employee; and will question the objectivity and expertise of the administrators who brought incompetency charges against the employee. Usually, the union will indicate that the administrator(s) bringing the charges hasn't taught school for many years, and, therefore, does not truly know good teaching methods. Also, they will claim that since the administrator(s) does not have training in the teacher's specific area of expertise, he/she is not competent to pass judgement on the performance of the teacher. Finally, they will present evidence if the lowest common denominator criteria has been violated [28,29].

The state's tenure commission will oftentimes rule in favor of the employee whenever there is any doubt in the commissioners' minds about the accuracy of management's evidence, the lack of adequate assistance having been provided, or the lack of sufficient time given to demonstrate improved performance. On the other hand, if comprehensive and accurate documentation of the termination specifications have been provided, and the teacher has been given adequate time to improve, management will usually be successful [30].

It goes without saying that termination of an employee for incompetency should be a last resort, for not only does an employee suffer embarrassment and stress, the employee may lose opportunities for future employment [31]. This situation, in turn, may drastically and negatively affect the fired employee's future life. Management must, nevertheless, do what it has to do, no matter how distasteful, to protect the interest of the students and the school district [32]. In the case of teacher incompetency, the decision has to come down in favor of protecting the students, since the only reason school districts exist is to educate the young.

Insubordination happens when an employee refuses to perform a task that does not violate the contract or is one that is not illegal or immoral [33]. If the employee refuses to perform that task after due warning by an administrator of impending discipline for refusing, the employee will be considered insubordinate [34]. Insubordination can be punishable by a variety of means, including termination if the insubordination is considered very serious or if there is a continuing pattern of an employee refusing to perform reasonable tasks. In most cases, firing an employee for serious insubordination will be upheld by any hearing body.

The most frequent cause of employee discipline is that of master contract violations. When a master contract violation occurs, it is management's right to discipline. Subsequently, it is the union's right to grieve management's actions.

Discipline for violation of the master contract involves management taking a specific disciplinary action and informing the employee (and sometimes the union) of the specific contract violation and the specific discipline that is to be administered. At this time the employee (or the union, in cases of class grievances—those which involve two or more members of the union in the same grievance situation) will file a grievance against management [35]. This begins the grievance procedure, which is spelled out in the master contract document.

A typical master contract grievance procedure will have a series of steps to be followed, and time limits will be included for each step of the procedure. Many grievance procedures will be similar to the example provided [36].

A TYPICAL MASTER CONTRACT'S GRIEVANCE PROCEDURE

The following four-step grievance procedure shall be available to members of the union for the purpose of resolving concerns which arise out of the interpretation and administration of the ratified collective bargaining master contractual agreement. It is the intent of this procedure to provide for the orderly settlement of alleged grievances in an equitable manner at the lowest possible grievance level [37].

(1) A grievance is a claim by a member of the union that there has been a violation, a misinterpretation, or a misapplication of any specific provision of the collective bargaining master contractual agreement [38].

(2) The grievant shall mean any member of the union or any group of union members, in a class grievance situation, alleging a grievance.

Time Limits and Recording

(1) Each written grievance shall include the name and position of the grievant, the specific article and the section of the master contractual agreement within which the grievance has occurred, the time and place where the alleged event(s) or party allegedly responsible for causing the existence of the said event(s) or condition(s) if known, and a statement of the nature of the grievance and redress sought by the grievant. The written grievance shall be signed and dated by the grievant [39].

(2) The grievance must be taken at Step One of the following procedures within five work days following the date that any union member knew or should have known of the act(s) or condition(s) upon which the grievance is based. Time limits at any step of the grievance procedure may be extended only by mutual consent between the Union and the School District's Director of Personnel. Should the time limits at any step be exceeded by the School District, the grievance may be processed to the next higher step of the procedure, but the grievant must proceed to the next step within the time which would have been allotted had the decision been communicated on the final day of the step. Should the grievant not meet the time limits of the grievance procedure, the

grievance will be considered as resolved at the last response and further appeal shall be barred [40].

(3) All time limits in the procedure refer to scheduled work days [41].

Procedure

(1) Step One—Immediate Supervisor: Within five (5) days of the alleged grievance, the grievant shall first discuss the alleged grievance with her/his immediate supervisor. The immediate supervisor will respond orally within five (5) days. If the grievant is not satisfied with the oral response, she/he may within five (5) days of being given the oral response, submit the grievance in writing to the immediate supervisor. The immediate supervisor shall respond in writing within five (5) days [42].

(2) Step Two—Director of Personnel: If the grievant does not accept the written determination provided by the immediate supervisor in Step One, the grievant must within five (5) days of receipt of that determination, file the alleged grievance with the Director of Personnel. The Director of Personnel shall respond in writing within (5) days [43,44].

(3) Step Three—Superintendent of Schools: If the grievant is not satisfied with the response at Step Two, she/he may within five (5) days of the receipt of the response, submit the grievance to the Superintendent of Schools. If the Superintendent so determines, she/he may ask the President of the Union to review all matters related to the alleged grievance. After reviewing the grievance, the Superintendent of Schools shall submit a written decision to the grievant within ten days of receipt of the grievance [45].

(4) Step Four—Grievance Arbitration: If the grievant is not satisfied with the response at Step Three, the grievant and the grievant's union, within five (5) days of the receipt of the response, can request arbitration of the alleged grievance. The payment of all expenses related to the arbitration shall be borne by the loser in the arbitration, except that the union shall pay the salary and expenses of all its members, and management shall pay the salary and expenses related to its members. In cases where the arbitrator rules partially in favor of both parties, all expenses related to arbitration shall be borne equally by both parties [46].

In following any grievance procedure, the procedure will only work well if the parties to the grievance:

- participate in problem-resolving behavior
- involve progressively higher levels of the procedure when the grievance cannot be settled at lower levels
- base actions on factual data
- govern themselves in an ethical and fair manner
- grieve only items that are based on specific contract violations
- attempt to obtain resolution at the lowest possible levels
- result in specific remedies that are fair and equitable [47]

From the standpoint of the union there are two techniques that can be utilized to put pressure on management if the labor/management environment remains an adversarial one. The union can (1) encourage its members to grieve anything and grieve often, and (2) automatically request arbitration, knowing that this will tie up management's time and be costly to the school district [48].

In order to counter these union tactics, management will attempt to (1) define limitations on contract grievance in the narrowest sense possible, (2) put very restrictive time limits on filing grievances and in carrying a grievance to higher steps of the grievance procedure, (3) deny any request by the union for an extension of the time limits, (4) restrict grievances to individual employees and not allow union or class grievances, and (5) prohibit binding arbitration [49,50].

Let's step back for a moment from the grievance process itself, and discuss progressive discipline, just cause, and due process.

PROGRESSIVE DISCIPLINE, JUST CAUSE, AND DUE PROCESS

Progressive discipline implies that the discipline administered to an employee, with the exception of very serious offenses, must be progressive in nature. That is, the discipline immediately administered cannot be discharge of the employee, but must follow a reasonable and rational sequence of disciplinary actions by the employer [51]. Generally, progressive discipline will follow a series of disciplinary steps similar to those listed below.

- As a first step, an oral warning or reprimand is given the employee following management's objective investigation of the alleged incident. Of course, this assumes the investigation will provide evidence that the employee's conduct required management to take disciplinary action.

• As a second step, a written warning or reprimand is issued. The written reprimand letter or document should include (1) the specifics of the incident, (2) the reasons for the warning or reprimand, (3) what behavioral changes are expected of the employee, and (4) what disciplinary actions may be administered if the employee continues the undesirable behavior.

• The third step will usually result in the employee being given time off with pay.

• The fourth step will usually result in the employee being given time off without pay.

• The fifth and final step usually results in the discharge or termination of the employee [52].

It should be carefully kept in mind that disciplinary action against an employee should be for corrective, not punitive, purposes [53]. The documentation for any employee's discipline should be accurate and precise. An example of a suspension letter written to an employee for excessive negative actions is provided in Figure 13.1.

Now that we have elaborated upon the meaning of progressive discipline, let's turn to the matter of just cause.

Just cause refers whether or not an administrator had just and proper cause to take the action which she/he took against an employee [54]. A typical just cause clause imbedded in a master contractual agreement might well read as:

> No employee shall be subject to corrective discipline, reprimand, discharge, demotion, or deprived of any employee advantages without just cause.

In simple common language, *just cause* means that the discipline meted out is justified because of the actions of the employee for which the disciplinary action was taken by an administrator. If the disciplinary action taken was excessive, the school district's administration will probably be ruled against. On the other hand, if the reviewing party feels that the disciplinary action taken was justified by the employee's actions, the school district's administration will probably receive a favorable ruling [55]. In just cause hearings, as in most matters, the documentation defending the action is crucial to achieving a favorable ruling on the matter.

Mr. _____
136 North Street
Anytown, New York 64315-4412

Dear Mr. _____:

The established and printed rules of this school district state: "employees are to be at their assigned work stations and performing their assigned duties at the regular start of the work day. On March 14, 19—, Principal Smith orally warned you about not reporting to work on time, and she indicated that you would receive a written reprimand if your tardiness continued. The reasons for the necessity of all employees reporting to work on time were reviewed with you by Principal Smith. On March 21, 19—, you again reported late for work and were again given a verbal warning by Principal Smith. She also gave you an additional verbal warning because of your tardiness on May 28, 19—. On April 6, 19—, Principal Smith gave you a written reprimand for failing to report to work on time in accordance with the work rules of the school district. This action was taken because you had previously reported late for work three times within the period of less than one month. She also indicated at that time that failure to correct your record of tardiness would make you subject to further and possibly more serious disciplinary action. Since the written reprimand by Principal Smith of April 6, 19—, your work record indicates that you were late for work on the following dates:

April 10, 19—Monday	April 17, 19—Monday
May 6, 19—Friday	May 13, 19—Friday
May 16, 19—Monday	

On each of these dates, Principal Smith was not given an adequate excuse for your reporting late for work. Since you have apparently chosen not to comply with the school district's normal and published work rules, since you were fully aware of these work rules, and since you apparently have chosen to continue your unacceptable behavior, I am suspending you from work for a two-week period, which shall begin on Monday, May 23, 19—. Upon returning to work, you will be expected to correct your tardiness and abide by the work rules of the district. Further incidents of tardiness on your part shall result in more severe discipline, including the possible termination of your employment.

Sincerely,
Jim Smith
Director of Personnel

cc. Personnel File

FIGURE 13.1. Sample suspension letter.

Once just cause is ratified as a part of a master contract document, this clause will provide the basis upon which an administrator must proceed with corrective discipline, and will be a criterion used in judging the appropriateness of an administrator's actions against an employee during grievance hearings, grievance arbitration, or even during litigation.

Let's now turn to the matter of *due process*. School district administrators often lose cases because they didn't follow due process guidelines. Sometimes they lose matters even when they did appropriately follow due process, simply because they did not sufficiently document their actions.

Due process refers to a procedure, which, when properly implemented, protects the rights of the individual employee [56]. It basically involves a set of criteria permit a determination of whether or not an employee was treated fairly and whether or not the employee had opportunities to be consistently heard and defended. Due process and just cause are both standards that must be met in dealing with matters of employee discipline.

The following criteria comprise the guidelines for adequate due process by the administrators of a school district in relation to the discipline of the school district's employees:

- The rule, expected conduct, or procedure to be followed was known to the employee, and it was considered reasonable.
- The employee was notified about the expected behavior and about probable disciplinary consequences for failure to comply with the expected behavior.
- There was a fair and objective examination of facts related to the alleged violation by the employee.
- Specific documentation was collected to verify and substantiate the employee's violation, and the employee was given a written copy of the charges.
- The disciplinary action is reasonable and consistent with the nature of the employee's violation, and the employee's previous employment record has been duly considered prior to administering the discipline.
- The employee has been given an opportunity for a hearing on the charges, and the employee has been told of her/his right of counsel and her/his right to call witnesses prior to the disciplinary action being taken. At the hearing the employee can present evidence on her/his behalf, and the employee has the right of cross-examination.

The notice of the disciplinary hearing must contain an explanation of all the rules related to the hearing.
* The employee shall be judged by an impartial third party [57].

Now that we have presented background information on progressive discipline, due process, and just cause, let's return to the major topic of grievances.

PREPARING FOR AND PROCESSING GRIEVANCES

In the grievance articles contained in most negotiated and ratified master contract agreements, there are very specific steps to be followed. Many times this grievance article will even deal with details related to the payment of an arbitrator, court recorder, and other grievance costs if grievance arbitration is included as a step in the grievance process.

In preparing for and processing a grievance hearing, the administrator should collect detailed documentation about the alleged grievance. The specific questions that should be answered as part of the grievance process should include documentation related to the following:

* Why is this a grievance?
* What specifically is aggrieved?
* Who is involved in the alleged grievance?
* Where did the alleged grievance take place?
* When did the alleged grievance take place?
* What specifically happened during the alleged grievance?
* Were there any witnesses to the alleged grievance? If yes, who were the witnesses?
* What recourse (demand) is the aggrieved employee seeking to resolve the grievance?
* Are there any past practices which may influence the outcome of this grievance? [58]

Once a grievance has been filed by an employee or an employees' union and it has gone the first level of the grievance procedure, it is then appealed by the employee to other levels of the grievance procedure. Management should develop a checklist to be followed when reviewing an appealed grievance. A simple checklist should cover the following:

* Have I collected all the information available at previous steps of the grievance?

- Have I held a personal conference with the employee who filed the alleged grievance, and have I listened intently to the employee's story?
- If necessary or wise, have I received the union representative's position on the matter?
- Have I taken notes on all the important facts?
- Have I made certain that I am clear on the recourse requested by the employee and/or the employee's union representative?
- Have I reviewed the grievance, the recourse desired and the pertinent facts with the employee in order that the employee understands these matters, and that the employee understands that I am accurate in the information I have recorded?
- Have I investigated the alleged facts with the employee's immediate administrator who took the action which is being grieved?
- Have I checked the time limits in the negotiated master contract's grievance procedure? Am I certain of the grievability of the issue to which I am to respond? Have I sought expert advise (legal or other) if I felt the need to seek it? Have I checked my facts and tentative decision with the school district's Director of Personnel before rendering a final decision?
- Have I answered the grievance within the time limits, and have I answered it by clearly stating my understanding of what is being grieved, what recourse is desired and the reasons for making the decision that I made?
- Have I explained to the employee, her/his right to appeal?
- Have I made certain that the action I promised was carried out accurately, completely, and in a timely manner?

If the negotiated master contractual agreement permits the arbitration of grievances as the final step in the grievance procedure, management should prepare a checklist of preparatory steps to be followed by administrators who will be involved in the grievance arbitration hearing.

- Study the grievance very carefully, reviewing its history through every step of the grievance procedure.
- Prepare a very clear statement of the issue in dispute, and identify the specific article and wording that is involved in the alleged grievance.
- Review the master agreement very carefully before going to the grievance hearing to assure yourself of the accuracy of the action

taken by the administrator and of the possible interpretation of the contract that could be used by the union.

- Assemble all the documents and papers you will need to present your position to the arbitrator, and make certain to have copies available in a well-organized format to hand to the arbitrator at the hearing.
- If the union possesses documents you need for the hearing, ask the union to provide you with copies or bring them to the hearing. If they do not, ask the arbitrator to subpoena them.
- Interview all the witnesses you intend to call, and with the help of the school attorney, make certain that your witnesses thoroughly understand the entire case and the importance of their own testimony. Coaching witnesses is not only wise, it is a crucial pre-hearing preparation step. Some witnesses, if not coached prior to the actual hearing, may panic and end up hurting your case.
- Develop a written summary of what each witness is supposed to prove; this procedure will assist you in making certain that no important item of testimony is overlooked.
- Study the case carefully from the union's point of view. Play the game of *"What ifs,"* and be prepared to counter any of the union's opposing evidence and/or arguments.
- Conduct a mock hearing, and have other administrators and the school district's attorney look for weak spots and previously overlooked details. Thus, these can be corrected before the actual arbitration hearing takes place. During this mock hearing have some members of your group present the strongest case possible from the union's point of view, and have other members serve as impartial third party mediators. Finally, have the school attorney vigorously cross-examine management's witnesses from the union's point of view.
- Find out as much as you can about the arbitrator, the way she/he conducts hearings, and any prior rulings that she/he has rendered in cases similar to the grievance case that will be arbitrated.
- Following the hearing, ask the arbitrator to render her/his award in a very short time period. If the grievance involves retroactive pay, the amount accumulates daily if the arbitrator ultimately rules in favor of the union's position.
- Although not part of the preparation for arbitration, it is important to end this discussion on grievance arbitration by providing very simple guidelines.

- If you win the arbitration, do not brag or flaunt your win in the face of the employee or the union. Remember, this is still your employee, and you will continue to live with the union and its representatives well into the future.

If the administration's action was not upheld in arbitration, make certain that you accept the decision without any thought of "getting even" with the employee or the union in the future. You win some and you lose some, and experienced unionists and management representatives who deal with the entire collective bargaining process understand and accept this. In fact, experienced hands on both sides of the table usually develop a great deal of respect for one another's skills and fairness over the long haul [59].

ESTABLISHING A CONTINUING WIN-WIN UNION/MANAGEMENT WORKING ENVIRONMENT

Once a master contract has been negotiated and ratified, a more important goal must be attained. That is, a continuous win-win, cooperative, and collaborative union/management environment must be initiated and continued on a long-term basis. This type of environment can only be created and maintained if both union and management representatives trust one another, generate accurate and honest communications, respect one another as professionals, and work very hard at the maintenance of the win-win environment [60].

Three practical suggestions will serve to illustrate means of achieving a win-win, collaborative, and cooperative environment:

(1) Establish routine weekly meetings of the union and management leadership. These meetings will provide the opportunity for both parties to anticipate and resolve potential problems, to communicate clearly the interests of both parties, and to build rapport between the leadership of both union and management.

(2) Establish a hotline for rumor control. In every organization, and certainly in a school district, many rumors arise. When these involve labor/management concerns, the leadership of both groups should immediately contact one another, establish factual information, communicate the facts to their members (and, if necessary, to the community), and quash the rumor before it causes any damage to the ongoing positive relationship that has been established between the union and management [61].

(3) Establish union/management work teams. These teams, whose membership is drawn from both union and management, can present a united and cooperative model. They can be used to arrive at data, to analyze data, and to make proposals for improving the work environment. Both groups will benefit from the establishment of such units as Quality of Work Life teams, Quality Circles, and Total Quality Management joint ventures.

In addition, these teams can display a joint effort on many non–union/management areas that will assist the students, the board of education, the administration, all union and non-union employees, and the community at large [62]. Having joint efforts to assist the community will especially pay big dividends in terms of improving the community members' attitudes toward both union and management.

SUMMARY

The operational stage of communicating and interpreting the master contract may seem a lesser endeavor after the task of achieving collective negotiations agreement, but it is an initial, critical step in the administration of the new contract. The dissemination of the tentatively agreed-upon contract to members of the administration is intended to achieve a basic understanding of the contents of the ratified master contractual agreement. Once the contract is ratified by both parties, a more intensive, article-by-article review is recommended to ensure uniform interpretation of the articles and the specific contractual wording. It is a training session for the administrators, and it will assist in setting the tone for an effective working relationship between management and the employees. Particular high-stress areas requiring attention include union rights, management rights, academic freedom, employee assignments, employee transfer, employee evaluation, unit membership, and the grievance process. Clear direction must be given to the administration to guide their day-to-day, detailed implementation of the contract's provisions. Regular communication and updates concerning the contract's implementation should be provided.

The intent of these efforts is to prevent the establishment of unintentional precedents, which can emerge from a single instance or multiple instances of past practice, thus nullifying, for all practical purposes, related contract articles. Precedents can be broken in two ways: language can be written into new contracts to eliminate an undesirable precedent, and management may create a diversity of interpretations related to the same action, which breaks the precedent through inconsistency.

Related to contract implementation are the steps involved in conducting a disciplinary procedure. Violations of the specific terms of the contract may include incompetency and insubordination. Proving incompetency and insubordination requires documentation, and the union may employ classic defense strategies (such as claiming administrative incompetency to judge teaching performance) to protect the employee.

Progressive administrative discipline underlies these procedures, and usually consists of oral warnings or reprimands, relief from duties with or without pay, and, finally, termination. The matter of just cause, language usually contained in the master contract, is also related to progressive discipline, and refers to whether or not an administrator had the right to take a particular action against an employee, and whether or not the discipline taken was appropriate. This clause will provide the administrative basis on which corrective discipline proceeds. Due process must also be observed as a standard for administrative procedure throughout the process of employee discipline.

A typical master contract grievance procedure involves definitions, time limits, recording information, and four procedural steps with various levels of appeal (immediate supervisor, director of personnel, etc.). Union grievance tactics in an adversarial climate may include the excessively frequent filing of grievances and automatic requests for arbitration.

The processing of grievances may be highly detailed in the master contract agreement and documentation of an alleged grievance must address such areas as the specific nature of the violation, persons, time and location, identification of witnesses, recourse demanded, and related past practice. Administrators responding to an employee grievance must ensure that due process and careful attention to detail and procedure have been followed, particularly in regard to the requirements of the master contract.

EXERCISES

1. What would be some effective techniques to train administrators on implementation of a new master contract?

2. Review the variety of administrative practices in your district, and determine which might be the most vulnerable to different interpretation and application, and thus likely to cause a problematic precedent.
3. Outline the steps of an imaginary contract violation (incompetency or insubordination) that would lead to employee termination.
4. Outline the steps of an imaginary progressive discipline situation.
5. Outline the types of data you would present at a grievance arbitration hearing.

REFERENCES

1. Kerchner, C. T. 1993. "Building the Airplane as It Rolls Down the Runway: Administrators Discover Labor Relations as the Linchpin to School Change," *School Administrator,* 50(10): 8–15.
2. Kearney, R. C. 1984. *Labor Relations in the Public Sector.* New York, NY: Marcel Dekker, Inc., p. 281.
3. Kearney, R. C. 1984. *Labor Relations,* pp. 283–284.
4. Helsby, R. D., J. Tener, and J. Lefkowitz, eds. 1985. *The Evolving Process—Collective Negotiations in Public Employment.* Fort Washington, PA: Labor Relations Press, p. 220.
5. Kearney, R. C. 1984. *Labor Relations,* p. 284.
6. Keane, W. G. 1996. *Win-Win or Else: Collective Bargaining in an Age of Public Discontent.* Thousand Oaks, CA: Corwin Press, Sage Publications, pp. 44–46.
7. Kearney, R. C. 1984. *Labor Relations,* p. 285.
8. Webster, W. G., Sr. 1985. *Effective Collective Bargaining in Public Education.* Ames, IA: Iowa State University Press, pp. 190–191.
9. Coleman, C. J. 1990. *Managing Labor Relations in the Public Sector.* San Francisco, CA: Jossey-Bass Publishers, p. 287.
10. Streshly, W. A. and T. A. DeMitchell. 1994. *Teacher Unions and TQE.* Thousand Oaks, CA: Corwin Press, Sage Publications, pp. 78–79.
11. Many, T. W. and C. A. Sloan. 1990. "Management And Labor Perceptions Of School Collective Bargaining," *Journal of Collective Negotiations,* 19(4): 283–296.
12. Webster, W. G., Sr. 1985. *Effective Collective Bargaining,* pp. 190–191.
13. Smith, S. C., D. Ball, and D. Liontos. 1990. *Working Together—The Collaborative Style of Bargaining.* Eugene, OR: ERIC Clearinghouse on Educational Management, University of Oregon, p. 59.
14. Helsby, R. D., J. Tener, and J. Lefkowitz, eds. 1985. *The Evolving Process,* p. 185.
15. Cimini, M. H. and C. J. Muhl. 1995. "Labor-Management Bargaining in 1994," *Monthly Labor Review,* 118(1): 23–38.

16. Coleman, C. J. 1990. *Managing Labor Relations,* pp. 184–185.

17. Kearney, R. C. 1984. *Labor Relations,* pp. 284–285.

18. Kearney, R. C. 1984. *Labor Relations,* p. 71.

19. Elkouri, F. and E. A. Elkouri. 1973. *How Arbitration Works.* Third Edition. Washington, D.C.: Bureau of National Affairs, Inc., p. 395.

20. Elkouri, F. and E. A. Elkouri. 1973. *How Arbitration Works,* p. 392.

21. Elkouri, F. and E. A. Elkouri. 1973. *How Arbitration Works,* p. 407.

22. Herman, J. J. and G. E. Megiveron. 1993. *Collective Bargaining in Education: Win/Win, Win/Lose, Lose/Lose.* Lancaster, PA: Technomic Publishing Co., Inc., pp. 163–165.

23. Richardson, R. C. 1985. *Collective Bargaining by Objectives: A Positive Approach.* Englewood Cliffs, NJ: Prentice-Hall, Inc., pp. 212–213.

24. Kearney, R. C. 1984. *Labor Relations,* p. 291.

25. Ibid.

26. Ibid.

27. Trotta, M. S. 1976. *Handling Grievances—A Guide for Management and Labor.* Washington, D.C.: The Bureau of National Affairs, Inc., pp. 24–25.

28. Paterson, L. T. and R. T. Murphy. 1983. *The Public Administrator's Grievance Arbitration Handbook.* New York, NY: Longman, Inc., p. 78.

29. Herman, J. J. and G. E. Megiveron. 1993. *Collective Bargaining in Education,* pp. 165–167.

30. Richardson, R. C. 1985. *Collective Bargaining By Objectives,* pp. 219–220.

31. Coulson, R. 1981. *The Termination Handbook.* London: Collier MacMillan Publishers, pp. 49–50.

32. Braun, R. J. 1972. *Teachers and Power—The Story of the American Federation of Teachers.* New York: Longman, Inc., p. 78.

33. Coulson, R. 1981. *The Termination Handbook,* pp. 100–101.

34. Paterson, L. T. and R. T. Murphy 1983. *The Public Administrator's Grievance,* pp. 72–73.

35. Kearney, R. C. 1984. *Labor Relations,* p. 289–297.

36. Webster, W. G., Sr. 1985. *Effective Collective Bargaining,* pp. 137–140.

37. Castetter, W. B. 1996. *The Human Resource Function in Educational Administration.* 6th ed. Englewood Cliffs, NJ: Merrill, pp. 589–593.

38. Webster, W. G., Sr. 1985. *Effective Collective Bargaining,* p. 194.

39. Trotta, M. S. 1976. *Handling Grievances,* pp. 100–101.

40. Trotta, M. S. 1976. *Handling Grievances,* pp. 98–99.

41. Paterson, L. T. and R. T. Murphy. 1983. *The Public Administrator's Grievance,* p. 52.

42. Paterson, L. T. and R. T. Murphy. 1983. *The Public Administrator's Grievances,* p. 51.

43. Webster, W. G., Sr. 1985. *Effective Collective Bargaining,* pp. 137–140.

44. Rebore, R. W. 1991. *Personnel Administration in Education—A Management Approach,* 3rd ed. Englewood Cliffs, NJ: Prentice-Hall, Inc., pp. 322–325.

45. Webster, W. G., Sr. 1985. *Effective Collective Bargaining,* p. 196.

46. Ibid.

47. Paterson, L. T. and R. T. Murphy 1983. *The Public Administrator's Grievance,* pp. 4–5.

48. Webster, W. G., Sr. 1985. *Effective Collective Bargaining,* pp. 206–207.

49. Webster, W. G., Sr. 1985. *Effective Collective Bargaining,* pp. 205–206.

50. Herman, J. J. and G. E. Megiveron. 1993. *Collective Bargaining in Education,* pp. 167–169.

51. Coulson, R. 1981. *The Termination Handbook,* pp. 73–74.

52. Coulson, R. 1981. *The Termination Handbook,* p. 122.

53. Justin, J. J. 1969. *How to Manage with a Union—Book Two—The Rules of Collective Bargaining, Grievance Handling, Corrective Discipline, Book One of How to Manage with a Union.* New York: Industrial Relations Workshop Seminars, Inc., pp. 294–295.

54. Paterson, L. T. and R. T. Murphy. 1983. *The Public Administrator's Grievance,* pp. 254–255.

55. Trotta, M. S. 1976. *Handling Grievances,* pp. 58–59.

56. Paterson, L. T. and R. T. Murphy. 1983. *The Public Administrator's Grievance,* p. 80.

57. Trotta, M. S. 1976. *Handling Grievances,* pp. 128–129.

58. Paterson, L. T. and R. T. Murphy. 1983. *The Public Administrator's Grievance,* p. 147.

59. Herman, J. J. and G. E. Megiveron. 1993. *Collective Bargaining in Education,* pp. 173–175.

60. Cimini, M. H. 1994. "Negotiated Changes in State and Local Government Contracts, 1993," *Monthly Labor Review,* 117(8): 3–10.

61. Ordovensky, P. and G. Marx. 1993. *Working with the News Media,* Alexandria, VA: American Association of School Administrators, pp. 22–24.

62. *Strategies for School System Leaders on District-Level Change.* 1994. "Dade County: A Stable Partnership in a Sea of Change." Alexandria, VA: Panasonic Foundation and the American Association of School Administrators, pp. 6–7.

.

MISCELLANEOUS ITEMS AND SUMMARIZING

Section Four consists of two chapters. Chapter 14, Miscellaneous Items, presents information about union ships and closed shops, power management, reality versus perception, fact versus propaganda, state and local relations with local union affiliates, and the importance of the initial master contract agreement. It also presents information on information leaks, information handling, expedited bargaining, zipper clauses, and limited or focused bargaining. Further it discusses forces that influence collective bargaining, certifying and decertifying unions, unfair labor practices, and bad faith bargaining. The chapter ends with a discussion of external contracting.

Chapter 15, Summary of Collective Negotiations, presents a listing of do's, don'ts, and maybe's of collective bargaining. It also presents information about the benefits and losses suffered by both labor and management. It ends by discussing the benefits and deficits of adversarial bargaining and win-win bargaining, and by elaborating upon the potential impact of school-based (site-based) management on the collective bargaining process.

Miscellaneous Items

CHAPTER 14 discusses a variety of important terms and matters that do not fit neatly into the first eleven chapters but which are of importance to those who are involved in collective bargaining, those who will become involved in collective bargaining, or those who are students of the collective bargaining process. These discussions begin with the differences between agency shop and closed shop, and they end with the topic of union management conflict over outside contracting. The chapter concludes with a summary, exercises, and references.

AGENCY SHOPS, UNION SHOPS, AND CLOSED SHOPS

An agency shop refers to a situation wherein the employees of a school district are not required to belong to the union that has the exclusive right to represent them in collective bargaining, but are still required to pay a service fee to the union [1]. The fee is intended to cover the costs of the union when the union is representing the employee in collective bargaining matters [2]. On rare occasions union and management have agreed that the individual employee can give an amount of money equal to the service fee to a charity of the employee's choice, rather than paying the money to the union.

The advantage of an agency shop is primarily that it allows employees who do not believe in unionism, or who are members of another union not given official recognition by the board of education or by an election, exclusive rights of representation; the freedom of choice to refuse to officially join a union that has gained exclusive representation rights [3]. Although the union officials would prefer that all members join their union, it does allow the union to collect fees for its work on behalf of the employees; and it eliminates the possibility of anyone getting a free ride. On the other hand, it does not allow the union to collect full dues, nor does it permit the union to use the agency shop fees for political purposes, such as lobbying legislators [4]. A closed shop is one in which all employees have to belong to the union *before* they can be hired by the school district [5]. A closed shop is illegal in most public school situations. The advantages of a closed shop are all in favor of the union that has been elected or recognized as the sole representative of the employees (at least of one category of employees, such as teachers) of a school district. It allows the union to collect full dues and to have wide discretion in the use of the money collected [6]. In closed shops, it is often impossible to hire anyone unless the hiring is done through the union hall. Obviously, this tremendously increases the power of the union leaders [7].

A union shop refers to a situation wherein all employees must belong to the union which has been recognized as the sole representative of the employees or at least one category of employees. All employees in that category have to belong to the union, but they do not have to join the union before they are hired [8–10].

TIMING + INFORMATION = POWER MANAGEMENT

The formula for success in collective bargaining depends on the party's possession of complete, accurate, and convincing information that will convince the other party, the mediator, the fact-finder, or the arbitrator that the party's position is the one to accept. This implies that the persons involved in the process of collective bargaining should (1) do their homework in great detail and in advance of the need for the information, (2) keep up-to-date on all changes that are taking place during negotiations in their school districts and in other school districts, and update their information accordingly, and (3) present their information in a clear and convincing manner.

Even though all of the information requirements are met, they are of little use unless they are presented at a time when the percent of success is maximized. To present excellent information in a convincing manner in the early stages of an adversarial negotiation is to waste the information, and doing so prematurely tips off the other party of your information and its intended usage. Also, to provide last best offer type of information to a mediator, when you are fully expecting that the impasse will go beyond the mediation stage, is again to waste the information and prematurely identify your ultimate position(s) [11,12].

REALITY VERSUS PERCEPTION
AND FACT VERSUS PROPAGANDA

During lengthy negotiations within an adversarial negotiating environment, it is often difficult for the members of the union, management, or the public to separate fact from propaganda. It is also often difficult for the members of both at-the-table negotiating teams to separate reality from perception.

Even though there may be an agreement between the parties that no information will be provided by either party until the total package is ratified as a master contract agreement, a well-used tactic during adversarial bargaining is the leaking of propaganda statements. Some typical propaganda tactics include [13]:

- The board of education is going to reduce the medical insurance.
- The board of education isn't interested in the children because they will not reduce class size.
- The board of education will not agree to any salary increase.
- The board of education's negotiating team is not bargaining in good faith.
- The chief negotiator hates teachers.
- The board of education is purposely acting inappropriately in order to provoke a strike with the hope that it can fire the employees for illegally striking.

The facts related to the above statements could well be as follows:

- Because of the escalating cost of medical insurance, the board has proposed that the employees pay for one-fourth of any premium increases.
- The board of education would like to decrease class size, especially at the early elementary level, but it does not have sufficient new monies to accomplish this.
- The management team's negotiating position is that it will not discuss salary increases until all other contractual items in contention are resolved.
- The board of education's negotiating team is bargaining in good faith because it has agreed to meet regularly, it listens intently to the union's proposals, and it offers rational counterproposals. It has not agreed to many items, but that is not a requirement for good faith bargaining.

- The board of education's chief negotiator is a lawyer whose wife is a teacher in another school district.
- The last thing the board of education wants is a strike, as it knows how a strike makes matters very complex and how it negatively effects all aspects of the school district for many years into the future.

During long, drawn-out, and difficult adversarial negotiations members of the negotiating team often have problems in adjoining reality and their perceptions [14]. This problem results from two situations: (1) when there exists serious animosity between individuals or multiple persons on either negotiating team, or (2) when the proposal/counterproposal activity is voluminous [15]. If either of these situations exist, frustration results and the parties to the at-the-table bargaining have difficulty in determining reality. Obviously, a skewed view of reality by any of the important players complicates matters, and makes the task of obtaining a TA (Tentative Agreement) that much more difficult [16]. In negotiations, the members naturally have different feelings about each item, and the emotions that evolve from the "underdog" attitude of those dealing (often for the first time) with management in a confrontational setting are upsetting.

UNION SUPPORT SYSTEM

Although the board of education's negotiating team sits at the table with the local union's negotiating team, its members must be aware that the local employees are usually not in complete control of what happens during the negotiations. Some of the influences involved in the local collective bargaining scene, using the teachers' unions of the AFT (American Federation of Teachers) and the NEA (National Education Association) as examples, are:

- The NEA or AFT will make a large databank of comparative information available to the local district's union officers. These data become powerful proposal and counterproposal tools during collective bargaining processes.
- The regional coalition of local union leaders may suggest that certain target districts be at the forefront of new foot-in-the-door proposals, which, if successfully negotiated, will become union demands in all the school districts in the near future.

- The state level will usually provide "Uniserve" directors to service the local district's union in a variety of ways. These Uniserve directors are full-time employees of the state union organization.
- Union stewards are usually local union officials that serve as the eyes and ears of the local union in each of the school district's buildings, but they usually are given training at the state level. They also work with the local union's officers through the state level to resolve many of the concerns the locals may have about the way the school district's administrators are managing the master contractual agreement.
- During at-the-table negotiations, the Uniserve director may well be the chief negotiator for the local union. If this is not the case, it is almost certain that the Uniserve director assigned to that local will be a very influential person in the settlement of the master contractual agreement. In all cases, the Uniserve director is a highly trained unionist. In addition, the state-level union has training sessions for all local union officers and for the local negotiating team members.
- Regional union members, and in serious conflict situations, state and national union leaders, will be present at the local school district to picket, pack board of education meetings, give media interviews, or conduct other activities intended to put pressure on board of education members, the superintendent of schools, the board of education's chief negotiator, and the negotiating team members to settle the contract in a manner which is favorable to the union's position(s) [17].
- During mediation, fact-finding and/or arbitration it is certain that the state-level union and perhaps the national-level union, will provide (1) relevant information, (2) consultation and advice, and (3) on-site officials from the state and/or national level(s).
- During grievance resolution sessions and especially during grievance arbitrations, the state-level union might have a full-time, state-level, union employed attorney present the union's case. At the very least, the union's attorney or Uniserve director will be actively involved in the preparation, strategy, and tactics related to the arbitration. This is a wise use of union resources, as the arbitration ruling will establish some precedental direction for the specific local school district in the future. More importantly, an

arbitration ruling against the union on an important matter that might effect numerous school districts is detrimental to the union [18–20].

CONTRACT LANGUAGE IS VERY IMPORTANT

Each word in a ratified master contract agreement is very important. The wording of each article during negotiations is a technically important matter. Some words, such as *shall* and *will,* are words that mandate compliance; whereas words like *may* or *should* allow the party flexibility when it comes to compliance. If the contract says, for instance, *shall* when it should have said *may;* or if the contract language stated *may* when it should have said *shall,* many problems could result during the management stage of the contract [21]. Either party could feel that the intent of the agreement was being violated. Unless there is a mutual agreement on the interpretation of the specific language at some period after the contract has been ratified, adversarial relations will appear and continue. Such a continuing adversarial relationship during contract management is harmful to both parties; and if the conflict state becomes public, this continuing relationship may cause the general public to lose faith in all the people who are supposed to be operating the district for the children's benefit.

Three examples of contractual language will serve to highlight the importance of very specific and clear contractual language.

Example—Class Size

- "Both parties agree that the maximum class size for grades one through three shall be twenty (20) pupils. In cases where the individual class reaches twenty-one (21) pupils, the board of education will immediately hire an additional teacher and split the class into two (2) classes."
- "Both parties agree that reasonable class sizes are important to the quality of teaching offered the students of Wonderful School District. Therefore, the board of education agrees to attempt to keep the maximum class size for grades one through three at twenty (20) pupils."
- "The board of education has the authority to determine class size"

In the first statement, the board of education *must* employ an additional teacher during any time period when any class in grades one through three reaches twenty-one students. This agreement could place the board of education in financial difficulty if it has a tight budget and quite a few classes end up with twenty-one or more students. In fact, if there were merely fifteen such situations and the average teacher's salary and fringe benefits equalled $40,000, it is clear that the unanticipated cost increase would amount to a total of $600,000. This could result in many classes having only eleven to fourteen students. All this is fine if the board of education assumes that classes in excess of twenty are detrimental to student achievement and the board of education has available funds to support such a contractual position without doing harm to other programs. Once agreed to in the master contractual agreement, it is clear that it is a *mandatory* action [22].

The second statement is permissive, even though it provides the directional philosophy that is held by the board of education about the matter of class size. On the other hand, the third statement leaves complete control of class size up to the decision-making power of the board of education.

Further analysis of these three statements indicates that the first statement favors the union, the third statement favors the board of education, and the second statement could be an agreed-to compromise statement reached during a win-win negotiating atmosphere. Whichever type of statement both parties ratify in a master contract agreement, it spells out the clear responsibility of both parties in the matter of class size.

IMPORTANCE OF THE FIRST NEGOTIATED MASTER CONTRACTUAL AGREEMENT

The first collective bargaining agreement that is ratified as a master contract is the single most important master contract that the two parties will ever ratify. This initial contract will set the stage for all future contractual negotiations in terms of the specific articles included and in terms of the specific language written into each article [23]. If articles or language are detrimental to either party to the negotiations or if the language is unclear, it may well take near-crisis situations to eliminate the article or the undesired language during future contract negotiations [24]. In the interim, during the management of the existing contract, adversarial relations may arise within a situation which has been historically one of a win-win employee/administrator atmosphere. This problem could arise simply because of unintended articles, too much power to one party, or inappropriate or unclear and cumbersome contractual language [25].

The most important initial contract articles are (1) recognition, (2) union rights, and (3) management rights. Also important are articles dealing with (4) class size (5) leaves, (6) academic freedom, (7) employee evaluation, (8) employee assignment, or (9) health insurance. Obviously, any article, in addition to the above, must be carefully analyzed before the contract is ratified, as it is one you will have to live with for a very long time [26].

INFORMATION LEAKS DURING NEGOTIATIONS

During critical stages of the negotiations it is very important to control leaks of information about at-the-table positions [27]. During the negotiation process, it is crucial that both negotiating teams go to their referent groups to give them a progress report or to get agreement about a change from the original demands provided by the referent group.

For the chief negotiator and the negotiating team members this is a very difficult decision that *must* be made. It not only involves what to share with the employees (in the union negotiating team's case) or with the board of education members (in the management negotiating team's case); but it involves decisions as to what can be shared and what can be withheld [28]. Sometimes, the immediate negotiations are at such a critical stage that any leak will cause a rupture, and in such situations it might be wise to hide important information from the referent group. This is a most difficult decision for a negotiating team to make, as very few people involved in negotiations feel that their referent group does not have the right to know where negotiations stand or the major areas of concern [29].

The reason for this dilemma, which could be ethical, political, and pragmatic in nature, is that almost all information shared with a referent group will be either purposely or accidentally leaked to the other party, the media, and/or the community at large [30]. This realization is balanced against the legitimate right to know by members of the negotiating team's referent group.

For some reason, a few members of any referent group will always feel a need to share information that others do not possess; and this sharing may be to friends, spouses, business acquaintances, neighbors or members of a like group from other school districts. As these people are provided with this information, they share it with others; and ultimately continuous sharing takes place [31]. If this sharing impedes progress at-the-table, makes an already complex situation more complex, or causes problems at any level, damage will take place and the energies of the negotiating parties will be focused on damage control rather than on bargaining.

WHEN AND WHERE SHOULD INFORMATION BE SHARED AND TO WHICH GROUPS

During negotiations there are continuous decisions that must be made related to the sharing of information. These decisions relate to (1) what information should be shared, (2) when should the information be shared, and (3) to which groups should the various types of information be shared.

If the parties have agreed to closed negotiations, as is the case in most districts, the only persons who will receive information during the process will be the negotiating team's referent group. This agreement is usually violated if the negotiations reach the impasse stage.

Media will receive information during two situations: (1) when both parties agree to a joint progress report of the negotiations during various stages of the negotiating process, and (2) when the negotiations reach the impasse stage. When impasse is reached, the media releases are done separately, and are usually slanted in favor of the position of the party releasing the information [32].

The general public is privy to the media releases, but are generally not informed about specific proposals during negotiations. Of course, there could be purposeful or accidental leaks to members of the community but, generally, the public is not given the contractual information until after the master contractual agreement has been ratified by both parties.

It is obvious that the specific information to be released is an important decision, as is the timing of that release [33]. If too much or too little information is released at the wrong time or to the wrong group(s), much damage can be done during the process of negotiating a master contractual agreement [34].

REOPENERS AND ZIPPER CLAUSES

Reopeners usually refer to the timeline, such as three months prior to the expiration of the existing master contract agreement, when negotiations are initiated on a successor contract. This timeline is agreed upon to allow both parties to the upcoming negotiations sufficient time, hopefully, to negotiate a successor contract prior to the date of expiration of the current master contract agreement [35].

A zipper clause is language within an existing master contractual agreement allowing re-negotiations of a specific article in the contract while all other contractual conditions remain in effect until the end date of the existing contract. Sometimes a situation will exist wherein a multiple-year ratified master contractual agreement will contain a zipper clause allowing yearly negotiations of the salary provisions [36].

In general, a zipper clause is negotiated into a master contract to avoid holding up the ratification of a total contract because of disagreement on a single provision. In the case of salary, the parties may agree to a compromised, first-year salary provision, but are reluctant to commit themselves for future years of the contract. Another situation that may lead both parties to agree on a zipper clause on salary provisions is one when neither party can predict the degree of increase in the cost-of-living and they want to reserve the opportunity to adjust future salary demands to a more certain resource future [37].

EXPEDITED BARGAINING

Expedited bargaining refers to a situation in which both parties to the negotiations agree to attempt to achieve a TA (Tentative Agreement) on a total contract over a very short period of time. Often the time period could be one week or less, and it usually occurs with both negotiating teams meeting at some location removed from the school district's environs. Both parties come very well prepared with information and rationale, which they share both freely and quickly. If successful, expedited bargaining accomplishes many good things, including satisfaction and trust between parties, a parsimonious use of resources, and the beginning or continuation of a win-win attitude that will permeate all activities of both parties throughout all aspects of the collective bargaining process [38].

FOCUSED OR LIMITED BARGAINING

This bargaining structure has an identical purpose to that of expedited bargaining—quick and win-win agreement on a master contract. In many cases, limited bargaining, like expedited bargaining, takes place at a motel or at some other off-school district location. In focused or limited bargaining, both parties agree to carry forth into the successor master contractual agreement most of the items currently contained in that agreement, and each party selects two or three areas where formal bargaining will take place.

FORCES THAT INFLUENCE COLLECTIVE BARGAINING

Collective bargaining does not take place in a vacuum. Both union and management will have forces impacting them during the stages of (1) preparing to negotiate, (2) negotiating at-the-table, (3) master contract ratification, and (4) contract management. The forces that will influence those responsible for collective bargaining include the following.

- The public is influential because of its attitude toward taxes and the degree to which they feel the school district is carrying out its educational charge. Depending on the public's attitude towards teachers, unionism, administrators, the superintendent of schools, and board of education members, it will lend a supportive or critical voice to the collective bargaining process [39].
- Business and industrial groups influence collective bargaining because of their supportive or non-supportive attitude towards the school district, its educational programs, or the taxes they pay to support the local school district.
- Political forces at the local, state, and national levels strongly influence collective bargaining in the terms of the legislation they pass and the amount of funds they supply to the local school district.
- Judicial agencies and quasi-judicial agencies influence collective bargaining because of the decisions they render related to collective bargaining and union/management powers and relationships.
- Governmental agencies located in the local school district can make a big difference in what happens during collective bargaining. The attitude of other governmental agencies towards the school district, the union, and management are important. If they are negative, this

will cause pressure on the collective bargainers. If they are positive, this will assist the collective bargainers.

* Media outlets certainly can influence collective bargaining by the degree to which they issue factual information, the degree to which they issue biased or incorrect information, and the degree to which they produce editorials [40].
* Students can influence collective bargaining, depending on how they feel they are being treated and serviced by the teachers and administrators of the district. Once these perceptions are shared with family members, neighbors, and friends, the collective bargaining will be either positively or negatively affected.
* Parents influence collective bargaining because of the attitudes they hold about how well their children are treated and educated, how well they feel they are treated by the school district's functionaries, and how well they feel their taxes are being utilized. They have great influence over non-parent others, who will give the parents credibility because they currently have children attending the schools.
* Taxpayers influence collective bargaining by the degree to which they are willing or unwilling to tax themselves to support the operation of the school district. The attitudes of retired community members who are on a fixed income and taxpayers who have no children of school age are crucial in many districts that have an aging adult population.
* PERB (Public Employment Relations Board) influences collective bargaining by promulgating rules to carry out the collective bargaining laws enacted by state legislatures. It also influences collective bargaining by its assignment of mediators and arbitrators, and by its compilation of rulings of arbitrators [41].

RECOGNITION CLAUSE

This clause, usually the initial clause or article in any printed master contractual agreement, is one which must be very carefully worded. It specifies which employees the union represents and which it doesn't represent, and gives sole representation rights to the union in all matters of collective bargaining throughout the length of the ratified master contractual agreement [42]. The contract is binding for its lifetime, but can be challenged by a vote to overthrow union legal action requested of the PERB by union members. It is crucial that management and confidential employees are listed as being omitted from the employees the union can represent [43].

CERTIFICATION AND DECERTIFICATION ELECTIONS

Although a board of education may accept a specific union as the official representation of a class of employees for the purpose of representation of those employees for all collective bargaining purposes, the union usually has to be selected through a certification election conducted by PERB (Public Employment Relations Board) [44]. New York State's Taylor Law contains the following wording in its section entitled Determination of Representation Status:

For purposes of resolving disputes concerning representation status, pursuant to section two hundred five or two hundred six of this article, the board or government, as the case may be, shall:

1. define the appropriate employer-employee negotiating unit taking into account the following standards:
   (a) the definition of the unit shall correspond to a community of interest among the employees to be included in the unit;
   (b) the officials of the government at the level of the unit shall have the power to agree, or to make effective recommendations to other administrative authority or the legislative body with respect to, the terms and conditions of employment upon which the employees desire to negotiate; and
   (c) the unit shall be compatible with the joint responsibilities of the public employer and public employees to serve the public.
2. ascertain the public employees' choice of employee organization as their representative (in cases where the parties to a dispute have not agreed on the means to ascertain the choice, if any, of the employees in the unit) on the basis of dues deduction authorizations or other evidences, or, if necessary, by conducting an election.
3. certify or recognize an employee organization upon (a) the determination that such organization represents that group of public employees it claims to represent, and (b) the affirmation by such organization that it does not assert the right to strike against any government, to assist or participate in such strike, or to impose an obligation to conduct, assist or participate in such a strike [45].

In most states a decertification election can be requested, and the election will be supervised by PERB (Public Employment Relations

Board) if the school district presents evidence that a substantial number of employees in the unit want to decertify, or if a substantial number of employees take it upon themselves to petition PERB to supervise a decertification election. Generally, a decertification election can only be called during a specifically stipulated period close to the end of the master contractual agreement in effect. Even if the decertification election is successful, the union previously certified would serve as the sole representative for collective bargaining purposes until the termination date listed in the existing master contractual agreement.

UNFAIR LABOR PRACTICE

Although other matters may be considered unfair labor practices by individual states, normally, an unfair labor practice can be charged against a union when (1) an employee organization or its agents deliberately interfere with, restrain, or coerce employees in the exercise of the rights granted them under the collective bargaining law, or (2) when the employee organization or its agents does not collectively negotiate in good faith with the public employer [46].

The public employer or its agents can be charged with unfair labor practice when (1) it conducts itself in the same manner as the union, using the unfair practices listed above, (2) it attempts to dominate or interfere with the formation or administration of any employee organization for the purpose of depriving employees of their rights under the collective bargaining law, (3) it attempts to discriminate against any employee for the purpose of encouraging or discouraging membership or participation in the activities of any union, and (4) it refuses to continue the terms of an expired agreement until a new agreement is negotiated.

Sadly, during serious adversarial negotiations, charges of unfair labor practices and/or bad faith bargaining are leveled against the other party solely as a tactical move. Usually, when this happens the other party to the negotiations levels countercharges. If the media covers these charges, unnecessary complications result and negative public opinions are formed.

BAD FAITH BARGAINING

Bad faith bargaining refers to a situation in which either party to the negotiations refuses to attend a reasonable series of meetings, refuses to meet with reasonable frequency, refuses to give serious consideration to the proposals of the other party, or refuses to make reasonable proposals or counterproposals. It should be emphasized, however, that if the above criteria are met, there is no requirement that either party must agree to any proposal [47].

UNION/MANAGEMENT CONFLICT WHEN SCHOOL DISTRICTS CONTRACT FOR SERVICES WITH OUTSIDE ORGANIZATIONS

Unions are very protective of jobs. This is understandable from the union's view, as every job retained means that another union member is paying dues to assist with the union's operations; it also means that the larger the union's membership, the greater the union's bargaining power. When contracts are let to non-school district commercial companies for things like food services, custodial services, maintenance services, or transportation services a red flag is raised in the minds of the unions' leadership and membership. Recently, the total operation of some schools has been handed over to commercial entities. This privatization also includes the supplying of teachers and administrators for the school district. Obviously, this would be of concern to the NEA and AFT leadership.

With the outsourcing of classified jobs and the privatization of the total operation of some schools, a whole new threatening dimension is inserted into the union/management dialogue [48]. If outsourcing and privatization proves to be more efficient, more productive, and more cost effective, what does the union do to counteract this trend? Does the union restructure to be more efficient, more productive, and more cost effective, or does the union mount a strong adversarial charge against management, coupled with an intensive internal and external media propaganda campaign? Only the future will determine the evolving union/management environment in our school districts; and only then will the roles to be played by union leaders and union membership become clear.

SUMMARY

A number of items and matters that affect collective bargaining require definition. Agency shop refers to an arrangement in which employees may remain non-union members but are required to pay a fee to the union for representational services. A closed shop, usually illegal, is one in which all district employees must belong to the union, even prior to employment. A union shop is one in which all employees must belong to the union, but not necessarily before they are hired.

The possession of complete, accurate, and convincing information regarding negotiations must be augmented by judicious and well-timed use during the negotiating sessions. Separating fact from propaganda during the negotiations process is frequently difficult, due to the leaking of rumors or the release of statements to the media. The NEA or AFT may support the local union's tactics and other strategies, and they can provide the local union with access to (1) a large nationally based databank of comparative information, (2) personnel such as Uniserve directors (who can serve as chief negotiators), (3) state-level training for local stewards, and (4) regional backup of both information and personnel in case of serious conflict situations.

Contract language is critical in that it defines mandatory terms, or permissive and flexible terms. The first negotiated master contractual agreement is the most important district document ever to be ratified, since it will set the stage for all future contractual negotiations. Key points requiring specific language include class size, leaves, academic freedom, employee evaluation, employee assignment, and benefit packages.

During negotiations, information leakages about tactics, stages of agreement or disagreement, or specific details about article proposals must be minimized, which may require the withholding of information from each side's referent group. Information should be shared with the media through a joint progress report.

Future negotiations may be affected by the establishment of reopeners, which set a timeline for successor contracts to be negotiated. A zipper clause is language within an existing contract which will allow re-negotiations of a specific article before the end of the existing contract. It is intended to avoid a holdup on items which one party or the other feels should be renegotiated sooner than the expiration date of the contract. Expedited bargaining is a streamlined approach to negotiations, when both teams come well-armed with information and push for a rapid Tentative Agreement. Focused or limited bargaining is similar in that the parties have a prior agreement to hasten the process by carrying forward most of the existing contractual articles, and limiting negotiation to only a few articles.

The forces impacting the negotiations process are many: the public, business and industrial groups, political forces, judicial and quasi-judicial agencies, government agencies, media, students, parents, taxpayers, and the Public Employment Relations Board. The recognition clause is a legal term, indicating which employees the union represents and which it does not, and gives sole representation rights to the union. Related to this is the legal selection process for that recognition status, done through a certification election conducted by the PERB. A decertification election, requested by union membership, removes the union as the sole representative, but this can only be done at the expiration of the existing master contractual agreement.

Unfair labor practices pertain to both union and management. If a union interferes with an individual's rights under the bargaining law, or if it does not negotiate in good faith, it may be charged with unfair labor practice. Likewise, the employer may be charged with the same violations if the employer attempts to interfere with the organizational rights of the employees. These charges are frequently leveled as a tactical move during adversarial bargaining. Bad faith bargaining occurs when either party refuses to meet, consider, make proposals, or offer counterproposals, or neglect or refuse to seriously consider the proposals of the other party during negotiations.

EXERCISES

1. Investigate the master contract, if any, or standard employee contracts in your school district. Note any of the particular contract language that is used and reflect on how it might impact the district's employee relationships. Are there any clauses that could cause a significant fiscal impact, such as class size caps?
2. Investigate the history of any previous contract negotiations or nonunion salary negotiations in your (or another) district. What were the issues? the resolution, if any?
3. What has been the role, if any, of the Public Employment Relations Board (PERB) in your (or another) district?

REFERENCES

1. Aaron, B., J. M. Najita, and J. L. Stern. 1988. *Public Sector Bargaining.* Washington, D.C.: Industrial Relations Research Associates, pp. 220–221.
2. Donley, M. O., Jr. 1976. *Power to the Teacher.* Bloomington, IN: Indiana University Press, pp. 132–133.

3. Ibid.

4. Splitt, D. A. 1991. "How Much Can Unions Charge Nonmembers?" *Executive Educator.* 13(9): 18.

5. Helsby, R. D., J. Tener, and J. Lefkowitz, eds. 1985. *The Evolving Process—Collective Negotiations in Public Employment.* Fort Washington, PA: Labor Relations Press, p. xxxiii.

6. Coleman, C. J. 1990. *Managing Labor Relations in the Public Sector.* San Francisco, CA: Jossey-Bass Publishers, pp. 200–201.

7. Herman, J. J. and G. E. Megiveron. 1993. *Collective Bargaining in Education: Win/Win, Win/Lose, Lose/Lose.* Lancaster, PA: Technomic Publishing Co., Inc., pp. 183–189.

8. Helsby, R. D., J. Tener, and J. Lefkowitz, eds. 1985. *The Evolving Process,* p. xii.

9. Coleman, C. J. 1990. *Managing Labor Relations,* p. 201.

10. Koppich, J. E. 1993. "Getting Started." In *A Union of Professionals: Labor Relations and Educational Reform,* edited by Kerchner, C. T. and J. E. Koppich. New York: Teachers College Press, pp. 194–195.

11. Webster, W. G., Sr. 1985. *Effective Collective Bargaining in Public Education.* Ames, IA: Iowa State University Press, pp. 81–86.

12. Neal, R. 1980. *Bargaining Tactics—A Reference Manual for Public Sector Labor Negotiations.* Richard G. Neal Associates, pp. 147–151.

13. Herman, J. J. 1991. "The Two Faces of Collective Bargaining," *School Business Affairs,* 57(2): 11–12.

14. Webster, W. G., Sr. 1985. *Effective Collective Bargaining,* pp. 56–57.

15. Webster, W. G., Sr. 1985. *Effective Collective Bargaining,* pp. 150–151.

16. Many, T. W. and C. A. Sloan. 1990. "Management and Labor Perceptions of School Collective Bargaining," *Journal of Collective Negotiations,* 19(4): 283–296.

17. Murphy, M. 1990. *Blackboard Unions—The AFT & the NEA 1900–1980.* Ithaca, NY. Cornell University Press, pp. 270–271.

18. Maier, M. M. 1987. *City Unions.* New Brunswick, NJ: Rutgers University Press, pp. 133–134.

19. Webster, W. G., Sr. 1985. *Effective Collective Bargaining,* p. 170.

20. Attea, W. J. 1993. "From Conventional to Strategic Bargaining: One Superintendent's Experience," *School Administrator,* 50(10): 16–19.

21. Castetter, W. B. 1986. *The Personnel Function in Education.* New York, NY: Macmillan Publishing Company, pp. 171–172.

22. Ibid.

23. Rebore, R. W. 1991. *Personnel Administration in Education—A Management Approach.* Third Edition. Englewood Cliffs, NJ: Prentice-Hall, Inc., p. 317.

24. Janes, L. 1984. "Collective Bargaining," *NASSP Instructional Leadership Booklet,* pp. 22–23.

25. Ibid.

26. Castetter, W. B. 1986. *The Personnel Function,* pp. 149–155.

27. Neal, R. 1980. *Bargaining Tactics,* p. 153.

28. Neal, R. 1980. *Bargaining Tactics,* pp. 73–75.

29. Rebore, R. W. 1991. *Personnel Administration,* pp. 309–310.

30. Webster, W. G., Sr. 1985. *Effective Collective Bargaining,* p. 76.

31. Webster, W. G., Sr. 1985. *Effective Collective Bargaining,* p. 138.

32. Smith, S. C., D. Ball, and D. Liontos. 1990. *Working Together—The Collaborative Style of Bargaining.* Eugene, OR: ERIC Clearinghouse on Educational Management, University of Oregon, pp. 55, 58.

33. Castetter, W. B. 1986. *The Personnel Function,* pp. 150–151.

34. Cimini, M. H., S. L. Behrmann, and E. M. Johnson. 1994. "Labor-Management Bargaining in 1993," *Monthly Labor Review,* 117(1): 20–33.

35. Webster, W. G., Sr. 1985. *Effective Collective Bargaining,* p. 216.

36. Webster, W. G., Sr. 1985. *Effective Collective Bargaining,* p. 217.

37. Herman, J. J. and G. E. Megiveron. 1993. *Collective Bargaining in Education,* p. 192.

38. Blakey, J. H. and K. A. Peterson. 1993. "Evergreen Process Keeps Peace at Contract Time," *School Administrator,* 50(10): 37.

39. Bascia, N. 1994. *Unions in Teachers' Professional Lives: Social, Intellectual, and Practical Concerns.* New York: Teachers College Press, pp. 1–8.

40. Ordovensky, P. and G. Marx. 1993. *Working with the News Media.* Alexandria, VA: American Association of School Administrators, pp. 22–24.

41. Kearney, R. C. 1984. *Labor Relations in the Public Sector.* New York, NY: Marcel Dekker, Inc., pp. 73–74.

42. Helsby, R. D., J. Tener, and J. Lefkowitz, eds. 1985. *The Evolving Process,* pp. 107–108.

43. Castetter, W. B. 1996. *The Human Resource Function in Educational Administration.* 6th ed. Englewood Cliffs, NJ: Merrill, p. 586.

44. Kearney, R. C. 1984. *Labor Relations,* pp. 50–51.

45. New York State Public Employment Relations Board. 1983–1984. *The Taylor Law.* Albany, NY: New York Public Employment Relations Board, p. 11.

46. Kearney, R. C. 1984. *Labor Relations,* p. 332.

47. Neal, R. 1980. *Bargaining Tactics,* pp. 203–204.

48. Greenwald, J. 1995. "The Battle to Revive the Unions," *Time,* 145(18): 64–66.

Summary of Collective Negotiations

CHAPTER 15 discusses the do's, maybe's, and don'ts of collective bargaining, the benefits for labor and management, the losses for labor and management, and the benefits and deficits of adversarial bargaining and win-win bargaining. The school-based management movement and its potential impact on collective bargaining precedes the closing summary and references.

Many years ago there were two farmers who worked adjoining pieces of land. One day they were out with their horses plowing the land and getting the soil ready for the spring planting. They began arguing about who owned the center strip of approximately one-half acre of land.

Until this day, they had always been great friends, and they had even helped one another by loaning horses and physically assisting each other with the planting and harvesting chores. In other words, their working history had been win-win.

But, for some reason, this day they became embroiled in a heated argument. Tempers flared for weeks, and when they finally began talking again, they ended up playing power games with the intent of beating the other man out of the contested property. This started the process of adversarial bargaining.

Farmer Jim proposed that Farmer Ken could keep the contested land if Farmer Ken would give him his prized team of Belgian plowhorses. Jim thought to himself "The Belgians are worth as much or more than the one-half acre of land." Jim realized the value of quid pro quo (receiving a value equivalent or greater than the value of what you give). Ken countered by explaining that if he gave up his horses he would have no method of plowing the land, and this would lead him and his family to financial disaster. So Ken counterproposed that if Jim would agree that the one-half acre of land belonged to him, he would give Jim one-half of all the vegetables produced on the one-half acre for the next five years.

Jim said he would seriously consider Ken's offer, but that he needed time to think it over and discuss it with his wife. After caucusing with his wife, Jim decided that he would reject Ken's offer. He stated that he would have to get something else from Ken for the land, or that Ken would have to give him something in addition to the produce from the one-half acre for the next five years.

After numerous proposals and counterproposals, Ken and Jim agreed that they could not find a way to settle their disagreement. They decided that Farmer Pete, one of their neighbors, was a fair man who both of them respected, and that they would ask him to assist them in reaching an agreement about the contested land, since they had reached an impasse. Farmer Pete served as a mediator at this impasse stage, but he wasn't able to get Jim and Ken to agree on any settlement of the dispute. Having attempted numerous times to get Jim and Ken to agree, Farmer Pete said that he would not continue to try to get the two men to reach agreement over the disputed one-half acre of land, but he did recommend that Jim and Ken ask Preacher Jack to study the facts in the matter and render a judgement that would be binding on both Jim and Ken.

Jim and Ken took Pete's suggestion, and Preacher Jack agreed to serve as fact-finder and arbitrator to resolve the dispute. Preacher Jack met with both men and had them agree to the value placed on the land. After looking at the value of other items either party would accept, such as five cows, another piece of land, a certain amount of labor, and other trade-off possibilities, Preacher Jack rendered his fact-finding report. He determined that since neither party seemed comfortable with any trade-offs for the land, that the land would be split in half. The one-quarter acre that adjoined Jim's land would be given to Jim, and the one-quarter acre that adjoined Ken's land would be given to Ken.

Both Ken and Jim felt the Preacher's decision was a fair one. However, before Preacher Jack left the two farmers he gave them a good lecture. He stated that the men had been friends for over twenty years and he stressed how they had always helped each other in times of need, how their wives were good friends, and how their children grew up together. He also told them that they were foolish to have let a little piece of land interrupt their friendship for the past seven months, and that if they used common sense, they would realize that their friendship and the friendship of their families was of much more value than the little one-half acre of contested land.

When the Preacher left, Jim and Ken began thinking about what the Preacher said, and they agreed that the friendly and helping relationship they had maintained for practically their entire lives was too valuable to lose. They decided to reignite that friendship by having a joint picnic for both of the families after Sunday's church service. They also invited Preacher Jack to join them.

It was towards the end of the picnic that Jim and Ken shook hands, looked each other in the eye and vowed never to be adversaries again. They had learned the value of win-win the hard way, and they weren't about to lose it again in the future.

This short fictitious tale spells out, in rather simple terms, the process of collective bargaining, and the value of a win-win collaborative approach. It also shows the danger of an adversarial approach to bargaining, and the value of mediation, fact-finding and arbitration if an impasse is reached during the adversarial bargaining process.

The dual goals of any aspect of collective bargaining are (1) to arrive at a fair and equitable agreement, and (2) to use a continuing win-win process as the best means of arriving at agreements. Win-win builds respect, caring, and honesty and, whenever possible, is the only way to go.

Now let's turn to the do's of collective bargaining. The do's shall be followed by a discussion of the maybe's and the don'ts of collective bargaining.

THE DO'S OF COLLECTIVE BARGAINING

If you are involved in any phase of the collective bargaining process, there are some do's that will enhance your chance of success [1]. Some of the most important ones include:

- Do think win-win and act win-win whenever possible.
- Do your homework, and collect all the data necessary prior to meeting with the other party.
- Do present your position(s) in a clear and simple manner in order to avoid any misunderstanding, and support your position with factual information and logical rationale.
- Do put yourself in the other party's shoes in order to understand fully where the other party is coming from and the needs of the other party.

- Do listen intently to the other party's position(s), and carefully study the data that the other party presents.
- Do be aware of any outside forces that may be influencing the collective bargaining.
- Do act honestly and ethically.
- Do treat the other party with respect and courtesy.
- Do request assistance such as mediation, fact-finding, and/or arbitration if your differences with the other party cannot be resolved without outside help.
- Do compliment the other party on their hard work leading to the agreement.
- Do commit yourself to working with the other party to initiate a win-win (if win-win has not already been initiated), and build upon it for the long term benefit of both parties, the students, the employees, the administrators, the board of education, and the community at large [2–4].

Along with some do's for collective bargaining, there are also some maybe's. These maybe's represent the gray areas, which must be decided on a case-by-case basis by the parties who are involved in collective bargaining.

THE MAYBE'S OF COLLECTIVE BARGAINING

The major maybe's to be considered during any phase of collective bargaining will be varied in number and type, and will depend on the current phase and state of the collective bargaining process that exists in the school district at a specific point in time. The major maybe's, however, will most certainly include the following:

- Maybe an attorney should serve as the chief negotiator for the negotiating team. The attorney should be very active in the wording of proposals and counters, and should serve as the resident expert in the caucuses with the purpose of offering advice on the legality of what is being proposed by either side.
- Maybe the union should allow a state's Uniserve director to serve as the chief negotiator for the negotiating team.
- Maybe the board of education's negotiating team should include some board member representation. Many persons, however, feel that having a board member as part of the negotiating team is a major mistake [5].

- Maybe the superintendent should sit in as a member of the board of education's negotiating team.
- Maybe the guidelines given by the board to its negotiating team should low ball what it would eventually feel is adequate.
- Maybe the guidelines given the union's negotiating team should high ball what the union would eventually feel is a fair settlement.
- Maybe the ground rules agreed to for negotiations should include no publicity, closed sessions, and TA'ing (Tentatively Agreeing) each article as it is agreed to by both parties.
- Maybe at the early signs of a possible impasse, both parties should request that PERB (Public Employment Relations Board) assign a mediator to the negotiations.
- Maybe a fact-finder should be selected if the mediator is not able to get both parties to agree.
- Maybe an arbitration panel should be selected if the fact-finder's recommendations are not accepted, and the public pressure exerted after publication of the fact-finder's findings is not sufficient to cause agreement to be reached between the two parties.
- Maybe both parties should choose to make the arbitration panel's rulings mandates for settlement.
- Maybe the union should involve its members in work-to-rule behavior if the contract negotiations reach a critical stage.
- Maybe the board of education's administrators should develop a detailed strike plan, if a strike appears to be imminent. It is important that the final strike plan be known to only a very few, and that it be kept confidential until it is actually put into use.
- Maybe the union should take a strike vote and eventually go on strike if it feels there is no other way to resolve the impasse.
- Maybe cooler and more logical heads can prevail and reach agreement by attempting new offers and using new strategies in the hopes of averting any serious long-term damage to union/management relations [6–8].

Now that the do's and maybe's of collective bargaining have been explored, one area of discussion remains. The don'ts of collective bargaining share equal importance with the do's.

THE DON'TS OF COLLECTIVE BARGAINING

The don'ts may somewhat differ from school district to school district, and they may differ within the same school district at different points in time and during different phases of the collective bargaining process. Be this as it may, there are some universal don'ts that are worthy of emphasis.

- Don't assume that any phase of the collective bargaining process is destined to be adversarial [9].
- Don't assume that the members of the opposite party have negative intentions, or that they can't be trusted.
- Don't think of collective bargaining as a battlefield, wherein the other party is the enemy and you must always be victorious.
- Don't ever participate in any phase of collective bargaining without doing your homework and being fully prepared.
- Don't look at the negatives, but find the sunshine at the end of the process.
- Don't give up on the other party prematurely.
- Don't be afraid to ask for outside assistance if both parties are stuck in neutral.
- Don't forget that the collective bargaining process is a long-term commitment to fairness and equity in the relations between employees and those who employ them. It is not a quick fix proposition [10].
- Don't allow any animosities, distrust, or personality conflicts to continue, and resolve them as quickly as possible. Also, develop harmonious long-term relationships between union and management whenever possible [11,12].

Now that we have briefly outlined the do's, maybe's, and don'ts of collective bargaining, let's turn to the topic of the benefits and losses for both labor and management involved in the process of collective bargaining.

THE BENEFITS OF COLLECTIVE BARGAINING FOR LABOR AND MANAGEMENT

It is quite obvious that many state legislatures assume collective bargaining is beneficial, as most states have passed collective bargaining laws. These laws permit employees in public employment situations, including public school districts, to bargain with their employer over the terms of some of the conditions of their employment, although states differ in the specific items about which they (1) mandate bargaining, (2) permit bargaining, and (3) prohibit bargaining [13]. A *mandated* area may be salaries, *permitted* areas may include class size or teacher load, and a *prohibited* area may be the right to strike. Regardless of what is permitted, mandated, and/or prohibited, collective bargaining has benefits for both labor and management. Some of these benefits include the following:

* Collective bargaining provides a uniform and continuous means of communication on matters of importance to both employees and their employer.
* Collective bargaining simplifies the number of unions or the numbers of employee-selected leadership personnel that management must contact to resolve issues. This simplification occurs when a specific union is certified, after an election supervised by PERB (Public Employment Relations Board) to determine that the majority of the employees in the designated unit desire that specific union to be their sole representative for collective bargaining purposes. It may also, however, have the effect of lessening the number of union leadership personnel for management to contact to resolve issues.
* Collective bargaining causes the two parties to negotiate a master contractual agreement, which spells out *in writing* the contractual details of the relationship between employees and administrators and between the union and management. This contract provides the day-to-day guidelines that guide the actions of both parties during the time the ratified contract is in effect.
* Collective bargaining allows for third-party assistance when a contractual agreement between the two parties reaches the impasse stage.
* Collective bargaining laws prohibit strikes or other actions that are harmful to the public's interest.
* Collectively bargained master contractual agreements contain procedures for resolving grievances which may arise during the time frame of the existing master contract agreement. In many cases, the master contractual agreement will permit an outside third party to assist in resolving grievances when the two parties cannot resolve the grievance themselves.
* Collective bargaining laws prohibit unfair labor practices by the union or by management.
* Collective bargaining laws, through the rules and regulations promulgated by the PERB (Public Employment Relations Board), provide a procedure designed to eliminate bad faith bargaining practices by either party to the negotiations.

- Collective bargaining laws provide the same representational freedom that has long existed in the private employment sector [14].

Not only are there benefits to be derived from collective bargaining for both labor and management, there are also some losses. Each individual involved will have to make a determination as to whether or not the benefits override the losses, or the losses override the benefits [15].

THE LOSSES OF COLLECTIVE BARGAINING FOR LABOR AND MANAGEMENT

- Collective bargaining results in some loss of individual freedoms for the individual employee. The whole essence of bargaining is group cohesiveness and constraints on the mass to bring the picture to the lowest (not highest) common denominator in employee-employer relationships.
- Collective bargaining tends to restrict the flexibility for decision making related to items that are negotiated into the ratified master contractual agreement, but does make for uniform handling of employees and eliminates the patronizing of favorites. This is, however, hardly a trade-off for bargaining.
- Collective bargaining often leads to a robotic type of by the book, day-to-day operations.
- Collective bargaining sometimes causes actions to take place which are not in the interest of the local union, especially when the local is tied into a unified structure with the union's state and national officials.
- Collective bargaining sometimes restricts management and the board of education from operating the district in the manner in which it should be operated.
- Collective bargaining, when it becomes extremely adversarial in nature, can destroy excellent employee/administrator relationships for years, can cause a hostile climate in which to educate children and youth, and can result in a loss of emotional and financial support from the community at large [16–18].

THE BENEFITS AND DEFICITS OF ADVERSARIAL BARGAINING

There is only one benefit to adversarial bargaining: one party wants to overpower the other party and, thus, gain more than it gives. The gains may not even be defensible, but they certainly will raise havoc with any future labor/management relations. In addition, when the other party reverses the power dimension, it is certain that the other party will take punitive action and get back as much or more than they lost during the last adversarial bargaining of a master contractual agreement [19].

THE BENEFITS AND DEFICITS OF WIN-WIN BARGAINING

If the two parties can collectively bargain and negotiate a master contractual agreement on the basis of collaborative action, and within a climate of trust, caring, respect, and mutual problem solving, there really should not be any deficits associated with a win-win approach to collective bargaining. The benefits will accrue to the employees, the administrators, the board of education members, the union and management, and the community at large. But, mostly, they will accrue to the benefit of the students of the school district, for they will attend schools that have an exceptionally positive school climate [20].

SCHOOL-BASED MANAGEMENT AND ITS IMPACT ON COLLECTIVE BARGAINING

Today, one of the most popular formats for restructuring schools is that of school-based management. The legislatures of the states of Kentucky and Texas have mandated it, as have many local school boards, and some superintendents. Some principals and teachers have received permission to attempt it. It matters little if the local school building does or does not wish to become the center of attention and accountability, the school-based management structure and process is increasing in implementation across the United States and internationally [21]. Although this popular reform movement holds much promise for the positive restructuring of schools, it has a dramatic potential to impact the way that collective bargaining has taken place in school districts [22–24].

In reality, many of the areas included in traditional ratified master contractual agreements become the business of a third party—that of school-based management committees comprised of teachers, parents, and the individual school building's principal [25]. Even though Kentucky does not have a state collective bargaining law, many of the school districts have included some of the items contained in the

Kentucky Reform Act in the decision-making power of the local school building's school-based management committee [26]. A glance through the major portions of the act related to school-based management (sometimes called school-site management or shared decision making in many locations), as outlined in Chapter 3, will illustrate the potential impact on the traditional collective bargaining decision-making structure, particularly for interviewing and hiring in Kentucky, and in Texas, legislative local-empowerment paired with language intended to preserve the absence of legal formal collective negotiations [27].

SUMMARY

Collective bargaining is a dynamic, important, and very serious process. Preparing for it, doing it, and living with its results will determine, in many aspects and to a large degree, the organizational structure that will exist in a school district and in the day-to-day procedures to be followed. Because of the impact on the school district's structure and procedures, the results of collective bargaining will have a significant effect on the climate and culture of the school district. In addition, the way it is conducted by union and management and the results achieved by it can strongly influence the attitudes of students, parents, taxpayers, and the citizenry of the school district. It is extremely important, and it must be handled carefully and wisely by all parties involved.

The innovation of school-based or site-based management, which promotes the direct involvement of employees and citizens in management decisions related to the individual school buildings, has been a main focus. If the school district allows school-based management teams authority over the selection of employees, the structure of the school day, and some budgetary areas, both union and management must take these matters seriously when managing or renegotiating a master contract. "Business as usual" approaches will not suffice. The environment has changed substantially, and the tenor of collective negotiations will be profoundly altered.

EXERCISES

1. Which of the "maybe's of collective bargaining" listed apply to your district?

2. Interview an administrator who has experience with collective bargaining to determine what they see as the benefits and drawbacks of the process. How do they perceive the win-win concept?

3. How as SBM impacted the negotiations process in your (or another) district?

REFERENCES

1. *Strategies for School System Leaders on District-Level Change.* 1994. "Dade County: A Stable Partnership in a Sea of Change." Alexandria, VA: Panasonic Foundation and the American Association of School Administrators, pp. 6–7.

2. Nyland, L. 1987. "Win-Win Bargaining Pays Off," *Education Digest.* L111(1): 28–29.

3. Maddux, R. B. 1988. *Successful Negotiation—Effective "Win-Win" Strategies and Tactics.* Los Altos, CA: Crisp Publications, Inc.

4. Thompson, B. L. 1991. "Negotiation Training: Win-Win or What?" *Training,* 28(6): 31–35.

5. Miron, L. F. and R. K. Wimpelberg. 1992. "The Role of School Boards in the Governance of Education." In *School Boards: Changing Local Control,* edited by P. F. First and H. J. Walberg. Berkeley, CA: McCutchan Publishing, p. 170.

6. Smith, S. C., D. Ball, and D. Liontos. 1990. *Working Together—The Collaborative Style of Bargaining.* Eugene, OR: ERIC Clearinghouse on Educational Management, University of Oregon, pp. 58–59.

7. Barrett, Jerome T. 1985. *Labor-Management Cooperation in the Public Service: An Idea Whose Time Has Come.* Washington, D.C.: International Personnel Management Association, pp. 29–30.

8. Herman, J. J. and G. E. Megiveron. 1993. *Collective Bargaining in Education: Win/Win, Win/Lose, Lose/Lose.* Lancaster, PA: Technomic Publishing Co., Inc., pp. 204–205.

9. Kerchner, C. T. 1993. "Building the Airplane as It Rolls Down the Runway: Administrators Discover Labor Relations as the Linchpin to School Change," *School Administrator,* 50(10): 8–15.

10. Keane, W. G. 1996. *Win-Win or Else: Collective Bargaining in an Age of Public Discontent.* Thousand Oaks, CA: Corwin Press, Sage Publications, pp. 31, 33.

11. Neal, R. 1980. *Bargaining Tactics—A Reference Manual for Public Sector Labor Negotiations.* Richard G. Neal Associates, pp. 39, 115, 193, 197.

12. Blakey, J. H. and K. A. Peterson. 1993. "Evergreen Process Keeps Peace at Contract Time," *School Administrator,* 50(10): 37.

13. Helsby, R. D., J. Tener, and J. Lefkowitz, eds. 1985. *The Evolving Process— Collective Negotiations in Public Employment.* Fort Washington, PA: Labor Relations Press, pp. 5–12.

14. Coleman, C. J. 1990. *Managing Labor Relations in the Public Sector.* San Francisco, CA: Jossey-Bass Publishers, p. 32.

15. Herman, J. J. and G. E. Megiveron. 1993. *Collective Bargaining in Education,* pp. 207–208.

16. Castetter, W. B. 1986. *The Personnel Function in Education.* New York, NY: Macmillan Publishing Company, pp. 137–138.

17. Richardson, R. C. 1985. *Collective Bargaining Objectives: A Positive Approach.* Englewood Cliffs, NJ: Prentice-Hall, Inc., p. 251.

18. Streshly, W. A. and T. A. DeMitchell. 1994. *Teacher Unions and TQE,* Thousand Oaks, CA: Corwin Press, Sage Publications, pp. 31, 33.

19. Smith, S. C., D. Ball, and D. Liontos. 1990. *Working Together,* pp. 18–19.

20. Smith, S. C., D. Ball, and D. Liontos. 1990. *Working Together,* p. 12.

21. Herman, J. L. and J. J. Herman. 1993. "A State-by-State Snapshot of School-Based Management Practices," *International Journal of Educational Reform,* 2(3): 89–94.

22. Nickoles, K. W. 1990. "Future Shock: What's Coming to the Bargaining Table," *School Business Affairs,* 56(12): 36–38.

23. Herman, J. J. 1992. "School-based Management: Sharing the Resource Decisions," *NASSP Bulletin,* 76(545): 102–105.

24. Herman, J. J. and J. L. Herman. 1995. "A Study of School-Based Management in Selected Southern States," *International Journal of School Reform,* 4(4): 89–94.

25. Herman, J. J. and J. L. Herman. 1992. "Educational Administration: School-based Management," *The Clearing House,* 65(5): 261–263.

26. Herman, J. J. and J. L. Herman. 1993. *School-Based Management: Current Thinking and Practice,* Springfield, IL: Charles C. Thomas, Publisher, pp. 158–159.

27. Miller, M. H., K. Noland, and J. Schaaf. 1990. *A Guide to the Kentucky Education Reform Act.* Frankfort, KY: Legislative Research Commission, p. 6.

APPLYING NEGOTIATION, MEDIATION, AND ARBITRATION TECHNIQUES WITHIN THE BROADER SCHOOL DISTRICT ENVIRONMENT

Section Five consists of two chapters. Chapter 16, Dealing with Conflicts Involving Internal Individual and Group Interests, addresses conflict between and/or among a variety of individuals and groups. Student, administration, employee, and board of education examples are provided.

Chapter 17, Dealing with Conflicts of Interest between External and Community Pressure Groups and the Board of Education and Administration, presents a variety of situations in which conflicts exist between external groups and school district personnel and officials. A variety of resolution strategies are provided in this chapter.

Dealing with Conflicts Involving Internal Individual and Group Interests

CHAPTER 16 discusses conflict resolution as a means of positive growth and provides a series of examples involving conflicts among students, employee/administration, board of education/superintendent, and board members themselves. It relates typical examples of conflicts of interest, including band boosters versus athletic boosters, extracurricular activities versus athletics, and conservative groups versus liberal groups (related to curricular programs). Changing staffing patterns of employees, changing evaluation procedures for employees, and implementing merit or performance pay are discussed, along with communicating with the community and the media during serious internal conflicts of interest. The chapter ends by discussing media coverage as a possible determiner of conflict resolution outcomes.

It should be noted that all of the examples are true incidents, but no actual identity of the individuals or school districts involved is provided.

CONFLICT RESOLUTION AS A MEANS OF POSITIVE GROWTH

Conflicts are often viewed as negative happenings. However, when the interests of two or more parties differ, the resolution of those differences can lead to (1) a very positive outcome, (2) growth through understanding other's views by the individuals and/or groups involved in the conflict, and (3) long-term beneficial communication and future conflict resolution skills by those involved in the conflict [1].

Many conflicts arise over time in any organization—this is also true of school districts—due to their very complexity. The interests of students, employees, teachers, administrators, board members, and classified personnel sometimes vary. Often these conflicts can and should be resolved in a manner that leaves the parties involved with respect for each other and with reasonably equitable solutions with which they can comfortably live [2]. A few examples of conflicts follow.

CONFLICTS: STUDENT EXAMPLES

At the elementary level, students sometimes participate in or create conflict situations. One of many examples that could be given is that of two or more students involved in a physical confrontation. One elementary principal developed a very appropriate learning experience, based upon the principle of progressive discipline, for young students who were involved in conflict situations [3]. Whenever a conflict arose between two students or among more than two students, each student had to meet with the principal and follow the following steps:

(1) At the first offense, the student had to communicate all matters related to the incident, describe her or his part in the conflict, discuss how she/he wished to be treated, determine ways in which the student's behavior deviated from the expected norm, and determine what she/he had to do to apologize and repair any damage done to the other party (parties) to the conflict. In addition, all of this had to be placed in writing by the student and mailed to the student's parents or guardian, with a copy placed in the student's cumulative file in the guidance office or the principal's office.

(2) At the second offense by the same student, all the above steps were followed and an additional step was added. This additional step involved calling the parent at home or at work and relating all of the above. The written documentation was also mailed, as in the first offense, with a copy placed in the student's cumulative record file.

(3) At the third offense by the same student, all of the above steps were followed, including the phone call and the mailed letter, but another step was added. The final step in this progressive discipline approach required the parent or guardian to come to the school during normal school hours (even if this meant missing work or bringing along younger siblings) to have the student go through all of the explanations in the presence of the parent or guardian, the student's teacher, and the school's principal. Again, written documentation was also placed in the student's cumulative file. Many, if not most, parents are very concerned about taking

off a day of work to come to school to hear their child talk about her/his misbehavior.

This procedure was developed by the principal, the teaching staff, and a representative group of parents and guardians. The procedure was placed in writing in a handbook, and it was provided to each child's parents at the beginning of every school year. It is a fair, creative, and effective method of resolving conflicts among the youngest students of the school district.

At the middle school level, the frequency of conflicts many times exceeds the frequency observed at the elementary level. In one instance, a group of older middle school boys and girls are intimidating some of the younger students into paying them their lunch money for protection. Once this is discovered, there are multiple actions that could be taken.

First, a meeting of all parents and guardians of the "protector students" should be called, and a routine course of action collaboratively developed if, or when, any further activities of this nature arise. Again, this consensus action plan would be placed in writing and provided to each student's parents or guardians.

Second, a student court could be organized by having the students elect their own representatives to meet with the faculty and administration to review any conflicts that arise. This court would only be advisory in nature, as it could have no legal basis for mandating corrective actions.

Third, a peer counseling program could be initiated. This has proven successful in many situations where conflict resolution among students has been successfully handled. This program would have limitations as to the types of conflicts that could be handled through this procedure, due to the actionability or seriousness of the offense [4–6].

Fourth, counselors and officers of the law could be called upon to meet with the serious offenders to indicate the negative consequences that could befall them if the behavior were to continue. This might be a program for only the most serious conflict situations.

At the high school level, conflicts usually become more serious in nature, such as rival gang activities that may take place within the school building or on the school grounds [7]. However, for those of a less serious nature, programs that work at the elementary or middle school levels may suffice.

In the case of rival gang conflicts that take place within the school's environment, a couple of very significant programs have been proven to have a high degree of success [8]. They are those that directly involve the clergy of the area with the gang members, and those that welcome the gang affiliation into the legitimate school activities.

Directly involving the clergy with the various gangs often has a positive effect on conflict resolution, and this is especially true of inner city schools or those schools whose students represent a variety of minority students [9]. Often, the clergy is an important instrument in the lives of the local adult community, and the clergy members, therefore, can enter the conflict situations with the support of the majority of the adults. The members of the clergy can interact with rival gang members by playing the roles of consultant, counselor, and big brother or big sister.

The interschool gang conflict can sometimes be successfully handled by the creative approach of accepting the gangs and turning them into clubs. They still retain the gang's name, symbols, and dress, but turn their gang efforts into creative and helpful pursuits [10]. Some examples of the gang/club's possible activities include the following: gangs can sponsor school events, some gang members can take on peer counseling roles, and the members can assist the school by meeting in an advisory council with non–gang members, teachers, administrators, and community representatives.

CONFLICTS: EMPLOYEE/ADMINISTRATION EXAMPLE

A middle school music teacher/band director's performance was evaluated as being unacceptable by the principal. The band director filed a grievance against the principal, and the teachers' union demanded removal of the unfavorable evaluation from the personnel file of the music teacher/band director. The superintendent, the personnel director, the chief negotiator for the union, and the school board's attorney met with the union's leadership and the union's legal counsel [11].

The result of this session was a review of the following evidence: (1) the middle school band had 280 students enrolled prior to the current band director being hired; and after two years under the current director, student enrollment had fallen below 100 students; (2) adjudication ratings in competition with other middle school bands at the regional and state levels fell from almost consistent "one" ratings to unanimous "three" ratings; (3) numerous written letters of complaints from parents of band students were presented; and (4) written observational notes from the principal's visit were provided.

After discussion, all parties agreed that there was a serious problem that demanded attention. Since the principal was not a music major, it was decided that two of the district-level administrators, who had expertise in the area of instrumental music, would observe the music teacher/band director as instructional classes took place, and would identify specific areas requiring remediation, as well as provide assistance to the music teacher/band director [12]. The two administrators assigned to assist the principal in the evaluation and remediation effort were the school district's personnel director, who had played first chair in a famous university's band, and the school district's media director, who had toured Europe with the band that he directed. It was agreed that the music teacher/band director would be given one year to improve to a satisfactory level, and evidence would be gathered to measure the degree, if any, of improvement made. The evidence decided upon included (1) progress on the remediation actions suggested and noted by the two school district's experts assigned to assist the principal in the evaluation effort, (2) no further loss in numbers of students enrolled, (3) a reduction in parent complaints, and (4) an increase in the adjudication ratings for the band during regional and state competitions.

This fair and timely conflict resolution prescription was agreed to by all parties involved. Ultimately, the union agreed with management on this issue.

CONFLICTS: BOARD OF EDUCATION/SUPERINTENDENT EXAMPLE

An escalating conflict was developing between the superintendent of schools and some of the school district's board of education members. The superintendent of schools accused the board of education of trying to micromanage the school district and usurp the superintendent's legitimate authority [13]. Some of the school board members accused the superintendent of not following their directives. Although both parties were uneasy about the conflict and both parties wanted to resolve their differences, they were unable to resolve the conflict among themselves [14]. Finally, they asked the executive directors of the state's superintendents' association and the state's school boards' association to meet with the superintendent and the board of education in an effort to mediate the difference and resolve the existing conflict.

Initially, the two individuals were called in to assist reviewing the written materials, jointly published by both associations, that outlined the factors involved in superintendent and board of education relation-ships [15,16]. They also shared a publication on ethics for school board members and superintendents of schools. They then worked with both parties to clearly identify the differences in positions and explored ways to resolve the existing differences [17].

The results of two Saturday sessions with the superintendent of schools and the school board members were twofold: (1) there was clarification and agreement on the appropriate roles to be played, and role discrepancies were eliminated, and (2) measurable goals were established that focused the attention of both parties on the attainment of positive outcomes that would benefit the students and the school district as a whole.

CONFLICTS: BOARD OF EDUCATION MEMBERS— INTERNAL CONFLICT EXAMPLE

A school district had a nine-member board that was split in every way and on everything conceivable. Although their board of education meet-ings were broadcast throughout the community and large groups attended each board of education meeting, their behavior and their language was less than exemplary [18]. The degree of conflict was clearly evident when one of the sitting board of education members died, and another of the board members refused to attend the person's funeral service.

Not only were the board of education members in constant dishar-mony, but this caused many of the school administrators to become dis-trustful of the board as a whole and of all individual board members. The administrators were becoming paranoid, and they didn't know when any decision they made would be criticized or overruled. Obvi-ously, this situation was reflected in poor morale among the teaching and classified employees of the school district which, in turn, impacted the education of children. Because so much energy was concentrated on political manipulations, the normal store of energy devoted to edu-cating and caring for students was reduced.

Something drastic had to be done to resolve this continuing conflict, as it could not be resolved by the parties, who were too emotionally involved for too extended a period of time. The solution was to hire a nationally known conflict resolution artist, and to get the agreement of all parties to attend a weekend session with the sole purpose of airing all views and complaints, identifying solutions to the conflict, and developing a means of monitoring behaviors. Should the conflict symptoms raise their heads, all parties to the weekend would involve themselves in mediation efforts to resolve the potential conflict before it became full-blown.

With numerous long hours of discussion, their actions proved beneficial, and all parties left the weekend feeling better about one another and pledging to behave in a more professional and positive manner in the future.

First, those individual board members who were in conflict with one another, or any administrator who was in conflict with a board member, were put in a room with the experienced conflict resolution specialist, who acted as observer/mediator, for as many hours as it took to rid each other of emotions, accusations, and distrust. In some cases there were hard words exchanged, in other cases, crying and hugging took place. But, eventually, there was a clearing of the air and a handshake. A threshold event took place when one member took five years of notes on others that had been kept as evidence of wrongdoing, and publicly destroyed each page as evidence of forgetting the past and starting over with a clean slate and a positive approach.

Second, a handwritten behavioral contract was signed and dated by every person in attendance; and consensus was reached that each person's behavioral contract would be provided to all others in attendance. Also, consensus was reached that all in attendance would be responsible for seeing that the author of the behavioral contract lived up to her/his contract.

Third, all board of education members were asked to, individually and without conversation with one another, list the wishes, goals, or objectives they desired the school district to achieve [19]. These lists were then collected and placed on newsprint around a large room for all to see. Hidden agendas were finally visible to all. Following the weekend, this list was dealt with at a public board meeting, and the board members voted to focus all of the board of education's, administration's, and total school district's efforts on the highest six priorities. Some of the listings were permanently eliminated, and the others would go through the same priority-setting procedure once the original six had been accomplished.

EXTRACURRICULAR ACTIVITIES VERSUS ACADEMICS

When such activities as a band performance and an athletic contest collide because of identically scheduled times and dates, a conflict of interest will arise that catches students in the middle. Of course, this situation can be avoided within the school's internal schedule by working out the time conflicts in advance of the school year. However, there are times, for instance, when a band adjudication is scheduled at a regional or state level and a successful athletic team is scheduled to play in a regional or state playoff contest during the same time period. In such cases, if a student is a band member and also on the athletic team involved, a conflict of interest arises that sometimes puts pressure on the student because of the demands of coaches and band directors as well as parents and booster support groups. This situation is exacerbated when one or more of the participating students are absent, such as students who are first chairs in the band as well as stars of the athletic team involved, and their absence will negatively affect the performance of either or both school units.

A successful way of resolving these potential conflicts of interest in advance of their arising is to adopt a policy, place it in writing, and distribute it to all school-sponsored groups. At its core, this policy should stress that individual students who are caught in this dilemma are the sole decision makers, and their decisions are to be free of pressure from outside persons. Finally, it should be emphasized that no punitive action shall be taken by any party because of the choice the student has made, and any punitive actions taken by a coach or band director shall be dealt with as a violation of school policy.

COMMUNICATING WITH THE COMMUNITY AND THE MEDIA

So many times is appears that the media sells papers by sensationalizing, emotionalizing, or obscuring facts by subjecture. One of the authors knows of ethical reporters who quit their jobs because an editor wrote a headline and modified a positive story to make it appear negative and sensational [20]. Obviously, if conflicts arise within school districts, these are fair game for the media to cover, but do not for a minute believe that all reporting of the conflict will be unbiased or factual. When this happens the school district and the conflicting parties are usually helpless pawns, and the only way to combat erroneous or sensationalized media reporting is to buy one's own newspaper and television outlet. Obviously, this is impossible.

MEDIA COVERAGE AS A POSSIBLE DETERMINER OF CONFLICT RESOLUTION OUTCOMES

It is doubtful if anyone feels that the media should not cover news events, even when they appear to be negative to the school district. The problem is one of combating unnecessary sensationalism, since many people still believe that if they read it in the paper, it is accurately and honestly presented.

The actions that the school district can take to lessen the blow of media sensationalism are few in number. A few suggestions will illustrate some positive actions a school district could take, and many districts have taken some or all of these.

(1) Meet with the news editors of newspapers and television stations, and tell them that they will be alerted as soon as any unusual events happen or when a major conflict appears to be developing. In turn, ask them to be factual in their reporting, and notify them, if they have agreed, when information they have printed or spoken is in error [21].

(2) Have a school district telephone hotline established with the phone number sent to every resident of the district and to every employee, with the suggestion that any time they hear information about which they are curious that they call the hotline for the facts. Those responsible for placing the information on the hotline must make one hundred percent certain that all information is factual, even when the event or incident places the school district in a bad light.

(3) If the district is covered by multiple newspapers and/or multiple television stations, delegate someone to maintain a yearly columnar inch report for newspaper coverage, and a number of minutes report of television news about the district. At the end of each year, give every newspaper a report card of columnar inches and percentage of news covered about the school district, and classify it as positive, neutral, or negative. Also, give them a report of the columnar inches and percentage of school district news covered that is considered factual and that is considered non-factual and sensationalized. Do the same, using minutes of coverage with the television stations.

Finally, always indicate the source of the most negative news and ask why, when covering the same school district's events and incidents as other media sources, their organization has the greatest percentage of negative reporting. If a source will not attempt to increase the positive percentage, the district can take out a paid add and place the factual report card analysis in the hands of the public.

(4) Have a district-level newspaper delivered to each resident once a month, with special issues delivered as hot issues arise. Again, by being completely factual on all matters, credibility will be established with the public over time, and the commercial media coverage will be somewhat neutralized.

(5) Invite the reporters into the district's schools for athletic events, open houses, lunch with the students, or any other positive contact source that can be utilized. In addition, ask the reporters and editors to become guest lecturers and speak to student English or journalism classes, and ask them to meet to share their expertise with students on career days.

(6) Finally, there is nothing like face-to-face, word-of-mouth contact to keep things positive and to neutralize negatives that might arise from conflict situations. Organize community meetings that are sponsored by citizens in their homes. Remember, however, this should be an ongoing activity, not one that is initiated only when conflict or a crisis exists.

SUMMARY

Consideration was given to the productive outcomes of conflict and to the inevitability of conflict in any complex organization, particularly schools. Equitable solutions are achievable, but require effort and imagination. Examples were presented that illustrated a resolution of conflict situations at the elementary, middle, and high school levels. A supervisory example was provided to illustrate administrator/teacher/union conflict. Escalating conflicts were demonstrated in scenarios of board/superintendent and internal board member conflict. Each case in the chapter involved the intervention of mediation from an appropriate professional level or source.

The chapter further described policy and procedural preventive measures applied to potential conflicts arising in the extracurricular/academic area. The chapter closed with a section on preventing and managing conflict with the media, with an emphasis on obtaining balanced reporting and on building relationships with media representatives.

EXERCISES

1. How would you go about organizing a representative group to develop a progressive discipline plan for the students of a school or school district?

2. Recall a student conflict situation in which you were involved or of which you are aware. How would you approach the conflict, and what actions would you take to ensure a positive result?

3. Did you agree with the methods utilized to resolve each of the conflicts of interest related in this chapter? What alternate methods would have worked?

4. If you were to be the person intervening in each of the conflicts related in this chapter, what specific steps would you have taken toward resolution?

REFERENCES

1. Katz, N. H. and J. W. Lawyer. 1994. *Preventing and Managing Conflict in Schools.* Thousand Oaks, CA: Corwin Press—A Sage Publications Company: p. viii.

2. Maurer, R. E. 1991. *Managing Conflict: Tactics for School Administrators.* Boston: Allyn & Bacon: pp. 110–129.

3. Blendinger, J., S. D. Devlin, and G. F. Elrod. 1995. *Controlling Agressive Students.* Fastback Series No. 387. Bloomington, IN: Phi Delta Kappa Foundation, pp. 11–22.

4. Miller, R. W. 1993. "In Search of Peace: Peer Conflict Resolution." *Schools in the Middle,* 2(3): 11–13.

5. Spence, D. and L. Vanderhoff. 1992. "Assistant Principals Lead Effort to Establish Peer Mediation Programs." *AP Special—The Newsletter for Assistant Principals,* 7(3): 1–3.

6. Shepherd, K. K. 1994. "Stemming Conflict Through Peer Mediation." *School Administrator,* 4(51): 14–17.

7. Frisby, D. and J. Beckham. 1993. "Dealing with Violence and Threats of Violence in the School." *NASSP Bulletin,* 77(552): 10–16.

8. Prothrow-Stith, B. 1994. "Building Violence Prevention into the Curriculum." *School Administrator,* 4(51): 8–13.

9. Lal, S. R., D. Lal, and C.M. Achilles. 1993. *Handbook on Gangs in Schools: Strategies to Reduce Gang-Related Activities.* Newbury Park, CA: Corwin Press—A Sage Publications Company, pp. 52–53.

10. Spring, J. 1993. *Conflict of Interests: The Politics of American Education.* 2nd ed. New York: Longman, pp. 165–169.

11. Giandomenico, L. L. and L. Shulman. 1991. *Working with Teachers Effectively: Communication, Relationship, and Problem-Solving Skills for School Principals.* Springfield, IL, pp. 83–100.

12. Lal, S. R., D. Lal, and C. M. Achilles. 1993. *Handbook on Gangs,* pp. 54–61.

13. Flinchbaugh, R. W. 1993. *The 21st Century Board of Education: Planning, Leading, Transforming.* Lancaster, PA: Technomic Publishing Co., Inc., pp. 366–370.

14. *School Boards: Strengthening Grassroots Leadership.* 1986. Washington, D.C.: Institute for Educational Leadership, pp. 41–44.

15. Carver, J. 1990. *Boards That Make a Difference.* San Francisco: Jossey-Bass, pp. 109–129.

16. Rogers, J. 1992. *On Board: A Survival Guide for School Board Members.* Bloomington, IN: Phi Delta Kappa, p. 9.

17. Stephens, A. B. 1995. *Conflict Resolution: Learning to Get Along.* Alexandria, VA: American Association of School Administrators, pp. 4–5.

18. *School Boards: Strengthening Grassroots Leadership,* pp. 41–44.

19. Herman, J. J. and J. L. Herman. 1994. *Educational Quality Management: Effective Schools Through Systemic Change.* Lancaster, PA: Technomic Publishing Co., Inc., pp. 120–122.

20. Herman, J. J. 1994. *Crisis Management: A Guide to School Crises and Action Taken.* Thousand Oaks, CA: Corwin Press—A Sage Publications Company, pp. 1–7.

21. Ordovensky, P. and G. Marx. 1993. *Working with the News Media,* Alexandria, VA: American Association of School Administrators, pp. 6–14.

Dealing with Conflicts of Interest between External and Community Pressure Groups and the Board of Education and Administration

CHAPTER 17 defines conflict of interest and provides examples. The chapter ends with a summary, exercises, and references. It should be noted that even though the examples provided are actual incidents known to the authors, the names of the individuals, groups, and school districts involved are not mentioned due to confidentiality.

DEFINITION OF CONFLICT OF INTEREST

A conflict of interest exists when two or more parties desire or demand differing actions or results because of disparate interests. Many persons perceive a conflict situation as a negative happening. However, many conflicts end in a positive manner, with each party gaining respect for the other parties' position and honesty, and the opening of clear and accurate communication lines that assist in avoiding future conflicts [1,2].

CONFLICT OF INTEREST PROBLEM-SOLVING TECHNIQUES

Although many problem-solving techniques could be reviewed, there is one particular technique that is extremely helpful in resolving conflict. The recommended technique is often referred to as the *Fishbone* or a *Cause and Effect Diagram*. The model provided in Figure 17.1 provides an illustration of a conflict of interest among students and teachers related to student tardiness. The mouth of the fish indicates the problem that must be addressed to resolve the conflict. The vertical spines indicate the possible sources of the problem, and the small horizontal spines indicate the causes and effects related to the problem. It should be noted that the number of spines will vary with the problem being addressed.

275

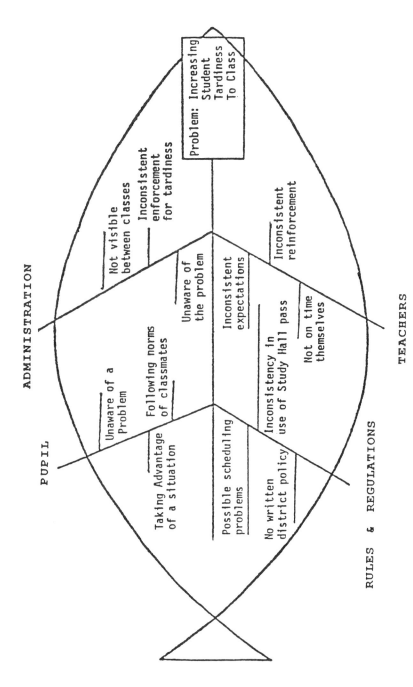

FIGURE 17.1. Fishbone analysis example of student/parent/educator conflict.

276

Once this technique is used to clearly identify the causes and effects, as well as the players, an action program can be developed by all involved parties with the goal of resolving the existing conflict. Once the action program is agreed to, all parties will know the solutions to be exercised, and since the solutions have been collaboratively arrived at by consensus, the parties will abide by the agreed upon solutions [3].

CONSENSUS-BUILDING TECHNIQUES THAT HELP RESOLVE CONFLICTS OF INTEREST

Three very useful consensus-building techniques will be reviewed: (1) the Delphi Technique, (2) the Fishbowl Technique, and (3) the Telstar Technique. Each of these formats are devised to cause consensus between and/or among large groups that are involved in conflicts of interest, and who come into the process with initial positions that are disparate.

Because these techniques are used with large groups, the length of time to reach consensus will vary considerably, based upon the complexity of the issues involved, and the initial disparity in views [4].

The Delphi Technique is one that can be utilized to reach consensus without face-to-face meetings of the participants. This technique can prove to be exceptionally helpful when the parties to the conflict are most disparate in their initial positions, and when the parties are highly emotional about the issues involved in the conflict. It is important that an outside intervener be utilized to carry out the Delphi's procedures. The Delphi process would proceed in the following manner:

(1) Step one would have the intervener send a letter to each involved party asking them to write down in a series of sentences the results that they wish to achieve, and then, a series of sentences indicating the specific resolutions that they would find acceptable. It is important that the proposed resolutions possess great specificity and clarity.

(2) The intervener/processor then collects these written responses, copies them and shares them with all parties involved in the process. At this time, she/he directs the parties to cross out the resolutions to which they cannot agree, modify the language, whenever feasible, to make those resolutions agreeable, and add written resolution statements that would compromise on areas of dispute.

(3) This process is continued until both parties have achieved agreement in writing, with specific wording, as a means of resolving their conflict of interest.

It should be noted that for this technique to be successful in conflict of interest resolution, there should be a prior agreement between both parties to work through the numerous sequences of exchanges until they reach consensus, and they also should reach prior agreement that an outside intervener/processor be solicited to assist the parties in this endeavor.

Included is a depiction of how a Delphi Technique would be utilized. The number of persons involved in the process will, obviously, vary with the size of the groups involved, and with the complexity of the variables as shown in Figure 17.2 [5].

The Fishbowl is a technique wherein the person facilitating the process has six to eight representative persons sitting in a circle or closely aligned rectangle. When large groups are involved in a conflict of interest, they are to select their discussional representatives. You will note in Figure 17.3 that an open chair is placed within the discussion area.

This technique is one where multiple parties to a conflict of interest elect representatives to speak for their interests with the other parties. Since members of large groups cannot all be involved in the discussions, a means has to be found to allow those individuals who are not selected to provide input and hear the discussions of the selected membership. This is accomplished by allowing all members of the conflicting group to observe and listen to the discussion of the selected members.

As members of the representatives discuss matters, negotiate and clarify positions, and attempt to attain consensus, an empty chair is provided so that any member of the audience may get into the discussion by sitting in the chair and expressing her/his views or provide helpful information. The one rule that the facilitator must outline before the process starts is that the person moving to the empty chair must immediately return to the audience after speaking. Obviously, once an individual leaves the open chair, others may occupy it for the same purpose, and under the same conditions. This process allows for large group participation, but it restricts the dialogue to a manageable number.

Finally, in situations where multiple meetings are held, members of the larger group can contact their spokesperson. These between-meeting contacts by members of the larger group can assist the spokesperson in assessing the attitudes of the group's membership towards the comments

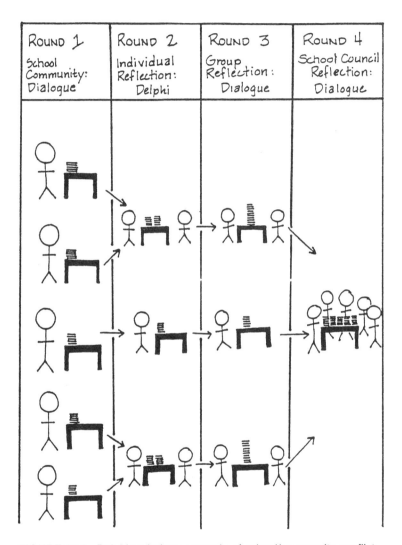

FIGURE 17.2. Delphi technique example of school/community conflict.

FIGURE 17.3. Fishbowl technique.

of the spokesperson, and will provide the spokesperson with a clear idea of which compromises the group's membership will accept to resolve the existing conflict [6].

The Telstar technique also requires a facilitator. It is a method of involving all participants, and it provides for a degree of involvement not normally afforded to all members of large groups in a conflict situation. This technique maintains a manageable number of discussants while providing a three-tiered interactive process. Tier one allows for six or eight discussants, tier two allows five referent members to sit directly behind and assist their discussant, and tier three allows all members of every group to hear the discussions, observe the behaviors exhibited, and discuss matters with their elected six-member team between meetings.

Normally, no more than eight discussants and eight six-member groups can be utilized. This will enable sufficient discussion towards a consensus decision, while allowing all other members of the groups to be observers and input providers. The likelihood of multiple required meetings is great when large groups are involved in complex conflict situations. This, in turn, requires all members of each group to contact their six-member team, and provide them with information and opinions between meetings.

The details of the procedure are as listed below. Remember that the groups who are parties to the conflict of must agree to have a facilitator work the process, and must also agree that they will stay the course until a consensus solution is ultimately reached.

Step one has the facilitator meeting with all groups to the conflict to explain the facilitator's role, the Telstar process, the requirement that each group selects six representatives, and that the group's members commit themselves to continue until the process terminates with a consensus agreement.

Step two has each group electing or selecting its six representatives. In *Step three* each group agrees to the initial meeting time, place, and date; and each group agrees that its representatives will continue to meet until a consensus resolution to the conflict is reached.

Step four the six representatives of each group are formed in a circle or a tight rectangular formation as indicated in Figure 17.4. At the first meeting, the behavior rules are made clear: (a) only the selected spokesperson for each six-member team can speak, and (b) any of the five members seated directly behind each spokesperson may stop the proceedings by calling "time out." At this point, all teams caucus, and discussions about tactics, information, or other matters are discussed by the five referent members and the team's spokesperson. Only that individual who called "time out" may again permit discussion to take place among the various groups' spokespersons by calling "time in." This process may continue throughout the meeting.

Step five all members of each of the groups may witness the discussions, and are free to contact their spokesperson and the five referent team members between meetings. Thus, they have an opportunity to give input, present their views, and provide information that can be used by their team during the discussion stage of the meetings [7].

These processes continue until a final resolution is reached. Telstar allows for a tri-level method of participation when large groups are in conflict with one another. The first level has direct spokespersons

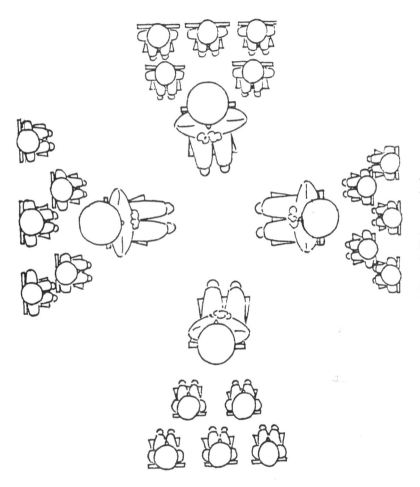

FIGURE 17.4. Telstar technique.

working towards a consensus solution, the second level permits five referent team members to assist the spokesperson for the group, and the third level allows every member of each group to observe the dialogue and to provide input between scheduled meetings.

Figure 17.4 illustrates this procedure. Notice the close proximity of the five persons who are serving as referents to their group's spokesperson.

Now that we have outlined some helpful problem-solving and consensus-building techniques, let's move on to some real life conflict or potential conflict situations. The first example discussed will illustrate a process utilized by one school district to avoid a very serious potential conflict of interest involving hundreds of persons.

BUYING HOUSES TO BUILD A NEW SCHOOL: AVOIDING CONFLICT

A school district that has absolutely no vacant land must build a new high school to accommodate curriculum improvements and an increase and projected future increase in student enrollments. In addition, the existing high school, with some renovation, would meet the needs of a burgeoning middle school student population. To build a new high school requires that as many as two hundred houses have to be purchased and removed from the land upon which they are situated in order to provide the necessary site. The various steps that were taken by the district's board of education and administration to solve this potentially highly emotional conflict of interest, involving hundreds of families, are listed below.

The first step was the formal announcement of the desire to build a new high school and the reasons for this need. The announcement also clearly indicated that in order to obtain the land to provide a site for this new high school, hundreds of homes would have to be purchased by the school district. Finally, the announcement stated the time and date of a public discussion of this matter in the district's field house, which seated a little over seven thousand persons. This announcement was covered by print and nonprint media in the area.

The second step involved a public meeting as previously promised and advertised [8]. The situation was again reviewed by the board and the superintendent, and they clearly indicated that there was at present no specific area of the district where the houses were to be bought. They then proceeded to have a lengthy question and answer period.

They also asked any resident who wished, to provide suggestions for how the board of education should best proceed with this project. Finally, they assured all members of the community that any discussion on this matter would take place at publicly called and advertised board of education meetings.

The third step involved the initial meeting after that held in the field house, where the board of education previewed all the suggestions provided by residents of the community, all suggestions provided by the employees of the school district, and all suggestions proffered by individual board members.

The fourth step involved a series of official public board of education meetings wherein the board members continued discussion of the issues involved and the possible solutions to the problem. Ultimately they arrived at a decision about how to proceed.

The fifth step involved activating the decision the board of education had decided upon. This action program included the following elements: (1) The board of education would hire three appraisers to appraise the properties to be purchased, and they would pay a ten percent premium price beyond the average of the three appraisers [9]. This was intended to allow a reasonable profit to be made by the property owner, but it eliminated the possibility of someone getting twice what the property was worth. (2) The board agreed to move the home of anyone wanting to retain their home to a school district of equal or higher quality, or (3) the board would take recalcitrant owners to court and begin condemnation proceedings on their properties [10]. The board clearly indicated that they absolutely did not want to exercise this third option if it could in any manner be avoided, but that they reluctantly would do this because the students must have a new high school building.

The sixth step, which took over nine months to accomplish, found all parties either selling their homes to the school district or having their homes moved to a school district of equal or better quality. Amazingly, because of the openness and clearly visible need, the board of education did not have to start court proceedings to condemn a single piece of property.

The final step involved recouping the ten percent premium paid in excess of the market value of the homes purchased. This was accomplished by taking out a full-page ad in the areas' newspapers advertising that any interested party could buy any of the homes listed by paying the district ten percent of the market value and moving the home to a new location.

This incident displays how forethought, planning, and open communication can avoid serious and emotional conflicts of interest from developing. One could only hope that all conflicts of interest could be resolved so well.

CONSERVATIVE GROUPS GET INVOLVED WITH CURRICULAR CONTENT

A staunchly conservative religious group insisted that Creationism be included in the school district's science curriculum, and other groups insisted that Evolution be the theory of human development to be taught. The school district's leadership had many meetings with the parties involved in this conflict of interest, and they finally negotiated a compromise agreement that both theories would be discussed [11–13].

CLOSING A SCHOOL BUILDING

No matter how student population shifts, or the extended age, relative inefficiency, and minimum degree of usefulness of a school building, in a small town or in a stable neighborhood, there is always a high probability of a conflict of interest developing among the school district's decision makers, the parents of the children attending that school building, and the residents of that school's attendance area. This conflict can evolve for a variety of reasons.

At the elementary level, the myth of a neighborhood school persists in this country. Many parents want to have their elementary age children attend a school that is close to home and located in their neighborhood. With the tremendous shifts in population to differing parts of the school district over time and with the changing demographic makeup of any elementary neighborhood school, it is clear that the numbers of elementary age children will not be a constant. In fact, in large metropolitan school districts, many schools utilize only one-half or less of the designed building capacity, while other schools in other sections will have student enrollment well in excess of the designed capacity of the school building.

At the secondary level, especially at the high school level, the small town or stable area will not want to see a school building closed that has had championship athletic teams, a prominent marching band, or a significant number of national merit scholars. All of this is a source of pride to the residents and students, and anything done to destroy this will normally cause a conflict of interest to arise.

School buildings usually have a fifty-year life expectancy, but this can be extended ten to twenty years by excellent maintenance upkeep and occasional remodeling. However, the need for constructing new schools and retiring old schools is one of education's immediate infrastructural requirements. Even when a school has gone way past its useful life expectancy, many old-timers will not want to lose the symbol of their high school glory days; and many others, although they have not been back in the school building for thirty to fifty years, will say "The school was good enough for me and it should be good enough for today's youngsters."

All of these attitudes combine to create a potentially hot issue within the student body, the parental group, and the school community at large. The task, then, is how to close a school building that is no longer useful, while avoiding a strong and far-reaching negative backlash from the community. One example of how this was handled will serve this purpose. The example involves closing a very old high school that, in the minds of many, depicted the best of everything that the school district had ever offered.

Step one—the board of education announced it would close high school X, while extolling its history and accomplishments, and emphasizing the deficits the school building possessed in terms of (1) health and safety, (2) inadequacy to house a modern set of curricular offerings, (3) inadequacy to utilize technology, (4) excessive maintenance costs merely to keep it operating without adding any improvements, and (5) how this was a cost/ineffective, and an educational/ineffective school facility.

Step two—the public received an invitation to attend a board of education hearing where all viewpoints and comments were welcomed. Again, at the beginning of the hearing, the rationale and factual information for the building's closure were reviewed. This meeting was a very lengthy one, and at the end of the meeting, the board of education promised to appoint a study and advisory committee of one hundred persons to study the facts and advise the board on this matter [14]. The board of education said that the committee would consist of volunteers, with the exception of ten persons who would be appointed by the board of education. These ten committee members would be appointed because of their specific areas of expertise, such as a contractor, a general, a construction manager, an architect, a health and safety specialist, and an instructional specialist. The board of education also indicated that the school would be kept in operation for the subsequent school year while the study was conducted by the advisory committee of one hundred, and until the board of education received the advisory committee's recommendation and made a final decision.

The advisory committee, after six months of study, reported to the board of education at a regularly called board of education meeting. All members of the school community were urged to attend. At the meeting, the advisory committee recommended closing the school, and the board of education thanked the committee for its hard work. At the end of the meeting, having allowed time for audience comments and individual board member discussion, the board voted to close the school building.

At this point the board of education asked for volunteers to serve on two advisory committees with board of education members and employees of the school district. One committee was to be made up of an equal number of members from the new school and members from the school to be closed [15]. The membership was to consist of parents, community members, and students, with some teachers from each school, the two high school principals, one *ex officio* central office administrator, and one *ex officio* board of education member. This committee's charge was to plan combined events for students and parents that would make the transition of all parties positive and comfortable.

This committee planned a variety of combined events, including teacher and student exchange days, joint parental booster and PTA meetings, joint school dances, joint pride days, and many other positive joint events.

The second advisory committee was to consist of some students and teachers from the school to be closed, some parents, and some school community members who had attended the high school in past years. In addition, an *ex officio* central office administrator was involved with the committee, and an *ex officio* board of education member was also to attend.

This committee planned a week-long, historical, joyful reunion. The activities included a dance, a dinner, an old timers recognition day, old timers athletic, band, debate and other contests, a student/parent/old timer picnic, a community recognition day, a large parade, and a final banquet that culminated with each person in attendance given a remembrance brick from the old building. During these activities, all graduates whose addresses were known and who had moved from the area were invited to attend, and a surprisingly high number of graduates did return to renew memories, acquaintances, and thank some of the long serving teachers. Finally, the new receiving school's PTA and student council obtained a sufficient number of bricks to have a memorial built to the old high school on the front lawn of the new building. A plaque was affixed to the triangular face of the memorial.

A good time was had by all, and the old school building was allowed to die a graceful death. Importantly, through extensive dialogue and input, through the use of a large number of persons on three committees, through a promise to let the school operate while the advisory committee studied the issue, and through the positive transition and historical recognition activities, a potentially hot and divisive conflict of interest situation was avoided.

CHANGING ATTENDANCE BOUNDARIES

A situation that is similar in many respects, but different in important other respects, is that of changing attendance boundaries. An actual example of changing a middle school attendance boundary will illustrate this matter. This example is one of a lose-lose initial result to a conflict of interest, but a long-term positive win for students, parents, community, and the school district.

This six-thousand-plus student school district possessed two middle schools. One was housed in a blue collar, low socioeconomic area that had a student capacity of eight-hundred students, the other was housed in a professional/owner, high socioeconomic area and had a designed capacity of one thousand students.

Over the years, the school in the blue collar community lost student-aged youth, and ultimately, ended up with a student population of three hundred and sixty students. On the other hand, the school located in the high socioeconomic area witnessed a large increase in student population, and, ultimately, ended up with a student population in excess of fourteen hundred students.

As the situation became more and more exacerbated, it was clear that even if the amount expended per pupil in the low enrollment school was doubled, the curriculum offerings could not be as comprehensive, the pupil-teacher ratio would be inefficient and expensive, the numbers of students needed to successfully compete in athletic and other co-curricular events were just not available, and the administrative overhead was too high. The high enrollment school, on the other hand, found itself with very crowded classes, an extremely high teacher-pupil ratio, and inadequate athletic facilities. The powerful and rich parents of students in the high enrollment school were very concerned and wanted the board of education to pass a bond issue to add additions to the existing high enrollment school.

To summarize the variables involved in this conflict of interest situation, it was clear that:

(1) The low attendance school could not offer curriculum choices to students equal to those offered to students in the high attendance school, no matter how much extra money per student was expended.

(2) The situation of overcrowding and having inadequate facilities to house the large middle school student population was untenable.

(3) This situation was extremely cost-ineffective.

(4) The parents of students in the high socioeconomic level area did not want some of their students transferred to the other middle school, which, by the way, was only three miles away. They, basically wanted them to stay with their own kind, and did not want their children associating with those other students. Their solution was to build additions to the current building, even though the site was not large enough to reasonably do this. Also, they were willing to expend much more money per pupil for students attending the low attendance middle school, as long as their children did not have to attend that school.

(5) Once the attitude of the parents of the students in the high attendance school became clear to the parents of the students in the low attendance school, they pressured the board of education and administration not to transfer any students from the high attendance school.

Even with all of these pressures placed upon them, the board of education decided to change attendance boundaries and transfer three-hundred-plus students from the high attendance school to the low attendance school in the subsequent school year. They explained their rationale as follows: the board did not want middle school student populations to exceed one thousand because students of this age would have problems adjusting in a large-population school building, the low attendance school was very cost-ineffective, and the site at the high attendance school was inadequate to house building additions.

Rumors flew about students being raped, gang activity, drug infestation, and other terribly negative matters that allegedly were taking place in the low attendance school. In addition, lawsuits were initiated to stop the board of education from making this attendance boundary change.

Both groups put extreme pressure on the board of education members and the superintendent of schools to take their side in the conflict. Although for the most part, parents and students from each site were all of the same race, certain dimensions of serious racial conflicts were evident. However, this was a socioeconomic war, not a racial war. Because of the ownership and political power of the residents of the high student enrollment area, threats were made to recall all board members and fire the superintendent. Obviously, the television and print media had a year-long field day.

Eventually, the case was taken to the state supreme court, and the court ruled in favor of the board of education. The board asked cool-headed and rational parents from both sides to get together and start to heal the wounds [16]. The PTA became an organization comprised of parents from both schools, and the students, initially skeptical and scared because of all the unpleasant rumors, started joining together in sports and other co-curricular activities. The teachers who were transferred from the high attendance school were given staff development training on how to handle the transition—especially how to handle any serious conflicts that arose between students or parents [17].

Finally, by the end of the first year of the transfer, things settled down, students became friends, the media retreated, and reluctant parents began accepting the reality and dismissing the rumors. Years passed, and an observer would never realize that this heated, abusive, serious conflict of interest had ever existed.

Incidentally, the recall of the board failed, and many of the board members were reelected and served numerous terms. This example illustrates that sometimes actions have to be taken that cannot avoid a conflict of interest, but doing the right thing will have a positive result over time.

SUMMARY

Less intrusive methods of conflict resolution described included the visual exercise of a Fishbone or Cause and Effect diagram, and a number of consensus building techniques. These included the illustrated

Delphi technique of successive looping and relooping of information among a cluster of experts; and the dialogue channeling and restricting strategies of the Fishbowl and the Telstar, the latter two being helpful in managing large groups. Hints to limit damage caused by escalating and unresolved conflicts of interest were provided.

EXERCISES

1. How would you go about developing a plan to intervene in an existing conflict of interest with a community group?
2. Think back to an intense conflict situation involving two community pressure groups. In retrospect, what do you believe could have been done to quickly and constructively resolve that conflict?
3. Did you agree with the methods utilized to resolve each of the conflicts related in this chapter?
4. If you were to be the person intervening in each of the conflicts related in this chapter, what specific steps would you have taken to resolve each one?

REFERENCES

1. Spring, J. 1993. *Conflict of Interests: The Politics of American Education.* 2nd ed. New York: Longman, pp. 165–169.
2. Herman, J. J. 1991. "Coping with Conflict." *The American School Board Journal,* 178(8): pp. 26–28.
3. Herman, J. J. and J. L. 1994. *Making Change Happen: Practical Planning for School Leaders.* Thousand Oaks, CA: Corwin Press—A Sage Publications Company, p. 81.
4. Herman, J. J. and J. L. 1994. *Making Change Happen,* pp. 46–49.
5. Ibid.
6. Ibid.
7. Ibid.
8. Ordovensky, P. and G. Marx. 1993. *Working with the News Media,* Alexandria, VA: American Association of School Administrators, pp. 22–23.
9. Herman, J. J. 1995. *Effective School Facilities: A Development Guidebook.* Lancaster, PA: Technomic Publishing Co., Inc., p. 13.
10. Herman, J. J. 1995. *Effective School Facilities,* pp. 95–96.
11. Molnar, A. 1993/1994. "Fundamental Differences." *Educational Leadership,* 51(4): 4–5.

12. Marzano, R. J. 1993/1994. "When Two Worldviews Collide." *Educational Leadership,* 51(4): 6–11.
13. Graves, B. 1992. "The Pressure Group Cooker." *School Administrator,* 4(49): 8–13.
14. Herman, J. J. 1993. "School-based management committees: A positive force in selling the need for and in planning new school construction." *Educational Facilities Planner,* 31(4): pp. 21–23.
15. Herman, J. J. 1995. *Effective School Facilities,* pp. 172–173.
16. Ledell, M. A, 1995. *How to Avoid Crossfire and Seek Common Ground: A Journey for the Sake of the Children.* Alexandria, VA: American Association of School Administrators, pp. 22–23.
17. Herman, J. J. and J. L. 1994. *Making Change Happen,* p. 49.

THE END PIECES

Section Six includes two chapters. Chapter 18, Union/Management—
The End Piece, discusses the past, present, and preferred future for
collective bargaining. It also relates information about moving from traditional negotiation techniques to the newer and preferred collaborative style. The value of getting to and maintaining a win-win, cooperative and collaborative style is promoted as the best route to future
collective bargaining successes, and it presents collaborative techniques that assist in arriving at win-win results.

Chapter 19, The Broader School District Environment—The End
Piece, discusses the past, present, and preferred future for school
district/community relations. Stress is once again placed on win-
win, cooperative and collaborative methods that will cause community members and school employees and officials to achieve a
successful and supportive learning environment for the children and
youth of the community.

Union/Management—The End Piece

CHAPTER 18 will discuss the past, present, and preferred future of collective bargaining in education; moving from the adversarial historical approach (though a more comprehensive history is provided in Chapter 2) to the preferred collaborative win-win approach, and getting to and maintaining a continuing win-win labor/management environment. The chapter concludes with a summary, exercises, and selected references.

THE PAST

Prior to the 1960s collective bargaining in education was a misnomer. For the most part, boards of education make yearly decisions about the salary schedules and the fringe benefits to be paid to teachers and other school district employees. In a few of the more enlightened school districts, boards of education met and conferred with the leadership of the teachers' association and the leadership of other employee groups prior to establishing pay scales and fringe benefits for the subsequent school years [1]. Generally, the board of education members would listen to the desires of employee groups, dismiss them from the meeting, discuss what they were willing to do, and establish the pay scales and fringe benefits that they felt was fair or desirable.

However, in the 1960s matters drastically changed in most school situations. Teacher groups became leaders of white collar unionism [2]. Prior to this time the National Education Association (NEA) envisioned itself and acted as a professional association concerned about matters of instruction and student welfare. Also, in the early 1960s, the American Federation of Teachers (AFT) had organized a few large metropolitan school districts. This effort by the AFT to usurp the NEA's membership and the complaints about the lack of significant progress in salary and fringe benefits for teachers, caused the NEA to become a more highly structured and aggressive union [3]. In fact, in the mid-1960s, the NEA decided that although administrators had historically been responsible for their high membership numbers (due to their strongly recommending that all teachers as well as all administrators join), the leadership decided that adminstrators could no longer hold membership in the NEA, and passed a resolution about their membership eligibility.

During this same period many states passed collective bargaining laws, allowing public school employees to participate in collective bargaining activities. Certification elections were successfully held, with the assistance of union organizers in numerous districts across the country, with the primary exception of most Southern states. Wisconsin implemented a statewide collective bargaining law in 1962; and Connecticut, Michigan, and Massachusetts passed similar laws in 1965. Since that time many other states have passed laws making collective bargaining legal for employees of school districts and other public employee groups [4].

Since this collective bargaining approach was new to most educators, the teacher organizations looked to established trade unions for leadership training. This led in many school districts to extremely adversarial bargaining stances. Boards of education, in many cases, disagreed with the right of teachers and other school district employees to bargain their employment conditions, picket, or be considered equally powerful during contract negotiations. On the other hand, teacher unions, especially the historically meek NEA, became demanding, aggressive, and insistent on achieving their demands, even when this led to a strike.

Although this adversarial environment continued in many situations, in the 1980s some boards of education and teacher and classified employee unions attempted a more enlightened cooperative and collaborative approach to collective bargaining [5]. This win-win approach was based on mutual problem solving and trust in the integrity of both the union's representatives and the board of education's representatives.

THE PRESENT

The present of collective bargaining in education presents a mixed bag. For the most part, there are fewer strikes by educational unions than there were in the 1960s and 1970s, but bitter strikes are still taking place in certain school districts. On the other hand, with thirty some years of history, some boards of education and some educational unions have shown some maturity in dealing with the collective bargaining process. They are more cooperative, they are sharing information with one another, they are dealing with mutual problem solving, they are filing fewer grievances, they are avoiding strikes, and they are gaining trust and appreciation from both the union and management.

Currently, in the mid-1990s, the external environment in which collective bargaining takes place has undergone substantive changes when compared to the environment of prior years. The following examples are dramatic and the changes involved will affect collective bargaining in the future.

(1) The adult population of most school districts has aged, and the great majority of residents do not have children in school. Therefore, they have very little personal motivation to be supportive of collective bargaining activities that are adversarial in nature.

(2) In most school districts, taxpayers are very reluctant to vote to raise their taxes in support of schools.

(3) Unions, in general across the country, have lost membership and power; and this is reflected in the general public's attitude towards teacher unions.

(4) The country has taken a definite political tilt towards conservatism.

(5) Many studies have indicated that the students in public schools are not achieving as well as students in other countries, or students in private schools in this country. This leads to criticism of management and employees, and, in turn, this leads to a lessening of support for schools.

(6) The economy has become more of a global one in nature, and this affects the ability to finance schools.

(7) The delivery systems for education are changing with the advent of technology, and this has implications for the numbers of teachers employed. In turn, this will affect the power balance between union and management [6].

THE PROJECTED FUTURE

Current models and controversial initiatives include privatization of schools where businesses contract to operate schools for a fee, voucher programs that exist in districts like Milwaukee, instruction delivered by a variety of distance learning delivery systems, choice programs where parents and students can select the individual school they wish to attend, and magnet schools for designated specialties and for creating a multicultural balance. In addition, alternative schools for students who possess certain needs or problems, and the push in some quarters to eliminate school boards as an antiquated concept, site-based management (that has been mandated in places like Kentucky and Texas), and numerous other changes that will affect the form and substance of collective bargaining in the future already exist [7,8].

Collective bargaining in education, having its beginnings in an industrial model, will have to change or it will experience a slow demise in the educational arena. Cooperative, collaborative, and win-win approaches to collective bargaining, where both union and management agree to approach contract negotiations and contract management as a task of mutual problem solving, are the light at the end of the future tunnel. If both, or either, union or management refrain from attempting to reach the light, it is the authors' belief that collective bargaining laws in most states will be drastically modified, and unions will have their bargaining power greatly reduced. The economic, political, and social context within which collective bargaining takes place has undergone major change; unions and management have to adjust their bargaining practices to accommodate these changes, or this process of collective bargaining will go the way of the dinosaurs [9].

If win-win is the preferred future method for collective bargaining in education, it is wise to explore this concept in greater depth. Moving from a traditional historical approach to collective bargaining in education to a win-win, cooperative and collaborative approach will take maturity, trust, and skill on the part of both the union and management leadership.

MOVING FROM THE ADVERSARIAL HISTORICAL APPROACH TO THE PREFERRED COLLABORATIVE WIN-WIN APPROACH

Two major issues that have existed in collective bargaining situations between teachers and classified school employees, and the boards of education and management groups are money and power [10]. If both union leadership and management leadership share accurate and honest information about the amount of money in the total budget and the amount available for employee salaries and fringe benefits, reasonable parties will have to agree that there is a finite amount of money available for all purposes [11,12]. The task facing both parties, then, is to achieve consensus on the amounts to be allocated for all purposes, including the amount available for salary and fringe benefits.

If both parties see collective and collaborative decision making as desirable, they can work together to solve problems, which can be translated into policies or standard operating procedures. It then becomes the responsibility of the union leadership, as well as management's leadership to see that the policies and standard operating procedures are adhered to by all employees.

Solving these two major foci of the collective bargaining process in the manner described above will allow a win-win, cooperative, and collaborative approach to take place. This approach, if continuously utilized, will also bring trust, respect, and further cooperation on a daily basis to all aspects of a school district's operations.

GETTING TO AND MAINTAINING A WIN-WIN LABOR/MANAGEMENT ENVIRONMENT

Getting to a win-win approach to collective bargaining will only take place if both parties to the negotiation realize that the external environment in which collective bargaining takes place has undergone dramatic changes. The parties will have to gain the maturity to understand that business as usual will not be successful. Once this is realized by both parties they can systematically go down the path of win-win, cooperative and collaborative collective bargaining. As this approach is continuously exercised, the entire human culture of the institution will change from one of distrust, grievances, and adversarial relations to one of trust, respect, and cooperative relationships. Figure 18.1 illustrates these changes [13].

The key issues to be decided in future labor/management situations are empowerment and school restructuring, which will lead to improvements in the achievement levels of students. Empowerment is a strong concept that basically leads to a collective decision about how much power each employee and collective employee and management group will be granted to deal with those matters that influence their working environment [14].

WIN/WIN	WIN/LOSE	LOSE/LOSE
COOPERATIVE	ADVERSARIAL	ENEMY OUTLOOK
COLLABORATIVE	SECRETIVE	ADVERSARIAL
TRUSTING	MISTRUSTING	NO TRUST
RESPECTFUL	ONE UPPMANSHIP	TOTAL WIN
PROBLEM SOLVING	POWER USAGE	FORCE ONLY
OPENMINDEDNESS	SECRETIVE	PARANOID
TOTAL SHARING	GUARDED	TOTALLY CLOSED
POSITIVE CLIMATE	SUSPICIOUS CLIMATE	WAR-LIKE CLIMATE

FIGURE 18.1. Indicators of Win/Win, Win/Lose and Lose/Lose Collective Bargaining Environments.

The degree of empowerment granted each of the employees is not the major issue with parents and the general public. Their concern can be stated in a simple question addressed to school employees and boards of education: *How are you going to restructure what you are doing in your schools to improve the education of our children and youth?*

Once both union and management have decided to use a win-win approach to collective bargaining and union/management relations, the parties can do many things to assist them in developing and maintaining a win-win labor/management environment. Some of the most successful things that they, collectively, can do to ensure this end result are the following:

(1) Both groups agree to involve themselves in team-building activities.
(2) Both groups take training in identifying, analyzing, and developing action programs to resolve problems.
(3) Both groups take training in clear communication techniques, such as "I" messages, negotiating meanings, and paraphrasing.
(4) Both groups take training in and practice consensus-building techniques.

(5) Both groups join together in assisting with community projects.

(6) Joint advisory committees are developed with equal membership from both the union and management.

(7) Weekly meetings are held between the leadership of both union and management for the purpose of solving minor problems before they become big problems.

(8) Both parties involve themselves in collective goal setting and collective action program deliberations.

(9) A hotline is established that enables the leadership to quell any negative rumors that arise. The leadership will then take responsibility for immediately informing their membership of the facts.

(10) Both groups will involve themselves in collective celebrations of success.

(11) Both groups will provide joint media releases as a means of avoiding media sensationalism, or when the media print information that gives the appearance that labor and management are at odds on some matter.

(12) Finally, both groups will join together to provide the community at large with positive news about the school district, the employees, the students, and the board of education [15].

Collective actions, such as the dozen listed above, will harness the energies of both parties to a positive agenda. As these actions continue, trust, caring, respect, and mutuality will grow, and a win-win, cooperative and collaborative approach to collective bargaining and labor/management relations will become internalized by employees, and become accepted as the only acceptable culture of the entire school district.

SUMMARY

The chapter briefly reviewed the transitions experienced by the unions, boards, and the collective bargaining process, as adversarial relationships evolved during the middle decades of the century. The present status of collective negotiations is again evolving, this time into a more cooperative and collegial relationship. The task of moving from an advesarial relationship to one of win-win cooperation was outlined, including descriptions of issues, process steps, and the required cultural changes of empowerment.

EXERCISES

1. Do a historical study of the origination and progression of collective bargaining in your school district.

2. Given the opportunity to work with the leadership of the union, board of education, and administration, what strategies and tactics would you utilize to get these leaders to initiate and maintain a win-win, cooperative and collaborative approach to collective bargaining and long-term labor/management relations?

REFERENCES

1. Herman, J. J. and G. E. Megiveron. 1993. *Collective Bargaining in Education: Win-Win, Win/Lose, Lose/Lose.* Lancaster, PA: Technomic Publishing Co., Inc., pp. 66–67.

2. Spring, J. 1993. *Conflict of Interests: The Politics of American Education.* 2nd ed. New York: Longman, pp. 165–169.

3. Streshly, W. A. and T. A. DeMitchell. 1994. *Teacher Unions and TQE.* Thousand Oaks, CA: Corwin Press, Sage Publications, p. 12.

4. Keane, W. G. 1996. *Win Win or Else: Collective Bargaining in an Age of Public Discontent.* Thousand Oaks, CA: Corwin Press, Sage Publications, pp. 4–6.

5. Streshly, W. A. and T. A. DeMitchell. 1994. *Teacher Unions,* p. 245.

6. Herman, J. J. and J. L. 1994. *Educational Quality Management: Effective Schools Through Systemic Change.* Lancaster, PA: Technomic Publishing Company, pp. 2–3.

7. Spring, J. 1993. *Conflict of Interests,* pp. 57–59.

8. McLaughlin, J. M. 1995. "Public Education and Private Enterprise: Where's This New Relationship Going?" *School Administrator,* 7(52): 7–13.

9. Kerchner, C. T. 1993. "Building the Airplane as It Rolls Down the Runway: Administrators Discover Labor Relations as the Linchpin to School Change," *School Administrator,* 50(10): 8–15.

10. Spring, J. 1993. *Conflict of Interests,* pp. 73–79.

11. Hargreaves, A. 1991. "Contrived Collegiality: The Micropolitics of Teacher Collaboration." In *The Politics of Life in Schools: Power, Conflict, and Cooperation,* edited by J. Blase, Newbury Park, CA: Sage Publications, pp. 68–69.

12. Herman, J. J. and G. E. Megiveron. 1993. *Collective Bargaining in Education,* pp. 206–209.

13. Herman, J. J. and J. L. 1993. *School-Based Management: Current Thinking and Practice,* Springfield, IL: Charles C. Thomas, Publisher, pp. 44–59.

14. Ledell, M. A, 1995. *How to Avoid Crossfire and Seek Common Ground: A Journey for the Sake of the Children.* Alexandria, VA: American Association of School Administrators, pp. 22–23.

15. Herman, J. J. and J. L. 1993. *School-Based Management: Current Thinking and Practice,* Springfield, IL: Charles C. Thomas, Publisher, pp. 245–246.

The Broader School District Environment—The End Piece

CHAPTER 19 discusses means of developing and maintaining a win-win environment for all parties, and it discusses conflict resolution techniques that are appropriate to use with various stakeholder groups. The chapter ends with a final summary, exercises, and references.

GETTING TO AND MAINTAINING A CONTINUOUS WIN-WIN ENVIRONMENT WITH AND BETWEEN ALL STAKEHOLDER GROUPS IN THE SCHOOL DISTRICT

Occasionally conflicts of interest will arise, and this is part and parcel of the challenges of operating a school district. The school district leaders cannot change this, but they can develop and utilize effective and successful methods of resolving conflicts of interests. The successful resolution to conflicts of interests, as they arise between and among individuals and groups, will result in a stepping stone towards a long-range, cooperative, win-win environment within which all parties work together for positive ends—especially that of effectively educating the children and youth of the school district [1]. The remainder of this chapter will address some significant points that will assist in the successful resolution of conflicts of interest.

CONFLICT RESOLUTION TECHNIQUES WITH VARIOUS STAKEHOLDER GROUPS

Appendix H: A Checklist of Steps Involved in Successful Conflict Resolutions provides an abbreviated set of hints on how to correctly resolve conflicts. A variety of techniques that can be utilized to successfully resolve conflicts of interest are listed below. They include legal recourse, arbitration, mediation, compromise, and collaboration techniques.

CONFLICT RESOLUTION AS A MEANS
OF POSITIVE GROWTH

There are numerous ways of resolving a conflict of interest. Some are through force and others are through constructive dialogue, cooperation, and consensus building [2]. The latter approach ends in a win-win resolution of the conflict for all parties involved, and it provides a means of positive growth and maturity of conflict resolution methods that remain as available resources to all individuals and all parties for use in the future.

Let's explore both the negative and positive characteristics of a variety of means of resolving conflicts of interests. The main methods, with their accompanying characteristics, are listed below, and by reviewing the characteristics, it should be clear that collaborative, win-win approaches are the most desirable, for a win-win approach will lead to the positive growth of all parties.

(1) Legal recourse should be used only as a last ditch effort to resolve a conflict of interest. It generally involves taking a black or white stand on the issues involved. In many cases it attempts coercive and intimidation tactics; and it almost always ends with a winner and a loser. This is clearly an adversarial approach, and the win-lose result will negatively taint the relationship between the parties into the foreseeable future.

(2) Arbitration is sometimes used to resolve a conflict of interest when the parties finally realize that they are unable to resolve the conflict without outside assistance. In the case of arbitration, the parties agree to hire an arbitrator to hear the facts and rationale presented by each party to the conflict, to review and interpret the information provided, and to render a judgement intended to resolve the existing conflict [3].

The parties can agree to advisory or compulsory arbitration. In the case of advisory arbitration either, or both, parties are free to reject the findings of the arbitrator. In compulsory arbitration, however, all parties to the conflict of interest are bound to execute the findings of the arbitrator.

Legal recourse and arbitration are methods utilized when a conflict of interest has to be resolved by force, and they usually end in a win-lose position for both parties. Let's now turn to more positive methods of resolving conflicts of interest.

(3) Mediation is sometimes used when the parties to a conflict of interest have agreed on some aspects of settlement, but who are unable to resolve all issues involved in the conflict. In mediation, an outside person or group of persons are hired to work with the parties in an attempt to resolve any remaining issues. The end result of a successful mediation intervention is that both parties reach agreement over all the issues in the final resolution of the conflict [4].

In general, the mediator will meet, individually, with the parties to the conflict of interest to determine (1) specific areas of agreement, (2) specific areas of disagreement, and (3) potential areas of compromise. Obviously, the mediator will collect any information that the parties can present to argue their case, and he will spend great amounts of time in discussing and practicing her/his listening skills. These separate conferences may continue for a considerable length of time before the mediator will bring the parties together.

During this back and forth caucusing activity, the mediator may float trial balloons to either or both groups, suggesting that if one party will give, or modify its position in one area, the mediator believes that she/he can get the other party to modify its position in another area. After some time has passed and the mediator is quite certain she/he has both parties warmed up to the give and take necessary for settlement of all issues, the mediator will bring both parties together and suggest a total settlement. In general, at this stage, both parties will agree to the suggested settlement.

It is crucial that the mediator congratulate both parties on their desire to settle their conflict of interest, and on their willingness to give and take on issues in order to reach the settlement. Shaking of hands and congratulations to all involved are in order, as everyone involved in the conflict resolution should go away feeling like a winner.

(4) Compromise is the next most positive technique to accomplish resolution of a conflict of interest between two or more parties. It is characterized by clear communication, sharing of rationale and information to defend each party's point of view, mutual give and take, and negotiation between the parties. The end result is that the parties, without the assistance of outside forces, involve themselves in discussions and compromise whenever feasible, and eventually end by discovering an acceptable balance that resolves the existing conflict of interest. Again, it is important that all

parties to the conflict of interest leave the environment perceiving themselves as winners [5].

(5) Collaboration is the highest, best, and most positive technique to utilize in resolving a conflict of interest between two or more parties. This technique displays the characteristics of cooperative problem solving, synthesis of information, and consensus resolution of all issues involved in the conflict. Not only do the parties end up feeling like winners, but they, in all probability, have developed increased trust in and respect for the other party(ies) to the conflict of interest [6].

MEANS OF STOPPING CONFLICTS OF INTEREST FROM CAUSING HARM

It is important to limit the harm caused by conflicts of interest between opposing parties. Some helpful hints to limit damage are listed below.

- STOP allowing conflicts of interest to divert the energies of the school district's personnel from attending to their primary function—educating the children and youth of the school district.
- STOP the parties to conflicts of interest from continuing and increasing, over time, negative relationships; and accomplish this by intervening with successful conflict resolution techniques.
- STOP the conflicts of interest from escalating by anticipating negative conflict situations before they arise, and by intervening early in existing conflict situations before the conflicts become emotional and irreparable.

UNRESOLVED CONFLICTS OF INTEREST—RESULTS

If conflicts of interests are left unresolved, they will fester and become increasingly heated and negative in nature. In fact, unresolved conflicts of interest will lead to some of the results listed below.

- a diversion of energies from the primary goal of educating students
- a long-term and increasing polarization of the parties to the conflicts
- a deepening of suspicion and mistrust among the parties
- a serious decrease of productivity, efficiency, and effectiveness within the school district and among the parties to the conflicts of interest

EVIDENT RESULTS IF CONFLICT RESOLUTIONS ARE SUCCESSFUL

On the other hand, the successful resolution of conflicts of interest will result in a much different and much improved list. Such a list will include the following results:

- clarification and resolution of the issues that were involved in creating the conflicts of interest
- improved problem-solving abilities of all parties to the conflict
- increased trust and respect among the individuals and parties to the conflict
- improved communications among the parties
- the efforts and resources of the school district's employees and of the stakeholders' groups will focus on the primary function of schools—that of providing high quality education to the children and youth of the community [7]

Now that we have listed some of the results of unresolved conflicts and those obtained when successful resolutions have been achieved, let's turn to some suggestions on how to judge whether or not conflicts have been constructively resolved. These guidelines will be especially helpful to the neophyte who has yet to become involved in resolving conflicts of interest.

METHODS OF JUDGING WHETHER OR NOT CONFLICTS OF INTEREST HAVE BEEN CONSTRUCTIVELY RESOLVED

Some important criteria that can be used to determine whether conflicts of interest have been successfully resolved appear below. Obviously, if these indicators are not present, then it is safe to assume that the conflicts of interest were not successfully resolved. Conflicts have been constructively and successfully resolved when:

- It is determined that the parties to the conflicts of interest have increased trust, communication, and problem-solving ability.
- The membership of both parties to the conflict are satisfied with the resolutions reached.
- All individuals and groups involved in the conflict have greatly improved their abilities to avoid future conflicts and/or to successfully resolve conflicts of interests before they become intense, emotional, and escalated in nature.

SUMMARY

The chapter focused on an array of techniques and strategies to successfully resolve conflicts of interest. A number of these were described, including legal recourse, arbitration, mediation, compromise, and collaboration—processes that determine potential areas of agreement and offer negotiated solutions. External solution processes, involving more formal interventions were provided. Hints on limiting the damage caused by conflicts of interest focused on rediverting resources and on prevention and damage containment; the results of unresolved conflicts of interest and the outcomes of successful resolution described opposite situations. Criteria which can be used to assess successful resolutions were provided.

A FINAL SUMMARY

In Chapter 1, beliefs about people were described as critically affecting the working relationships of people and groups. Stages of group growth and the definition of a winning team laid the groundwork for fruitful collective negotiation relationships. Chapter 2 reviewed the history of the development of unions, providing a focus on the NEA and the AFT. Contemporary information on union mergers and new directions were given. Chapter 3 discussed a variety of means of empowering employees. Such innovations as Quality of Work Life (QWL) and Quality Circles (QC) were discussed, and extensive information was provided on school-based management. Employee recognition and the advantages of creating union/management teams were stressed.

In Chapter 4, the involvement and needs of stakeholders, clients, and the larger community were discussed, with attention focused on the impact of the bargaining process, whether positive or negative, on these groups. Client input was recommended to obtain client information and desires prior to beginning the bargaining process and throughout its four phases: before negotiations, during negotiations, impasse declaration, and master contract ratification. Chapter 5 presented strategic and tactical planning information, linking it to union and management examples. Chapter 6 focused on choosing and analyzing the negotiation's team members, with emphasis on the preparation and collaborative attitude of team members. Pre-negotiation training was stressed as being essential, and specific team member's roles were described. Content area information and background information on opposite team members was to be gathered.

Chapter 7 expanded on this collection of background information, recommending investigation of state law, existing policies, the history of grievance arbitration, and comparable districts' information. Compilation and continuous updating of this information was also recommended. Chapter 8 addressed preparing to go to the bargaining table, and noted the need to determine the level of exclusive representation. An example of a positive relationship with union and management was provided. The development of a notebook to contain key negotiating information was recommended, and predetermined structures, strategies, and tactics for bargaining were recommended. Rationales and supporting data of all proposals had to be developed.

Chapter 9 considered conduct at and away from the table, recommending the establishment of ground rules and determination of the procedures for exchanging proposals. Team member roles must be integrated with successful at-the-table strategies to best present proposal packages. Chapter 10 addressed the preparation and strategizing required when dealing with an impasse situation. Mediation, fact-finding, and arbitration were described in detail, and tactics to successfully negotiate these stages of bargaining resolution were related.

Chapter 11 investigated arriving at lose-lose through the scenario of a strike, and it presented a plan for administrative preparation aimed at minimizing the impact of a strike on the district. Description of union tactics and recommended administrative countertactics were provided. Chapter 12 addressed finalizing and communicating the signed master contract, through the stages of Tentative Agreement to final ratification. Two scenarios: (1) win-win and (2) adversarial were presented as background contrast of the differing processes in achieving that agreement. Presentation, publicizing, and distributing the final contract suggested the need for careful strategies.

Chapter 13 considered the operational stage of communicating and interpreting the master contract; the initiation and implementation of such areas as union and management rights, and cost and non-cost articles. The chapter stressed the requirement for a close review of each item of the contract to prevent erosion of the agreement through the setting of harmful precedents. Chapter 14 covered a number of related items and matters that affect collective bargaining, including laws on employee representational services, contract language, security during bargaining, and re-openers or zipper clauses. The forces impacting the negotiations process, and unfair labor practices and bad faith bargaining were described.

Chapter 15 offered a summary of the do's, maybe's, and don'ts of collective bargaining, and a description of the benefits and losses associated with win-win and lose-lose negotiations. Chapter 16 addressed conflicts involving internal district individuals and groups, and provided examples of typical conflicts in educational settings. Similarly, Chapter 17 addressed conflicts of interest external to the district, involving the community and the media. Again, examples were provided, and a number of models of strategies were offered. Chapter 18 reflected upon the past, present, and future of collective bargaining in education, moving from the historical aspect to the preferred collaborative win-win approach. Chapter 19 discussed means of developing and maintaining a win-win environment for all parties, and addressed various means of resolving conflicts of interest.

In the Introduction, the reader was promised a how-to-do-it road map, which would present practical details on all the important aspects of collective bargaining at the local school district level. It proposed to set the stage by discussing how administrators and employees live and work together in the school district environment. Subsequent chapters detailed all of the strategies, tasks, events, and influences that bear on the collective bargaining process; from the initial certification election of a union through the preparation for, negotiation of, and administration of a union/management collective bargaining agreement. The book focused on administrators, teachers, and non-teaching employees; and on union and management groups who participate in the dynamic, emotional, and intellectually stimulating and draining process called collective bargaining. It also focused on win-win, win-lose, and lose-lose situations that affect the individuals and groups who work within the school district and which, subsequently, affect those who are served by the employees of the school district.

It is the authors' hope and belief that as groups continue to mature in this dramatic process, they will recognize the power and benefits of a win-win approach. For only by win-win, collaborative action between the employees, employees' unions, the school district's administrators, and the school district's board of education will the clients of the district be well served. School exists solely for the purpose of education of the children and youth, and it is with this in mind that we charge those of you who read this volume to only utilize win-win strategies and tactics.

Win-win reaps benefits for the students, the employees, the management and the community at large. Be a winner—join the win-win bandwagon.

EXERCISES

1. A conflict of interest exists between two powerful individuals, one of whom is the chief executive officer of a large corporation and the other is the superintendent of the school district. You have been selected to intervene and to facilitate a resolution to this conflict. What specifically would you do to resolve this conflict?
2. A conflict of interest exists between the board of education and a large community group, and you have been selected to facilitate a resolution to this conflict. What specifically would you do to resolve this conflict?
3. Consider a past conflict in which you were involved or with which you are familiar. What techniques(s) might have facilitated a better resolution to the situation?

REFERENCES

1. Herman, J. J. and J. L. 1993. *School-Based Management: Current Thinking and Practice,* Springfield, IL: Charles C. Thomas, Publisher, pp. 69–70.
2. Herman, J. J. and J. L. 1991. *The Positive Development of Human Resources and School District Organizations.* Lancaster, PA: Technomic Publishing Co., Inc., p. 155.
3. Herman, J. J. and G. E. Megiveron. 1993. *Collective Bargaining in Education: Win-Win, Win/Lose, Lose/Lose.* Lancaster, PA: Technomic Publishing Company, pp. 125–128.
4. Herman, J. J. and G. E. Megiveron. 1993. *Collective Bargaining in Education,* pp. 120–122.
5. Ertel, D. 1991. "How to Design a Conflict Management Procedure that Fits Your Dispute." *Sloan Management Review,* 32(4): 30–41.
6. Katz, N. H. and J. W. Lawyer. 1994. *Resolving Conflict Successfully: Needed Knowledge and Skills.* Newbury Park, CA: Corwin Press—A Sage Publications Company, pp. 36–51.
7. Fields, J. C. 1993. "Unlocking the Paralysis of Will: Leaders Can Use School Efficacy to Unleash a 'Can-Do' Spirit." *School Administrator,* 5(50): 8–13.

Example Provisions from Local School Districts; Master Contracts Related to Insubordination, Incompetency, Contract Management, and Grievance Procedures

POLICY FOR INSUBORDINATION, INCOMPETENCY, OR CONTRACT MISMANAGEMENT BY MANAGEMENT PERSONNEL

MANAGEMENT personnel shall be those who are not allowed to be members of the employee union for those subordinate to the level of the administrator.

When a proved situation arises that the management person has violated a responsibility called for in her/his personal contract, the superintendent shall hear the administrator and the person bringing charges against her/him.

The administrator can bring to the hearing any witness she/he shall determine to be appropriate to the resolution of the situation. The person bringing the charges must present hard evidence that the infraction did, in fact, take place. The use of witnesses shall be expected and reasonable.

GRIEVANCE PROCEDURE

Definition

A "Grievance" is a claim, based upon a teacher's or group of teachers' belief that there has been a violation, misinterpretation, or misapplication of any provision of the Agreement. The "Grievance Procedure" shall not apply to any matter which is prescribed by law, State Regulation, over which the Board is without power to act. No Board prerogative shall be made the subject of a grievance. A grievance may be filed by the Association only when the grievance applies to more than one building and a group of teachers with a common complaint have requested such action.

Procedure

Since it is important that grievances be processed as rapidly as possible, the number of days indicated at each step should be considered as maximum and every effort will be made to expedite the process. The time limits specified may, however, be extended by mutual agreement.

In the event a grievance is filed on or after 1 June, which, if left unresolved until the beginning of the following school year, could result in irreparable harm to a party in interest, the time limits set forth herein shall be reduced so that the grievance procedure may be exhausted prior to the end of the school term, or as soon thereafter as is practicable.

Level One

A teacher with a grievance shall first discuss it with her/his immediate supervisor or principal, within ten (10) school days from the time of the incident over which the teacher is aggrieved or has reasonable knowledge of the incident. At her/his option, the teacher may invite an Association representative to be present while the grievance is discussed. Every effort shall be made to resolve the grievance informally. If the grievance is not resolved, the matter shall be reduced to writing by the grievant and submitted to the same principal/supervisor. The grievance must be reduced to writing, on the proper grievance form, two (2) school days from the time of the discussion between the grievant and her/his supervisor. Within two (2) school days after the presentation of the written grievance, the principal/supervisor shall give her/his answer in writing to the grievant. That Association shall receive a copy.

Level Two

In the event that the aggrieved person is not satisfied with the disposition of her/his grievance at Level One, or in the event that no decision has been rendered within two (2) school days after the presentation of the grievance, she/he may file the grievance in writing with the Association or its representative within five (5) school days after the decision at Level One, or lack of, at Level One.

The Association shall make a judgment on the merits of the grievance. If the Association decides that the grievance lacks merit, or that the decision at Level One is not in the best interests of the educational system, it shall notify the teacher and the principal, and the matter insofar as the Association is concerned is terminated.

If the Association decides, in its opinion, the grievance has merit, it shall refer such grievance in writing to the Superintendent, or such person as the Superintendent may designate, within five (5) school days after the receipt of the grievance from the grievant. Copies shall also go to the Superintendent or her/his designate, the appropriate Director and the Principal/Supervisor.

Within five (5) school days after the Superintendent or designate receives a grievance, she/he shall meet with the aggrieved teacher and a representative or representatives (maximum of 5) of the Association, in an effort to resolve her/his grievance. If the grievance is transmitted directly to the Superintendent or designate (omitting Level One), she/he shall meet with the Association within five (5) school days. The decision on the grievance shall be rendered in writing within five (5) school days after such hearing; copies sent to the aggrieved, the Association, the principal/supervisor, the appropriate Director, and the Superintendent.

Level Three

If the grievance is not settled at Level Two, it may be referred in writing to the Board of Education within five (5) school days after receipt of the decision at Level Two. The Board shall hold a hearing, or designate one or more of its members to hold a hearing, or otherwise investigate the grievance, or prescribe such other procedures as it may deem appropriate for consideration of the grievance. The Association shall have an opportunity to present its view at this level within twenty (20) school days to the Board, or its representative, as it may authorize. Within twenty-five (25) school days after receipt of the grievance, the Board shall render a decision on the grievance and present it in writing to the aggrieved teacher, the Association, the Principal/Supervisor, the appropriate Director, and the Superintendent.

Level Four

(1) If the grievance is not settled at Level Three, the Association may, within ten (10) school days, after the receipt of the Board's decision at Level Three, request that the grievance be submitted to arbitration. The request for submission to arbitration shall be made by written notice to the Board.

(2) Within ten (10) school days after the date of a written request for arbitration, a committee of the Board, or its designated representative, and the Association, may agree upon a mutually acceptable arbitrator. If the parties are unable to agree upon an arbitrator, within the ten (10) day period herein provided, either the Board or the Association may, within twenty (20) school days after the date of the written request for arbitration, request the American Arbitration Association to submit a list of qualified arbitrators. The arbitrator shall then be selected according to the rules of the American Arbitration Association.

(3) The arbitrator shall hear the grievance in dispute and shall render her/his decision in writing within thirty (30) days from the close of the hearing. The arbitrator's decision shall be submitted in writing and shall set forth her/his findings and conclusions with respect to the issue submitted to arbitration. The arbitrator shall confine her/his decision to the particular

case submitted to her/him. Both parties agree to be bound by the award of the arbitrator and agree that judgment thereon may be entered in any court of competent jurisdiction.

(4) The arbitrator shall have no authority except to pass upon alleged violations of the express provisions of this Agreement and to determine disputes involving the application or interpretation of this Agreement.

The arbitrator shall construe this Agreement in a manner which does not interfere with the exercise of the Board's rights and responsibilities, except to the extent that such rights and responsibilities may be expressly limited by the terms of this Agreement.

(5) The arbitrator shall have no power or authority to add to, or subtract from, or modify any of the terms of this Agreement and shall not substitute her/his judgment for that of the Board where the Board is given discretion by the terms of this Agreement. The arbitrator shall not render any decision which would require or permit an action in violation of the Michigan School Laws. The termination of probationary teachers shall not be subject to arbitration.

(6) The arbitrator's fees and expenses shall be shared equally by the Board and the Association. The expenses and compensation of any witnesses or participants in the arbitration shall be paid by the party calling such witnesses or requesting such participants.

(7) A complaint or dispute involving the discharge or demotion of a teacher on continuing tenure shall not be subject to the grievance and arbitration procedure, but shall be presented, heard, and resolved pursuant to the provisions of Act 4, Public Acts of Michigan, 1937 (Ed. Sess.) as amended (Tenure of Teachers Act).

(8) All arbitration hearings shall be held in the school district.

Rights of Teachers to Representation

(1) Members of the Association involved in the Association's business shall continue to enjoy the good faith and professional treatment they have enjoyed in the past.

(2) The Association shall have the right to be present and to state its view at all stages of this grievance procedure. Either party at any level may be represented by counsel, but reasonable notice shall be given the other party in advance if counsel is to be present.

(3) Nothing contained herein shall be construed to prevent any individual teacher from presenting a grievance and having the grievance adjusted at Level One, without the intervention of the Association, if the adjustment is not consistent with the terms of this Agreement, provided that the Association has been given the opportunity to be present at such adjustment.

Miscellaneous

(1) Levels Two and Three of this Grievance Procedure may be passed to the next level for any reason as determined by the Board, or its representative (e.g., no authority to make the judgment, a decision has been rendered in a similar previous decision). However, a hearing must be held at one of the above levels.

(2) It is assumed that grievance problems will be handled at a time other than when the teacher is at work, and that members of the Association will be present to process grievances promptly. In the event that this is not possible due to conflicts in schedules (unwillingness of witnesses to testify after hours), or for other reasons, the grievance will be processed during the working day, and the Association for the teacher (if the Association will not be present) will pay the cost of its member and witnesses, and the Board will pay its witnesses. If Level Four is imposed, all costs will be shared equally by the Association and the Board (if there are any costs).

(3) If more than one teacher has a similar complaint, which has been individually discussed as provided in Level One, the Association may file a grievance to be commenced at Level Two, in lieu of individual grievances.

(4) Failure at any level of this procedure to communicate the decision of a grievance within the specified time limit shall permit the Association to proceed to the next level of the procedure.

(5) Failure to file the grievance in writing, as specified in Level One, or to forward it as specified in Levels Two, Three, or Four, shall mean the grievance is waived.

(6) If the employee elects to be represented, she/he must still be present at any level of the grievance procedure where her/his grievance is to be discussed, except that she/he need not be present where it is mutually agreed that no facts are in dispute, and that the sole question is the interpretation of this Agreement.

(7) The filing of a grievance shall in no way interfere with the right of the Board to proceed in carrying out its management responsibilities, subject to the final decision on the grievance.

(8) The Association is prohibited from processing a grievance on behalf of an employee or group of employees without her/his (their) consent.

(9) Grievance decisions with individual employees which appear in conflict with this Agreement may be grieved by the Association beginning with Level Two.

(10) All documents, communications, and records dealing with the processing of a grievance shall be filed separately from the building personnel files of the participant.

Examples of Cost and Power Analyses of Master Contract Proposals

AS proposals are presented by either party (union or management) to the collective bargaining process, it is crucial that each proposal is analyzed for its costs and its power relationships. The cost analysis is especially crucial if a multiple-year contract agreement is to be ratified.

Three examples will illustrate the importance of these analyses of proposals.

EXAMPLE ONE

The union's negotiating team proposes changing the health insurance paid by the school district to coverage of spouse and to full family coverage from single employee coverage. Since it is anticipated that the master contract will eventually be ratified, the cost impact will be as follows.

Analysis

(1) Current base year's cost per single employee	$1,450
(2) Added cost per spouse = +$950	$2,400
(3) Added cost per full family = +$1,450	$2,900
(4) Average increase in premium over the past five (5) years = 18%	
(5) Anticipated number of single employees = 1,000	
(6) Anticipated number of spousal coverage = 800	
(7) Anticipated number of full family employees = 800	

(1) Current base year's cost =		$1,450,000
(2) Future year one's cost =		$3,976,600
Base year	$1,450,000	
Spouse $950 × 800	760,000	
Full family $1,450 × 800	1,160,000	
TOTAL BASE:	$3,370,000	

Anticipate yearly 18%
premium increase   ×   18
PREMIUM INCREASE   606,600

GRAND TOTAL $3,979,600
(3) Year two's cost: $4,692,388
    (18% premium increase × $3,976,600 = $715,788)
    ($3,976,600 + $715,788)
(4) Year three's cost $5,537,018
    (18% premium increase × $4,692,388 = $844,630)
    ($4,692,388 + $844,630)

Note the tremendous escalation of costs to the district if the board of education ratifies a three-year master contract that includes this additional health benefit. The benefit request is a reasonable one, but the cost may be prohibitive.

EXAMPLE TWO

The board of education's collective bargaining team proposes that all teachers be required to attend one week of staff development activities prior to the beginning of school for the students. During this week, the board's team proposes that the teachers will be paid the substitute teachers' daily rate of forty dollars ($40) rather than their daily contracted salary rate.

Analysis

(1) *Power* is in favor of the board of education in that it, in essence, is requiring an extra week of work at a reduced pay rate.
(2) *Cost to the board* for 400 teachers = $80,000
    (400 × 40 = $16,000 × 5 days)
(3) *Cost to teachers* for 400 teachers = $376,000
    The average teacher salary computed on a daily basis is $228 and they will be working for $40. This is a loss per day of $188.
    ($188 × 400 teachers = $75,200 × 5 days)

EXAMPLE THREE

The union proposes that no board policy or administrative rules and regulations shall be adopted or promulgated without the union first having received the proposed policy or rules and regulations at least one calendar month prior to adoption. Also, the union will be given the opportunity for a hearing, if it so chooses, on the matter prior to the adoption at a legally constituted board meeting.

Analysis

If the proposal is accepted as part of a ratified master contractual agreement, the union is gaining significant power in that it obtains a review procedure prior to any important board of education policy or rules and regulations action. It also gains a public hearing that can be utilized to strategize a negative media event opposing the policy or rules and regulations if the union chooses to be in opposition.

The board of education loses power and has nothing to gain from agreeing to this proposal.

A Format for Analyzing Fringe Benefits and the Costs of Master Contract Articles

THE first thing needed is a series of several grids upon which up-to-date information is posted in such a manner that each cell becomes a cost item based upon the number that is reflected therein. Here is an example of a "scatter grid" for a public school district showing the total number of employees that would be impacted by the contract settlement. The example below is for your study and understanding and one that will enable you to prepare a similar grid showing the number of teachers in each cell represented by the number of years of teaching credit (in the district), down the column and across the columns showing the degree status your district honors for pay purposes.

No. Teachers	BA	+15	+30	MA	+15	+30	Ed.S.	Ed.D.
1	12			6	1			
2	15	10	5	6	11			
3	5	20	21	11	11			
4			25	7	7			
5	2	3	26	22	10	5	1	6

You can also use this same grid for the cost of various leave days during the prior year of school. By substituting the numbers in the cell with the facts of cost for substitutes, you can also cost-out the days being used and numbers being requested. The grid on days *not* taught will be extremely valuable for the management team. It shows the number of teachers that used each of the columns for leave during the year.

No. Days	Funeral	Sick	Personal	Pregnancy	Misc.
1	12	3,532	121	11	15
2	45	2,128	265	35	26
3	5	1,120	11	11	26
4	5	189	0	7	8
5	1	102	0	20	5

When more than five consecutive days are used for any purpose, a tally must be kept and rows added to the grid as the numbers are finalized. This grid already shows that the regular teachers were absent from the classroom for 142 funeral days, 12,414 sick days, 684 personal days, 242 pregnancy days (short term), and 202 miscellaneous days, including court appearances, etc. (Don't forget your sabbatical leave costs should also be added to this grid.)

Using this grid, the cost of an increase can be computed rather easily on a computer spreadsheet by merely plugging in the increased costs (by cell) and using the number of teachers as the multiplier for the product to be printed in a like grid. The totals will show you where the costs are highest for the purpose of devising your counterproposals.

A separate grid needs to be developed by the fringe benefit office in order that the same type of information will be available for costing the fringe benefits.

Type of Coverage	Single	Spouse	Family	Other
BCBS	462	322	621	0
Major medical	12	106	0	0
Dental	2	60	0	0
Life	0	20	121	11
Optical	25	7	7	0

In this grid, you will use the cost of Blue Cross/Blue Shield for a single member times the 462 persons and the product would go into the cell as follows: $$$$$ × 462 and follow this same scheme in each cell of the grid. When a proposal is made, the new product would go into the cell. There will be some shifting of costs, therefore only the column's total will provide the correct data for decisions to be made.

Main Points of Kentucky's Reform Act of 1990 Related to School-Based Decision Making

KENTUCKY LAW: KRS CHAPTER 160, SECTIONS 14 AND 15

Section 14: School-Based Decision Making

(1) January 1, 1991, the school board shall adopt a policy for implementing the school-based decision making approach, and policies related to KRS 160.340 must be amended to further implement this approach related to professional development activities (sections 2 & 3 of HB 940).

(2) Each participating school shall form a school council composed of 2 parents, 3 teachers and the principal or administrator. More can be added, but the proportion must remain the same. Parents cannot be related to any school employee.

  (a) Teachers shall be "elected" for 1 year terms by a majority of teachers.

  (b) Parents shall be "selected" by the members of the PTO of the school; or, if none exists, by the largest organization of parents formed for this purpose.

  (c) The principal or head teacher shall chair the council.

The Council's and Principals' Responsibilities Include:

  (1) Set school policy to provide an environment to enhance students' achievement and meet the goals of Sections 2 and 3 of this act. The principal shall be the primary administrator and instructional leader of the school; and, with the assistance of the total school staff, shall administer the policies established by the school council and school board.

  (2) All staff "may" be participants. The staff shall divide into committees according to their areas of interest. A majority of each committee's members shall "elect" a chair to serve a one year term. Each committee shall submit its recommendations to the school council for consideration.

(3) The council and each committee shall determine the agenda and frequency of meetings. The meetings shall be open to the public with the exceptions provided in KRS 61.810.

(4) Within the funds available from the school board, the council "shall" determine the number of persons to be employed in each job classification at the school, and can make personnel decisions on vacancies. It cannot recommend transfer or dismissals.

(5) The council "shall" determine which instructional materials and student support services shall be provided in the school.

(6) From a list of applicants recommended by the superintendent, the principal "shall" select personnel to fill vacancies, after consultation with the school council.

(7) To fill a principal vacancy, the school council "shall" select from among those persons recommended by the superintendent, and the superintendent "shall" provide additional applicants upon request.

(8) The council shall adopt a policy to be implemented by the principal in these additional areas:

   (a) Determination of curriculum, including needs assessment, curriculum development, alignment with state standards, technology utilization, and program appraisal within the local school board's policy.

   (b) Assignment of "all" instructional and non-instructional staff time.

   (c) Assignment of students to classes and programs.

   (d) Determine the schedule of the school day and week subject to the beginning and ending times and school calendar set by the school board.

   (e) Determine the use of school space during the school day.

   (f) Plan and resolve issues regarding instructional practices.

   (g) Select and implement discipline and classroom management techniques; including the roles of students, parents, teachers, counselors and principals.

   (h) Select extracurricular programs and determination of policies relating to student participation based on academic and attendance requirements, program evaluation and supervision.

(3) The Local Board Policy on School-Based Decision Making "shall" also Address:

   (a) School budget and administration (discretionary funds; activity and other school funds; funds for maintenance, supplies and equipment; and accounting and auditing).

(b) Assessment of individual student progress, including testing and reporting of student progress to students, parents, the school district, the community and the state.

(c) School improvement plans, including the form and function of strategic planning and its relationship to district planning.

(d) Professional development plans developed pursuant to Sections 12 and 13 of this act.

(e) Parent, citizen and community participation including the relationship of the council with other groups.

(f) Cooperation and collaboration within the district and with other districts, public agencies and private agencies.

(g) Requirements for waiver of district policies.

(h) Requirements for record keeping by the school council.

(i) A process for appealing a decision made by a school council.

(j) In addition, the school board "may" grant to the school council any other authority permitted by law.

(4) The school board "shall" make liability insurance available to all members of the school council when performing duties as school council members.

(5) After the effective date of this act, any school in which two-thirds (2/3) of the faculty vote to implement school-based decision making may do so.

(6) By June 30, 1991, each school board shall submit to the Chief State School Officer, the name of at least one (1) school which has decided to implement school-based management. If no school so votes, the school board "shall" designate one (1) school to implement it.

All schools shall implement school-based management by July 1, 1996. However, by a majority vote of the faculty, a school performing above its threshold level requirement, as determined by the Department of Education, may apply to the State Board for exemption from this requirement.

(7) The Department of Education shall develop sample guidelines to assist local boards in the development of their policies, and it shall provide professional development activities to assist schools in implementing school-based decision making.

(8) A school that chooses to have a different school-based model than the one outlined, can request an exemption by describing the model, submitting it through the board of education to the Chief State School Officer and the State Board for approval.

Main Points of Texas' Reform Act of 1990 Related to School-Based Decision Making

SENATE BILL 1
(JUNE, 1990)

21.7532 Campus Performance Objectives

(a) For each school year, the principal of each school campus, with the assistance of parents, community residents, and the professional staff of the school . . . shall establish academic and other performance objectives of the campus for each academic excellence indicator adopted under Section 21.7531 of this code. . . . The objectives must be approved by the district's board of trustees.

(b) In this section, "parent" means a person who is a parent of or person standing in parental relation to a student enrolled at a school . . . and who is not an employee of the school or the school district. . . . "Community resident" means a person 18 years of age or older residing in the attendance area of a school . . . but this does not include a person who is a parent of a student enrolled in that school or a person who is an employee of the school or the school district.

21.930 District-Level Decision Process

(a) The board of trustees of each school district shall adopt a policy to involve the professional staff of the district in establishing and reviewing the district's educational goals, objectives, and major district-wide classroom instructional programs.

(b) The board shall establish a procedure under which meetings are held regularly with representative professional staff and the board or board designee.

(c) The board shall adopt a procedure . . . for the professional staff within the district to nominate and elect the representatives who will meet with the board or board designee as required under the provisions of this section. . . . Two-thirds of the elected representatives must be classroom teachers. The remaining representatives shall be campus-based staff.

(d) This section does not prohibit the board from conducting meetings with teachers or groups of teachers other than the meetings described by this section.

(e) Nothing in this section shall be construed as creating a new cause of action or as requiring collective bargaining.

HOUSE BILL 2885
(MAY, 1991)

TEC §21.931

(a) Each school district shall develop and implement a plan for site-based decision making not later than September 1, 1992. Each district shall submit its plan to the commissioner of education for approval.

(b) Each district's plan:

(1) shall establish school committees;

(2) may expand on the process established by the district for the establishment of campus performance objectives; and

(3) shall outline the role of the school committees regarding decision making related to goal setting, curriculum, budgeting, staffing patterns, and school organization.

(c) A school committee established under this section shall include community representatives. The community representatives may include business representatives.

(d) The commissioner may not approve a plan that the commissioner determines contains one or more provisions that may be construed as limiting or affecting the power of the board of trustees of the school district to govern and manage the district or as limiting the responsibilities of the trustees.

(e) The commissioner shall identify or make available to school districts various models of implementing site-based decision making under this section not later than January 1, 1992. . . . The commissioner shall arrange for training in site-based decision making through one or more sources for school board trustees, superintendents, principals, teachers, parents, and other members of school committees.

(f) Nothing in this section may be construed as creating a new cause of action or as requiring collective bargaining.

SENATE BILL 351
(APRIL, 1991)

TEC §11.273: Waivers and Exemptions

(a) Except as specifically prohibited under subsection (e) of this section, a school campus or district may apply to the *commissioner of education* for a waiver of a requirement or prohibition imposed by law or rule that the campus or district determines inhibits student achievement.

(b) An application under this section must include a written plan developed by the campus principal or district superintendent, as appropriate, and faculty of the campus or district that states the achievement objectives of the campus or district and the inhibition imposed on those objectives by the requirement or prohibition and shall be approved by the district's board of trustees.

(c) The *commissioner* may grant a waiver under this section for a period not to exceed three years. A prohibition on conduct that constitutes a criminal offense may not be waived.

(d) A school campus or district for which a requirement or prohibition is waived under this section for a period of three years may receive an exemption from that requirement or prohibition at the end of that period if the campus or district has fulfilled the achievement objectives submitted to the *commissioner*. . . . The exemption remains in effect until the *commissioner* determines that achievement levels of the campus or district have declined.

(e) A school campus or district may not receive an exemption or waiver under this section from requirements imposed by federal law or rule, including requirements for special education or bilingual education programs. . . . A school campus or district may not receive an exemption or waiver under this section from a requirement or prohibition imposed by state law or rule relating to:

(1) curriculum essential elements, excluding teacher methodology used by a teacher and the time spent by a teacher or a student on a particular task or subject

(2) restrictions on extracurricular activities

(3) health and safety

(4) competitive bidding

(5) elementary class size limits

    (6) minimum graduation requirements

    (7) removal of a disruptive student from the classroom

    (8) suspension or expulsion of a student

    (9) at risk programs

  (10) prekindergarten programs

  (11) educational employee and educational support employee rights and benefits . . . or

  (12) special education or bilingual education programs

(f) A school district or campus that receives a waiver under this section for textbook selection may select for purchase a textbook not on a state-adopted multiple list. . . .

(g) The *commissioner* in considering exemptions or waivers shall provide as much regulatory relief as is practical and reasonable to campuses or districts that are considered high performing.

Management's Confidential Contingency Plan for Use During a Strike

(1) A special confidential "hotline" is established by which you can report any strike activities which are taking place at your site, and from which you can receive the latest status report from management's central strike control. The phone number is (906) 432-1161 (fictitious phone number).

(2) From this date forward, administrators hearing rumors or possessing pertinent information should immediately report the same to the superintendent of schools. The superintendent shall immediately share this information with the school district's chief negotiator, and the superintendent shall make a judgement as to whether or not to share this information with the board of education president (or with the board member selected as the primary communication contact person for the board of education). The board president will then decide whether or not to share this information with other board members, and the chief negotiator will decide whether or not any specific administrators will be informed—this decision by the chief negotiator will be on a "need to know" basis.

(3) Parents, student, community members or employees who phone with questions or comments are to be told that a public "hotline" has been established by the board which will be connected to a recorder which will provide the latest updated information on the situation and on the progress to date. Also, please ask them not to attempt to phone board members or administrators, because they have great responsibility to carry out during this time of crisis. Finally, assure them that the hotline messages will be updated at least once per day and sooner if that is required. This public "hotline" number is (906) 321-0567 (fictitious phone number).

(4) Daily during the strike, each administrator is to be prepared to follow this regimen:
   • Hand deliver a daily report on the form outlined in Figure F.1 to the superintendent of school's office by 5:00 P.M. daily.

Prepare for a brief 4:30 P.M. meeting daily in the superintendent's office.

School _____   Date _____

9:00 A.M. Report

Number of *employees* present _____

Number of students present (report only if we attempt to continue student instruction during the strike) _____

Do you have pickets? _____   How many? _____
Any unusual union activity (explain)? _____
1:30 P.M. Report
Number of *employees* present _____
Number of students present _____
Do you have pickets? _____   How many? _____
Any unusual union activity (explain)? _____
4:00 P.M. Report
Number of employees present _____
Number of students present _____
Do you have pickets? _____   How many? _____
Any unusual union activity (explain)? _____
Reported by (administrator's signature): _____

FIGURE F.1. Daily strike report.

(5) Also, during the strike, it should be understood that:
  • Any questions from the media are to be referred to the district's chief negotiator and spokesperson, and the chief negotiator will automatically be forwarding appropriate releases to the media covering our school district.
  • Any media representative wishing to visit within any school building shall be accompanied by the building principal or by the administrator in charge of the building at the point of the requested visit. This requirement is put in place to have an eye witness to what the media representative sees, and to check the accuracy of the media representative's report. It also is being put in place, since frequently the presence of a media representative will be cause for heightened union activity.
  • Any communication with teachers or with the teachers' union representatives is to be handled *in writing solely by the district's chief negotiator.*
  • Any contact with attorneys shall be by the district's chief negotiator or the superintendent of schools.
  • All communication with the board of education president or with board of education members shall be through the superintendent of

schools, or from the superintendent of schools to the board president and the board president will communicate with the other board of education members.

- All communication with other governmental agencies, including the police and other school districts, shall be through the chief negotiator after the chief negotiator has reviewed the communications with the superintendent of schools.

- Non-public school officials shall be contacted by the superintendent of schools, and the superintendent of schools shall make any necessary decision as to future transportation and other traditional services provided by the school district to the non-public schools by the school district. The same procedures will prevail in regards to the special education and vocational education students who are transferred into or out of our school district for their instruction.

- The *only spokespersons* for the school district are the district's chief negotiator and the superintendent of schools, and the board members have agreed that their *sole spokesperson* shall be the president of the school board.

- Do not discuss any matters related to negotiations or the strike with any teacher or non-administrator, regardless of friendship or respect patterns which you may have with those individuals.

(6) Principals and other administrators must understand that:
- Since we start school earlier for secondary school students, if teachers do not show for work on the first day, call the transportation office to arrange for secondary students to be returned home, after receiving permission to do so by the superintendent. The superintendent can reach the radio stations and cancel elementary school classes, and also cancel school for the remainder of the day. This is the procedure for the second day of the school year as well. An announcement will be made at that point if school is being cancelled until further notice.

- If teachers walk out during the day, call the central office for assistance until students are picked up by the bus. Secretaries, aides, administrators, and other available non-teacher personnel will be sent to your buildings. PTA presidents and PTA members will be contacted only if sufficient supervision is not available by utilizing the school district's employees.

- All teachers, teacher aides, cafeteria workers, and transportation employees who report for work shall be paid for the initial two days. Thereafter, they shall be notified in writing by the individual buildings' principals (for teachers, aides and cafeteria workers), and by the director of transportation service (for transportation employees) that they are laid off until further notice. This is not intended to be a punitive step, but the money that will be saved will be required when the school days missed are made up later. Also, explain to these dedicated employees that we can't afford to pay them if there is no work for them to do at this time.

- All fringe benefits of striking employees shall be continued only upon payment of the costs by the individual employee. The assistant superintendent for business affairs will forward a letter, which is also signed by the superintendent of schools and the president of the board of education, to each striking employee, so informing them.
- If custodial or other employees absent themselves in support of the teachers' union, all buildings shall be completely closed down. The assistant superintendent for business shall be authorized to hire off-duty police or other appropriate individuals to maintain security on a twenty-four hour basis, if this action is deemed necessary. If necessary, administrators shall devise a plan to cover all buildings with administrators for day, afternoon, and evening shifts.
- If the strike continues beyond the second day, an administrators' meeting shall be conducted to deal with how to provide interim instruction, and with means of cutting all overhead and other costs to a minimum level. All administrators should give prior thought to this need area. All after school activities, except in the event of a complete shutdown, shall take place as scheduled when the individual building's principal and the director of co-curricular activities are assured of proper supervision and normal arrangements.

(7) Further, during the strike:
- Paychecks for previous work completed shall be distributed through the buildings in accordance with normal procedures.
- Pickets are to be permitted *only outside* of school buildings. If pickets attempt to enter the building or otherwise become unruly, immediately call the superintendent or the chief negotiator and they will decide whether or not to have the assistant superintendent for business call the police for assistance.
- Daily, file an incident report in the format shown in Figure F.2.

(8) During the strike, principals should:
- Maintain a complete log (names, addresses, phone numbers, and topics) of any person making contact with the administrator.
- Report any unusual incident that takes place. The principals should take a photo or videotape to document the incident.

(9) The assistant superintendent for operations shall inform the director of transportation, the director of custodial and maintenance services, and the director of food services of the arrangements which specifically apply to their operational areas.

Building _____Reporter _____Date _____
The following is an account of all activities which took place at this building today. It includes pertinent information regarding any unusual incidents which occurred and any information available describing strangers on school building grounds. Also, the names of those persons involved in the incidents, and a statement of any threats received or vandalism observed or discovered. Please, use the camera that you were issued to take photos of the people involved or the damage incurred.
Time of incident _____
Activity _____
_____
_____
_____

FIGURE F.2. Incident report.

(10) Greater and in-depth planning shall be shared at a meeting immediately following the initiation of the first day of the strike. Before administrators are asked to attend a central meeting, there will be a replacement assigned to their facility.

(11) During any strike situation, administrators and board of education members are under a great deal of stress. Now that we have our strike plans in place, let's discuss the conduct of board of education members and administrators during the strike.

Union's Confidential Work Stoppage, Prestrike, and Strike Plans

SOMETIMES contract negotiations become protracted, and the union leadership decides to put pressure on the board of education and its negotiating team by devising and carrying out tactics designed to put pressure on the board of education to settle the contract in terms that will be favorable to the union. If the win-lose strategy is subscribed to by the union's leadership, the following examples will illustrate some of the tactics that they could use to assist them in becoming the winner in a win-lose game.

PRESTRIKE TACTICS

A wide variety of prestrike tactics could be enacted by the union. Eight examples will illustrate tactics that are frequently utilized:

(1) Having friends of the union (uses spouses of members or union members from neighboring districts) write letters to the editors in newspapers distributed in the school district. These letters to the editors will indicate how badly the board is treating its teachers or other employees in regard to negotiation positions taken or in comparison of contract items received by employees of other school districts that are superior to those offered by the board of education.

(2) Picketing board of education meetings, and picketing around school buildings prior to the start of the school day and immediately following the end of the school day.

(3) Teachers refusing to provide homework to students or to meet with parents after the school day.

(4) Coaches and sponsors indicating that they will not sign a supplemental contract to carry out their duties during the next school year unless a master contractual agreement is agreed to and signed by the board of education.

(5) Having friends of the union pack public board meetings and put pressure on the board to sign-off and agree to a new master contract agreement. When possible, the union will notify all media sources in the hopes that

they will publicize the meeting at which the board of education is roundly criticized for its erroneous stands during contract negotiations.

(6) The union will file unfair labor practices charges against the board of education in the hopes that the general public will believe that the board has been unfair to its employees during the contract negotiations. This again will lead to free media publicity that will reach the residents of the school district.

(7) The union will file a bad faith bargaining charge against the board of education in the hopes that the general public will perceive that the board of education has not acted properly during the contract negotiations. This will also lead to free media publicity that will reach the residents of the school district.

(8) The union leadership will play some dirty tricks by trying to assemble real or unreal stories and rumors about whomever they feel is the strongest person or persons who are holding strong against some of the union's contract demands. The individuals usually targeted are the chief negotiator for the board of education, the board of education members, or the superintendent of schools. Usually, only one target is chosen, as to criticize all parties will make the union look like it has no focus, and the public might perceive the union as blaming everyone but itself for the failure to reach a master contract agreement without adversarial and negative situations happening.

WORK STOPPAGES

Often when the above tactics have not proven helpful and the time spent on negotiations has found the union with very limited success, the leadership might attempt another more disruptive tactic—that of work stoppages. For the most part, the tactic of work stoppages will be in the form of teachers or other employees taking sick leave. A most effective tactic is one in which all teachers from a single school building call in sick for a specific day. This tactic may be rotated among all the individual school buildings in the school district, disrupting normal routine and costing a great deal of money for substitute teachers. About all the board of education can do is insist on doctors' excuses (although, legally, the board of education cannot demand them unless this has been a traditional operational policy), or the board might ask for court relief (which is probably not going to be a successful approach to the problem).

STRIKE PLANS

Assuming none of the above tactics have proven successful in getting the board of education to agree to the union's contract demands, the union will prepare its strike plans. These plans will be carried out whenever the union feels it will be to its advantage to initiate them. The purpose, again, is for the union (and hopefully the community) to put sufficient pressure on the board of education that they will give into the union's contract demands. Some of the specific planning will include the following.

(1) Begin the strike immediately before the start of a new school year. This, hopefully, from the union's standpoint will cause the parents of students to put a great deal of pressure on the board of education.

(2) Actually start the school year, but have the coaches and sponsors refuse to sign supplemental contracts and execute their traditional duties. This will bring much pressure by the participating students and from the parental booster groups for settlement to take place.

(3) Begin the school year for one week, and then take the membership out on strike. This will prove to be doubly harmful, as many parents with school-aged children both work.

(4) Begin a media and propaganda rumor campaign that will place the board of education in the worst light possible within the community.

(5) Organize pickets at every site.

(6) Hold media interviews whenever the media will go along with the union's request.

(7) Pack every school board meeting with "alleged" angry parents and citizens.

(8) Call on the resources of the state union organization, and, sometimes, the national union organizations when a big win becomes important to all three union levels.

(9) Set up a hotline to keep the negotiation information current from other school districts in the area that are also still involved in contract negotiations.

(10) Establish committees to oversee that the complete set of tactics decided upon are carried out in a speedy and accurate manner. Some committees might well include (a) media coordination, (b) picketing coordination, (c) union membership morale and actions coordination, (d) meetings with community residents coordination, (e) pressuring of individual board members coordination, and (f) getting student support coordination.

The major concern of the union is that of making the board of education and the board's negotiating team look like the "bad guys", while avoiding the community painting the union in the same light. If the union is unsuccessful in this matter, it could become the loser—not only during the current negotiations, but many years into the future.

A Checklist of Steps Involved in Successful Conflict Resolutions

DIRECTIONS: Place an "X" in front of each box as you complete each step in the conflict resolution checklist below.

❏   (1) Have you entered the conflict situation with the goal of arriving at a win-win resolution for all parties to the conflict?

❏   (2) Have you developed strong communication links with all parties to the conflict?

❏   (3) Have you achieved the trust of all parties to the conflict?

❏   (4) Have you determined the actual position(s), including those beneath the surface, of each party to the conflict?

❏   (5) Once you have determined the positions of each party, have you analyzed areas of agreement, areas of disagreement, and possible areas for future compromise?

❏   (6) Have you made certain that you and all parties to the conflict of interest understand the circumstances that brought about the conflict?

❏   (7) Have you determined the outcome(s) that you are going to find acceptable to yourself?

❏   (8) Have you determined the specific role or roles that you are going to play (discussion leader, mediator, fact-finder, arbitrator, consensus builder)?

❏   (9) Have you obtained the agreement of the parties to the conflict of interest to a set of behavioral ground rules to be used during the conflict resolution process?

❏ (10) Have you legitimized the interests of all parties to the conflict, and have you convinced the opposing parties that each party's interests are legitimate?

❏ (11) Have you legitimized the feelings and perceptions of all parties to the conflict?

❏ (12) Have you insisted that all parties to the conflict view it as a mutual problem to be resolved, not as a win-lose struggle?

❏ (13) Have you insisted that each party to the conflict take the other parties perspective, and determine why and how the opposing party should act if their party was sitting in the other party's position?

❏ (14) Are you willing to float trial balloons or propose experimental solutions to the conflict?

❏ (15) Have you insisted that compromises be made to resolve the conflict of interest?

❏ (16) Have you proposed package deals in which several issues are dealt with as part of a whole resolution?

❏ (17) Have you insisted on causes or intermissions during the dialogue sessions in order that the participants can reflect on the conflict, what they are learning from it, and the advantages to them of resolving the conflict?

❏ (18) Have you clarified for all parties to the conflict the consequences that would accrue to each party if the conflict would be permitted to continue in a negative manner?

❏ (19) Have you focused the attention of all parties to the conflict on the long-term benefits and outcomes to each party by resolving the existing conflict of interest?

❏ (20) Do you insist on much dialogue, paraphrased meanings, negotiating positions, and reaching agreement by consensus—not by power positions or threats to the other party?

❏ (21) Once the parties reach a consensus solution to the conflict, are you certain the solution is fair and equitable; and that it leaves both parties with respect for one another and with *wins?*

Absolutes   are those bargaining proposals from which the negotiators will not retreat.

Academic Freedom   means the scholarly right of teachers to teach and behave professionally according to their own determination of instructional and professional appropriateness.

Accidental Death and Disability Insurance   is a fringe benefit intended to provide emergency insurance coverage for employees who experience a fatal or catastrophic accident.

Administration   is one of three basic means of operation in management. It is the skill to direct others in the accomplishment of the institution's goals.

Administrator   is a person employed to take day-to-day responsibility for the operation of a unit, such as a school building, or of a program, such as special education.

Adversarial Bargaining   happens when both sides continually make attempts to gain power from the other side. It can occur because of conflicting personalities of the chief negotiators, because of tight money in economically strapped times, or because of inside or outside pressures to settle or not to settle a contract.

AFL   is the American Federation of Labor.

Agency Shop   refers to a situation wherein all employees are required to pay a service fee to the union, but they are not required to become members of the union. The fee is intended to cover all the costs of the union when the union is representing the employees in collective bargaining matters.

American Arbitration Association   is a professional group that will supply a list of arbitrators to both parties.

American Federation of Teachers (AFT)   is an AFL-CIO international union; its membership is mostly urban. It represents the professional, economic, and social concerns of teachers, as well as other public employees.

Arbitrability refers to the negotiable status of individual contract items; arbitrability may be questioned by either party. If the question of arbitrability is raised and a review by the arbitrator of existing contractual language and the state's collective bargaining laws and its supplemental rules and regulations causes the arbitrator to rule that a certain item is not arbitrable, the party who questioned the arbitrability of the item scores a big tactical win. Most times, however, the arbitrator will not be questioned on the arbitrability issue; and when she/he is, the ruling generally is one that states the item is arbitrable.

Arbitration is a voluntary (both sides agree) or compulsory (the law in some states) method designed to settle disputes, whereby an outside agent (impartial third party) reads documentation presented, conducts a hearing, and renders a decision as to the final settlement of a contract. The decision is usually final and binding.

Arbitrator is an impartial third party to whom parties in dispute present their differences for decision.

Assessed Property Valuations are data which provide negotiators with information related to the taxable value of the property that exists in the school district, and its future potential to increase or decrease the income from a district's property tax.

Association of State, County, and Municipal Employees (ASCME) is an employee organization that draws membership from the ranks of mainly classified school district employees.

Authority is the expressed right to complete tasks assigned by upper levels of management.

Bad Faith Bargaining refers to a situation wherein either party to the negotiations refuses to attend a reasonable series of meetings, refuses to meet with reasonable frequency, refuses to give serious consideration to the proposals of the other party, or refuses to make reasonable proposals or counterproposals.

Bargaining Chip Proposals are meant to be giveaways or bargaining chips.

Bargaining Notebook is a compilation of data consolidating all of the information that the local bargaining team requires as reference information during the process of negotiations. Major items include copies of the state's bargaining law, the current master contract agreement, financial status, etc.

Bargaining Process is a set of meetings, caucuses, and document preparations for proposals and counterproposals, which will be completed when both teams agree to each proposal and receive approval of the proposed contractual agreement by both of their respective referent groups.

Bargaining Rules are those rules by which any negotiation team operates, depending on the directions given by the official body (board of education, in the case of the management's negotiation team), which precedes the overall guidelines provided to the negotiation team, and to the specific style and role to be played by the negotiation team's chief negotiator and spokesperson.

Bargaining Team refers to those members who are selected or elected to represent the union or the management during the process of negotiating a collective bargaining master contractual agreement.

Bargaining Units are employee groups recognized by employers, or designated by an authorized agency, as the organization for conducting collective negotiations.

Belief is something accepted as true or accurately perceived as being true.

Board of Education is the policy setting local body which carries legal responsibility for the official decisions related to the education of the children within a school district and for all decisions related to the operation of the local school district. Boards of education may be either elected or appointed, and their memberships usually vary between five and eleven members.

Bonded Indebtedness is the amount of money owed to pay off bonds (principal and interest).

Caucus refers to a private (union team or management team) single party meeting held during negotiations, when proposals and counterproposals are considered, and strategies and tactics are discussed.

Certification Election is a supervised employee election which results in the formal designation of an organization to act as exclusive representative for all employees in the bargaining unit.

Certified Employees are those employees who hold professional state-level certification; usually teachers and administrators.

Chief Negotiator is the person appointed to do all the communication at the table for one side or the other in the presentation of proposals or counters and to discuss content and intent of the language. She/he is empowered to call caucuses, initial (temporarily approve) all items as agreed upon, set the calendar for at-table bargaining, and, in general, be responsible for the conduct of the team at the table.

Class Grievance   is a complaint that may be filed when it is felt that the grievance relates to a group of union members rather than to a single individual.

Classified Employees   are those school district employees who are not required to be certified; it refers to such employees as custodians, food service workers, transportation personnel, etc.

Clients   in the context of the book, refers to the students first, and secondly, to the community at large. The community constitutes the parents and all other taxpayers who have a stake in the outcome of the bargaining being done.

Closed Hearing   refers to the type of impasse procedural hearing that may occur if either party objects to a public, open hearing. Most experts in the field recommend closed hearings. This also refers to closed negotiating sessions.

Closed Shop   refers to a situation wherein any person wishing to become employed by the school district must become a member of the union prior to being hired. Closed shops are prohibited in public school settings.

Co-Curricular Activities   are those activities in which students participate that are not part of the main course of study, such as athletics.

Collective Bargaining   is the legally required process wherein both the school district board of education's negotiation team and the exclusive representatives of a union's negotiation team meet, confer, and bargain in good faith for the purpose of executing a written master contractual agreement that incorporates all of the agreements reached during the bargaining process.

Collective Bargaining Law   is the statute governing representation of certified employees and governing the employer-employee negotiations.

Comparative Data   refers to economic and noneconomic statistical information about neighboring or demographically and financially similar school districts; those systems to which the negotiating district will have to be ultimately compared.

Contract Arbitration   refers to the situation when an outside arbitrator comes into the school district as a step in an impasse procedure. In this case, the union and management cannot reach agreement on one or more proposed master contract articles, and an arbitrator is hired to come in to resolve the outstanding contractual issues in order that a total master contract agreement can be reached and ratified. Contractual arbitration can be mandated or permissive, depending on the specific state's laws and regulations governing collective bargaining.

Contract Article   refers to individual provisions of a master contract, such as salary or a particular benefit.

Contract Erosion   refers to the result when management is not following both the strict interpretation of the contract and the direction of her/his supervisor in the operation of the contract following ratification, by allowing union members a freedom not allowed in the contract.

Contract   is a written document between an employer (the Board of Education) and an employee organization, usually for a definite length of time, defining the conditions (salaries, etc.) of employment, the rights of both parties to the contract, and the procedures to be followed in settling disputes or other issues arising during the course of operating the contract.

Contract Language   refers to the specific terminology and written technical structure of the master contract. Some words, such as shall and will, are words that mandate compliance; whereas words like may or should allow the party flexible decision-making power when it comes to compliance.

Contract Management   is the administrative process that ensures that the employees receive all benefits of the negotiated contract and that the day-to-day operations conform to the contract language.

Contract Ratification   occurs when employees of a particular group vote in an open meeting to accept a contract offer, and when the board of education also votes to accept it.

Contract Violation   is a misinterpretation of the wording of the master contract which results in action bringing about a charge by the offended party of noncompliance with the contract.

Cost of Living Index   is an economic percentage indicator used in the expression of normal living expenses, including inflation.

Cost/Benefit Analyst   is a member of the negotiation team who carries the basic responsibility of determining the financial cost of every potential proposal being developed by management's negotiation team. This person also is responsible for determining the financial cost of every at-the-table proposal being made by the union's negotiation team.

Counterproposal   is a proposal made in response to a proposal from the other side in collective negotiations.

Court Recorder is a person who is sometimes hired when fact-finding procedures are taking place, in order to have a verbatim record of the proceedings. A court recorder is also sometimes hired during arbitration hearings.

Decertification Election is formal procedure removing the negotiations representation status of an employee organization.

Delphi Technique is a consensus-reaching technique which can be employed without participants meeting together; it is characterized by successive rounds of written responses and reactions to issues.

Demographic Data includes pupil population figures, density across grade levels, age of residents, average family income, etc., which are collected about the school district and its students in order to inform the fact-finding procedure.

Dental Insurance is a fringe benefit intended to provide preventive, diagnostic, and basic dental care services for employees.

Dividing and Conquering is a technique used when the union team's members represent different interests; to create proposals which are divisive in nature and aimed at internally polarizing the individual union negotiating team members.

Documentation is the administrative recording of each step in the employee disciplinary process. Documentation must take place at every step of the disciplinary process, and the documentation must be in writing with a copy to be placed in the employee's personnel file and a copy given to the employee.

Due Process is the act of following legal steps to ensure that employees are treated fairly and according to law.

Economic Contract Proposals involve fund expenditure, such as salary or fringe benefits proposals.

Employee and Union Rights are those rights which are specified in the collective bargaining law of the state and those rights written into a ratified master contractual agreement between union and management.

Employee Compensation means wages and fringe benefits provided to employees as part of contractual obligations.

Employee Evaluation refers to the performance assessment of individual workers in the school district.

Employee Leaves are release times, given with or without pay, to employees desiring temporary relief from job assignment for such purposes as sick leave, maternity leave, sabbatical leave, etc.

Employee Termination   refers to the discharge of an employee by the school district, within existing and legally appropriate personnel procedures and guidelines.

Employee Transfer   refers to the reassignment of employees, usually between buildings or classroom assignments.

Employment Conditions   refers to such conditions as contract time, length of work day, length of work year, etc.

Empowerment   is the process of allowing employees to make decisions related to assigned work tasks, involving them in the creation of ways to maintain a productive and satisfying work environment, and involving them in day-to-day problem solving and decision making.

Exclusive Representation   is the right and obligation of the employee organization designated as the sole representative authorized to negotiate for all district employees.

Expedited Bargaining   refers to a situation whereby both parties to the negotiations agree to attempt to achieve a TA (tentative agreement) on a total contract over a very short period of time. Often the time period could be one week or less, and it usually occurs with both negotiating teams meeting at some location removed from the school district's environs.

Fact-Finding   is in the impasse phase of bargaining. This resolution procedure usually follows mediation and precedes arbitration. It is used to allow an outside individual or panel to review all presented documents from each side of the conflict, and to make a determination as to her/his recommended settlement, whether in money, empowerment, or policy.

Fall Back/Alternative Proposals   are those proposals which are readied in advance to be used in case of abandonment or modification of original at-the-table proposals.

Federal Mediation and Conciliation Service (FMCS)   is a federal agency that provides independent mediation to groups involved in negotiations or labor disputes, and it supplies arbitrators and factfinders upon request.

Financial Impact   refers to the economic effect of a union negotiation proposal, for example, an across-the-board salary increase.

Financial Status   refers to the income and expenditure status of the district's budget, its historical allocations, and the amount of money available for all purposes—including negotiations.

Fishbone Diagram is a problem-solving technique used to visually identify cause and effect.

Fishbowl is a technique in which multiple parties to a conflict of interest elect representatives to speak for their interests with the other parties to the conflict.

Focus Groups are comprised of employees and management, and are usually assembled to deal with a specific problem that is facing the school district. Focus groups usually meet for very short periods of time; and the task of a focus group is usually one of isolating a problem, analyzing the variables that impact the problem, and brainstorming possible solutions.

Focused/Limited Bargaining has as its purpose one which is similar to that of expedited bargaining—that of quick and win-win agreement on a master contract. In many cases, limited bargaining, like expedited bargaining, takes place at a motel or at some other off-school district location. In focused bargaining, both parties agree to carry forth into the successor master contractual agreement most items that are currently contained in that agreement, but each party selects two or three areas where formal bargaining will take place.

Fringe Benefit Costs are those costs accruing to specific employee benefits, such as health insurance coverages.

Fringe Benefits are those benefits the employee receives but which do not become direct salary. Fringe benefits usually consist of paid holidays; health, life, dental, vision, and other insurances; retirement provisions, severance considerations, workman's compensation, unemployment compensation, leaves of absence, etc.

Future Items are those new desired items introduced into current negotiations that are not expected to be met, but which do establish a future agenda that can be pushed during subsequent contractual negotiations of replacement master contractual agreements between union and management.

Good Faith Bargaining occurs when the board of education's or union's negotiating team agrees to meet regularly, listens intently to the other side's proposals, and offers rational counterproposals.

Grievance Arbitration is the study of mandated or suggested rulings by an arbitrator when there is disagreement about the specific management actions taken which may or may not violate the actual wording or the intent of the written and ratified master contractual agreement.

Grievance Handling is a step-by-step process followed by management which assures that employees will be handled with consistency and fairness. A grievance becomes a quasi-legal document once submitted, and must be handled as such.

Grievance is an employee complaint or problem of dissatisfaction with some aspect of employment. It may be solved by means already bargained into the contract, depending on the scope of the existing grievance procedure.

Ground Rules are those mutually agreed upon rules under which the bargaining proceeds. They usually involve such things as place and time of meetings, who attends meetings, etc.

Health Maintenance Organization (HMO) is a type of employee health coverage that limits the range of health care providers in order to make the coverage more cost effective.

High Ball Proposal is an exaggeratedly overinflated negotiations demand, intended to achieve a greater negotiating range; this usually occurs during adversarial negotiations.

Horizontal Salary Step is a salary placement reflecting an employee's degree level or level of training.

Hot Issues are those issues sometimes headlined and dramatized to give a biased perception that all negotiations issues are of this nature.

Impasse is a term used to define persistent disagreements between the employee organization and the employer, requiring further steps to be taken by an outside force to bring about settlement through appeal procedures.

Impasse Procedures vary from state to state; some allow either party to declare impasse and request a mediator from the state's PERB (Public Employment Relations Board) or other state agency that has been designated to oversee the collective bargaining of public agencies in the state. Procedures include mediation, fact-finding, and arbitration.

Incompetency is failure to perform to the levels or standards or efficiency accepted by the profession.

Instruction Expert is the one who knows the what and why of the instructional programs being offered in the district, and this expert can alert the management's negotiation team to the impact, positive or negative, of any instructionally related proposal that the team is considering bringing to the table.

Insubordination is failure to follow a legal, ethical, and reasonable request or demand of a person in a supervisory or administrative position who can bring about disciplinary procedures against the employee who is insubordinate.

Interest Arbitration   is aimed at achieving a settlement of the terms and conditions of a new bargaining contract. It is a process conducted by an outside third party, and it may lead to recommended or mandated terms of settlement.

Item-by-Item Arbitration   addresses arbitration of individual contract articles, and the arbitrator may rule in favor of one party on some items, and in favor of the other party on other items in dispute.

Just Cause   is a determination made that the action taken by an employer had reasonable evidence to take discipline against an employee, and that the specific discipline was justified.

Labor Arbitration Reports   is a publication of the Bureau of National Affairs, and lists information about arbitrators. Other sources are the *Martindale-Hubbell Law Directory,* or the *Summary of Labor Arbitration Awards.*

Last Best Offer Arbitration   occurs when the arbitrator must rule in favor of a single party's total last best offer, and the arbitrator cannot rule on an item-by-item basis.

Last Best Offer   is the final contract proposal offered by either side in negotiations.

Lose-Lose   is a term utilized to describe an adversarial relationship between labor and management that deteriorates to the point that an employee strike is called; the end result of which is a long-term loss, in many respects, for both labor and management.

Low Ball Proposal   is an exaggeratedly underinflated negotiations demand, intended to achieve a greater negotiating range; this usually occurs during adversarial negotiations.

Management   is the collective body of individuals who are employed to oversee and to operate the day-to-day affairs of a school district within the policies and directives of a board of education.

Management Rights   are those statutory (or otherwise established) rights or prerogatives of employers, such as personnel decisions, which are to be made without consultation with or notification to the employee organization(s).

Mandated Subjects   of collective bargaining are those items required to be collectively bargained by a state's law, usually including matters of salary and fringe benefits.

Master Agreement is a formal written agreement detailing all of the specific details reached between the union and management. It is the end result of successfully concluded negotiations.

Master Contract is the document bargained and agreed to by both sides in the negotiations process. This term is sometimes used instead of the term *master agreement.*

Master Contract Violation is a process that usually involves management taking a specific disciplinary action and informing the employee (and sometimes the union) of the specific contract violation and the specific discipline that is to be administered. At this time the employee or the union, in cases of class grievances (those which involve two or more members of the union in the same grievance situation), will file a grievance against management. This begins the grievance procedure which is spelled out in the master contract document.

Maternity Leave is a fringe benefit for pregnant employees which allows time off from the employee's job assignment, usually without pay.

Mediation is an impasse process conducted by a third party to attempt to resolve the differences between the two parties' bargaining proposals, usually through a federal or state mediation agency. Recommendations by mediators are customarily advisory and not binding on either party. In the process, mediation is usually synonymous with facilitation of reconciliation and is used as the first step to bring about settlement.

Mediator is an impartial third party who tries to reconcile an impasse between employer and employee organizations.

Medical Insurance is a fringe benefit intended to cover regular medical care for employees, including preventive care and outpatient services.

Multi-Contract Bargaining refers to the process in which individual contracts are negotiated separately with each group of unionized employees.

National Education Association (NEA) is the nation's largest professional teacher organization.

Need is a requirement. It also can be used to define the difference or discrepancy between the *what is, what should be,* or *what could be* state of affairs.

Negotiation is the active and formal give and take between members of a union negotiation team and a management negotiation team, which ultimately ends in a master contract governing the provisions, activities, and accommodations agreed to by both union and management.

Negotiations Guidelines are those guidelines provided to the negotiating team by its referent group (board of education or union membership), which govern the parameters of negotiations.

Negotiations Status Notebook is a running diary of the status of proposals, intended to serve as a reference to the negotiating team during bargaining.

Noneconomic Contract Proposals do not involve fund expenditure.

Observer is a member of the negotiation team responsible for observing the behavior of the opposite negotiating team's members.

Official Minutes are the official narrative record of negotiations proceedings, usually electronically recorded and transcribed.

Open Hearing refers to the type of impasse procedural hearing which may occur if both parties agree to open the process to the public; the arbitrator, however, may or may not agree to allow the hearing to be open.

Packaging Proposals involves combining those proposal items that have some relationship into one group, and insisting that all interrelated items are bargained as a unit.

Past Practice is a means of grievance handling by considering the manner in which a similar problem was previously handled.

Per Pupil Expenditure is a budgetary and negotiations figure which reflects dollar expenditure on a student unit cost base; all costs, such as salary and operational costs, are included in the calculation.

Permissive Statement is language within the master contract that indicates actions or specifics which may be met; there is an intent of guidance and latitude in the decision-making process.

Permissive Words such as *could* or *should* are particular contractual terminology, and indicate noncompulsory requirements.

Permitted Subjects include practically anything that can be agreed to by both parties, and which are not contradictory to any existing law.

Picketing is the constant presence of dissenting, sometimes striking, employees at various key administrative locations (such as the central office), usually carrying signs and intending to attract media attention and to gain support.

Post Hearing Brief is a written document filed by either the union, management, or both, elaborating on the points made at the arbitration hearing, and adding additional information to support their position.

Posturing is an at-the-table technique which implies presenting an artificial position or attitude in negotiations in order to pretend that you feel strongly or take seriously an item may not be one about which you feel strongly or about which you are not truly serious. Posturing is intended to throw the opponent off balance in her/his deliberations.

Potential Strike Items are those items could trigger a strike if they are entered into the arena of negotiations. They might well deal with such items as the right of administrators to evaluate the degree of employee performance, with the right of management to make employee assignments, or the amount of new dollars that will ultimately be allocated to settle the contract with the employees' union.

Power Impact refers to the noneconomic effect of a union negotiations proposal, especially with reference to any impact on managerial purview.

Precedent is a detail which has been a common practice in the organization. It can be a resultant action or determination made in a prior situation closely related to the one being considered at the time.

Progressive Discipline is a definitive step-by-step process whereby the employee is given more severe discipline each time the same (or very similar) violation of management's rights takes place. The first step may be a verbal reprimand, the second will constitute both a verbal and written reprimand, the third a deduction in pay, and, lastly, the dismissal of the employee from the organization.

Prohibited Subjects normally include the right to strike. In some cases such items as hiring, supervision, job assignment, recruitment, discharge of employees, and evaluation of employees are prohibited by the state's collective bargaining law.

Proposal Analysis involves analysis of the other party's proposals and counterproposals in order to prepare adequate counters and to anticipate items that may be approved or items that may be areas of disagreement.

Proposal is a suggested negotiations item, such as a specific salary increase, which is part of a negotiations package.

Public Employee Relations Board (PERB) is the state agency appointed to oversee collective bargaining.

Pupil-Teacher Ratio is the number which reflects the average number of students assigned to an individual classroom teacher.

Quality Circles generally are groups of six to eight employees who identify problems within their workplace; develop potential solutions to each problem; present their proposed solution to management and, if management approves, implements its solution.

Quality of Work Life can be defined as a *philosophy* which states that employees are capable of and desirous of improving their work environment and level of production; as a *goal* which attempts to make the work environment for employees the best possible work environment, and as a *structure and process* which involves employees in continuously improving the quality of their work life.

Quid Pro Quo proposals are those proposals by which the negotiating team determines they can obtain something of equal or greater value than those they would give as a compromise to the other team.

Rationales are logical justifications which accompany negotiations proposals, and they are accompanied by comprehensive and convincing data.

Reopeners usually refer to a timeline, such as three months prior to the expiration of the existing master contract agreement, when negotiations are initiated on a successor contract. This timeline is agreed upon to allow both parties to the upcoming negotiations sufficient time, hopefully, to negotiate a successor contract prior to the date of expiration of the current master contract agreement.

Recognition Clause is the initial clause or article in any printed master contractual agreement. It specifies which employees the union represents and which it doesn't represent, and it gives sole representation rights to a specific union in all matters of collective bargaining throughout the length of the ratified master contractual agreement.

Recorder is a member of the negotiation team who has the responsibility for accurately and comprehensively keeping a written record of every significant discussion or agreement point made at-the-table by the union, management, or by both parties.

Restructuring is the name given to any idea that dramatically changes the structure of school districts or changes the manner in which they operate.

Retroactive Pay is an amount, accumulated daily, which the arbitrator may ultimately award to an employee after a disciplinary action process, if she/he rules in favor of the union's position.

Sabbatical Leave is a fringe benefit provided for employees who request leave for scholarly purposes, such as pursuit of advanced degrees. Frequently these employees continue on the payroll at a reduced salary rate, as an inducement for such pursuit.

Salary Differential refers to the monetary difference paid to teachers with advanced degrees or years of service.

Salary Schedule is an array of employee salaries coded by years of experience and/or to level of professional preparation.

School-Based Management is a structure and a process which delegates greater decision-making power related to any or all of the areas of instruction, budget, policies, personnel, and all matters related to governance, to the local school building level; and it is a process which involves a variety of stakeholders, including employees, in the decisions which relate to the local individual school building's programs and operations.

Sick Leave is a fringe benefit provided for employees for personal illness, or, sometimes, for illness of a family member.

Sick Outs are when union members use sick leave or personal leave, in concert, on the same day in the hopes that a normal school day will be interrupted. Sometimes there will be a staggered usage of this tactic wherein the employees in one building will all call in sick or take personal leave one day, another building's teacher staff will do this on another day, and so forth. This tactic is usually utilized after a lengthy impasse, to apply pressure on the school board to settle a contract.

Sidebar Agreements refer to actions taken away from the official negotiation's meetings by the chief negotiator for both the union and management.

Single-Contract Bargaining refers to the process in which one contract is negotiated on behalf of all groups of employees, regardless of their individual union affiliation.

Spokesperson is the person selected to be in complete control of communication at the table. This person must possess the ability to think on her/his feet, be able to manage conflict and disagreement within the team and between the union and management teams, must possess leadership skills that will cause consensus within the team members, and will share responsibility for the training and overall preparation for upcoming negotiations with the various negotiation team members.

Stakeholders are the local community residents, including parents, students, or other persons who have an interest or stake in what takes place in the school district.

Strategy is the design to achieve a clearly defined goal. It is the *what* to be achieved, while a tactic is the *how* or maneuvers used to achieve the goal.

Strike is a temporary cessation of work by a group of employees, undertaken in order to communicate a grievance, achieve media and community recognition, or to enforce a threat related to negotiations demands.

Strike Plan is an emergency backup plan intended for damage containment and for effectively dealing with typical employee tactics during a strike. It usually addresses such critical areas as coverage/supervision of students in each school, and specific countermeasures and contingency strategies.

Sunshine Law is a statute in many states which requires open public-sector meetings, such as board of education meetings.

Superintendent of Schools is the CEO (Chief Executive Officer) of a school district.

Supervision is one of the three basic operations in management; the function of assisting others in improving upon their abilities.

Tactic is a maneuver or action designed to achieve a goal or objective.

Target District is one which the regional, state, or national union selects to establish some negotiations or contractual precedent.

Taylor Law is the labor negotiations law in New York that heavily penalizes striking teachers and which defines an impasse as when both parties fail to achieve an agreement at least one hundred and twenty days prior to the end of the fiscal year of the public employer.

Teamsters are a separate, mostly transportation-related (trucker), union.

Telegraph means a mannerism displayed in negotiations by people who transmit their feelings by verbal cues or by tone of voice.

Telstar is a technique involving all participants in a conflict of interests, providing for a degree of involvement that normally is not afforded to all members of large groups that are in a conflict situation. This technique maintains a manageable number of discussants within a three-tiered interactive process.

Tentative Agreement (TA) is an agreement between the two bargaining teams that later has to be ratified by the union membership and the board of education in order to become official.

Throw Away Proposals are proposals which are seriously presented, but are not considered absolutely necessary to secure before reaching a contractual settlement with the other party to the negotiations. These proposals assist in the give and take that accompanies every negotiation.

Total Quality Management (TQM) is a philosophy, goal, and process involving continuous improvement of products and services. It deals with quality goals and a value-added concept of quality, involving all stakeholders in decision making and customer satisfaction.

Transcript is a verbatim record of the proceedings of an impasse hearing. In cases where a transcript is allowed, there should be a prior agreement as to which parties, besides the arbitrator, are to receive transcripts, and who will pay the expenses of the court recorder and for the preparation and distribution of the transcripts.

Tripartite Arbitration Panel is an arbitration panel consisting of three arbitrators; one selected by the union, one selected by the board of education, and one selected by the two previously named arbitrators.

Tripartite Bargaining is bargaining that refers to the negotiations between the spokesperson and her/his team members; the bargaining between the union team and the management team at the table; and the bargaining between the negotiating team and its referent group (union membership or board of education).

UAW is the United Auto Workers of America.

Unfair Labor Practice is a labor practice that can be charged against a union when (1) an employee organization or its agents deliberately interfere with, restrain or coerce employees in the exercise of the rights granted them under the collective bargaining law, or (2) when the employee organization or its agents does not collectively negotiate in good faith with the public employer. The public employer or its agents can be charged with an unfair labor practice when (1) it conducts itself in the same manner as in the union's unfair practices listed above, (2) it attempts to dominate or interfere with the formation or administration of any employee organization for the purpose of depriving employees of their rights under the collective bargaining law, (3) it attempts to discriminate against any employee for the purpose of encouraging or discouraging membership in, or participation in the activities of any union, and (4) it refuses to continue the terms of an expired agreement until a new agreement is negotiated. Management can also file a charge of unfair labor practice against a union.

Union is the official recognized bargaining unit that has the authority to collectively bargain a master contractual agreement with the management of a school district, and which has the authority and responsibility to represent all union employees on a day-to-day basis.

Union Rights refers to those rights, such as representation, that accrue to the union.

Union Shop refers to a situation wherein employees are required to join the majority union organization recognized by the board and by the National Labor Relations Board or comparable state's governing agency as the exclusive employees' representative. This is generally not permitted in public education situations.

Union Steward   is the individual elected by the members of the union to serve as their representative, usually at the building level.

Union/Management Relations   refers to the interface, both officially and unofficially, between formal representatives of a union or of management. The degree of positive interface, to a large part, determines the working environment within which collective bargaining and the day-to-day operation of a school district takes place.

Union/Management Teams   are various-sized groups comprised of official representatives of the employee's union and the official administrative representatives of the school district. The union/management teams meet for a variety of time periods depending on the issue upon which the team is focusing.

Uniserve Director   is a full-time, state-level union employee assigned to one or more local school district-affiliated union groups.

Vertical Salary Step   is a salary placement reflecting an employee's years of service in the district.

Vertical Work Team   is a type of team which is vertically representational of top-to-bottom levels of the school district, with single or multiple members drawn from the ranks of central office personnel, supervisors or coordinators, principals, teachers, and classified personnel.

What-If Game   is the anticipation of the union's or management's proposals and the potential reactions that the other party's negotiating team may have to the proposals.

Win-Lose   is a term utilized to describe an adversarial relationship between labor and management in which as one party wins a point, matter, or condition, the other party loses.

Win-Win   is a term that indicates a positive and collaborative relationship existing between management and labor that is highly beneficial to both parties.

Wordsmith   is a member of the negotiation team who carefully prepares the wording of each proposal offered by the management's negotiation team, and is responsible for the detailed analysis of every word of every proposal brought to the table by the union's negotiation team.

Work-to-rule   actions are those whereby employees are instructed by the union leaders to refuse to perform any duties not specifically mandated by the contract. In many cases, this means that teachers will not provide homework, will not meet with students who require help after normal school hours, and will not meet with parents to discuss their child's progress at any time, other than during normal school hours.

Worst Case Scenario is the most disastrous thing that could be predicted to happen with regard to the results of negotiations.

Zipper Clause is language within an existing master contractual agreement which allows re-negotiations of a specific article in the contract while all other contractual conditions remain in effect until the end date of the existing contract. Many times a situation will exist wherein a multiple year ratified master contractual agreement will contain a zipper clause which allows yearly negotiations of the salary provisions in the existing master contract.

Aaron, B., J. M. Najita, and J. L. Stern. 1988. *Public Sector Bargaining*. Washington, D.C : Industrial Relations Research Associates.

AASA. *A new look at empowerment*. (1990). (AASA Stock Number 021-00278). Washington, D.C.: American Association of School Administrators.

America 2000: *Voices from the field*. 1991. Washington, D.C.: William T. Grant Foundation Commission on Work, Family, and Citizenship, and the Institute for Educational Leadership.

"Are Trade Unions and Human Resource Management Incompatible?" 1995. *Manager Update*, 6(3): 25–27.

Attea, W. J. 1993. "From Conventional to Strategic Bargaining: One Superintendent's Experience," *School Administrator,* 50(10): 16–19.

Bacharach, S. B. and E. J. Lawler. 1984. *Bargaining—Power, Tactics, and Outcomes*. San Francisco, Ca: Jossey-Bass Publishers.

Bacharach, S. B., J. B. Shedd, and S. C. Conley. 1989. "School Management and Teacher Unions: The Capacity for Cooperation in an Age of Reform," *Teachers College Record,* 91(1): 97–105.

Bailey, W. J. 1991. *School-Site Management Applied*. Lancaster, PA: Technomic Publishing Co., Inc.

Barrett, Jerome T. 1985. *Labor-Management Cooperation in the Public Service: An Idea Whose Time Has Come*. Washington, D.C.: International Personnel Management Association.

Barth, R. 1990. *Improving Schools from Within*. San Francisco, CA: Jossey-Bass, Publishers.

Bascia, N. 1994. *Unions in Teachers' Professional Lives: Social, Intellectual, and Practical Concerns,* New York: Teachers College Press.

Beamer, J. B. 1985. "An Introduction to the Public Employees Relations Act," Address by the Chairman of the Public Employment Relations Board of Iowa. *Public Employment Relations Act,* pp. 13–18.

Bennis, W. and B. Nanus. 1985. *Leaders: The Strategies for Taking Charge*. New York: Harper & Row.

Benson, N. and P. Malone, P. 1987. "Teachers' Beliefs about Shared Decision Making and Work Alienation." *Education,* Spring: 244–251.

Blakey, J. H. and K. A. Peterson. 1993. "Evergreen Process Keeps Peace at Contract Time," *School Administrator,* 50(10): 37.

Blendinger, J., S. D. Devlin, and G. F. Elrod. 1995. *Controlling Aggressive Students.* Fastback Series No. 387. Bloomington, IN: Phi Delta Kappa Foundation.

Braun, R. J. 1972. *Teachers and Power—The Story of the American Federation of Teachers.* New York: Longman.

Brock, J. 1982. *Bargaining Beyond Impasse—Joint Resolution of Public Sector Labor Disputes.* Boston, MA: Auburn House Publishing Company.

Bucholz, S. and T. Roth. 1987. *Creating the High Performance Team.* New York, NY: John Wiley & Sons.

Carver, J. 1990. *Boards That Make a Difference.* San Francisco: Jossey-Bass.

Castetter, W. B. 1996. *The Human Resource Function in Educational Administration.* 6th ed. Englewood Cliffs, NJ: Merrill.

Challenges for School Leaders. 1988. Alexandria, VA: American Association of School Administrators.

Cimini, M. H. 1994. "Negotiated Changes in State and Local Government Contracts, 1993," *Monthly Labor Review,* 117(8): 3–10.

Cimini, M. H. and C. J. Muhl. 1995. "Labor-Management Bargaining in 1994," *Monthly Labor Review,* 118(1): 23–38.

Cimini, M. H., S. L. Behrmann, and E. M. Johnson. 1994. "Labor-Management Bargaining in 1993," *Monthly Labor Review,* 117(1): 20–33.

Cloyd, S. 1990. "Involving School Board Members in Negotiations," *School Business Affairs.* 56(12): 24–27.

Coleman, C. J. 1990. *Managing Labor Relations in the Public Sector.* San Francisco, CA: Jossey-Bass Publishers.

Coulson, R. 1981. *The Termination Handbook.* London: Collier MacMillan Publishers.

Davis, W. M., et al. 1990. "Collective Bargaining in 1990: Health Care Cost a Common Issue," *Monthly Labor Review,* 113(1): 3–10, 27–29.

Doherty, R. E. and W. E. Oberer. 1967. *Teachers, School Boards, and Collective Bargaining: A Changing of the Guard.* Ithaca, NY: New York State School of Industrial and Labor Relations, Cornell University, p. 120.

Donley, M. O., Jr. 1976. *Power to the Teacher.* Bloomington, IN: Indiana University Press.

Eberts, R. W. and J. A. Stone. 1984. *Unions and Public Schools.* Lexington, MA: D.C. Heath and Company.

Elkouri, F. and E. A. Elkouri. 1973. *How Arbitration Works.* 3rd ed. Washington, D.C.: Bureau of National Affairs, Inc.

Elsea, S. W., D. A. Dilts, and Haber, L. J. 1991. "Factfinders and Arbitrators in Iowa: Are They The Same Neutrals?" *Journal of Collective Negotiations,* 19(1): 61–67.

Ertel, D. 1991. "How to Design a Conflict Management Procedure that Fits Your Dispute." *Sloan Management Review,* 32(4): 30–41.

Feiock, R. C. and J. P. West. 1990. "Public Presence at Collective Bargaining: Effects on Process and Decisions in Florida," *Journal of Collective Negotiations,* 19(1): 69–70.

Fields, J. C. 1993. "Unlocking the Paralysis of Will: Leaders Can Use School Efficacy to Unleash a 'Can-Do' Spirit." *School Administrator,* 5(50): 8–13.

Fisher, R. and W. Ury. 1981. *Getting to Yes—Negotiating Agreement Without Giving In.* Boston, MA: Houghton Mifflin.

Flinchbaugh, R. W. 1993. *The 21st Century Board of Education: Planning, Leading, Transforming.* Lancaster, PA: Technomic Publishing Co., Inc.

Fox, M. J., Jr. and D. Cooner. 1990. "Arbitration: Preparing for Success," *Journal of Collective Negotiations,* 19(4): 254.

Freeman, R. B. and C. Ichniowski. 1988. *When Public Sector Workers Unionize.* Chicago, IL: The University of Chicago Press.

Frisby, D. and J. Beckham. 1993. "Dealing with Violence and Threats of Violence in the School." *NASSP Bulletin,* 77(552): 10–16.

Genck, F. H. and A. J. Klingenberg. 1991. *Effective Schools Through Effective Management.* rev. ed., Springfield, IL: Illinois Association of School Boards.

Giandomenico, L. L. and L. Shulman. 1991. *Working with Teachers Effectively: Communication, Relationship, and Problem-Solving Skills for School Principals.* Springfield, IL.

Glickman, C. 1990. "Pushing School Reform to a New Edge: The Seven Ironies of School Empowerment," *Phi Delta Kappan,* 72(1): 68–75.

Gorton, R. A., G. T. Schneider, and J. C. Fisher. 1988. *Encyclopedia of School Administration & Supervision.* Phoenix, AZ: Oryx Press.

Granof, M. 1973. *How to Cost Your Labor Contract.* Washington, D.C.: The Bureau of National Affairs, Inc., p. 32.

Guillén, M. F. 1994. "The Age of Eclecticism: Current Organizational Trends and the Evolution of Managerial Models," *Sloan Management Review,* 36(1): 75–86.

Guthrie, J. W. and R. J. Reed. 1986. *Educational Administration and Policy-Effective Leadership for American Education.* Second Edition. Boston, MA: Allyn & Bacon.

Hampton, D. R., C. E. Summer, and R. A. Webber. 1987. *Organizational Behavior and the Practice of Management.* Glenview, IL: Scott, Foresman and Company.

Hargreaves, A. 1991. "Contrived Collegiality: The Micropolitics of Teacher Collaboration." In T*he Politics of Life in Schools: Power, Conflict, and Cooperation,* edited by J. Blase. Newbury Park, CA: Sage Publications.

Heisel, W. D. 1973. *New Questions and Answers on Public Employee Negotiation.* Washington, D.C.: International Personnel Management Association.

Helsby, R. D., J. Tener, and J. Lefkowitz, eds. 1985. *The Evolving Process—Collective Negotiations in Public Employment.* Fort Washington, PA: Labor Relations Press.

Hendrickson, G. 1990. "Where Do You Go After You Get To Yes?" *The Executive Educator.* 12(11): 16–17.

Herman, J. J. 1988. "Map the Trip to Your District's Future," *The School Administrator,* 45(9): 16, 18, 23.

Herman, J. J. 1992. "School-based Management: Sharing the Resource Decisions." *NASSP Bulletin,* 76(545): 102–105.

Herman, J. J. 1992. "School-based Management: Staffing and Budget Expenditures." *School Business Affairs,* 58(12): 24–25.

Herman, J. L. and J. J. 1995. "Total Quality Management (TQM) for Education." *Educational Technology,* 35(3): 14–18.

Herman, J. J. 1989. "Strategic Planner: One of the Changing Leadership Roles of the Principal," *The Clearing House,* 63(2): 56–58.

Herman, J. J. 1989. "A Vision for the Future: Site-Based Strategic Planning," *NASSP Bulletin,* 73(518): 23–27.

Herman, J. J. 1989. "External and Internal Scanning: Identifying Variables That Affect Your School," *NASSP Bulletin,* 73(520): 48–52.

Herman, J. J. 1989. "School District Strategic Planning (Part I)," *School Business Affairs,* 55(2): 10–14.

Herman, J. J. 1989. "Site-Based Management: Creating a Vision and Mission Statement," *NASSP Bulletin,* 73(519): 79–83.

Herman, J. J. 1989. "Strategic Planning—One of the Changing Leadership Roles of the Principal," *The Clearing House,* 63(2): 56–58.

Herman, J. J. 1989. "A Decision-Making Model: Site-Based Communications Governance Committees," *NASSP Bulletin,* 73(521): 61–66.

Herman, J. J. 1989. "School Business Officials' Roles in the Strategic Planning Process (Part II)," *School Business Affairs,* 55(3): 20, 22–24.

Herman, J. J. 1990. "Action Plans To Make Your Vision A Reality," *NASSP Bulletin,* 74(523): 14–17.

Herman, J. J. 1990. "School Based Management: A Checklist of Things to Consider," *NASSP Bulletin,* 74(527), 67–71.

Herman, J. J. 1991. "Coping with Conflict," *The American School Board Journal,* 178(8): 26–28.

Herman, J. J. 1991. "The Two Faces of Collective Bargaining," *School Business Affairs,* 57(2): 10–13.

Herman, J. J. 1992. "Strategic Planning: Reasons for Failed Attempts," *Educational Planning,* 8(3): 36–40.

Herman, J. J. 1993. "Conducting a SWOT Analysis: Strategic Planning for School Success," *NASSP Bulletin,* 77(557): 85–91.

Herman, J. J. 1993. "School-based management committees: A positive force in selling the need for and in planning new school construction." *Educational Facilities Planner,* 31(4): 21–23.

Herman, J. J. 1993. "TQM for Me: A Decision-making Interrogatory." *School Business Affairs,* 59(4): 28–30.

Herman, J. J. 1994. *Crisis Management: A Guide to School Crises and Action Taken.* Thousand Oaks, CA: Corwin Press—A Sage Publications Company.

Herman, J. J. 1994. "Determining the Critical Success Factors," *NASSP Bulletin,* 78(559): 108–110.

Herman, J. J. 1995. *Effective School Facilities: A Development Guidebook.* Lancaster, PA: Technomic Publishing Company, p. 13.

Herman, J. J. and J. L. 1991. *The Positive Development of Human Resources and School District Organizations.* Lancaster, PA: Technomic Publishing Co.

Herman, J. J. and J. L. 1993. *School-Based Management: Current Thinking and Practice,* Springfield, IL: Charles C. Thomas, Publisher.

Herman, J. J. and J. L. 1994. *Making Change Happen: Practical Planning for School Leaders*. Thousand Oaks, CA: Corwin Press—A Sage Publications Company.

Herman, J. J. and J. L. 1991. *Educational Quality Management: Schools Through Systemic Change*. Lancaster, PA: Technomic Publishing Co., Inc.

Herman, J. J. and J. L. Herman. 1992. "Educational Administration: School-based Management," *The Clearing House*, 65(5): 261–263.

Herman, J. J. and J. L. Herman. 1995. "A Study of School-Based Management in Selected Southern States," *International Journal of School Reform*, 4(4): 89–94.

Herman, J. J. and R. Kaufman. 1991. "Making the Mega Plan," *American School Board Journal*, 178(5): 24–25, 41.

Herman, J. L. and J. J. 1993. "A State-by-State Snapshot of School-Based Management Practices," *International Journal of Educational Reform*, 2(3): 89–94.

Herman, J. J. and G. E. Megiveron. 1993. *Collective Bargaining in Education: Win/Win, Win/Lose, Lose/Lose*. Lancaster, PA: Technomic Publishing Co., Inc.

Hoy, W. K. and C. G. Miskel. 1987. *Educational Administration*, 3rd ed. New York, NY: Random House.

Huber, J. and J. Hennies. 1987. "Fix on These Five Guiding Lights and Emerge from the Bargaining Fog," *American School Board Journal*, 174(3): 31–32.

Janes, L. 1984. "Collective Bargaining," *NASSP Instructional Leadership Booklet*. Reston, VA: National Association of Secondary School Principals.

Johnson, D. W. and F. P. Johnson. 1982. *Joining Together—Group Therapy and Group Skills*. 2d ed. Englewood Cliffs, NJ: Prentice-Hall.

Justin, J. J. 1969. *How to Manage with a Union—Book Two—The Rules of Collective Bargaining, Grievance Handling, Corrective Discipline, Book One of How to Manage with a Union*. New York: Industrial Relations Workshop Seminars, Inc.

Katz, N. H. and J. W. Lawyer. 1994. *Preventing and Managing Conflict in Schools*. Thousand Oaks, CA: Corwin Press—A Sage Publications Company.

Katz, N. H. and J. W. Lawyer. 1994. *Resolving Conflict Successfully: Needed Knowledge and Skills*. Thousand Oaks, CA: Corwin Press—A Sage Publications Company.

Kaufman, R. and J. J. Herman. 1989. "Planning that Fits Every District: Three Choices Help Define Your Plan's Scope," *The School Administrator*, 46(8): 17–19.

Kaufman, R. and J. J. Herman. 1991. *Strategic Planning in Education: Revitalizing, Restructuring, Rethinking*. Lancaster, PA: Technomic Publishing Co., Inc.

Kaufman, R., J. J. Herman, and K. Watters. 1996. *Educational Planning: Strategic, Tactical, Operational*. Lancaster, PA: Technomic Publishing Co., Inc.

Keane, W. G. 1996. *Win Win or Else: Collective Bargaining in an Age of Public Discontent*. Thousand Oaks, CA: Corwin Press—Sage Publications.

Kearney, R. C. 1984. *Labor Relations in the Public Sector*. New York, NY: Marcel Dekker, Inc.

Keith, S. and R. H. Girling. 1991. *Education, Management, and Participation—New Directions in Educational Administration*. Boston, MA: Allyn & Bacon.

Kennedy, J. D. 1984. "When Collective Bargaining First Came to Education: A Superintendent's Viewpoint," *Government Union Review*, 5(1): 26.

Kerchner, C. T. 1988. "A New Generation of Teacher Unionism," *Education Digest,* L111(9): 52–54.

Kerchner, C. T. 1993. "Building the Airplane as it Rolls Down the Runway: Administrators Discover Labor Relations as the Linchpin to School Change," *School Administrator,* 50(10): 8–15.

Killion, J. P., J. P. Huddleston, and M.A. Claspell. 1989. "People Developer: A New Role for Principals," *Journal of Staff Development,* 10(1): 2–7.

Koppich, J. E. 1993. "Getting Started." In *A Union of Professionals: Labor Relations and Educational Reform,* edited by Kerchner, C. T. and J. E. Koppich. New York: Teachers College Press, pp. 194–195.

Lal, S. R., D. Lal, and C. M. Achilles. 1993. *Handbook on Gangs in Schools: Strategies to Reduce Gang-Related Activities.* Newbury Park, CA: Corwin Press—A Sage Publications Company, pp. 52–53.

Lavan, H. 1990. "Arbitration in the Public Sector: A Current Perspective," *Journal of Collective Negotiations,* 19(2): 154.

Ledell, M. A, 1995. *How to Avoid Crossfire and Seek Common Ground: A Journey for the Sake of the Children.* Alexandria, VA: American Association of School Administrators.

Lewis, A. 1988. *Restructuring America's Schools.* Alexandria, VA: American Association of School Administrators.

Maddux, R. B. 1988. *Successful Negotiation—Effective "Win-Win" Strategies and Tactics.* Los Altos, CA: Crisp Publications, Inc.

Maier, M. M. 1987. *City Unions.* New Brunswick, NJ: Rutgers University Press, pp. 133–134.

Many, T. W. and C. A. Sloan. 1990. "Management And Labor Perceptions Of School Collective Bargaining," *Journal of Collective Negotiations,* 19(4): 283–296.

Marzano, R. J. 1993/1994. "When Two Worldviews Collide." *Educational Leadership,* 51(4): 6–11.

Maurer, R. E. 1991. *Managing Conflict: Tactics for School Administrators.* Boston: Allyn & Bacon.

McGregor, D. M. 1960. *The Human Side of Enterprise.* New York, NY: McGraw-Hill Book Co.

McLaughlin, J. M. 1995. "Public Education and Private Enterprise: Where's This New Relationship Going?" *School Administrator* 7(52): 7–13.

Miller, M. H., K. Noland, and J. Schaaf. 1990. *A Guide to the Kentucky Education Reform Act.* Frankfort, KY: Legislative Research Commission.

Miller, M. H., K. Noland, and J. Schaaf. 1990. *A Guide to the Kentucky Education Reform Act.* Frankfort, KY: Legislative Research Commission.

Miller, R. W. 1993. "In Search of Peace: Peer Conflict Resolution." *Schools in the Middle,* 2(3): 11–13.

Miron, L. F. and R. K. Wimpelberg. 1992. "The Role of School Boards in the Governance of Education." in *School Boards: Changing Local Control,* edited by P. F. First and H. J. Walberg. Berkeley, CA: McCutchan Publishing.

Morgan, G. 1989. *Creative Organizational Theory: A Resourcebook*. Newbury Park, CA: Sage Publications.

Muhl, C. 1995. "Collective Bargaining in State and Local Government, 1994." *Monthly Labor Review,* 118(6): 13–17.

Murphy, M. 1990. *Blackboard Unions—The AFT & the NEA 1900–1980*. Ithaca, NY: Cornell University Press.

Namit, C. 1986. "The Union Has a Communications Strategy—And Your Board Should, Too," *American School Board Journal*. 173(10): 30–31.

Neal, R. 1980. *Bargaining Tactics—A Reference Manual for Public Sector Labor Negotiations*. Richard G. Neal Associates.

Neal, R. G. 1988. "At Arbitration Hearings, Justice Favors the Well Prepared," *Executive Educator,* 10(11): 17–18.

New York State Public Employment Relations Board. 1983–1984. *The Taylor Law.* Albany, NY: New York Public Employment Relations Board.

Nickoles, K. W. 1990. "Future Shock: What's Coming to the Bargaining Table," *School Business Affairs* 56(12): 36–38.

Ordovensky, P. and G. Marx. 1993. *Working with the News Media*. Alexandria, VA: American Association of School Administrators.

Panasonic Foundation and the American Association of School Administrators. 1994. "Building Labor and Management Coalitions," *Strategies for School System Leadership on District-Level Change*. 1 (2) Seacaucus, NJ: Issue series of the Panasonic Foundation in collaboration with the American Association of School Administrators, pp. 2–6.

Panasonic Foundation and the American Association of School Administrators. 1994. "Dade County: A Stable Partnership in a Sea of Change." *Strategies for School System Leaders on District-Level Change,* 1 (2) Seacaucus, NJ: Issue series of the Panasonic Foundation in collaboration with the American Association of School Administrators, pp. 1–12.

Panasonic Foundation and the American Association of School Administrators. 1994. "Using Internal and External Coalitions." *Strategies for School System Leaders on District-Level Change,* 1 (2) Seacaucus, NJ: Issue series of the Panasonic Foundation in collaboration with the American Association of School Administrators, pp. 1–12.

Paterson, L. T. and R. T. Murphy. 1983. *The Public Administrator's Grievance Arbitration Handbook*. New York, NY: Longman, Inc.

Peters, T. J. and R. H. Waterman. 1982. *In Search of Excellence: Lessons from America's Best-Run Companies*. New York: Warner Books.

Plauny, L. 1992. "Compared to What? Developing a Teacher Compensation Comparison Standard," *School Business Affairs,* 58(8): 16–20.

Prothrow-Stith, B. 1994. "Building Violence Prevention into the Curriculum." *School Administrator,* 4(51): 8–13.

Rebore, R. W. 1991. *Personnel Administration in Education—A Management Approach*. Third Edition. Englewood Cliffs, NJ: Prentice-Hall, Inc.

Richardson, R. C. 1985. *Collective Bargaining by Objectives: A Positive Approach.* Englewood Cliffs, NJ: Prentice-Hall, Inc.

Rogers, J. 1992. *On Board: A Survival Guide for School Board Members.* Blooming-ton, IN: Phi Delta Kappa.

Ross, V. J. and R. MacNaughton. 1982. "Memorize These Bargaining Rules Before You Tackle Negotiations," *American School Board Journal,* 169(3): 39–41.

Rush, H. M. F. 1987. "The Behavioral Sciences" in *Training and Development Handbook,* edited by R. L. Craig, 3rd edition. New York: McGraw-Hill, pp. 135–167.

Rynecki, S. B. and J. H. Lindquist. 1988. "Teacher Evaluation and Collective Bargaining—A Management Perspective," *Journal of Law & Education,* 17(3): 489–490.

School Boards: Strengthening Grassroots Leadership. 1986. Washington, D.C.: Institute for Educational Leadership.

Schwerdtfeger, R. D. 1986. "Labor Relations Thrive When You Control Collective Bargaining," *American School Board Journal.* 173(10): 41–42.

Seifert, R. 1990. "Prognosis for Local Bargaining in Health and Education," *Personnel Management.* 22 (June): 54–57.

Sergiovanni, T. J., and J. H. Moore. 1989. *Schooling for Tomorrow.* Boston: Allyn & Bacon.

Shepherd, K. K. 1994. "Stemming Conflict Through Peer Mediation." *School Administrator,* 4(51): 14–17.

Sleemi, S. 1995. "Collective Bargaining Outlook for 1995," *Monthly Labor Review,* 118(1): 3–21.

Smith, S. C., D. Ball, and D. Liontos. 1990. *Working Together—The Collaborative Style of Bargaining.* Eugene, OR: ERIC Clearinghouse on Educational Management, University of Oregon.

Spence, D. and L. Vanderhoff. 1992. "Assistant Principals Lead Effort to Establish Peer Mediation Programs." *AP Special—The Newsletter for Assistant Principals,* 7(3): 1–3.

Splitt, D. A. 1991. "How Much Can Unions Charge Nonmembers?" *Executive Educator.* 13(9): 18.

Spring, J. 1990. *The American School 1642–1990: Varieties of Historical Interpretation of the Foundations and Development of American Education.* 2nd ed. New York: Longman.

Spring, J. 1993. *Conflict of Interests: The Politics of American Education.* 2nd ed. New York: Longman.

Stephens, A. B. 1995. *Conflict Resolution: Learning to Get Along.* Alexandria, VA: American Association of School Administrators.

Streshly, W. A. and T. A. DeMitchell. 1994. *Teacher Unions and TQE,* Thousand Oaks, CA: Corwin Press—Sage Publications.

Tait, R. C. 1995. "Contract Negotiations Without Ill Will," *School Administrator,* 52(9): 30–31.

Taylor, B. O. and D. U. Levine. 1991. "Effective Schools Projects and School-Based Management." *Phi Delta Kappan,* 72(5): 394–397.

Thompson, B. L. 1991. "Negotiation Training: Win-Win or What?" *Training,* 28(6): 31–35.

Toch, T. 1991. "Public Schools of Choice." *American School Board Journal,* 178(7): 18–21.

Trotta, M. S. 1976. *Handling Grievances—A Guide for Management and Labor.* Washington, D.C.: The Bureau of National Affairs, Inc.

U.S. Department of Education—Office of Educational Research and Improvement, Programs for the Improvement of Practice. 1993. *A Guide to Developing Educational Partnerships.* Special report prepared by Naida C. Tushnet, Southwest Regional Laboratory. GPO, October.

Urban, W. J. 1985. "Merit Pay and Organized Teachers in the U.S.A." In *Politics of Teacher Unionism: An International Perspective,* edited by M. Lawn . New York: Croom Helm.

Venter, B. M. and J. Ramsey. 1990. "Improving Relations: Labor Management Committees in School Districts," *School Business Affairs.* 56(12): 20–23.

Ventner, B. M. and L. A. McFerran. 1992. "Don't Use Our Health Insurance: Paying Employees to Forgo Dual Coverage," *School Business Affairs,* (58)2: 10–13.

Webb, L. Dean, J. T. Greer, P. A. Montello, M. S. Norton. 1987. *Personnel Administration in Education—New Issues and New Needs in Human Resource Management.* Columbus, OH: Merrill Publishing Company.

Webster, W. G., Sr. 1985. *Effective Collective Bargaining in Public Education.* Ames, IA: Iowa State University Press.

Zack, Arnold. 1980. *Understanding Fact Finding and Arbitration in the Public Sector.* Washington, D.C.: U.S. Department of Labor, Labor Management Services Administration.

academic freedom, 206, 221, 236, 244
accidental death and disability
    insurance, 147
action plan, 33, 70, 77–79
action programs, 43, 75, 77, 128,
    277, 285
administration, 18, 21, 31, 8, 45, 220,
    263, 265, 284
administrators, 20, 30, 39, 48, 159,
    243, 257, 267, 269, 272, 288, 296
adolescent stage of group growth, 10,
    12
"adopt-a-school" programs, 57
adversarial approach, 49, 54, 56–57,
    78, 83, 98–99, 101, 103, 106,
    109–111, 113, 122, 126, 131, 153,
    182, 189–190, 196–197, 213, 222,
    231, 243, 251, 254, 295, 296–297,
    304–305
adversarial bargaining, 8, 67, 97, 109,
    119, 138, 227, 230–232, 242, 249,
    256
adversarial relations, 4, 41, 122, 183,
    234, 236, 299, 301
agency shop, 84, 93, 229, 243
alternates, 100, 104, 108
alternative schools, 298
American Arbitration Association, 169,
    193
American Association of School
    Administrators, 30, 40
American Federation of Teachers,
    1, 19–22, 24, 98, 232, 243–244,
    295

arbitration, 49, 89, 111, 132, 159, 161,
    164, 169, 170–173, 176, 189, 193,
    198, 212, 218–219, 220, 222, 233,
    251–253, 303–304, 308
arbitrator, 87, 129, 163, 169–171, 173,
    193, 198, 212, 217, 219, 230, 240
article, 106, 113, 137, 140, 197, 204,
    206, 221, 234–236, 244
asking for the moon, 128
assessed property valuation, 90
assistant principals, 110
Association of State, County and
    Municipal Employees, 1, 99
at the table, 95, 101
at-the-table, 67, 83–86, 88–89, 92–93,
    95, 102, 104–110, 112, 114, 120,
    126, 128–130, 137, 142, 144–146,
    150, 153–154, 167, 176, 189, 195,
    231–232, 236, 237, 239
athletics, 110, 263, 269, 289–290
attorney, 103, 111–112, 115, 233, 252,
    266
auditory care, 141
bad faith bargaining, 120, 227, 242, 245
bargaining chips, 137, 141, 154
bargaining notebook, 68, 119, 124,
    127, 130–131, 142, 152, 164, 172
bargaining units, 83, 206, 221, 242
behavioral rules, 67, 111, 114
beliefs, 3–9, 12, 75, 79
benefits, 5–7, 23, 49, 63, 72–75, 79,
    84, 86, 90–92, 95, 109, 124–125,
    127, 142, 143–146, 154, 180, 186,
    235, 244, 295, 298

board of education, 3–5, 31, 37, 39, 48,
    54, 59, 60, 71, 76–79, 138, 221,
    253, 256, 257, 263, 267, 268–269,
    272, 284, 285, 287–288, 290–291,
    295–297, 301
bond issue, 90–91, 95, 290
boosters, 270, 288
boycotts of business, 178
budget, 31, 37, 39, 60, 73, 86, 89–90,
    92, 94, 99, 109, 113, 124, 132,
    168, 172, 195, 205, 258, 298
bureaucracies, 26, 29, 31
business, 40, 55, 57, 62–63, 71
business manager, 110–112
calendar, 58, 59, 60, 105, 114
capital outlay, 63
caucus, 101, 107, 109, 114, 138, 252,
    281, 305
Cause and Effect Diagram, 275, 291
central office, 36, 288
certification, 91, 121, 122, 241, 245,
Chicago Federation of Labor, 21
Chicago Teachers' Federation, 21
chief negotiator, 5, 88, 99, 101, 104,
    106–107, 109–111, 114, 142, 147,
    149, 154, 181, 183–184, 190,
    194–196, 198–191, 203–207, 231,
    233, 236, 244, 252, 266
child care leave, 147
class size, 84, 90, 129, 180, 231, 234,
    235, 236, 244, 254
classified employees, 1, 49, 56, 77,
    243, 263, 268, 296, 298
clients, 1, 58, 59, 60, 62–64, 308
climate, 40, 43, 58, 75, 92, 123,
    257–258
closed shop, 84–85, 93, 227, 229–230,
    244
co-curricular activities, 56–57, 90, 95,
    99, 177, 185, 289, 291,
collaboration, 23–24, 28, 30, 38, 43,
    46–48, 54, 56, 63, 75, 78–79, 98,
    100, 105, 107, 113–114, 120, 133,
    138, 153, 197, 220, 251, 265,
    295–296, 298–299, 303–308

community, 4–8, 18, 30–31, 45, 48,
    54–59, 63, 71–74, 77–78, 92, 109,
    122, 127, 152, 167, 175, 177, 182,
    184, 186, 191, 193, 197, 204, 221,
    236–237, 240, 252, 256–257, 263,
    266, 268, 272, 275, 285, 287–289,
    301, 307–308
comparable school districts, 83, 85, 89,
    91–92, 94, 113, 125, 131–132,
    141, 164, 172, 192
comparative information, 49, 61, 67,
    72–73, 88, 108, 114, 168, 232,
    244
concessions, 23
conditions of employment, 98, 141,
    154, 296
conflict resolution, 4, 5, 7, 8, 47, 263
consensus, 27, 39, 75, 79, 102, 265,
    269, 277–278, 281, 284, 291,
    299–300, 303–306
consumer price index, 124
content area experts, 114
contingency plans, 185
contract arbitration, 62–63, 70–71, 87,
    93, 127, 162, 163, 172, 208
contract articles, 83, 85, 88, 94, 113,
    120, 139, 153, 184, 190–191,
    196–198, 221, 231, 244
contract language, 109, 138, 169, 191,
    198, 206, 221, 234, 236, 244
contract management, 55, 56, 63, 159,
    184, 204–207, 219, 221, 298
contract violations, 159, 203, 207–208,
    210, 213
cost of living index, 86, 166, 238
cost/benefit analyst, 102–103, 114
counselors, 265, 266
counterproposals, 68, 73, 101, 104,
    106, 119, 125, 129, 132, 137, 139,
    141–142, 145, 147–148, 168, 154,
    231–232, 243, 245, 252
culture, 27, 36, 40–41, 46, 258, 299,
    301
curriculum, 32, 34, 59, 99, 184, 263,
    284, 286–287, 290

custodial and maintenance personnel, 99, 103, 243, 287
data, 40, 43, 71–72, 83, 93, 98, 120, 138, 144, 221
decertification election, 121, 241, 245
decision makers, 35, 40–41, 270, 286
decision making, 23, 25, 27–28, 30–32, 35–37, 43, 46, 77, 98, 132, 256, 258
Delphi Technique, 277, 278, 292
Deming Award, 40
Demographic data, 71, 168, 172
dental insurance, 141, 148
department heads, 110
discharge, 214
disciplinary action, 208, 213, 215, 222
discipline, 88, 203, 209, 210, 213–217, 222
distance learning, 297
dividing and conquering, 145–146
documentation, 209–210, 214, 216–217, 222
downsizing, 26, 28
dropouts, 72, 75
due process, 203, 213, 216–217, 222
dues, 230, 241
economic items, 109, 140, 168
elementary, 22, 265, 272
elementary level, 22, 90, 231, 264–265, 272, 286
employee assignments, 127, 131, 206, 216, 221, 236, 244
employee evaluation, 31, 84–85, 142, 154, 191–192, 195, 206, 221, 244, 267
employee leaves, 142, 154, 236, 244
employee recognition, 1, 37, 45, 308
employee termination, 142, 154
employee transfer, 206, 221
employee turnover, 92
employment conditions, 141, 154, 296
empowerment, 1, 25–26, 28–30, 32, 34, 42, 46–49, 258, 299, 301, 308
enrollment, 60, 75, 95, 286, 289
erosion of the contract, 207

exclusive recognition, 121
Executive Order 10988, 21
executive session, 180
expedited bargaining, 227, 238–239, 244
expenditure, 86, 93, 99, 102, 124, 127
external data, 71–72
external scanning, 70–71
extra duties, 131
extracurricular activities, 263, 272
fact-finding, 63, 89, 111, 125, 127, 129, 159, 161–164, 167, 170, 172, 176, 189, 192, 198, 230, 233, 251–253
fall back proposals, 119, 130
Federal Mediation and Conciliation Service, 162
finance, 5, 7, 53, 55, 59, 63–64, 72, 85, 89, 102, 108–111, 114, 145, 149, 163, 167
financial audits, 124, 132
financial example, 166, 172
financial experts, 97
Fishbone, 275, 291
Fishbowl, 277–278, 292
flexibility, 154, 165–166, 172, 184, 191, 198
focus groups, 33, 61
focused or limited bargaining, 244
food services, 99, 103, 110, 243
gangs, 265, 266
goals, 4–5, 8–9, 11–12, 27, 29, 47, 123, 269
Good faith, 141, 153, 231, 242, 245
governance, 25, 29, 31–32, 37, 74
governmental agencies, 185, 239, 241, 245
grievance, 49, 61, 67, 72, 73, 85–89, 93, 106, 108, 112, 124, 142, 154, 159, 204–206, 210–212, 218–219, 222, 233, 255, 297, 299
grievance arbitration, 83, 85, 87, 124, 162–163, 172, 203, 207, 216, 218, 233
grievance articles, 217

grievance clause, 203
grievance hearings, 216
grievance mediation, 132
grievance procedure, 206, 208, 210,
    217–218, 221–222
ground rules, 68, 137, 138, 139, 140,
    153, 231, 253
health insurance, 125, 141, 143–147,
    150, 231, 236
Health Maintenance Organization, 143
high ball proposal, 190, 197
high school, 22, 265, 272, 284–285,
    287
high-cost items, 129
hiring, 18, 84
hot issues, 129
hotline, 175, 185, 220, 271, 301
impasse, 49, 55, 57, 62–63, 64, 83,
    86–87, 89, 111, 125, 127, 129,
    132, 140, 153, 159, 161–163, 164,
    167, 169–171, 189, 191–192,
    194–95, 197–198, 230, 237, 253,
    255, 308
income, 93, 99, 109, 124
incompetency, 203, 208–210, 222
individual signoff, 140
infiltrating, 185
information leakages, 236, 244
information network, 92
injunction, 183
instruction, 29, 30, 32, 34, 37, 58, 74,
    86, 99, 103, 110, 112, 114,
    122–123, 130, 177, 186, 205, 267,
    288, 295
insubordination, 88, 203, 208–210, 222
internal scanning, 70–73
interpersonal communications, 39
item-by-item bargaining, 163, 172
items for the future, 129
job actions, 176–179
job assignment, 84
job security, 6, 54
joint sessions, 192
just cause, 203, 213–214, 222
Kentucky, 257–258, 298
Kentucky Education Reform Act
    of 1990, 34, 258

kindergarten, 151
Labor Arbitration Reports, 169
labor movement, 6, 19, 23, 99
language analysis, 61–62, 108, 114,
    183, 209
last best offer, 119, 126, 132, 164, 169,
    172, 230
laws, 99, 108, 114, 142, 154, 162, 169,
    172, 175, 179, 181, 191, 240
layoff, 92, 186
legal recourse, 208, 303, 308
legislation, 34, 53, 63, 71, 93, 167,
    230, 240–241, 254, 257–258
levels of appeal, 222
library and media service, 110
life insurance, 147
limited bargaining, 239
local, 73
local union affiliations, 19, 21, 31, 61,
    90
loosely coupled organizations, 25, 37
lose-lose, 4–5, 8, 159
low ball proposals, 190, 197, 253
magnet schools, 298
management rights, 27, 85, 130, 142,
    154, 191, 203, 206, 221, 236
management team, 4, 191, 203
mandates, 84, 88, 93, 102, 108, 235,
    244, 253, 255, 298
mandatory arbitration, 89, 171
Martindale-Hubbell Law Directory,
    169
master contract, 4–5, 9, 60, 63, 72–74,
    84–91, 93, 98, 109, 120, 121, 124,
    128, 130–132, 138, 141, 150, 154,
    159, 163, 166, 171, 178–179, 183,
    189–190, 195, 197–198, 204,
    206–207, 209–210, 216–217, 220,
    222–227, 231–235, 238–239,
    255–258
maternity leave, 148
media, 57, 63–64, 122, 129–132,
    140, 153, 175, 177, 178, 180,
    182, 185, 196, 197, 198, 204,
    233, 236, 237, 242, 243, 244,
    245, 263, 270, 271, 272, 275, 284,
    291, 301

mediation, 63, 89, 111, 125, 127, 159,
161–162, 164–165, 169–170, 172,
176, 189, 191, 197, 230, 233, 251,
252, 269, 303, 305, 308
mediator, 129, 161, 164–165, 167, 170,
172, 191, 197, 219, 230, 240, 253,
269
meet and confer, 21, 84, 93
membership, 17, 23, 243, 296, 297
middle school, 265–266, 272, 284,
289, 290
militancy, 21
minutes, 125, 132, 140, 153, 155, 197
mission, 11–12, 28
monitoring, 70
morale, 45, 56–58, 64, 122
motivation, 26–27, 29
multicultural, 298
multiple contractual negotiations, 100,
103
National Association of School
Superintendents, 20
National Education Association, 1, 19,
20, 21, 22, 24, 98, 232, 243, 244,
295, 296
National Labor Relations Board, 84
need, 26
needs, 3, 6, 9, 12, 26, 63
needs assessment, 40, 42, 61, 69,
71–72
negotiating sessions, 190
negotiating team, 97–98, 100, 107,
109–113, 132, 190–193, 231–232,
237, 241
negotiation schedule, 154
new item proposal, 141, 154
newspapers, 271–272, 285
non-cost example, 109, 127, 129, 140,
148, 153–154, 166, 198
non-binding arbitration, 198
non-public schools, 185
non-verbal behavior, 108, 110
objectives, 43, 128–129, 131, 148–149,
154, 176, 269
observational experts, 98
observers, 102–103, 107, 114, 139
operational procedures, 87

optical insurance, 141, 148
oral warning or reprimand, 213, 222
organizational theory, 25
output, 41
outside parties, 171
outsourcing, 243
ownership, 36, 47, 48
package signoff, 140
packaging, 137, 140, 153
packing of board meetings, 180, 185
paid holidays, 147
paraphrasing, 108
parental choice, 71
parents, 32, 48, 55, 57, 63, 71–72,
77–78, 240, 245, 258, 264, 265,
286–288, 289–291
past practice, 83–87, 89, 93, 207–208,
217, 221–222
payroll, 186
pensions, 21
per pupil expenditures, 168
permissive subjects of bargaining, 84,
88, 93, 102, 108, 235, 244, 255
personal business, 176, 207
personality conflicts, 137, 145, 147
personnel, 114, 204–206, 209, 211,
218, 266, 267
personnel policies, 85, 93, 205
phone banks, 62
picket, 54, 57, 175–178, 185–186, 233
policies, 22–23, 29, 31, 48, 76,
86–89, 99, 124, 132, 206,
270–271, 299
politics, 8, 19, 22–23, 28, 31, 55, 71,
268, 291, 298
positioning, 137, 145–146, 154, 190
post-hearing briefs, 168, 170–173,
192–193, 198
posturing, 137, 145–146, 154
power factors, 60
pre-negotiation information, 142, 146,
164
pre-negotiation preparations, 97, 114,
108, 119, 122, 153, 155
precedents, 87, 93, 159, 203, 205–208,
221
preferred future, 69, 70, 74

preferred future vision, 69–70, 74–75, 77, 79
principal, 27, 29–30, 32, 47, 58, 77–78, 83, 110, 205, 257, 264, 265, 266, 267, 288
prior agreements, 127
privatization, 297
problem solving, 9–11, 13, 37–39, 100, 133, 138, 153, 155, 257, 275, 297–298, 306–307
procedural questions, 196
professionalism, 17, 23, 29–30, 32, 269
prohibited subjects of bargaining, 84, 93, 255
propaganda, 175, 227, 231, 243–244
Proposal packaging, 154
proposal rationales, 198
proposals, 68, 73, 92, 100–106, 112, 119, 125, 129, 130–133, 137, 140–142, 144–147, 150–154, 168, 172, 232, 237, 243, 245, 252
Public Employee Relations Board, 83, 121, 124, 161–165, 169, 172, 191–192, 197, 240–241, 245, 253, 255
public relations, 185, 205
public sector employees, 53
public support, 20, 129
pupil-teacher ratio, 90, 92, 102, 129, 289, 290
quality, 29, 41, 47
Quality Circles, 25, 38–42, 48, 50, 221, 308
Quality of Work Life, 25, 39–42, 50, 221, 308
questionnaires, 61, 64
quid pro quos, 68, 119, 130, 133, 137, 147, 149, 154
ratification, 63–64, 87–88, 106, 110–111, 119, 141, 152, 159, 166, 178, 179, 181, 183, 189, 193–198, 203–205, 208, 211, 217, 221, 231, 233–236, 238–240, 244, 255
rationales, 129, 130, 141–144, 165–166, 172, 238
re-openers, 238, 244
recognition clause, 119, 121, 240, 245

recorder, 102–103, 114, 144, 211
recruitment, 84–85, 195
referent group, 236, 244
reform, 29, 31, 34, 257
reopeners, 104
representation rights, 21, 229, 240–241, 245
resource persons, 139
restructuring, 29, 31, 40, 42, 257, 299
retroactive pay, 219
revenues, 168, 172
sabbatical leave, 147
salary, 5–6, 8, 18–22, 49, 53, 63, 73, 75, 79, 84, 86, 90–92, 127–128, 132, 142, 145, 148–149, 166, 178, 182, 190–192, 195, 212, 231, 235, 238–254, 298
salary schedule, 91, 95, 109, 124, 131, 143, 146, 150, 151, 166, 295
sanctions, 21
school attorney, 219
school choice, 297
School-Based Management, 25, 29–31, 34–36, 41–42, 48, 76–79, 227, 249, 257–258, 298, 308
school-site budgeting, 29
scope of bargaining, 83
seniority, 151
service fee, 84, 229
settlement, 191–192, 305
sick leave, 93, 176
sick outs, 176, 185
side bars, 68, 127, 132, 137, 147, 149, 153–154
signing-off, 124
single contract bargaining, 107
special education, 90
spokesperson, 68, 101, 103, 106, 111, 114, 137–138, 144–145, 153, 175, 178, 280–281, 284
staff development, 31, 123, 291
staffing, 35, 37
stages of group growth, 12
stakeholders, 1, 40–41, 53–55, 60, 63, 71, 74, 79, 303, 307–308
state level, 61–62, 71, 73–74, 88, 91, 126–127, 145, 161, 270

statute, 163, 179
statutes, 121, 163, 172
stewards, 199, 244
strategic and tactical planning, 67, 69,
    79
strategic goals, 42, 70, 75, 77–78
strategic objectives, 70, 75, 77
strategies, 109, 114, 127, 129, 131,
    137, 145, 147–149, 152, 154,
    176, 194
strike, 4–7, 21–22, 84, 119, 127, 131,
    159, 175, 181, 185–186, 231–232,
    241, 255, 296–297
strike plan, 175–176, 181, 185
strike vote, 179, 194, 198
students, 3–8, 13, 26, 30–32, 34, 41,
    45, 54, 55, 56, 58, 59, 60, 63, 71,
    79, 100, 102, 120, 123, 127, 129,
    175, 177, 179, 197, 210, 235, 240,
    245, 258, 263–264, 267, 270, 272,
    284, 286, 287–291, 295, 297, 301,
    306
student weighting, 90
student enrollment, 168
student loads, 123
substitute employees, 39, 149, 185
Summary of Labor Arbitration Awards,
    169
sunshine laws, 180, 195
superintendent, 3–5, 19–20, 27, 53, 97,
    99, 103–107, 110–111, 115, 122,
    181, 182–183, 186, 194–195, 198,
    203, 212, 233, 239, 253, 257, 263,
    266–267, 268, 270, 272, 284, 291
supervisors, 53, 83–84, 212, 272
suspension, 214–215
table data, 94
tactical plan, 69, 76, 77
tactics, 127, 128, 129, 131, 137, 145,
    147, 148, 149, 152, 154, 164, 176,
    185, 244
target district, 112, 232
tax base, 53, 73–74, 94–95, 100, 125,
    145
taxes, 8, 55, 90–92, 163, 168, 239–240
taxpayers, 4–8, 48, 73, 145, 180, 240,
    245, 258, 297

Taylor Law, 161, 241
teacher aides, 90, 103
teacher load, 254
teacher militancy, 17–18
teachers, 122–123, 141, 175–177, 180,
    182, 184, 186, 197, 205, 209, 230,
    231, 234, 239–240
teams, 1, 3, 11, 12, 25–28, 47–49, 67,
    77, 93, 120, 138
Teamsters, 99
technology, 123, 287, 297
telegraphing, 102, 110, 145
television, 271, 291
Telstar Technique, 277, 280, 281, 292
Tentative Agreement, 112–113, 137,
    140, 152–153, 155, 159, 169, 183,
    189–190, 194, 197, 203, 221, 232,
    238, 244, 253
termination, 209–210, 214–215, 222
Texas, 257–258, 298
Texas Educational Opportunity Act
    (House Bill 72), 34
Theory X, 26–27
Theory Y, 26–27
Theory Z, 27
throw away proposals, 119, 131
time limits, 211, 218, 222
Total Quality Management, 25, 40–42,
    221
trade unions, 1
training, 32, 38–41, 109, 123
transcript, 171, 173, 193
transformational change, 42
transportation services, 99, 103, 151,
    243
trend analyses, 69–70, 73, 79, 83, 86,
    92–93
tripartite bargaining, 126, 162
trust, 23, 27, 36, 49, 56, 257
unfair labor practices, 120, 227, 242,
    245, 255
unions, 5, 21, 22, 31, 32, 37–39, 41,
    46, 48, 50, 230
union dues, 243
union representatives, 4–5, 256
union rights, 206, 221, 236
union shop, 84–85, 93, 227, 230, 244

union steward, 58, 196, 233
Uniserve Director, 61, 233, 244, 252
verbal and non-verbal behavior, 137
verbal warning, 215
vertical teams, 32, 33
violation, 163, 172, 209, 211, 216, 222, 234, 237, 245
vision, 11–12, 69, 75, 77
vocational classes, 90
voucher, 297
wage, 98, 163, 166, 180
wait time, 108
walkouts, 21
what-if scenarios, 176, 179, 185
win-win approach, 4–13, 79, 83, 97, 119–120, 133, 153, 159, 190, 197, 220, 227, 249, 251, 252, 257, 295–304

win-win negotiating environment, 67, 119, 189
win-lose, 4, 7–8, 13, 97, 119, 138, 304
winning team, 11–12
witnesses, 168, 171–172, 216–219, 222
wordsmith, 97, 102–103, 114, 145, 149
work environment, 1, 25, 28, 31, 38, 54
work-to-rule, 57, 177, 185, 253
working conditions, 5, 8, 56
workload, 114
worst-case scenario, 126, 185
written reprimand, 214–215
zipper clause, 227, 238, 244

JERRY J. Herman , Ph.D., is currently a management and training consultant. He has experience as a teacher at the elementary, junior high, senior high, community college, and university graduate school levels. He has been a principal, an elementary curriculum coordinator, a secondary curriculum coordinator, a school district's research coordinator, an assistant superintendent of schools, and a superintendent for 20 years in school districts in the states of Michigan and New York. In addition, he as been a university professor of administration and planning an a university administrator.

He has served as a consultant to numerous school districts and other education-related organizations. He has made numerous presentations to a wide variety of instruction- and management-related organizations and has served on several national committees dealing with educational issues.

Jerry has authored in excess of 150 journal articles for numerous national journals and has written twenty-two books on the topics of team building, instruction, human relations, community relations, finance, crisis management, strategic and tactical planning, and union/management relations. He has taught graduate courses on most of these topics, and he has served as the chair of over fifty doctoral dissertation research committees dealing with school-related instructional and management matters. In addition, he has been active with his own research related to these matters.

Janice L. Herman, Ph.D., is currently Head of the Department of Educational Administration at Texas A&M University—Commerce. She has served as a teacher of many different subjects and at many different grade levels, both overseas and in the states. She has also been a principal and a state of education department evaluation specialist, as well as a teacher in Virginia, Texas, Nebraska, and Thailand.

Janice has authored numerous articles in national publications. In addition, she has served on many state-level committees, and she has served as a graduate professor of educational leadership. She has presented at numerous national and state conventions and has served as a consultant to a variety of school districts and universities.

Together, the Hermans have held a wide variety of professional positions in Alabama, Kentucky, Virginia, Ohio, Texas, Michigan, New York, Iowa, and abroad. They have both been members of teacher unions. Janice Herman has played a leadership role at the building level with a teacher's union; Jerry Herman began his experience with collective bargaining in 1965 in the state of Michigan. He has served as an at-the-table negotiator; and he has experienced numerous contracts with various union groups that include teachers, transportation employees, school aides, food service employees, custodial employees, maintenance employees, and administrative employees. They have both made many national presentations and have written books and numerous articles on the topics discussed in this book. It is from their many years of experience and their broad experiences in dealing with solving a wide variety of major problems, intervening in conflice situations between and among various individuals and groups, and in involvement with a variety of unions in collective bargaining environments that this book has evolved.